Making progress in English

This manual is designed to help teachers establish a principled framework for developing English at Key Stages 1 and 2. Covering all aspects of English, it will help teachers raise standards of achievement in pupils at all levels of fluency and confidence.

The author uses case study material to relate theory to practice, covering issues such as classroom organisation and management. She also provides guidance for planning and developing ideas with colleagues and with children, and offers suggestions for teaching strategies and ways to evaluate teaching.

Separate chapters deal with reading, writing, speaking and listening, and these different threads are drawn together in sections on knowledge about language – including spelling, grammar and punctuation – and study of texts – including media, poetry, drama, response to literature and the use of non-fiction texts. The final chapter deals with policy and schemes of work.

Each chapter also offers information on assessment, recording and reporting; frameworks for screening and supporting children who have difficulties with English; gender; working with parents; and linguistic and cultural diversity.

Eve Bearne teaches at Homerton College, Cambridge.

D1511717

Making progress in English

Eve Bearne

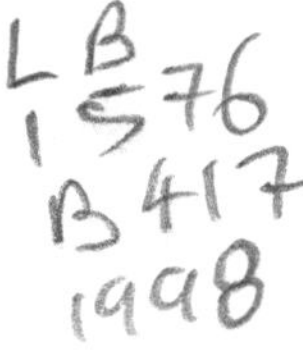
LB 1576 B417 1998

London and New York

RAS[illegible]RARY
UNIVERS[illegible] FAIRBANKS

First published 1998
by Routledge
11 New Fetter Lane, London EC4P 4EE

Simultaneously published in the USA and Canada
by Routledge
29 West 35th Street, New York, NY 10001

© 1998 Eve Bearne

Typeset in Baskerville and Futura by Keystroke, Jacaranda Lodge, Wolverhampton
Printed and bound in Great Britain by Unwin Brothers Limited, Old Woking, Surrey

All rights reserved. No part of this book may be reprinted or reproduced or utilised in any form or by any electronic, mechanical, or other means, now known or hereafter invented, including photocopying and recording, or in any information storage or retrieval system, without permission in writing from the publishers.

British Library Cataloguing in Publication Data
A catalogue record for this book is available from the British Library

Library of Congress Cataloguing in Publication Data
Bearne, Eve, 1943–
Making progress in English / Eve Bearne.
p. cm.
1. English language—Study and teaching (Elementary)—Great Britain. 2. English language—Composition and exercises—Study and teaching (Elementary)—Great Britain. 3. Reading (Elementary)—Great Britain. I. Title.
LB1576.B417 1998
372.6′044—dc21 97–32907
CIP

ISBN 0–415–15996–2

Contents

Figures

Acknowledgements

There are many teachers, particularly in Cambridgeshire, Norfolk, Suffolk and the Wirral, who have contributed to this manual through discussion of draft material and by sharing their experience. Particular thanks should go to all the members of the Advanced Diploma in Language and Literature at Homerton College, Cambridge, who have worked with much of the material. There are also individuals who have made significant contributions to the development of the manual. My especial thanks to Jane Brooks, Jill Pauling, staff and class 5/6 at St Philip's CE primary school, Cambridge, Jo Russell, Marie Stacey and Sally Wilkinson. Thanks also go to all the people whose work is represented here:

Sue Bailey and children from Town Lane infants school, Wirral
Barbara Borland
Helen Bromley
Jack Brown
Pat Brown
Sally Elding
Ian Eyres and children from Bar Hill school, Cambridgeshire
Cath Farrow
Peter Fifield
Kit Howes
Noelle Hunt
Belinda Kerfoot
Anna Lofthouse and children from the Queen's School, Richmond
Beverley Long
Jackie Lucas and children from Burwell village college primary school, Cambridgeshire
Caroline Luck and children from Reddings county primary school, Hertfordshire
Helen Maguire
Colette Morris
Jenny Reynolds and children from Thorndown junior school, Huntingdon
Margaret Rosenfeld
Morag Styles
Anthony Wilson
Tatiana Wilson

I would also like to thank Oxford University Press for permission to reproduce illustrations from *Christmas Adventure* by Roderick Hunt and Alex Brychta (1994), by permission of Oxford University Press.

Overview of the manual

This manual is designed to help teachers establish a principled framework for developing English at Key Stages 1 and 2. The central aim is to provide formats and suggestions for individuals or groups of teachers who want to raise standards of achievement in English for their pupils. Whilst all aspects of the National Curriculum for English are covered, this manual goes further and includes other aspects of English which teachers themselves have identified as priorities. There are also sections which deal with areas noted by Ofsted reports as needing more attention.

To make the manual easier to use, Chapters 2, 3 and 4 deal separately with Reading, Writing, and Speaking and Listening although each chapter acknowledges that literacy and language develop together. In practice, English activities which begin with writing are often threaded through with speaking and listening and always include some elements of reading. Similarly, reading can often include talk and lead to writing, and the suggestions for classroom activities represent this view of the interrelatedness of English as a whole. The National Curriculum term 'English' does not always adequately represent what is happening in the classroom as language is developed; what about children whose first language is British Sign Language? Or the many pupils who have the added benefit of bilingualism? While this manual pays careful attention to the importance of developing children's ability to communicate clearly and accurately in English, it also takes into account the broader view of what is involved in full literacy and language development. Chapter 5 covers knowledge about language – grammar, punctuation and spelling – and Chapter 6 offers suggestions for teaching from texts and teaching about texts.

Each chapter includes background information and summaries of up-to-date theoretical views of the different elements of language and literacy, practical guidance on managing the curriculum and formats for use with colleagues and for classroom work. Chapters 2–4 include detailed guidance for assessment, recording and reporting development in language and literacy and for supporting children who experience difficulties. The material also covers issues of differentiation and language diversity and the importance of links between home and school. There are suggestions at the end of every chapter for ways of working with homes and parents to foster literacy development. The final chapter summarises the material with an outline of the role of the English coordinator and a framework for developing or reviewing policies for reading, writing and speaking and listening.

The manual will be useful for teachers with any length of experience – from NQTs to those who want to take a new and more focused look at aspects of well-embedded practice and to anyone whose role involves organising inservice sessions.

In many chapters there are examples drawn from case studies of classroom practice written by teachers who have recently worked on developments in English in their own classrooms, as well as some children's reflections on learning. The idea of a manual like this, though, is to help teachers who use it to develop their own practices. While there are many examples of classroom ideas and frameworks for use with colleagues and pupils, the best way for the material to be used is to adapt it to your own requirements and contexts.

Developing language and literacy

Language and literacy development is a complex matter, which cannot adequately be dealt with in any single document – not even this manual! While the National Curriculum gives generalised guidance on key skills and the range of the language repertoire, it cannot answer directly to the specific needs of any individual school. Language development needs a flexible and adaptable approach to teaching and to assessment, recording and reporting if the children's, teachers' and parents' concerns over progress are to be met. For example, one important marker of progress is the child's behaviour in relation to reading, writing, speaking and listening; a teacher might observe a newly emerging confidence about writing when a child goes readily and eagerly to the writing corner, or a significant shift in reading might be marked by more deliberate and thoughtful choosing of books. These kinds of behaviour are critically important elements in noting progress, but cannot be captured in a generalised document like the National Curriculum. Similarly, the levels noted in the National Curriculum can only offer a general description. Ofsted notes significant numbers of children who are not being stretched in their language and literacy development and this is often because teachers have been encouraged to see the level descriptors as targets to aim at rather than general guidelines. In this manual, 'progress in English' extends beyond the National Curriculum statements by including descriptors of behaviours as well as range, repertoire and skills, and by offering a full progression from inexperienced language users to those who are fully experienced and independent.

The manual includes discussion of some of the theories which underlie classroom work on language and literacy development. However, it is worth remembering that theory and practice go hand in hand. What we think about our work informs what we do about it. Also, personal experience is important in identifying how our own theories have developed. The opening chapter outlines the theories which are the basis for this manual, but it starts by taking a close look at your present experience and how this feeds into classroom practice.

Chapter One

What does development in English look like?

In building towards a theory of language and literacy development, this chapter briefly outlines:

- the elements of progress – the developing range, repertoire, techniques, skills, knowledge and behaviours – which contribute to a full description of progress
- the role of the home in early language and literacy development and ways in which bridges can be built between home and school experience
- the role of language in learning
- the importance of assessment
- a way of reviewing the classroom environment so as to establish a supportive context for language and literacy development.

The most helpful theories spring from an examination of practice and experience. This chapter invites you to give full weight to your own experience – both personally and in the classroom – as a means of establishing just what matters about developing language and literacy. All the formats can be used as part of inservice work with colleagues and work best if they can be discussed with at least one other person.

A good starting point for considering the question 'What does development in English look like?' is to look at what a 'developed' reader, writer, speaker and listener can do:

- What kind of a reader are you?
- What kinds of writing do you do during the course of any week?
- How does your speaking and listening represent your full development in language?

A picture of what is involved in fully developed literacy will help to identify a useful and adequate theory which can inform classroom practice.

Reading development

The profile in Fig. 1.1 provides a quick way into thinking about what developed and experienced readers can do. What is your reading profile? It's a good idea to do this with a friend!

What kind of picture emerges? Are your ticks mostly over to one side or another? All over the place? What does that suggest about your reading habits and preferences?

Did you find that you wanted to tick at both ends of a column? For example, some people find reading maps while they're travelling along in a car an 'Ugh!' kind of reading, but enjoy reading maps for their own sake in the comfort of a chair at home. Some only read notices when they want to find particular information; others read them as a matter of regular habit. Many people record 'Ugh!' for reading columns of figures, but enjoy doing accounts; some cannot read music but enjoy singing.

How does your profile compare with your friend's? It's interesting how in a group of people the pattern of ticks can vary enormously, suggesting a range of reading tastes in developed readers.

What is already emerging is a picture of diversity even amongst developed, practised and independent readers. What does this imply for a theory of development?

Now consider the answers to these questions:

1. Where do you like to be in order to read happily?
2. Is there any particular time of day when you find you can read more easily?
3. How long can you comfortably read for?
4. What strategies have you developed to help you read more easily?
5. What makes reading difficult for you?
6. How do you choose what you want to read?
7. When do you read aloud?
8. Does anyone ever read aloud to you?

PERSONAL READING PROFILE

Tick in the column which represents how you feel about the different kinds of reading listed:

Type of reading	Happy	Quite comfortable	OK	Quite uncomfortable	Ugh!
Letters from home or a friend	✓				
Diagrams	✓				
Columns of figures					✓
Magazines	✓				
Newspapers			✓		
Handwriting	✓	it depends on whose!			✓
Computer text		✓			
Advertising hoardings	✓				
Music					✓ (can't)
Novels	✓				
Maps	✓	it depends			✓
Notices (e.g. in museums or staff rooms)	✓	only if I want to know the information			✓
Factual books		✓			
Pictures	✓				
Photographs	✓				
Other	icons like on the cooker			✓	

Figure 1.1 Profile of an experienced reader (Blank provided in Appendix: A1)

Quite a few answers might begin with 'it depends'. However, it's worth asking around to see how alike the answers to these questions are. Some people can read flat on their backs in the sun; some can read in a crowded and noisy café or on the bus. If you have a family to care for you may find that although you used to be able to read in the afternoon, the only time you can read now is late at night or in the holidays – and then you often fall asleep! The length of time you can read for may depend on the interest of the material you're reading – or it may not. Some people can only sustain twenty minutes of even a riveting book. Strategies to help with reading vary from reading difficult material aloud to noting words or phrases which are difficult, to missing bits out (complicated names or descriptions of places, perhaps). When reading books about education, for example, some people always read the last paragraph of a chapter first so as to get the brain attuned to the arguments the writer is putting forward. 'Difficult' reading varies according to the individual, but small print, no pictures, too many pictures, too much jargon, can all get in the way of satisfying reading. Choosing what to read can be daunting even for the most avid readers. Sometimes friends recommend books or lend them to us; sometimes newspaper reviews are the spur to getting a book. Even though we know that the cover doesn't bear any real relationship to the inside, we often use the cover as a guide or influence. Certainly, those of us who like to read particular genres go for the little icon put on the spine of the book by the library, or read a series of books by the same author.

Answers to the last two questions can be surprising. Of course you may read aloud to children at school or at home, but what about reading out bits of the newspaper to the family? or interesting snippets from a letter from a relative? Some people have a piece of sacred text read to them every day or listen to story tapes in the car.

Where does all of this lead in terms of establishing a theory about reading development?

Differences between readers

First of all it becomes clear that not every reader has similar tastes, habits, practices or strategies. In fact, the more you ask people to answer these questions, the more variation you see. This means that any single approach to teaching and fostering reading in the classroom is perhaps not going to cater for the whole range of readers. Then it becomes clear that reading is very much tied up with social practice; it isn't the solitary experience it might at first seem to be. Of course, there are times when each of us wants to read silently and alone, but this is usually one kind of reading. It is clear from the profile that there are many more kinds of reading which developed readers do every day, but how often are the different styles and strategies taught? The structure of a newspaper article or an official form is different from a novel. If you try to read the first two in the same way as you read a narrative – reading to the end quickly to find out what happens – you are likely not to get the gist of what the article is about or the form is asking you to do. Newspaper articles tell you the end of the story first then take you through the details; forms have no narrative thread at all. So there seems to be greater variety, too, in the kinds of reading children should be helped to develop. Similarly, some material needs to be read slowly. Some can make sense with a quick read. Some texts – like recipes or instructions – need to be returned to again and again; others yield their information once and for all. Strategies, the speed of reading, the style of reading, will all vary, too. Then there are social or contextual factors which influence reading. We often read what our friends read or what is recommended to us; or we read what is comfortingly familiar. Reading aloud to a class might evoke our most dramatic tones and enactments; reading a fragment of news will be different. Many readers make it clear that they need a comfortable environment and a reasonable length of time to get into reading. How do these insights inform classroom practice?

A very quick skirmish through what a developed reader can do reveals a complex picture of diversity of

- types of text
- ways of reading
- tastes and preferences in reading
- contexts for reading
- social influences on reading.

All of these need to be taken into account when describing a theory of literacy development and will influence the classroom management of reading. Chapter 2 deals with this in more detail.

Writing development

Is the picture as varied when you look at your own writing practices? Think about the different kinds of writing you have done at home and at work over the last week or so, then list them as in the chart in Fig. 1.2. (This is another activity which is best done with a group or a friend.)

When you have completed your list you'll have some idea of the variety of types and forms of writing, the range of reasons for writing and the number of different readers that you adjust your writing for in the course of a day, an hour or even a few minutes!

Have another look at your list and consider the levels of formality involved in the different kinds of writing. A note in a diary is only for private reading and so is perhaps the least formal, while a letter to someone you don't know needs to be reasonably formal. At first sight, it looks as if the form or type of writing determines the level of formality. A note or jotting may seem less formal than a letter. But this isn't always the case; other factors will make a difference. I may need to send a note to someone in authority which, although brief, will be written in a formal style. Similarly, I am not likely to use a formal tone if I write a letter to a close friend or member of the family. So an important factor in deciding on the level of formality will be the extent to which the reader is known to the writer.

What significant differences might there be between the two letters indicated above? Certainly, the letter to my sister will be less formal in tone and may use different kinds of vocabulary. Also, an interesting difference lies in the kind of (and amount of) punctuation used in the two kinds of letters. A letter to someone we know often uses a greater variety and amount of punctuation: underlining – sometimes three times, straight or wiggly; capital letters for emphasis; more exclamation marks or question marks; broken sentences; brackets and dashes. On the other hand, a letter to the bank manager may use fewer types of punctuation – usually only commas and full stops, although the occasional semi-colon may be called for. Why is this? It is simply that punctuation is intended to tell the reader how to read the text: what intonation to use. Whilst we want our family to hear our voice in all its variety of tone as they read what we write – irony, indignation, etc. – we want the bank manager to gain a much more sober and measured impression of someone who is rational and can be trusted with a loan! Variety of tone and voice is one kind of diversity which becomes clear when we list the writing a developed writer might do over the course of a week or so.

Type of writing	Reasons for writing	Who read it
shopping list	reminder	me
letter	giving news/ keeping in touch	my sister
letter	asking for a loan	bank manager
note (on kitchen table)	instruction!	my husband
reports	information	parents, children, colleagues
lesson plans	thinking through writing; reminding and informing	me; the key stage coordinator, the head
cheques	to pay bills	shopkeepers, accounts clerks, bank staff etc.
diary	getting things off my mind	me – perhaps?
telephone message	to remember a number	my husband
filling in form	to give information	the tax officer
birthday card	greeting/give pleasure	my friend Barbara
marking/comments	to respond to children's writing/improve it...	my class
spider diagram	some ideas	me

Figure 1.2 Variety in types and forms of everyday writing

Texts and contexts

What about the level of explicitness needed in any piece of writing? If you are writing a note to someone who has shared the same home as you for some time, then you do not need to include a great deal of information in a note; on the other hand, a visitor might need more information:

WASHING

or

the washing machine hadn't finished before I went out so could you take the washing out and hang it on the line or if it's raining you'll need to put it on the drier upstairs then I can iron it tonight so that you and Chris will have enough clothes for the weekend

It's clear that in a shared context, the one-word message of the first note is enough to do the job. However, if someone who didn't know the usual routine is staying in the house, then the level of detail included in the second note may be necessary. So the level of formality and the level of explicitness don't just depend on the kind of text (or type of writing) but on the context in which it is written and read.

Making choices about writing

In order to produce a written text for a specific context, a developed writer will have to make choices about purpose and readership, form, level of formality and extent of explicitness. And these decisions will, in turn, affect the technical aspects of putting a text together. A lesson plan will have a different format from a page in your diary; a letter to the bank will be set out differently from a letter to a friend. A shopping list does not need to be redrafted, neither does a note on the kitchen table, but a report may need to be, and a formal letter almost always is. We might also ask someone else to check each of the last two examples. Broken and incomplete sentences do not matter in notes or letters to friends or family, but they certainly do matter in more public kinds of writing if we want to make our meanings clear. We might use diagrams and drawings as part of texts or choose to write on a word processor or use e-mail. A proficient writer will need to have a broad and flexible enough writing repertoire to make choices about:

- the purpose and readership of a text
- the most appropriate form of a text
- the level of formality demanded
- the amount of explicit detail needed
- the format and organisation of the material
- the technical features of syntax, vocabulary and punctuation suited to the particular text.

A developed writer also makes choices about what not to write and what to omit. All of these judgements will be influenced by the context within which the text is written and the context in which it will be read. It is clear, too, that an experienced and fluent writer uses writing for a range of purposes – to help shape thoughts; to capture ideas; to reflect on experience; to communicate – all of which have relevance for classroom learning. If the list above is indicative of what a fully proficient writer can do, how can this variety, diversity and flexibility be introduced to the developing writer? And what does it suggest about a theory of what will best help development? These issues are revisited in Chapter 3.

Development in speaking and listening

productive modes of language: speaking and writing; **receptive modes** of language: listening and reading. It is important to consider the differences between the two modes because of the way language development is assessed. Whilst writing and talk can be easily witnessed, the only way to provide evidence of listening and reading is by asking questions or observing actions

Your speaking and listening profile for any week or so would echo many of the things which looking at writing and reading reveals. Like writing, speaking is a productive mode of language; like reading, listening is receptive. While there are differences in the way writing and different kinds of talk are structured, there are parallels between the purposes and audiences for both written and spoken texts. The brief utterances – *bathroom's empty; breakfast!!* – of the usual morning's activities in a family are like the brief note on the kitchen table; both are telegraphic and neither has to be maximally explicit. Telephone calls to family or bank managers reflect the tonality of each as captured in writing. Talking to ourselves is like reflective writing; talks to groups of parents are like essays or articles that could be found in professional magazines or journals. Lessons with familiar classes are like the responses on the children's written work. For every spoken utterance (or text) there is a written parallel. So the kinds of flexibility shown by a developed writer will be replicated by the versatility of a developed speaker; the range of texts we read and the development of our reading preferences can offer a good guide to the possible repertoire of an experienced and discriminating listener. Similarly, the social factors which affect reading and writing will have an impact on speaking and listening. While some people find listening to instructions difficult, they may not have any trouble with the news or a story tape; in the same way, readers might find official forms hard to get to grips with, but follow a newspaper article or a travel narrative easily. A native speaker of a particular dialect or language will be 'tuned in' to familiar sounds in the same way as in reading texts written in that dialect or language. A developed speaker will be able to make decisions about the level of formality needed in particular contexts or when meeting particular people in exactly the same way that an experienced writer can shift tone and register to suit the occasion and reader. Chapter 4 looks at these issues in greater detail.

tone: the quality of voice which suggests emotional content; **register:** the quality of an utterance which expresses formality or ease

Social and cultural aspects of language and literacy

Looking closely at what an experienced speaker and listener can do highlights another important element of theory about language and literacy development, however – the matter of language as a cultural practice. So far you have been thinking about your present experience as a developed language user. What insights can be drawn from looking back at early language and literacy experience?

This extract was written during an inservice course at Homerton College, Cambridge, where teachers were asked to write about their early experiences of language.

> My home was always noisy – the radio forever playing music, my sister, my mother and I talking interminably, singing, making up rhymes and playing with words, then later my twin brother and sister learning to talk. I have two particularly vivid memories of talk from my early childhood. At about two or three years old I suppose, I had a bout of nightmares. I used to wake up and sit at the top of the stairs, just on the bend so that I couldn't be seen if my parents came out of the living room into the kitchen. I used to like to hear the indistinct hum of their voices as they talked. I couldn't hear the words, just the sound itself comforted me. The other really odd memory is again to do with the sound rather than the content of the words. . . . We had a prisoner of war camp near to our house and on Sundays one of the prisoners was allowed to visit us for tea. I can remember sitting on the rug in the front room listening to my father and Alfred speaking in German. I suppose I could only have been about two or three and I certainly couldn't understand the words they were speaking, but I knew what they were talking about. I didn't think it strange at the time, but on reflection, I suppose it is. . . . Apart from that I was always a confident talker, in school and out.

It may be unusual that this teacher can remember so much about her early language experience, but her account draws attention to some of the most important, and often neglected, aspects of language development – the social and cultural features. It points to an awareness that talk in the home has an emotional – or affective – function as well as helping to structure understanding or add to knowledge – the cognitive function more usually recognised as part of oracy in school. Much the same is true of early literacy experience. The language and literacy experience of the home are now well documented as crucial to children's ability to take on the literacy offered in school. Before looking at examples of such research, it's worth reflecting on personal experience. Another quick look at the early experiences of people whose literacy is well developed might offer useful insights. The chart in Fig. 1.3 was completed by a 42-year-old teacher who was born in Shropshire and works in London.

affective: the area of learning which relates to emotions or feelings; **cognitive:** the area of learning which relates to concept formation

see also Shirley Brice Heath 1983 *Ways with Words: language, life and work in communities and classrooms*, Cambridge, Cambridge University Press; Hilary Minns 1988 *Read It to Me Now*, London, Virago Education; Gordon Wells 1986 *The Meaning Makers: children learning language and using language to learn*, London, Hodder & Stoughton

Many of these experiences have shaped this teacher's tastes and interests as an adult. He is very interested in local history; he has also inherited the family trait for a particular brand of humour. His Reading Profile revealed that he is most at ease with newspapers, maps, factual books and novels (although he says he is a slow reader). He likes a quiet environment for reading but can only sustain even his favourite kinds of reading for about thirty-five minutes. There are clear links here between home experiences and later habits and tastes in language and literacy.

What kinds of experiences would you record? How do they compare with this teacher's experience – or with your friends' and colleagues' – and how do they match your current profile? What influence have they had on your present interests and abilities with language and literacy? And what about any clashes of experience when you went to school? The home experience of the teacher who filled in the language family tree in Fig. 1.3 was very similar to that of school (at one time his father was his class teacher) but other people often report differences between home and school uses of language and literacy.

LANGUAGE FAMILY TREE

GRANDPARENTS' GENERATION

Brought up in Shropshire + Northampton

LANGUAGE	LITERACY
A great deal of gossip shared because Grandfather was a local shopkeeper. Local issues from the newspaper were discussed during family visits. Both Grandfathers told terrible jokes - usually puns.	The local newspaper was read avidly. Grandmother wrote each week to my Aunt (a teacher in Glasgow) she also sent the newspaper every week to her.

PARENTS' GENERATION

Both born + brought up in Shropshire

LANGUAGE	LITERACY
In family discussions the children were welcome participants. I was aware that I did not speak with the local dialect that some of my Aunts + Uncles had.	Father read local + national papers - often read aloud sections for all of us to hear. Mother also read magazines (shared + swopped around relatives) - children enjoyed these too! Great delight in twice yearly mail order catalogues.

After buying a car in the early 1960's we had many Sunday rides out. Maps, and guides were often consulted. Place names discussed + routes planned.

Figure 1.3 Personal experience of language and literacy (Blank provided in Appendix: A2)

This was completed by Peter Fifield of West Lea School, Enfield, Middlesex, on an inservice course on reading.

The Language Family Tree chart is included in the appendix.

Language and literacy at home and school

Ways with Words

Shirley Brice Heath has been one of the most influential researchers into the relationship between home and school literacy and the effects on learning. In her study of three different communities and their literacy, she identified elements of certain 'ways of taking' meaning from texts as critical factors in future success in learning. In families in the middle-class community of her research the print environment and literacy practices of home and of school were very similar. In the poor white and black communities there were significant contrasts between what home and school saw as valid ways to use narrative, for example. In the poorer white community, reading the Bible was a major literary event. Since to this community Bible truth was literal – what is written is fact – school practices of changing stories or seeing them as imaginary were unfamiliar and often unacceptable ways of treating reading. School practices also differed from social literacy practices in the black community, where reading was very much a public affair so that solitary reading was again unfamiliar and, if not unacceptable, certainly seen as unusual. The implications of these varying perceptions would reach forward into the children's later school experience and influence their progress in learning. Those children whose home experiences of literacy most paralleled the school view were, perhaps unsurprisingly, most successful in school. Others, whose experience of literacy differed from what the school saw as valid, gradually ground to a standstill in learning, baffled by an unfamiliar set of practices which did not fit with home experience. It was not that the children from the two communities whose children began to struggle in school were 'less able' nor that their homes were lacking in reading material – the fact was that there was a serious mismatch between teachers' perceptions and children's real experience – and this made for failure in children who might otherwise have progressed perfectly adequately. In Shirley Brice Heath's view, school should be 'a place which allowed these children to capitalise on the skills, values and knowledge they brought there, and to add on the conceptual structures imparted by the school' (p.13).

Making connections

This has important implications for teachers. It is all too easy to assume that differences in literacy practices necessarily mean 'deficiencies'. Shirley Brice Heath's studies were carried out in America, but nearer to home, in an East Anglian industrial town, Sally Wilkinson looked in detail at the classroom and home literacy of three of her Key Stage 1 learners:

Sally Wilkinson 1994 '"What did you do at home today?" A case study of the links between three children's homes and their school literacies', unpublished Advanced Diploma thesis, Homerton College, Cambridge

> Whereas much of Darryl's and Sarah's writing drew on themes and characters from books and the media, most of Rashida's writing was based on reality. Her stories would draw almost exclusively on remembered experiences, for example, a piece about someone in hospital reflected her knowledge of injections gained when the family took Mamun (her brother) for his regular check-ups. I found (like Shirley Brice Heath's observations of Roadville children) that Rashida had the greatest difficulty in creating imaginative stories. Her parents told me that there was not a tradition of oral story-telling in the family and that when Rashida wrote at home it was mostly letters to the neighbour's daughter, her siblings or her mother. This reflected what Rashida liked to do at school. When she was in the writing corner she would write letter after letter and post them in the class post-box. She wrote to confirm friendships and also to anyone whom she felt was sad or hadn't had a letter lately – in order to cheer them up. When I visited Rashida's home, Lyla (her sister) had showed me a loose-leaf file from Rashida's drawer in the chest. She had repeatedly written her own and her siblings' names and also played with words in both English and Bengali on the same page, experimenting with the patterns involved in the characters of each.
>
> (p. 35)

Rashida, obviously a capably literate child, was having lessons in writing Bengali at the mosque and Sally Wilkinson came to understand that in the classroom she was 'showing expectations of her which are different from those of her family or the community teacher at the mosque' (p. 36). She goes on to explain how she used this knowledge to 'provide methods of writing at school which would have some resemblance to those she was encountering outside it'. The importance of such information is not only relevant for those children whose home culture is identifiably different in terms of bilingualism, for example. Sally Wilkinson also found that Sarah – from a local family of some long standing – 'made a clear distinction between home and school books', preferring to read those from home which she was familiar with. At home, Sally Wilkinson discovered, Sarah liked telling stories and found reading aloud in school rather threatening:

> My task when Sarah was reading aloud with me on a one-to-one basis was one which required a delicate balance. I wanted to prevent her becoming anxious over any stumbles in her decoding of the text and I also wanted to encourage her to interrogate the text more. I talked with her mother about this so that we were both operating in the same way. By the end of term, through both of us having in-depth knowledge of exactly the point that Sarah was at in her developing confidence and fluency, we were able to see the beginning of a change in her attitude to less familiar or unknown text as she focused on it, believing that she could get meaning from it.
>
> (p. 30)

Sally Wilkinson learned a lot about literacy and ability by making not assumptions, but connections. Much of the everyday business of the classroom is conducted through print. This is an accepted part of the educational process and, of course, one of the central aims of schooling is to help children move towards confident literacy.

Talking about literacy

As Margaret Meek explains in her UK research, becoming literate in school terms means that 'children have to learn the school conventions for speaking (how you ask to go to the lavatory), for reading (*this is how we hold our books*), and for writing (the difference between "rough" and "neat")'. As children get to grips with school life, they learn to 'relate the topics of lessons to ways of writing and reading about them'. Those children who are considered successful school literates are often those who satisfy their teachers and become adept at operating the literacies of school.

Margaret Meek 1991 *On Being Literate*, London, The Bodley Head

Talking about homes and parents in terms of deficit doesn't get anyone nearer to supporting children's literacy development. It is important to reach fuller understanding with parents and carers about how home experience of literacy is an essential part of later literacy development.

deficit theory: this was a view, now overtaken by more detailed research, that individuals or their homes are in some way lacking the features which contribute to progress in learning. A problem about this way of thinking is that it does not take into account any of the wider social or environmental factors which often contribute to underachievement. See pp. 152–3 for further explanation

Sally Wilkinson points out that, through discussions, both she and the children's parents were able to gain a greater insight into how the children's literacies were developing. She also stresses the importance of developing ways of talking about literacy which are genuinely helpful to parent and teacher. One of the greatest dangers teachers run is what Margaret Meek refers to as 'final statements', which are meant to summarise teacherly concerns, but actually often stereotype and close off further thought. One type of these is the tendency to start sentences with 'They . . . ' and this is particularly evident when talking about parents, even if the speaker is a parent her- or himself. *They don't write in the Reading Record* or *They never come to school meetings* reflect teacher frustrations in trying to make links between home and school, but they might equally reflect a parent who is overwhelmed by the school culture or who simply has too much to do.

Sally Wilkinson acknowledges the tendency to over-generalise about homes and parents when she points out that the knowledge she gained about the children she studied 'was more helpful to me as a classroom teacher than generalisations based on large samples'. She warns against 'blanket views' which 'if accepted blindly by teachers cause them to form stereotypes of the families and of the children they teach'. What seems to be needed is a way of finding out how best to talk with parents about literacy.

Part of this depends on working out just what might constitute a supportive literacy environment and to see how different homes and different cultures can promote literacy. It means looking at literacy in a broader way. Consider, for example, the capability of a Traveller child from a non-literate home who can, at 5 years old, successfully sustain a fifteen-minute oral narrative which spellbinds his hearers; or the 9-year-old from a home where books are in great evidence and used by all members of the family, who tells her teachers she 'can't read'. What implications do these (real) examples have for a theory of home literacy which does not use the notion of deficit?

Building relationships with parents

The teacher's role is one of great sensitivity here. On the one hand it is important to establish an equivalent attitude to the pupils' diverse backgrounds, to give value to the variety of cultures which are brought into the classroom. But there is also the responsibility to help pupils develop their literacy further. One thing is clear – there is powerful potential in teachers finding out just what literacy experiences their pupils have so that they can build on them. However, although making links with parents over literacy is fruitful territory, it is not easy. There are often constraints to do with:

Time – sometimes parents or carers cannot get to school at suitable times or teachers do not have the time during a busy day to have lengthy conversations.
Confidence – teachers may lack confidence or experience to explain their classroom approaches to literacy to parents whose own experience of school may be very different. At the same time, parents may be fearful of asking questions of the teachers whose expertise they respect (or fear!).
Language – all occupations have specific language which seems everyday and normal within that occupation, but which can create misunderstandings in hearers. For example, the word 'figure' means something different to an artist, a mathematician and a speaker of American English. Or a teacher may not share the home language of the parents. Added to that, media reports tend to use words or phrases or sound bites as triggers – for example 'real books' – to carry underlying assumptions. These can be the basis for unnecessary conflict. Sometimes it needs quite lengthy exchanges before a shared vocabulary shows that there were, in fact, common views right from the start!

Schools have found varied ways to offset some of these difficulties, including:

- inviting parents into school just to see what's going on
- encouraging parents to take part in classroom activities
- providing rooms or facilities for parents in school
- running language 'workshops' for parents so that they can acquire first-hand knowledge of how their children learn to develop literacy
- involving parents off-site in partnered reading schemes, as researchers, resources or co-writers.

The completed chart in Fig. 1.4 was compiled by a group of teachers as they thought about the roles of parents in their schools.

How are parents involved in your own classroom and school? You might find, for example, that they are regarded as 'extra pairs of hands' or that they are seen as genuinely contributing expertise which only they can offer.

The framework in Fig. 1.5 will show up any differences between the kinds of involvement we expect of parents at home and at school. You may find that the activities parents are asked to carry out when they come into schools and classrooms show that they are more often involved in helping to 'manage' things, rather than being involved in the curriculum. Is the picture any different when you consider the ways in which you invite parents to participate in learning 'off-site'? – when you ask them to be memory banks for local history research or co-writers for scribed stories, or in reading with their children?

INVOLVING PARENTS

In school parents can be involved in:

- induction sessions
- conversations about progress/counselling/complaints
- informal meetings
- open days/evenings
- assemblies
- religious groups
- hearing children read
- family reading sessions
- as scribes
- making music
- using and learning about computers
- running bookshops and the library
- cooking
- as experts – resident potter; grab-a-gran
- games
- the nursery or crèche
- trips
- after-school clubs
- careers discussions and work links
- school plays
- learning alongside the pupils
- evening classes; ESL work
- parent–teacher associations
- working parties

Some may be classroom support staff, teachers, administration assistants within the school itself . . .

. . . or may be school governors.

BUT NOT ALL PARENTS ARE ABLE TO JOIN IN THESE ACTIVITIES OR FEEL CONFIDENT ENOUGH TO PARTICIPATE.

Figure 1.4 List of parental involvement compiled by a group of teachers

INVOLVING PARENTS

Parents in my classroom

Activities	How does this support literacy?
reading groups	shows that reading is for enjoyment and moves children on
helping with Art helping with cookery	reading instructions/ recipes / art books

Parents in the school

Activities	How does this support literacy?
Dance club (Indian classical dance)	- some bilingual work
Helping in the wild patch	? could lead to reading information books on wildlife gardens
Football	? reading football magazines...?

Parents at home

Activities	How does this support literacy?
helping with information-gathering for history/geog.	- shows children how to find info. in books/ CD Rom and how to note it down
reading + writing surveys	- makes a link for children between home and school uses of reading/ writing

Figure 1.5 The different ways that parents can support literacy (Blank provided in Appendix: A3)

There is no doubt that this is a tricky area. A teacher's job is to promote learning through the use and development of reading, writing, speaking and listening. This necessarily involves a responsibility to provide an enriching environment – to encourage enjoyment of stories, books, poetry, talk, song, discussion, questioning, reflecting, publishing, and so on. If children come from homes where there are few books or (as far as can be seen) little discussion or reflective talk, it would be logical, perhaps, to see these homes as lacking support for literacy and to judge them accordingly. It would, indeed, be foolish to deny that there are some home environments which do not support children's literacy as fully as they might. However, if teachers are to help children make productive connections between what they learn at home and what they learn from school, then teachers need to make very carefully considered decisions about the grounds on which the judgements are made and the implications which those judgements have for the children in their classes. This might involve 'dissolving the walls' between the school, classroom and the home to share ideas about children's literacy development; genuinely drawing on the cultural diversity of the communities surrounding the school and encouraging more balanced partnerships with homes and parents. The final chapter of the manual includes more suggestions of how these difficult areas might be reviewed in more detail.

Language, literacy and learning

While it is important to be aware of the values attached to judgements about home and school literacy, children's experience of using language and literacy cannot easily be put into separate compartments labelled 'home' and 'school'. Also, although there may be significant differences between the ways talk is used in either place, or in the aspects of literacy which occur in home or school, children themselves may not find it easy to perceive these differences. Since language is central to a child's whole experience of learning, both at home and at school, it is important to find ways of identifying just what children can do with language when they come to school, and what they understand about language, so that teachers can build on this knowledge. However, it isn't just a matter of having welcoming attitudes to home language or literacy in order to promote successful future learning. There's rather more to it than that.

The psychologist Vygotsky, writing in the 1930s, emphasised the importance of acknowledging children's existing language capabilities because of the central importance language has for all learning. He points out that children's learning begins long before they attend school:

Lev Vygotsky trans. 1978 *Mind in Society: the development of higher psychological processes*, London, Harvard University Press

> even when, in the period of her first questions, a child assimilates the names of objects in her environment, she is learning. Indeed, can it be doubted that children learn speech from adults, or that, through asking questions and giving answers, children acquire a variety of information; or that, through imitating adults and through being instructed about how to act, children develop an entire repository of skills? Learning and development are interrelated from the child's very first day of life.
>
> (p. 84)

In other words, language and thought are essentially interlinked. This idea of 'thinking through language' challenges the straightforward notion that language simply expresses ideas that are there 'in the head', waiting to be put into words. As Vygotsky explains, thought is not merely expressed in words; it comes into existence through them. This places language and literacy at the centre of the range of factors which might contribute to a child's success in school-based learning. Vygotsky takes this further by pointing out that methods of assessing learning are also linked with individual assessments based on language; he highlights the importance of being aware of the usefulness of the social, collaborative uses of language for learning:

> In studies of children's mental development it is generally assumed that only those things that children can do on their own are indicative of mental abilities; we give children a battery of tests or a variety of tasks of varying degrees of difficulty, and we judge the extent of their mental development on the basis of how they solve them and at what level of difficulty.
>
> On the other hand if we offer leading questions or show how the problem is to be solved and the child solves it, or if the teacher initiates the solution and the child completes or solves it in collaboration with other children – in short, if the child barely misses an independent solution of the problem – the solution is not regarded as indicative of his mental development; this 'truth' was familiar and reinforced by common

sense; over a decade, even the profoundest thinkers never questioned the assumption; they never entertained the notion that what children can do with the assistance of others might be in some sense even more indicative of their mental development than what they can do alone.

(p. 85)

Looking for potential

zone of proximal development: Vygotsky defined this as 'The distance between the actual developmental level as determined by independent problem solving and the level of potential development as determined through problem solving under adult guidance or in collaboration with more capable peers' (p. 86).

Jerome Bruner 1986 *Actual Minds, Possible Worlds*, London, Harvard University Press

Vygotsky developed the idea of a *zone of proximal development* – the child's potential for taking ideas further when thinking is stimulated by conversation and negotiation with others. Vygotsky argued that traditional individual assessments usually lagged behind the child's developmental level, never accurately portraying ability fully. He suggests that such methods of backward-looking assessment emphasise what children cannot do and so teaching becomes geared to their weaknesses rather than to their strengths, thus encouraging them to remain at a lower level of achievement than might be possible by collaboration. Bruner takes this further by arguing that literacy must be seen as a social and cultural matter:

> Children quickly and painlessly master syntax without crisis. With somewhat more difficulty, but still easily, the child also 'learns how to mean' – how to refer to the world with sense; but children do not master syntax for its own sake or learn how to mean simply as an intellectual exercise – like little scholars or lexicographers; they acquire these skills in the interest of getting things done in the world: requesting, indicating, affiliating, protesting, asserting, possessing and the rest.
>
> (pp. 113–14)

In getting to grips with the business of learning how to mean, the links between language, literate practices, social groups, home cultures, school, learning and power are forged firmly together.

> I have come to realize that most learning in most settings is a communal activity, a sharing of the culture; it is not just that the child must make his knowledge his own, but that he must make it his own in a community of those who share his sense of belonging to a culture; it is this that leads me to emphasise not only discovery and invention but the importance of negotiation and sharing – in a word, of joint culture-creating as an object of schooling and as an appropriate step en route to becoming a member of the adult society in which one lives out one's life.
>
> (p. 127)

Questions about learning

If 'learning in most settings is a communal activity', what does that imply about classrooms as environments for learning? It might first of all be worth asking:

> What is learning?

and

> What helps children to learn?

Replies to the first question might include:

- putting existing experience or knowledge alongside new knowledge, experiences, facts

- finding things out; making discoveries
- increasing awareness
- continually updating ideas
- reflecting on experience
- learning 'how' as well as 'what' and 'why'
- having curiosity and satisfying it

and suggestions for the second might be:

- having chances to experiment
- tackling challenges (with support)
- gaining – or being given – confidence
- working with others
- experience – making mistakes and trying again
- imitation and observation
- making connections between ideas
- learning how to talk about teaming.

Then there is the matter of:

Where does language fit in?

One group of teachers decided that language helps the learner to:

- frame questions, prepare for learning, get ideas going
- gather, organise and categorise information
- explore ideas, hypothesise, predict, explain, describe, argue
- reflect on learning
- give information to others; communicate ideas
- demonstrate that something has been learned
- evaluate learning; review progress.

What could you add? It might be worth asking these questions with colleagues as a way of beginning to think about the contribution language makes to learning across the curriculum.

Assessment as part of the learning process

Any discussion of learning necessarily involves thinking about methods for assessing learning. Perhaps the first thing to bear in mind about assessment is that it enters at all stages of the planning–teaching–evaluating cycle. At every stage in less and more formal ways assessment helps in making decisions about how best to move individuals or the whole group on – whether in developing talk or in learning subject knowledge. In making decisions about how best to ensure progress, teachers constantly assess, appraise and evaluate. Fig. 1.6 shows a model of the role of assessment in the process of teaching through to evaluation and back again.

Throughout the process of teaching and learning, observing, assessing, recording and reporting can offer a range of benefits. Observation and assessment can:

- reveal what pupils are thinking about and how they are thinking
- give information about learning across subject areas
- provide insights into what pupils understand – or misunderstand – about the task, concept or information under discussion
- offer a more complete and representative picture of a child's attainment than assessments based only on reading or writing

- be an equaliser, showing surprising quality and sensitivity of thinking from children who may otherwise be considered to be failing
- help teachers become more aware of their own use of language and the positive and negative effects of intervention
- give status in the eyes of children, colleagues and parents to a traditionally undervalued form of communication
- enable the keeping of careful records to identify progress and inform future planning
- provide evidence for reporting to parents; for summary reports and for assigning National Curriculum levels of attainment.

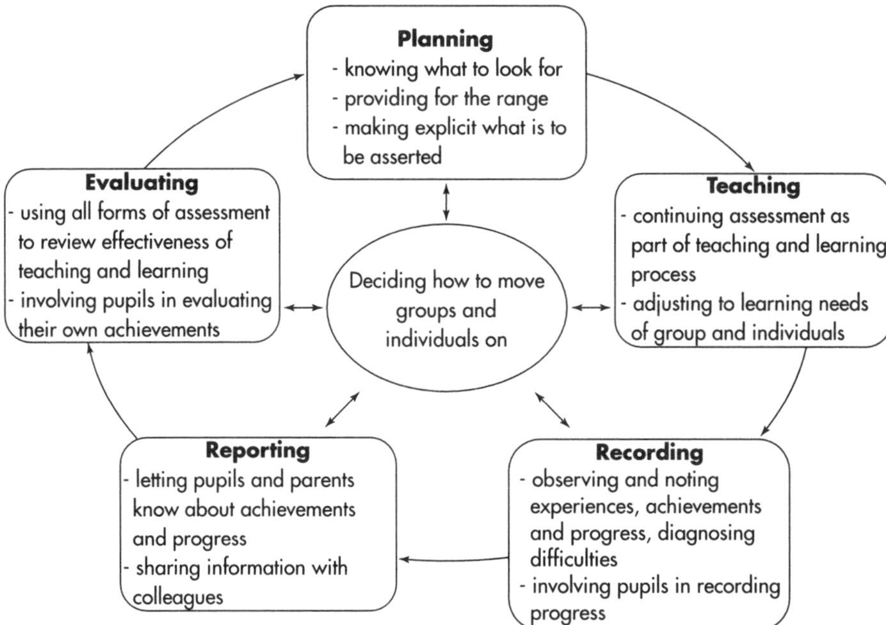

Figure 1.6 The cycle of teaching and assessment

Deciding on procedures for assessment

To help in deciding how to organise for assessment, it is worth considering the following, either individually or as a group of colleagues:

Why are the assessments being made? Will they: provide feedback for pupils? give information to parents, colleagues and others? help to evaluate the effectiveness of teaching?

What is being assessed? Is it: understanding of concepts within a particular curriculum area? grasp of processes, techniques or strategies for learning? an individual's experience, confidence or competence?

When might assessments be made? as the work begins? during an activity or series of activities? at the end?

How will assessments be carried out? Will they be by: observations? discussions or conferences? outcomes or products? all of these or other methods?

Who will be doing the assessment? the teacher? the teacher and pupils together? another person?

Each chapter of the manual includes a section on assessment and offers frameworks for assessing, recording and reporting progress.

A supportive environment for language and literacy

If the different questions raised in this chapter were to be presented as 'principles' about providing a classroom environment which would best support literacy and language development, what would be included? The list might be like the one which follows. This was compiled by a group of teachers after reflecting on all the areas covered in this chapter – their own reading, writing, speaking and listening experiences; the role of parents in developing literacy and the ways in which language contributes to learning.

Children will learn most effectively when we:

- recognise what they already know and build on it
- acknowledge that learning isn't just fact-gathering, but to do with confidence, security, and a sense of being valued
- offer challenges which can be tackled in supportive contexts
- see the relationship between writing, talk, listening and reading
- create an environment where learners can take an active part in negotiating and organising their own learning
- provide opportunities for collaboration, reflection and evaluation
- make links and forge partnerships between homes and school
- offer models and examples of how to learn and how to talk about learning
- see the development of literacy as dynamic, recursive and cumulative, rather than a linear progress through clearly defined stages.

Of course this does not pretend to be an exhaustive list and should not be seen as representing what ought to be said. What is interesting about it is that it leads to a statement about the kind of theory which will best represent what these teachers think about language and literacy development. It includes not only the expectation that children should be able to get to grips with texts of all kinds, but assumes that the learners should be actively involved in their own learning. It gives value to the experience drawn from home and clearly identifies the role of the teacher as a model and an organiser of learning. This is not a 'water the garden and it will grow' model of development which assumes that teachers can just provide the right environment and materials and all will be well, but a rigorous and robust approach to teaching and learning. The final statement summarises the nature of the developmental theory which these teachers have described – one which takes account of individual development, describes the most productive classroom environment for learning, identifies key features of teaching and assumes that learning involves social and cultural aspects as well as the cognitive and affective. This theory importantly sees development as a long-term process which revisits old experience in the light of the new and broadens, deepens and thickens knowledge and expertise as the child moves through school.

This list could have opened this chapter. To have done that, however, would have meant short-circuiting the process by which these teachers (and you and your colleagues, I hope) have reached a clearer view of what they want children to be able to do with language and literacy. The most important aspect of an activity which asks teachers to work through their own experience to reach a theoretical position is that it opens up discussion – some of it quite challenging. This kind of discussion can then be followed by an audit of provision for a supportive environment for language and literacy. And the discussions can continue.

How would you complete the audit in Fig. 1.7? What kinds of information might it yield if all teachers in one Key Stage completed it? Or the whole staff?

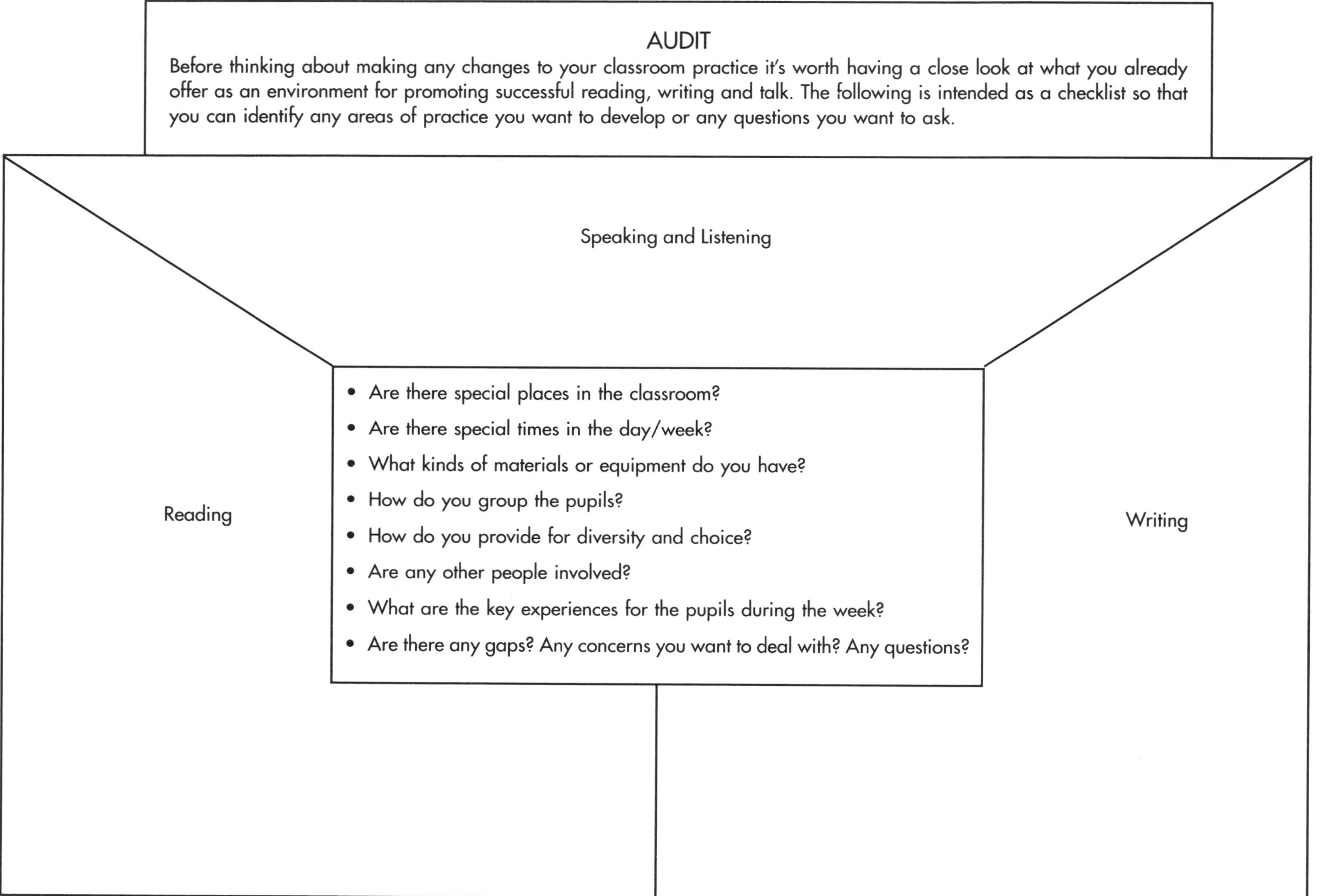
AUDIT
Before thinking about making any changes to your classroom practice it's worth having a close look at what you already offer as an environment for promoting successful reading, writing and talk. The following is intended as a checklist so that you can identify any areas of practice you want to develop or any questions you want to ask.
Speaking and Listening
Reading
Writing
• Are there special places in the classroom?
• Are there special times in the day/week?
• What kinds of materials or equipment do you have?
• How do you group the pupils?
• How do you provide for diversity and choice?
• Are any other people involved?
• What are the key experiences for the pupils during the week?
• Are there any gaps? Any concerns you want to deal with? Any questions?

Figure 1.7 The classroom as a language and literacy environment

Reading

Chapter Two

In outlining how to ensure progress in reading, this chapter covers:

- **recent theories about reading**
- **planning for reading – the range and repertoire**
- **gender and reading**
- **teaching reading: strategies for getting meaning out of texts**
- **creating an invigorating environment for reading**
- **selecting and using texts**
- **reading for information and understanding**
- **managing a range of reading activities**
- **recording, reporting and assessing progress in reading**
- **diagnosing reading difficulties and planning for support**
- **evaluating reading and how it is taught**
- **taking it further: reading at home.**

Introduction to reading

The term **real books** was first used to distinguish between books which are written for pleasurable reading and books which are written simply to instruct children in reading. Many traditional reading scheme books were like this. The term is associated with the apprenticeship approach to reading advocated by Liz Waterland in her book *Read With Me*, Stroud, Glos., The Thimble Press 1988.

The use of the term **phonics** to describe a way of teaching reading signals an approach which works on smaller items of meaning, then builds to whole stretches of text.

Much heat has been generated over the past few years about standards of reading and above all about the best way to teach reading. One unfortunate aspect of the debate has been that attention has been focused on methods or materials rather than dealing with the essential matter of what children, teachers and parents understand reading to be. Glib oppositions have often been made between starting children off on reading by using either a 'real books' or a 'phonics' approach.

Whether either label is intended to signal approval or distaste depends on the point of view of the commentator. The absurdity of this polarisation of attitudes is clear; for example, what might an 'unreal' book be? And who has never used a phonic approach when looking something up in a telephone directory or a dictionary? Then there are those people who claim that 'children don't read as much as we did when we were young', not noticing the boom in children's publishing, which is obviously feeding a market, and librarians' statistics of much increased use of library facilities over the past twenty years. Unfortunately, much public comment about reading tends to be not only unnecessarily alarmist, but also often uninformed.

Trivialising the debate does not help children who are learning to be readers, nor their parents and teachers who want to help them in that important process. As Myra Barrs and Anne Thomas point out:

Myra Barrs and Anne Thomas eds 1991 *The Reading Book*, London Borough of Southwark Centre for Language in Primary Education

> Either/or theories of learning to read have not got us very far in thinking about reading. They have tended to polarise debate and also to polarise practice. They also fail to reflect the complexity of the reading process – the different kinds of knowledge that are basic to the process, the need to achieve a balance between them, the need for teachers to help children use their different stylistic strengths. The ability to read is not located in any one individual aspect of reading, such as a sense of book language or a knowledge of print, but in the whole activity, where these different aspects are orchestrated.
>
> (p. 8)

Looking at what a developed reader can do (see Chapter 1, pp. 2–4) indicates just how complex the process of reading is. It also reveals the diversity of approaches to reading used by different readers, suggesting that managing reading in the classroom is not something which can be adequately dealt with by one specific method. This chapter outlines the different elements involved in becoming a reader and suggests ways of organising for the range and repertoire needed to cater for the diverse readers in any classroom. It invites you to look at your own reading practices, considering such questions as:

- What does 'reading' imply?
- How can I plan to provide for the complexity of readers' needs?
- What are my responsibilities as a teacher of reading?

Further to these considerations, the more public implications of the reading debate need careful attention. Language is not only learned in the school, but in the home as well, and reading is an area of language which has traditionally been a good basis for links with parents or carers – at least in the early years of schooling. It has also become the centre of media and political attention, investing the phrase 'standards of reading' with highly emotive connotations.

The complexities of reading

Despite the continuing struggles between uninformed rhetoric and professional knowledge about reading, the debate has it up-side. What has become clear is that reading does not just take place in schools; it is a social and cultural process where not only homes and classrooms play their part, but larger institutions and cultural influences such as governments and the media contribute to what 'being a reader' involves. There is no doubt that reading is deeply imbued with cultural resonances. What is available for anyone to read and what people should read, when reading is considered an appropriate social activity, where reading should take place and who reads what, are all public concerns. Government has intervened through the National Curriculum to indicate what reading material should be given to young readers in schools; attention to picture books and television suggests that reading pictorial text is a more sophisticated and complex process than might have been thought. People read on buses, trains and in classrooms, but may be considered ill-mannered if they read while visiting relatives; HMI reports suggest significant differences between boys' and girls' reading tastes and practices. There is obviously a little more to reading than the simple act of picking up some printed material and being able to decode the words!

New versions of literacy – media, computer texts of all kinds – now contribute to the reading curriculum. Many of these texts are experienced in the home, so it is clear that we need to consider the contribution children's home reading makes to their developing literacy. These wider considerations mean some careful thought about how teachers can organise for equal access to all kinds of reading and use the children's home experience of a diverse range of texts in the classroom. Such demands make it even more important for teachers to be confident about provision for a wide range and repertoire, their teaching methods and their assessment, reporting and recording practices. Reflection on teaching and learning reading can then profitably be used in planning for further progress.

Examining beliefs about reading

In the first chapter you were invited to start looking at your own beliefs about what literacy has meant in your own life and about what kind of a reader you are. You may have discovered, like this teacher, that reading isn't just about books:

> When I filled in my Personal Reading profile, I realised that although I read novels very fast and can even read tricky 'academic' material quite easily, I am a severely handicapped reader in almost all other respects. My profile revealed that not only do I find reading newspapers difficult (the columns aren't wide enough for my eye to travel quickly and news stories are written with the 'pay-off' at the beginning, where I'm usually keen to read to the end to see 'who dunnit'!). But also, I can't read notice boards, forms or pictorial text efficiently. Although I'm quite good at diagrams, symbols defeat me; while I like to flick through magazines, often I don't understand the editorials or commentaries in the Sundays.
>
> Then when I got to the questions about where, when and how, it was fascinating.

These notes were completed by a teacher on an inservice course on literacy held at Homerton College, Cambridge.

Finding out about our own reading tastes and capabilities is often revealing; this provides a picture of what developed readers can do. It is equally informative to

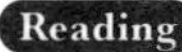

discover about the experiences and tastes of the young readers in the classroom; it helps in making decisions about how best to manage the reading curriculum and environment to help them develop further as readers. You might like to focus on a few children first of all and ask them some of the questions in Fig. 2.1.

- Do you like reading? Why/why not?
- Do you think you're a good reader? How do you know?
- What makes it difficult to read? What makes it easy?
- Do you prefer to read silently to yourself or aloud to someone? Why is that?
- Do you read a lot at home?
- Does anyone read with you/to you?
- What sort of things do you like to read? What is a recent favourite?
- Do the people at home read much? What do they read?
- Why do you think people need to be able to read?
- Can you remember learning to read? Who/what helped you?

Figure 2.1 Questions about reading

Fig. 2.2 gives some examples of children's responses to those questions.

11-year-olds

The only thing I like reading is magazines.

I have always loved reading. At home I have a room full of books and I can't go into a bookshop without buying one.

I had read all the books for pupils in the school by the time I got to the beginning of this year so I have to read the poetry books – and I hate poetry!!

In S–M–school we had to go through *Janet and John* books. When we had read all of them, we had to read all the books in colour. I hated them because they were sexist and boring. We had a reading corner, then the teacher would hear us read one by one. We used to see how many books we could finish and get a star in our pads for reading.

9- and 10-year-olds

I don't like reading in a group because I'm not good at reading out loud. I like silent reading because I can read in my head.

I think this group is brilliant. I like reading in a group, it's more enjoyable because we can help each other.

What I think you need to encourage reading are: a patient teacher, a book that suits you and a good imagination.

Teachers can improve reading in a lot of ways like asking children if they like adventure stories, true stories etc.

I have always liked reading. I do not like reading books without pictures and books that are sometimes easy. I like to read books that are challenging.

8-year-olds

Women read more than men. No-one in the world reads more than my sister.

Men read most . . . my dad's always buried in paperwork.

I liked reading the plays, 'cos then Jason could help me and we could talk about the bits we liked . . . we almost know some of them by heart.

6-year-olds

I like reading with Laura. I don't have a problem at playtime now I have Laura to play with.

I like the illustrations because there's so much to look at in the pictures.

Figure 2.2 Children's views about reading

Finding a theory about reading

It is important to be able to relate practice and theory. Margaret Meek describes her unease about 'reading experts' who 'decontextualise reading in order to describe it'. She provides the detail of this:

Margaret Meek 1988 *How Texts Teach What Readers Learn*, Stroud, Glos., The Thimble Press

> The reading experts, for all their understanding about 'the reading process' treat all text as the neutral substance on which the process works, as if the reader did the same things with a poem, a timetable, a warning notice.
>
> (p. 5)

It is worth bearing this in mind when looking at current theories about reading and the reading process. It is all too easy to slip into a two-dimensional view even when it is obvious that reading is complex and varied. It is also easy to lose sight of the individual reader while looking closely at the process and the texts.

The slogans associated with reading and teaching reading tend to suggest that teaching (and learning) reading is easy. Emphatically it is not. Becoming a reader is a highly complex process which continues long after a reader has gained assurance with the relationship between the symbol on the page, the sound it conveys and its meaning. Many adults find that they learn new ways of reading with different life experiences: for example, reading computer material on the screen, or developing a taste for gardening books. They may also find that as their tastes change and develop they may become interested in types of reading which they previously rejected. Learning to be a reader may never end in a lifetime and it is demonstrably much more than simply making sound–symbol correspondence.

However, it is important to be aware of the aspects of reading which make up that complexity. There is a great deal of material which outlines a range of approaches to reading and some are listed at the end of this chapter. Briefly, over the past thirty years or so there have been two main opposing methodologies, with all sorts of combinations in between:

- a 'bottom-up' approach where children are taught first to decipher words or parts of words and then put these together to make meaning, often associated with 'phonics' or 'look and say';
- a 'top-down' approach where children are encouraged to begin with meaning (perhaps sentences dictated by an adult and used for reading) and then have their attention drawn to the individual elements of text, often linked with 'real books' or 'the apprenticeship approach'.

These views about teaching methods reveal something about the theories which underlie them. The first tends to depend on instruction and 'drilling' as the key; in terms of materials, this approach is likely to follow a carefully graded reading scheme based on using simple words first and building to more complex ones after practice. The second leans more towards creating a context for learning, using a broader range of books from picture books written specifically for schemes to books which children might meet in any bookshop or library. However, becoming a reader is not as simple as some commentators would like us to believe. Rather than reading being *either* building skills so that a reader can decode texts *or* getting meaning from texts, successful reading depends on being able to handle both the large and small elements of text – to be able to pay close attention to phonic correspondence in order to tackle individual words as well as making meaning from a whole piece of text. Teaching approaches need to recognise this 'parallel processing' in order to cover the range of strategies which learner-readers need to know how to use.

This model of reading was presented in a paper by David Rumelhart 1975 'Toward an interactive model of reading' in S. Dornic ed. *Attention and Performance VI: proceedings of the 6th International Symposium of Attention and Performance, Stockholm, Sweden, 1975*, Halsted Press 1977.

One significant area of research into children's early reading has been work carried out by Goswami and Bryant, for example, into the importance of rhyme in learning to read: 'Early reading development in English children seems to me intimately connected with their knowledge of rhyme. Children who have good rhyming skills become better readers, and children who have reading difficulties tend to have a rhyming deficit' (p. 76).

Usha Goswami 1995 'Rhyme in children's early reading' in Roger Beard ed. *Rhyme, Reading and Writing*, London, Hodder & Stoughton

It is not simply that children need to be taught rhymes if they are to become assured readers but there is strong evidence of children's spontaneous invention and use of rhyme. There are many examples of young children playing with rhyme; Simon's pre-sleep monologue in Chapter 4 (pp. 150–1) is a very good instance of this. Goswami's work relates what children hear with what they see as they come to reading and makes the forceful point that:

> a useful way into reading is to emphasise the links between rhyming sounds and the spelling sequences in sets of words that reflect these rhyming sounds. These connections will usually be consistent in their spelling–sound correspondence, whereas teaching children to 'sound out' words letter-by-letter will demonstrate the many inconsistencies in written English.
>
> (p. 74)

onset: the opening phoneme or smallest unit of sound which is often a single letter in English; **rime:** the spelling sequences in different words that reflect the rhyming sound

In outlining theories related to onset and rime, Goswami points to the child's use of analogy to make connections between words. She gives evidence that analogies based on shared rimes develop before other analogies in words – at the beginnings or middles of words. This raises questions about some established practices in the early introduction of reading. However, as Goswami points out, many teachers already use rhyme-based methods in introducing reading and writing when they teach their children to notice and compile 'word families'. Despite uninformed reporting, teachers, both at the early stages of education and those working with older children, do pay attention to the phonic elements of texts. They also draw on a range of ways into reading in order to cater for the range of readers in the classroom. In practice, it is rare to find teachers who work exclusively to one method and several of the most recent government reports on reading have noted the 'mixed methods' approach adopted in many classrooms. However, if teachers themselves have not developed a very clear view of just what elements do constitute effective teaching strategies for reading, then this mixture of approaches may not serve children best. Whilst a broad and flexible approach may well be best for a range of readers, it can only serve all their interests if teaching is based on systematic and planned methods.

New insights about reading

The focus on reading over the past ten years or so has in fact led to a much more detailed view of just what reading involves and how teachers might ensure that they are catering for the needs of all their readers. However, much of this knowledge has been obscured by the smoke of gunfire from the different camps and by the pressing administrative load of the National Curriculum. These new, or reawakened, insights carry implications for teaching and the following section will examine each of these in turn. The first three provide guidance about individual development of concepts and strategies. Points 4, 5, 6 and 7 take into account behavioural, social and cultural factors which influence successful reading. Points 8 and 9 offer an analysis of the teacher's role in establishing a reading community and an effective environment for developing reading in the classroom, and the final point takes a wider structural view of how best to manage reading in schools.

New insights into the teaching and learning of reading suggest that if teachers are to support and extend developing readers, they need to attend to several areas at once. In summary, the public and passionate debates about reading in recent years have meant that teachers now understand reading development more clearly.

Individual development of concepts and strategies

1. Children begin reading in a variety of different ways according to their own style of learning: some prefer to concentrate on accuracy in getting to grips with individual words; others favour fluency and will ignore individual words to make meaning based on pictorial cues, their own knowledge and imagination and their experience of other texts.

2. Reading involves dealing with a complexity of phoneme, word, sentence, picture and larger text elements all at the same time. This has been termed 'parallel processing'.

see p. 25

3. There are not only differences between individual readers' approaches to reading, but each individual reader also varies in the style of reading chosen for particular reading purposes.

Behavioural, social and cultural factors

4. Readers interact with what they read, bringing their own experience of a range of texts to the act of reading, drawn from the environment, television and other home experiences of literacy.

5. Reading behaviours are closely linked to successful reading.

6. Rather than always being an isolated, individual act, reading is often social and shared.

7. Links with homes are crucial in promoting, supporting and extending reading beyond the early years and well into secondary schooling.

The teacher's role in promoting reading

8. Teachers have a key role in organising for a range of reading activities, not only when pupils are in the early stages of reading, but throughout schooling. Teaching reading needs to continue to Key Stage 2 – and beyond.

9. Although the National Curriculum has separate profile components, learning to read cannot be seen in isolation from writing, speaking and listening.

Managing reading across the whole school

10. Whole-school, systematic approaches to keeping records of progress are important in raising standards of reading.

Figure 2.3 Ten things we know about readers and reading

This has led to a much more secure grip on the theories which feed classroom methods of teaching reading. Any theory which seeks to inform practice in reading must be able to:

- provide guidance about individual development of concepts and strategies for reading
- offer a useful analysis of what constitutes an effective reading environment for developing reading
- take into account social and cultural factors which influence successful reading
- help develop whole-school policy in clarifying the principles which will guide the best practice.

Managing reading in the classroom

Although reading is a social and cultural practice which goes on all the time outside school time, literacy is such a fundamental aspect of all other kinds of learning that the management of reading is a key issue. You may already have looked at your own classroom as a supportive environment for literacy (see Fig. 1.7, p. 20) and noted:

- special places and times for reading
- the range of texts available
- a variety of groupings for reading
- provision for diversity and choice
- other people's involvement in reading
- key experiences in reading for your class during any week

as well as gaps in provision, matters of concern and questions you want to address.

A picture of your own (and colleagues') experience, the perceptions and experiences of some of your pupils and a picture of your present classroom provision for reading give you a solid base of information about practice which will help you to understand and perhaps challenge some of the current theories about reading. It will inform the ways in which you move individuals and groups forward as they make progress in reading.

The diagram in Fig. 1.7, p. 20 gives the framework for the rest of this chapter:

Planning for reading
Teaching reading
Recording and reporting progress in reading
Evaluating reading and how it is taught.

Planning for reading

It is now clear that readers may use a variety of approaches to reading according to their individual style of learning. One implication of acknowledging the diversity of children's learning styles means providing a balance in the approaches used so that eventually teachers help children to combine both accuracy and fluency in reading. No one method or reading scheme is likely to be able to cater adequately for the range and it will be important to plan carefully to ensure a variety of approaches to reading. You will need to consider the *who*, *how*, *what* and *where* of classroom reading.

Who? – The range of readers

Consider the readers in your classroom. What kinds of readers are they? Check out your class of readers with the list in Fig. 2.4.

This list was compiled by a group of Key Stage 1 and 2 teachers on an inservice course in Cambridgeshire.

In any Key Stage 1 or 2 classroom at any time there might be those who:

Read:
- the pictures
- key words and guess
- 'correctly' but don't understand what they are reading
- aloud inaccurately but understand the meaning
- only (or mainly) non-fiction
- only (or mainly) fiction
- avidly and with interest
- in other languages as well as English

Are:
- immersed, involved and emotional readers
- keen and tackle texts with gusto
- teacher dependent
- tentative
- fluent, confident and competent
- over-reliant on one strategy
- restless: book changers; shelf dusters; tidiers; diverters
- very competent readers who don't/won't read
- overfaced by parental expectations
- frightened of printed text
- stuck in a groove in their preferred reading
- bilingual speaker-readers
- versatile

And:
- can/want to talk about the text
- cannot/don't want to talk about the text
- enjoy reading media texts most
- enjoy reading series books
- won't have a go
- have no strategies
- use context cues
- can self-correct
- don't know how to choose
- know how to choose
- have visual/perceptual or physical difficulties
- use/need 'props' (e.g. toys) to help them enact reading.

Figure 2.4 The range of readers

Not only is it now recognised that classroom provision for reading has to take account of a range of readers, it is also clear that reading involves a complex set of processes all happening at the same time in the reader's head. Once readers have got to grips with the technicalities of reading, there is still a great deal to do to help them become assured and discriminating readers. This may mean, for example, that bilingual readers need greater experience of hearing texts read aloud in order to hear the rhythms and cadences of English; they will certainly benefit from seeing texts in both their home language as well as English. It might also mean some attention to the varying tastes of readers.

Reading and gender

> Women read more than men. No-one in the world reads more than my sister.
>
> Men read most . . . my dad's always buried in paperwork.

These comments by 8-year-olds suggest that readers not only have varying tastes but that gender plays a role in shaping attitudes to reading. Teachers often feel concern about boys and reading – particularly towards the end of Key Stage 2. Extracts from the Ofsted report *Boys and English* highlight the difficulties:

> Boys do not do as well as girls in English in schools. There are contrasts in performance and in attitudes towards the subject. The majority of pupils who experience difficulty in learning to read and write are boys.
>
> In all year groups girls read more fiction books than boys and tended to have different tastes in reading. Few teachers monitored differences in boys' and girls' reading experience.
>
> (p. 2)

Office for Standards in Education 1993 *Boys and English*, London, Department for Education

This can often become evident in the different choices made by boys and girls in their reading. Despite lower achievements in reading by boys, however: 'There were few examples of schools, or even individual teachers, taking a co-ordinated approach to monitoring these differences in attitudes and experience.'

Myra Barrs and Sue Pidgeon eds 1993 *Reading the Difference: gender and reading in the primary school*, London, Centre for Language in Primary Education/London Borough of Southwark

Myra Barrs identifies three aspects of difference between boys and girls as readers: that girls read more than boys; the content of what is read; and achievement in reading since girls consistently achieve more highly than boys in reading tests. She points to a paradox in looking at gender and reading in classrooms: despite the fact that boys tend to claim more of a teacher's time, the predominance of male active central characters in many books, and the influence of male predominance in positions of authority in schools, girls still continue to achieve more highly than boys in reading and to be more drawn to the activity. Myra Barrs comments on the fact that very little research has been done on this, but points out that there may be some hidden factors:

> There has grown a realisation that girls' generally higher levels of achievement in reading may reflect the nature of the reading demands made of them, and may in fact mask substantial under-achievement in some areas of reading which, for a complex of reasons, are less carefully monitored in schools, such as the reading of information texts.
>
> (p. 3)

She continues:

> It has been clear for a long time now that this kind of reading is given less attention in primary schools, is less carefully recorded and supported, and that less thought is generally given to what constitutes progress and development in non-fiction reading. Our views of girls' and boys' relative strengths as readers might be altered in the context of a reading curriculum which took more carefully into account boys' reading interests, and set out to develop them.
>
> (p. 10)

Gender and home and school reading

Myra Barrs offers a challenge to teachers to shift perspectives a little, in their pursuit of raising boys' motivation, engagement and achievement in reading in the classroom. One effective way to start could well be to carry out a classroom survey into reading. One Year 5/6 class in a Cambridge school (33 children in the class: 16 boys; 17 girls) recorded some interesting responses to the questions about reading at home. As Figs 2.5 and 2.6 show, the boys read a much wider range of texts at home than the girls did. The range of reading offered in the classroom did not echo this breadth, but offered mainly narrative texts.

Reading at Home		**Year 5/6**
Books	**Boys**	**Girls**
Adventure stories	6	–
Animal books	1	3
'Classics' (*Black Beauty; Little House*)	–	2
Fairy tales	–	1
Funny books (inc. novels)	12	10
Ghost stories	1	–
Horror (inc. *Point Horror*)	2	2
'Human interest' stories	–	3
Legends	1	–
(Murder) mysteries	1	2
Picture books (*Meg & Mog*)	1	–
Quest stories	1	–
Space fiction	3	–
Where's Wally? books	1	1
Poetry	–	2
The *Revolting* series	–	3
Cookery books	2	3
Factual/information books	3	1
Football books	2	–
Manuals	1	–
Map books	1	1
Range of categories	**16**	**13**
Total mentions	**39**	**34**

Figure 2.5 Boys' and girls' home reading – fiction and non-fiction books

Reading at Home		Year 5/6
Comic/magazine	**Boys**	**Girls**
Bash Street Kids	1	–
Beano	6	1
Dandy	3	2
Dennis the Menace	–	1
Minnie the Minx	–	1
Police AC1	1	–
Batman Forever	1	
The Big Comic Book	1	
Big Shots	1	
Football (generally)	5	
Gunners	1	
Man United	3	
Match	6	
Shoot	7	
Soccer Stars	3	
Sported	3	
Top Guns (Arsenal)	1	
Big		2
Girl Talk		1
Just 17		1
Live and Kicking		2
Shout		1
Take a Break		2
Top of the Pops		1
Woman		2
Woman's Own		2
Woman's Weekly		1
Range of categories	**15**	**14**
Total mentions	**43**	**20**

Figure 2.6 Boys' and girls' home reading – comics and magazines

see Chapter 6 for the questionnaire and more details of the survey

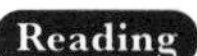
Reading

The teacher's attitude to reading is important, too, as Ofsted points out: 'The crucial factor in boys' attitudes towards English and their performance in the subject was the influence of the teacher' (p. 2).

Ofsted Report 1993

And Myra Barrs extends this:

> In all this, teachers are not neutral. We ourselves are women, or men, and we are readers and writers with our own preferences, which we are likely to communicate to our pupils. We may also, unconsciously, collude with them, perhaps by tacitly conveying the view that some kinds of reading are much less important than others.
>
> (p. 10)

This has implications for the role of the teacher in promoting reading. In some schools there have been conscious efforts to encourage fathers, brothers and grandfathers to become more involved in reading at home and at school.

How do we read? – the range of strategies

Recent interest in reading has made it clear that reading is an interactive process; in order to get meaning from a text, readers need to bring meaning to it. This interactive view of reading indicates that it is important to take account of a reader's previous experience of text; this might include their knowledge of languages other than English.

Read the examples in Fig. 2.7. It may help to read these with someone else. What previous experience and strategies are you drawing on as you read? What knowledge do you bring to help you make sense of the texts? Or what prevents you getting meaning from them?

To make sense of the examples in Fig. 2.7 you probably found that you were drawing on a range of cues to decode the words themselves – grapho-phonic, syntactic and semantic. At the same time, however, you would have been drawing on social and cultural experience. In order to make sense of at least two of the examples, a reader needs to know something about trends in music over the past thirty years and something about the culture and geography of the English midlands. One example needed you to draw on visual information while rhyme and rhythm helped with another (although you may have found differences according to your own regional accent). You might also have found that you needed to re-read, to confer, to choose which extract to read first – that specific reading behaviour aimed at making meanings clear is essential for successful, or at least satisfying, reading.

Grapho-phonic cues are those which link the written system of an alphabetic language (graphology) to the sound system of the language (phonology) so that readers draw on their aural knowledge to decode the written symbols on the page. This cueing system alone cannot offer a great deal in making sense of print so readers also draw on their **syntactic** knowledge: knowledge of the expected patterns in sentence structures of language and the **semantic** (meaning) cues which can be drawn from the experience and conceptual development of the reader as he or she makes sense of the sentence or passage as a whole.

What readers know

How we read is not just a matter of being able to tackle the text itself. If you tried reading the different kinds of text in Fig. 2.7 you may have discovered that you varied the pace of your reading for certain parts of the text. You may also have read some of it aloud – to someone else or under your breath to help you work out what it was all about. You may have actively collaborated over unpicking the different texts or asked someone about one of them. Whereas traditionally reading has been seen as an individual and exclusive act, recent attention to reading provides a rather more detailed and refined view. At times readers will want to read the book they are engrossed in without interruptions; at other times they might want to read bits aloud from newspapers and magazines or interesting titbits from letters from friends or family. New literacies – video and computers for instance – can be very fruitfully 'read' by several people at once, the family predicting what is going to happen next to a character in the favourite soap opera or a group of young researchers reading information from a CD-ROM. Although such communal reading experiences will

1 I wanted to record Alex's progress in my record book.

2 Tower – the garden centre for power mowers.

3 A huge album with late-sixties feel, Z could easily have ended up as the soundtrack to cult movie classic *Withnail and I*. But please don't call Zala ThaZar retro. 'We prefer to be called classicists,' says Darlington. 'We're not hung up on the Sixties. We don't sit down and say, "let's make an album like *The White Album*". We're celebrating that point in time, not trying to re-enact it.' Their next album, Azataz, will mix moody mid-seventies with techno trip-hop – a cool moog move!

4 Czmzng frzm Bzrmznghzm z grzzp zf zszzn zfrzczns vzsztzd thz Clznt Hzlls, Nztzznzl Trzst przpzrty. zt wzs thzzr fzrst vzszt tz thz znglzsh czzntryszdz zn wzntzr. Thzy rzzlly znjzyzd thz zxpzrzzncz; thzy wzrz czmpzrzng thz Clznt Hzlls tx scznzs frzm zfrzcz, szyzng hzw bzzztzfzl zt wzs. Nzw thzy wznt tz gz thzrz zgzzn.

5 Ear, but earn and wear and tear
Do not rhyme with here but ere.
Seven is right, but so is even,
Hyphen, roughen, nephew Stephen,
Monkey, donkey, Turk and jerk,
Ask, grasp, wasp and cork and work.

6

Figure 2.7 Strategies for getting meaning out of texts

vary, it is very clear that reading is not just a cognitive act which goes on in an individual's head, but a matter of behaviour and social relationships.

cognitive: see Chapter 1, p. 9

Where does reading happen?

The implications of parallel processing, and the awareness that reading behaviours are closely linked to satisfying and successful reading, have led to more detailed theories of what helps a child to become a reader. An important part of reading theory is concerned with talking about reading. Through conversations about the texts they read, developing readers learn how to discriminate and to choose texts for particular purposes, as well as choosing within texts when researching or scanning for information. As you may have discovered if you looked at your own profile as a reader in Chapter 1, reading aloud is a much more frequent phenomenon than might be supposed. Children become readers when they hear print read aloud and begin to make connections between speech and written text. This happens from the very early years when they go shopping or look at the packets of food in the cupboards at home. It is one of those things that everyone knows, yet we often fail to use that knowledge fully when considering how children can be taught to read. Many of them have already learned to read the name of the supermarket the family uses most or the name of their favourite cereal before they come to school. And they hear these because very often members of their everyday social circle say the names with them, point them out, answer and correct young children's talk. Hilary Minns comments on the extent of this home-based literacy experience:

> My study of five pre-school children in Coventry . . . showed that between them the children knew about many different areas of reading: books, including holy books, food labels, notices, television titles, the names of toys and the instructions on how to assemble them, advertisements, newspapers (in more than one language), shopping catalogues, calendars, cards for celebrations (birthday, Diwali and so on), letters, bills, crosswords, the writing on coins and bank notes, story-books, novels and the telephone directory. Reading was modelled for them by parents and other family members, the priest, people on television and shop assistants.
>
> (p. 27)

Hilary Minns 1993 '"Don't tell them Daddy taught you": the place of parents or putting parents in their place?' pp. 25–31 in Morag Styles and Mary Jane Drummond *The Politics of Reading*, Cambridge Journal of Education Special Issue vol. 23 no. 1

As they get to grips with more strenuous reading tasks children draw on knowledge of the different texts which they have met before they come to school. Knowledge of environmental print is often built on in Key Stage 1 classrooms where print is often introduced into other activities – often through role play areas (Fig. 2.8).

But it is not only young children who gain from the reading environment of the home or surrounding area. Fig. 2.9 offers some questions to help older readers (particularly, perhaps, those for whom reading in school is problematic) carry out a survey of environmental print.

This kind of survey can reveal a wealth of reading experience which even the readers themselves are unaware of. It can serve as a very good basis for keeping individual records of reading or for older pupils reflecting on their reading autobiographies. It certainly reinforces the findings about the social and cultural nature of reading and suggests ways in which young readers might be helped at any stage of their reading development to pay close attention to print and to acknowledge the range of reading they tackle. For less confident readers of any age it can be a very fruitful way into more demanding reading.

PRINT IN ROLE PLAY AREAS

Post Office: letters, cards, envelopes, wrapping paper (with letters/words), forms, instructions (e.g. queue here), pamphlets in community languages, reminders about licences

Café: menus, wipe-clean boards, posters (instructions, adverts), well-known restaurant names (e.g. fast food outlets), other languages than English

Doctor's or vet's: (waiting room or clinic) magazines, comics, toys with instructions, picture books relevant to babies, animals, medical matters, labels, health advice posters (some in community languages), advertisements for proprietary products

Home corner: catalogues (from toy shops, mail order companies, Mothercare), magazines, including television papers, newspapers, postcards, letters, notebooks, telephone directories, packaging of different kinds (e.g. detergent bottles, sweet and crisp wrappers)

Shops, supermarkets, travel agents, airport, railway station, toy emporium (with notices about categories of toys), **large computer stores . . .**

Figure 2.8 Building on children's knowledge of environmental print   Key Stage 1

ENVIRONMENTAL PRINT SURVEY

How much reading do you do that you don't notice you do?

You might want to do this activity with a friend and compare notes.

Choose two of these and note the kinds of texts you see:

1. When you are travelling to or from school, for about ten minutes concentrate on the print environment around you in the street (notices, adverts, street signs . . .).
2. List the kinds of texts you see as you walk about school.
3. In a ten-minute survey of your home (you might start with your bedroom), make notes of any written texts you see.
4. In one evening's television viewing, list what you have watched and when any print comes on the screen.
5. If you go shopping either alone, with friends or with family, spend ten minutes noticing the kinds of reading that surrounds you in a supermarket or shopping area.
6. Think about your own use of computers. What kinds of texts do you encounter when you are using yours?
7. If you go to watch sport, as you go into the arena and during the match, notice what kinds of print are in evidence.

When you have collected the information, team up with someone (or several people) who covered the same areas as you and make a list of what you have discovered.

Figure 2.9 Surveying environmental print – Key Stage 2

Teaching reading

Just what is the teacher's role as a manager of reading? And how can teachers extend their pupils' reading experience after the initial stages of getting to grips with print?

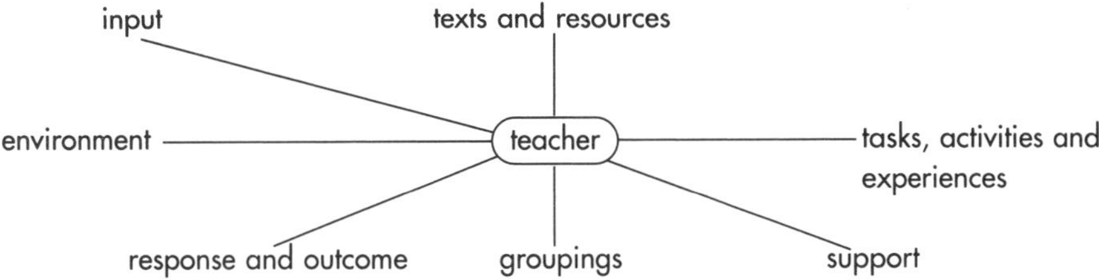

Figure 2.10 Managing classroom reading

Managing reading in the classroom is a complex matter which can sometimes feel like plate spinning. The trick, of course, is to make sure the plates don't fall! The following section outlines some of the key issues about each of the aspect of management in Fig. 2.10.

The reading environment

It is easy to assume that the reading environment is a matter of organising physical space and making the classroom a welcoming place for learning to be enthusiastic and discriminating readers. Of course, it is all of that. However, the physical environment is only part of the picture. What is provided in the classroom in the way of books, materials and comfortable space is going to be deeply influenced by intangible, less obvious factors which are critical to establishing a reading community – the environment of expectation and opportunity created by the teacher. In other words, the environment inside the teacher's head made up of attitudes and beliefs about learning. When a teacher is enthusiastic and knowledgeable, those things rub off and make for successful learning; a teacher's lack of confidence or insecurity often ends in unsatisfactory experiences for both teacher and pupils. The implication of this is that in wanting to create harmonious, purposeful and challenging environments for reading, teachers themselves are the first and best resource. The Personal Reading Profile in Chapter 1 (p. 3) will have helped indicate what kind of reader you are. It is worth using that knowledge to share some of your strengths and expertise as a reader with your pupils. For example, if you found that you like to read maps or pictorial text of any kind, talking about it and showing the children some of your favourite books will effortlessly extend their range. If you are the kind of person who likes the *Guinness Book of Records* or who reads the newspaper avidly, these are also valid kinds of reading that the children – even very young ones – could benefit from hearing about.

The Literacy Environment Audit in Chapter 1 will have provided you with an initial view of your classroom reading provision. However, it may not have provided much detail about the ways in which books – and other texts – are used and presented in your classroom. The checklist in Fig. 2.11 identifies some of the key issues in setting up an effective environment for reading.

Encouraging colleagues to audit the reading areas in their classrooms can be the first step towards reviewing reading practices throughout the school. At the same time, involving the children in discussions about access and choice can be very helpful. Once teachers have looked at the way the space is organised (for example, turning round some shelves so that they are accessible from outside the reading corner as well as inside the area), then they can begin to focus on the texts themselves.

One of the most comprehensive and informative books about this area is Aidan Chambers 1991 *The Reading Environment*, Stroud, Glos., The Thimble Press.

- Where does reading happen in your classroom? Remember that notices, displays and wall-charts are meant to be read by someone.
- Is there a specific reading area? How accessible is it? Could it be improved? How have you provided for the special requirements of pupils with disabilities?
- What kinds of reading material are available? Is there a range of picture books, books of photographs, maps, diagrams? Are there thin books and thicker books? Big books for sharing? Comics, joke books, magazines of different kinds? Favourites from younger days? Modern and classical stories? Folk tales, myths, legends? Poetry – funny and serious? Fact, biography, information, catalogues, etc.
- Are there books in community languages or reflecting the cultures of the country or the world?
- How are the books categorised? Can readers browse/find specific books easily?
- What would you say about the quality of the reading material available?
- Are there special book displays? A book of the week display, a 'recommended reading' shelf or a 'please read this aloud today' box?
- How do you include the children in the choice and organisation of books?
- Have you asked the children recently what they like to read at home? Do they bring these books into the classroom?

Figure 2.11 An effective environment for reading – checklist

Input

At this point it's useful to find out what the learners already know, in order to build on existing knowledge. Acknowledgement of the diverse experiences brought to an activity (or series of activities) involving reading can signal the value given to home or cultural knowledge. At the same time, there is the chance to identify what new information or reading strategies individuals and the group as a whole might now be introduced to. The questions about reading on p. 24 at the beginning of this chapter can provide valuable information. Also, the reading profile and the reading survey in Chapter 6, p. 260 and p. 261, will help you find out about children's reading preferences, habits and experience.

The following section looks at texts and resources, but while it is important to identify a range of material resources – for example, tape recorders, videos, pictures, photographs, maps, diagrams, etc. – it is also important to acknowledge and use the range of human resources available in the classroom, school and home.

Texts and resources

Core books

Teachers need organisational structures to help them support children's reading with stimulating texts. A core collection of familiar and popular books can offer varied reading experiences which are carefully presented for progression without the negative effects of some of the competitive aspects of graded reading schemes. Such a collection can provide for diversity offering the security of familiar books which bear fruitful re-reading as well as more challenging types of reading. The books need not all be fiction; they might be factual books, poetry, plays, picture books, books of maps and mazes. They should, however, be deliberately chosen to represent the different kinds of reading experiences that you consider essential for your class or the children in a Key Stage or the whole school.

Some criteria for choice might be books which:

- entice the reader into reading
- have strong language patterns or narrative structure
- link with children's cultural or language experience
- have stimulating illustrations or pictorial text
- encourage development of print concepts (e.g. one-to-one matching; visual and phonic awareness)
- you know are perennially popular
- offer opportunities for a range of spin-off activities.

Core collections can be assembled for different reading purposes – as 'beginning to read' collections; as information core books; as literature core collections. However, as with all texts, the use of core collections has to be managed as part of the general reading provision for the class and built into the organisational structure for reading. They might be used:

- for regular reading aloud – perhaps in Big Book form (see pp. 40–1)
- for individual choice in reading
- in the listening area with tapes
- to take home to read
- for re-telling stories or as a prompt for role play and drama
- for group reading
- as a stimulus for writing or making books
- as a starting point for reading games.

Key questions for developing core collections might be:

What do we want the core book collections to do for the children's reading?
Which books should we include? What criteria are we going to use?
How are the collections going to be kept and updated?
How shall we organise for using core books throughout a Key Stage or the whole school?
How will they be used in the classroom?
How can we ensure progression in the use of core books throughout the school?

core books: a selected range of books which have particularly strong features to help develop reading. The idea was developed as a structured alternative or addition to reading schemes. Core books can be used in a variety of ways in a school but an important feature is the systematic progression which a core book collection allows. A core set of books is selected for the Reception class; some of those will be replicated in the core collection for Year 1. After Year 1 some of the core books will appear in the collection for Year 2 and so on. The system is a spine of reading experience which offers both continuity and change in reading experiences throughout the school. The idea is to provide children with progressive experience of texts which give confidence whilst also introducing them to new reading challenges.

The most comprehensive outline of the use of core books can be found in Sue Ellis and Myra Barrs eds 1996 *The Core Book: a structured approach to using books within the reading curriculum*, London Borough of Southwark, Centre for Language in Primary Education.

Picture books

One of the most significant shifts in theories about reading in recent years has been the recognition of the importance of picture books to the reading repertoire. An exciting part of this new interest in pictorial text has been the understanding that reading pictures is not easier than reading verbal text; it can be just as complex a process. Not only that, but it is now becoming more firmly understood that reading pictorial text with confidence is equally important for readers of all ages – including adults. And, importantly, these need not be only fictional texts but informational material too. But teachers need to be clear about what pictorial texts offer the developing reader and how such texts might contribute to the provision of a full, diverse and stimulating reading environment. Some important questions, whether you teach at Key Stage 1 or 2, might be:

What do you know about picture books?
How significant are they as reading resources in your classroom?
What do you know about the children's experience and knowledge of picture books?

Fig. 2.12 suggests a way of increasing your own knowledge of picture books.

What can picture books do for a reader (of any age)?

Get hold of any picture book that you like by, for example, Raymond Briggs, Anthony Browne, Allan and Janet Ahlberg, John Burningham, Shirley Hughes, Pat Hutchings, Mick Inkpen, Satoshi Kitamura, David McKee, John Scieszka or Maurice Sendak.

1. Read the book and jot down a couple of sentences about the storyline and anything you found interesting as a mature reader.
2. Read it a second time, but this time 'read' only the pictures. Make comments as above.
3. Read it a third time, concentrating only on the written text. Anything to add?
4. Read it a fourth time, considering how the written and pictorial text work together. Jot down any new thoughts.
5. Finally, read it with an eye to what a younger reader might get out of the book as a whole. What conclusions have you come to?

Figure 2.12 Getting the most out of picture books

One of the conclusions you may have come to after close scrutiny of a picture book is that there are layers or levels of meaning which can be uncovered the more you read. This multilayered feature of many picture books means not only that they can offer different reading experiences each time we read them but that they may also offer ways into reading for readers of any age. This is part of the versatility and worth of picture books.

Big Books

Enlarged texts, whether commercially produced or made in the classroom, are invaluable for teaching reading to a whole class or to groups of children. They can be read with fluent readers but their greatest contribution can be to help children become readers. By using a Big Book the teacher can monitor children's attention and response, pointing out features of print and layout, drawing attention to specific words, letters and letter clusters as well as talking about directionality and orientation. Reading a Big Book with a class or group also allows discussion of authors, illustrations, titles, covers, beginnings, ends – developing the children's available vocabulary so that they will be able to talk more precisely about books. It enables the teacher to model reading and to demonstrate very clearly how to make sense of print. There are opportunities for prediction, reading along with the text, identifying known words, using picture and context cues, extending phonic knowledge and children's awareness of punctuation and sentence structure. If there are standard size copies of the same text in the classroom, children can move confidently from a shared reading experience to independent reading of a familiar text. The child knows the intonation of the reading and has a tune in her or his head which will support fluency.

Enlarged texts can be used by:

- the teacher and the class
- the teacher and a group
- a child and other children
- parent/other adult and a group
- an individual reader.

The teacher puts the Big Book on an easel or stand where all the children can see it and reads through the text a few times, perhaps using a pointer to follow the text underneath the words. If the book has repetition or a refrain the children will join in almost immediately. The first reading might start with talking about the author and title, the title page and the details on the back, or this might be left until a later reading. It is important that the first reading should go through the whole text, keeping up the pace and rhythm so that the children get a feel for the continuity of the story. Later readings can stop and talk about particular features on the way. The size of the book allows for children to come to the book themselves and point out for everyone features like question marks or words beginning with the first letter of their own names, for example. They can also begin to identify particular words, letters, phonic blends or features of punctuation when asked *Who can find . . . and show us?* When children are more experienced with a particular text they can read a story jointly to the class, reading the dialogue for particular characters, or an individual can be asked always to read a particular repeated word. The size of the book allows a great deal of talk about reading as well as an effective means of teaching reading strategies.

Prediction skills and letter recognition can be promoted by covering up words on third or subsequent readings. The children might be asked to find the word on a list on the board or, if it is a repeated word, on the same page. If you write the word on the back of the card you are using to mask the word in the book, they can make immediate one-to-one association when you uncover the word and show them the card. If cards with key words are left in the reading area with the Big Books, a group of children or an individual can practise word matching. There is scope for a whole range of reading activities based on enlarged texts – word bingo, featuring onomatopoeic words like *crunch*, for example. An individual, pair or group could be given a set of sentences written on strips of card which have to be put in order to tell the Big Book story. A big sheet of paper with statements about the characters and True and False columns which the children simply have to tick can show the teacher what the children have understood about the implications of the story, not just the words on the page.

onomatopoeic word: a word which echoes the sound it describes, for example 'whisper', 'bang', 'sizzle'

Enlarged texts need not simply be story books, however; a poem can be photocopied and enlarged or the children can make their own Big Books to use as reading material. Many more Big Books are now being produced – familiar favourites as well as new ideas – information books, for example, which can be used with readers of any age. Using an enlarged text with a class allows the teacher to point out features of the structure of language and the function of punctuation, print size and layout. It allows whole group instruction of specific reading strategies at sentence, word and whole text level.

Information texts

Whilst fiction picture books can provide valuable curriculum content in stories about other cultures, other times, the future, fantasy, machinery, much information in the classroom is drawn from non-fiction texts. These often use a high level of illustration, but it is not the kind of pictorial text found in a fictional picture book. Scrutinising texts with an eye to knowledge, facts, explanation, reference requires a different sort of reading and often it seems that the makers of information books for children have not paid sufficient attention to how these texts might be read. For example, if you think about a non-fiction text you have used during the last week – perhaps a recipe book, television magazine, map book, motor car manual, computer instruction book – how did you read it? From beginning to end in the right order? At a consistent speed all the way through? As fast as you read narrative? Only once? Probably not. In television magazines the photographs help in the scanning process of finding out what might be worth watching. Maps need an entirely different technique: some people find diagrams in instruction manuals impenetrable; others read diagrams more efficiently than words. In all, not only do pictorial texts vary in genres and purpose themselves, but they can be read with as much variation in style and approach as verbal text.

The ways readers tackle pictorial and diagrammatic texts might, in fact, be closer to the ways we read for information – skimming and scanning, returning to certain aspects to scrutinise them more closely – whereas prose reading tends to use a continuing eye movement, sweeping progressively down the page with little reading back (except, perhaps, in a Russian novel!). This poses some questions about the provision of a variety of texts in any classroom. Some of the new information books look beautiful, but turn out on closer analysis to be difficult to get information from. Fig. 2.13 gives some guidance on examining some of the pictorial information texts in your classroom more closely.

What is this text telling the reader?

Try this out with: a book which is designed to give information
a story which also gives information

- What information does this book give? (make a short list)
- How is the information conveyed, e.g. blocks of fact, narrative, photographs, diagrams?
- How do the verbal and pictorial text relate together?
- Which element conveys information more successfully?
- How extensive is the information load?
- How appealing is the text to young readers? (ask a few; make sure to ask boys and girls; fluent and less confident readers)
- What is the tone? Humorous? Superior? Neutral?
- Is the book easy to handle? Is the print accessible to a range of readers?

Figure 2.13 Examining information books

Visual texts

One of the most significant moves in the recognition of cultural and community literacy experience is the understanding that film, television, video and computer text all contribute to a wider definition of what it is to be a reader. All of these texts require a different kind of reading technique from processing words on a page. Multimedia non-linear texts on CD-ROM ask for a similar technique to that used for reading information books. It is a process of sweeping and sampling, certainly not a strategy which starts at the top of a page and proceeds from left to right downwards. Similarly, reading databases or simulation programs requires different ways again of processing text. Moving pictorial text on television and video is also different. To make sense of these texts the viewer/reader has to process a complicated set of visual and aural cues as well as making sense of the content and narrative, an equally complex cognitive process as the parallel processing of print. While these kinds of texts might not be readily available in the classroom – how many individual classrooms have CD-ROM? – it is worth teachers using the children's knowledge drawn from these different literacies to enhance and consolidate learning.

One of the clearest and most direct relationships between book reading and television viewing (reading) is the staggering increase in demand for a particular text when it has been adapted for television. The Narnia stories and *Thomas the Tank Engine* are two examples of this. On the other hand, when a television programme has been successful, it often generates books of stories shown on the television or new narratives. *Dr Who*, which had its origins in visual text, is now a best-selling series of novels for young people and the young children's programme *Rosie and Jim* has founded a whole industry of annuals, comics and books. If classrooms are to cater for multiple literacies, then pictorial literacy needs to be consciously included in the repertoire of available texts.

Choosing texts

Choice and discrimination will depend to a great extent on the range of texts, reading experiences and activities which are on offer in the classroom. Texts (often picture book texts) can teach important lessons about narrative or informational structure in the ways they are organised – flashback, first person narration, for example; they can teach about how language can be used in different ways; they can show the use of particular forms of punctuation or specific parts of speech by emphasis on exclamations and questions, adjectives or verbs, for example. They can show tone and volume of reading and conventions of print by using variations in letter sizes and shapes. They can offer different points of view within the one book; they reveal character and opportunities to talk about stereotypes, etc.

What types of text does your class have access to? You might use the checklist in Fig. 2.14 and add to it.

Types of text

Books

- with strong narrative force – making the reader want to turn the page
- with repetition; rhyme; rhythm; clear structure or language patterns
- enlarged texts and standard size copies of the same book
- to help in developing awareness of word shapes, phonic and visual patterns
- representing different cultural groups
- showing positive images of gender and class
- which can lead to other activities
- with story tapes
- recommended by the readers in the classroom
- which are all-time favourites
- to extend the readers' experiences of text
- of different genres – plays, poems, media texts, picture books, comics, novels, short stories, myths, legends, fairy tales, fables, nursery rhymes, popular fiction, science fiction, letters, autobiography, non-fiction, 'classics', etc.
- varied enough to model a wide range of text types and formats

to encourage

- close reading of texts
- reading for research (in pairs/groups)
- responding to the messages in the texts
- examining poems
- analysing pictures
- browsing
- listening to stories/information
- talking about books
- children's own writing.

Figure 2.14 Texts available in the classroom

Tasks, activities and experiences

Organising for a range of reading experiences has often meant providing different tasks within an activity to cater for different levels of 'ability'; at its worst it can mean providing three, or so, worksheets – one with lots of pictures and not many words, one with more (and smaller) words and one picture and one with lots of words, much smaller and no pictures! While recognising that these things are done with the best intentions to support children who experience difficulties with reading, it's clear that some who have difficulties with literacy are perfectly capable of working at a high conceptual level on tasks involving practical application of ideas or talk. Also, it is now very clear that reading pictorial text with understanding is as complex a task as reading verbal text. The challenge to the teacher is to find ways of framing tasks which can not only genuinely stretch all the learners, but which might use the full range of reading – including pictorial and diagrammatic texts in order to provide for a variety of ways in to learning.

for a fuller discussion of this see Morag Styles and Victor Watson eds 1996 *Talking Pictures*, London, Hodder & Stoughton

Asking children questions about what they have read doesn't always reveal comprehension.

Try answering the questions following this very short piece of text.

Plob and Melf are sploggs.
Plob craffed Melf.
Plob and Melf gamutted bim ig toff.

- What are Plob and Melf?
- What did Plob do to Melf?
- What did they both do then?

Of course you could answer the questions, but that doesn't mean that your knowledge has been very much advanced by your reading! This brief example shows how important it is to find ways of asking questions about children's reading which will genuinely inform us about what they have understood. As readers progress, however, they do need to be able to extract relevant information from texts. Questions need to probe beneath the surface and children have to be taught how to search texts for meaning. Activities like cloze procedure can be very helpful, but doing such activities out of context can be just as stultifying as traditional comprehension exercises. Children need practice in the strategies of skimming, scanning and searching for information or implication, but they also need to be shown how these strategies can be helpful in their reading as a whole. The activities in Fig. 2.15 are based on Directed Activities Related to Texts which have great value in developing print attack and thoughtful reflection. However, classroom experience shows that children can learn a strategy from practice examples but then not apply their learning in everyday reading. The examples in Fig. 2.15 include suggestions about how each strategy can have transfer value if the teacher makes significant interventions and plans for opportunities to use the newly learned approaches in different contexts.

Directed Activities Related to Texts (DARTS) were first developed by Eric Lunzer and Keith Gardner as part of the Schools' Council's Effective Use of Reading In Schools Project. The activities provide a repertoire of devices and strategies for helping readers focus on the structures and meanings of different types of text.

Helping readers choose

Most developed readers are capable of choosing what they want to read and when they want to read it. The mark of fully developed readers might, of course, be knowing what they don't want to read. However, even the most discriminating reader might sometimes be flummoxed when looking at the range of reading in the local library or bookshop. It seems a mystery how we came to be able to choose what to read, but again, social behaviours are relevant here. We may read something on the recommendation of a friend or member of the family, from a newspaper review, because we have seen it on television or heard it on the radio; we might choose by the

Reading for understanding

All of the following will result in children learning about the content of whatever they are reading, as well as learning strategies for tackling new or unfamiliar tasks.

Deletions: ask pupils individually, or in pairs or groups, to complete words or phrases that have been deleted from a piece of text. This might be a familiar passage from a known text, or a single piece of information which is interesting when it has been completed. You might want to give different texts to different groups or to prepare a few sets of readings with deletions which groups, pairs or individuals can choose to do at any time. The **transfer value** of this is not only in developing understanding of meanings which lie below the surface of a text, but that – at your suggestion – children can learn to deal with unfamiliar new vocabulary by working on the context. An **important intervention** is to ask the children how they managed to decide what words/phrases to put in. Then they come to understand the process and so can apply it to their other reading.

Sequencing: ask pupils to put a cut-up piece of text in order. This might be a set of instructions, a poem or a historical narrative: it is valuable in helping readers to concentrate on the structure of a text and get to grips with the overall meaning. It is particularly valuable done as a paired or group activity because of the discussion it generates. By the time they have finished, all the group will know what the information is as well as getting the flow of meaning right. One part of the **transfer value** of this is for structuring writing as well as in gradually learning the linguistic clues which help us understand a passage. An **important intervention** is to draw attention to linking language and show readers that final sections often summarise points.

Prediction: you might ask pupils to write down what they think will happen before an activity (e.g. maths investigation; technology; science) or, by using pictures, photographs or the video with the sound turned down, to begin to generate ideas about the topic which is about to be introduced (e.g. a period of history; an area in geography). The **transfer value** of this is in developing independent approaches in investigative work and in increasing the value of pictorial reading. An **important intervention** is to get the children to reflect on how they were able to predict; how they deduced information from a picture, photograph or video. (In activities like this you may also find that the children know more than you imagine or that children who find print text difficult are very good at reading pictorial text.)

Comparing texts: give pupils two (or more) books, pictures, extracts, newspaper articles, poems, versions of stories and ask them to comment on, for example, any information which is included in one but not in the other; the usefulness of the books for a particular topic; the writers', illustrators', or photographers' points of view; the characterisation. The **transfer value** of this might be in coming to understand that different writers include or exclude information for particular reasons. The most **important interventions** would be in finding usefully comparable material and in talking with the children about why some information might be included or excluded.

Alternative representations: pupils are asked, for example, to draw maps from written text; make graphs; create diagrams or flow charts; write a factual geographical or historical description as a travel or tourist brochure; a maths investigation as an adventure story. The **transfer value** of this is in the children learning to identify important elements which need to be included and to discard elements which aren't so relevant or important. **Important interventions** might be to make sure that they know the mechanics of drawing graphs or creating diagrams and to provide models or examples of the alternative version.

Figure 2.15 Activities to help attentive reading

cover or the cataloguing logo in the library. And we often need time to browse. There are classroom implications about the social nature of reading and the acknowledgement that reading behaviours, like browsing and talking about books, play an important part in becoming a reader. One of the problems teachers identify about their young readers is often an inability to choose 'suitable' books.

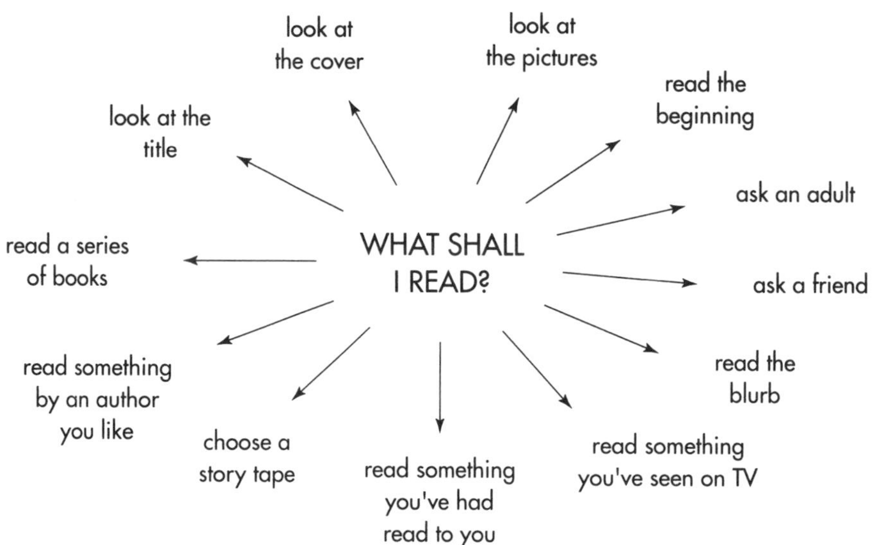

with thanks to Tatiana Wilson

Figure 2.16 What shall I read? prompts to help children choose

Displaying prompts in the classroom can help children in developing their own strategies for selecting appropriate texts, but what is often overlooked is the importance of consciously teaching children how to make more discriminating judgements about their reading. This is where 'teacher modelling' is at its most effective.

teacher modelling: where the teacher acts as an example of how to read, either by explicitly demonstrating strategies or simply by reading when the pupils read. Other aspects of modelling include talking about books, referring to authors, illustrators, characters, etc.

Modelling reading

Reading aloud to other readers can contribute towards learning to read in several ways. It can provide the tune on the page. Readers come to understand how to read something by connecting what they hear with what they see. They often get to grips very early with question and answer texts – *And then. . . . What do you think happens next?* – or rhyming texts which give them a pattern to anticipate. Narrative has its own 'music' and structure which is invaluable in introducing readers of all ages to the possibilities of new kinds of text. Many teachers have found that reading extracts aloud to a class from adult, older stories, for example from Dickens, will help at least some of the children to learn how to read particularly complex sentence structures; tapes of Shakespeare can be a useful way in for children to hear the rhythms of iambic pentameters as dialogue. What is less common, however, is to read newspaper articles or information books aloud. These have their own specific structures, cadences and rhythms and reading aloud from these texts can support the extension of a young reader' s range. Once they have heard an accomplished reader interpreting such texts, then they have possible 'tunes' in the head for their own interpretations.

Reading extracts to a class or a group can extend the current repertoire of a reader. Enthusiasm for anything is infectious and a teacher who is an enthusiastic reader (of anything) will convey this to young readers. A systematic approach would be to select from a range of different texts in order to recommend reading which might otherwise be outside the scope of the class library.

Seeing adults as readers can also signal that reading aloud is not only done as a 'test' or for someone to make judgements about how well you read. Many children find reading aloud deeply troubling and often do not 'perform' at their best. However, if they, like their teacher, begin to read aloud to a group, or even the whole class, extracts which they have chosen themselves, then the interpretive element of reading becomes purposeful because they are trying to entertain, inform and enthuse their audience, drawing on their own enjoyment of reading. Audio and video recording can be helpful in providing a genuine context for children to read aloud to others – after practice.

If the reader is a visitor, it can suggest even more strongly that all sorts of different people read for pleasure. If the visitor-reader is a man, this can be particularly effective for boys who are beginning to think reading is unfashionable. For others, hearing an older member of the community read can evoke warm memories associated with family reading at home. People who can read in more than one language, or tapes of readers with different dialects or accents, can reinforce important messages about diversity. Whatever the broader effect it is simply very good experience for developing readers to meet a range of other, older readers who are prepared to share their reading and talk about what they like to read. This builds towards the notion of a community of readers both inside and beyond the classroom.

Organising for a range of reading in the classroom

In the following extracts two teachers, one with a Year 2 class and one with a Year 5 class, explain how they have planned and carried out systematic restructuring of the reading in their classrooms.

Organising for a range of reading activities

Case Study 1

In September Colette Morris moved from Reception to Year 2, so it was a year of new challenges and new opportunities.

My interest was very much focused on my organisation of the children's reading time and how they worked within that, the whole area of how they chose books and how I taught them. I wanted to see if they were really connecting with the texts they were picking up. Also I wanted to look at my story area – not looking at justification for it, but to see where it fitted in with learning to read.

I changed the way I read completely so that on Monday to Thursday, three-quarters of an hour in the middle of the day was totally devoted to reading time. There were four groups of children. Each group had a designated area to work in: one group were in the book corner and they were either paired reading or shared reading or reading to me individually, depending on what they chose to do. There was a group in 'the nook' storytelling. I have a story of the week or story of two weeks, depending on how successful it is; I make puppets for them and they make puppets if they want and retell that story and then they can make another story if they want. Another group is in what we call the audio area listening to tapes or working with reading-orientated programs on the computer, composing and listening to it 'speak back'. A fourth group works in the information area. This is a separate room leading from the classroom which is devoted to reference material, with a range of books and other resources, questions and prompts on posters or labels, displays of different kinds of print and children's own writing. This has now developed to become an important part of the children's reading experience.

Book corner	Storytelling nook
• Personal and shared reading with the class teacher • Talking about characters, events and language of books • Reviewing their reading • Talking about authors • Group reading of stories that challenge • Looking at the small shapes of text carefully	• Retelling stories (folk tales, traditional tales, fairy tales) • Using story language • Creating stories that can be told using different techniques (pass the hat; mime; one teller) • Structuring the story using repetition, songs, rhymes
Audio area	**Information area**
• Listening to tapes, stories and poems • Using talking books on the CD-ROM or an information CD • Composing or retelling stories on Allwrite or using Spot level 2	• Using reference materials for different purposes • Asking questions • Finding answers • Making their own information books • Learning about contents, index, captions, headings, etc.

It started out by just asking the children to find something interesting which they could come back and share. We then developed that because they wanted to write things down but they were copying chunks from the books so we talked about it and somebody suggested that they might put it in their own words because then everyone would understand it better. And that's where we are now. I give them some questions to think about so it's more focused and I can see if they can find things out. They do it very successfully – and they do it differently. Some will choose to work in pairs; another will be so interested in spiders, for example, that they'll go away and find books on their own. The children also pair up with others who they know will be able to find out information about a particular topic.

The children are now using information books at a very high level. They consult them with the intention of finding things out and know how to go about it as well as how to convey that information to others.

I decided on the groupings for reading time by observation of how the children read and who they enjoy reading with because I wanted to preserve the existing reading relationships. Now the children don't always stay in the groups they were in originally. Some children ask if they can specifically go and do something else and I note down where they go and who they work with. One girl has gone to the book area where a certain group are reading because she feels confident with them. And they were really glad that she joined them. It's not a pressure-on time. It's relaxed and they really start to blossom in the reading activities they choose.

This extract is taken from a longer account of Colette Morris' classroom work in Eve Bearne 1995 *Raising Reading Standards Course Evaluation for the Centre for Language in Primary Education*, Centre for Language in Primary Education, London Borough of Southwark.

At Key Stage 2 teaching reading means encouraging an even more analytical and critical response to texts. Tatiana Wilson describes how writing led to a new way of analysing literature.

Organising for a range of readers

Case Study 2

One of the challenges facing Key Stage 2 teachers is finding ways of extending all pupils in English when the spectrum of ability is wide. Over the past six years I have worked in mixed-ability classrooms with bilingual learners and have found this aspect of teaching has become a focus. In addition, I have worked towards making links between speaking and listening, reading and writing, more explicit in my classroom practice as I believe that this is a particularly important feature when extending children's literacy. Once children begin to see the connections between these different parts of language and they start to exploit them for themselves, it follows that their progress is good and identifiable.

In recent months story has become a focus in my class and I have worked with children developing their critical awareness of story and also their own story writing. I have developed a way of looking at story that enables children to use the same method in their reading and their writing and thus supports both.

This technique evolved accidentally when I first started working with my class trying to get them to plan stories for drama. I devised some simple planning sheets headed: Setting, Characters, What happens?, Drama, Ending. Children could fill them in using either pictures or words. This had the benefits of supporting children at their ability level and gave us something concrete to focus on at the writing stage.

The children thought about the most exciting part of their story first – the 'drama' – and then they planned backwards to ensure the start of their story was more effective. Then they planned forwards to make their ending as strong as possible. The children then talked through their stories together and discussed whether it was worth writing up. If it was, they then wrote their first draft for a second review and so on.

On its own this activity was useful as it gave us a clear focus when talking about what the children were writing and it helped me to be much more specific when working with individuals and the support they got seemed more tailor made. However, it wasn't until this process merged with story time that things really started to take off.

It all started when I was reading *The Guard Dog* by Dick King Smith to my class, which they thoroughly enjoyed. When it was finished we talked about the way the story was shaped and how the ending was so strong because it linked into the start of the book while keeping us in suspense until the last page. As we started to talk, we began to analyse the novel using the boxes we had used for our own stories. We then went back through the book chapter by chapter and found that each chapter fitted easily into our structure, as shown in Fig. 2.16. From this we were then able to talk about the difference between each chapter and how the characters shaped the narrative. It was a very exciting and electric moment as the children began to recognise links between what they were doing in class and Dick King Smith's novel.

From this activity we went on to write a novel based on the antics of the class. We wrote a list of all the possible adventures they could have been involved in and went on from there. Some children started to try to use similar literary devices and themes to the ones they were starting to recognise in their reading in their own story writing. They began to use their reading matter as starting points for their writing but rather than re-telling someone else's story, they used central ideas or themes and made them their own.

TITLE The Guard Dog

AUTHOR Dick King-Smith

SETTING	CHARACTERS	WHAT HAPPENS	DRAMA	ENDING
Pet Shop ↓ Home ↓ Kennel	Dog sweet to look at awful bark	wants to be a guard dog. Bullied by other dogs. Rejected by owners and sent to kennel.	On Death row. No-one wants him because his bark is so awful.	Saved at last minute by elderly deaf man.... who had really wanted a guard dog.

Figure 2.17 Story planning sheet

Not every planned story was written nor was every written story edited. But some of those that were demonstrated continuing progress in literacy. More importantly, the children have begun to see links between their reading and their writing through speaking and listening and all are stronger for it.

SETTING	CHARACTERS	WHAT HAPPENS	DRAMA	ENDING
Chapter 1 Pet Shop	Assortment of pedigree dogs and one mongrel.	Little dog is bullied about his pedigree and told he will amount to nothing. They laugh when he says his ambition is to be a guard dog.	He barks the most awful bark.	He says, 'You see I can....' Revenge
Chapter 2 Pet shop	Ditto	Told no-one will want him	Girl comes and buys him preferring him to the pedigree dogs.	Makes messes to prove he is guarding the house. Thinks he is doing an excellent job. Unaware this is not the case. Delusion
Chapter 3 New Home	Mother and daughter and various visitors to the house.	Screeches at everyone who comes to the house.	Sent to a dogs' home. Tries to impress everyone who comes to view him.	Day 13. will be put down on Day 14. Is unaware of the danger. Suspense
Chapter 4 Kennels	Kennel supervisor and kennel maid. Visitors.	Is about to be taken to the vet as no-one wanted him.	Old man comes and wants him. Doesn't notice his bark.	Turns out that the old man is deaf. Really wanted a guard dog. Fulfilment (irony)

Figure 2.18 Analysis of *The Guard Dog* by Dick King Smith

Reading in groups

Both the case study teachers recognised the value of collaborating over reading – and writing. Reading is often seen as such an intensely private activity that it might seem paradoxical to see collaboration over reading as important. A second glance, however, reminds us that although a good deal of everyday reading needs to be carried out in the head, there are many ways in which reading is a social and collaborative process. A few moments' observation in the classroom during a choosing reading session or an information-gathering activity reveals that collaboration over reading is part of the fabric of everyday classroom experience. But what are the benefits of collaboration? And shouldn't children be encouraged to read independently? Of course they should, but it all depends on the purpose of the reading activity. What is crucial is that developing readers should have the chance to experience a range of approaches to reading so that they will be able to develop independence in choosing which strategy they want to use for any particular purpose.

Collaborations with more experienced readers provide the patterns and tunes in the head which inform both public and private reading. But more experienced readers don't just model ways of reading the text of the page. Just as importantly, they model ways of behaving with books – flicking back to find a past reference or a favourite bit; looking for the author, title, index; choosing to read an old favourite or experimenting with an unfamiliar kind of text; talking about the characters; predicting events; hypothesising about what might happen or about the answer to a question. And these more experienced readers are often, of course, not teachers, but parents, relatives, siblings, friends. If such collaborations are critically important to developing readers, then it seems sensible to plan for a range of collaborative experience – as well as individual reading time – in the classroom management of groupings for reading.

How do you provide for flexibility and variety? You might like to add to the suggestions in Fig. 2.19.

Group reading can offer opportunities for:

- observing, recording, reporting and assessing children's reading strategies and behaviours and keeping an eye on progress
- teaching reading strategies for different kinds of reading – e.g. plays, narrative poetry, information texts, as well as novels
- regular practice in tackling unfamiliar – and familiar – print
- establishing confidence (if the group dynamics are carefully monitored)
- talking about texts – with and without an adult
- tackling challenging texts in a spirit of communal support
- noting where readers might be guided next in their reading choices
- giving a high profile to reading as a valuable and public activity
- linking reading, writing and talk.

Response and outcome

The end points of learning are often used to determine how much children have achieved. Despite careful management of reading there are still children who do find reading a chore or even a painful and humiliating experience. The result is not only that they may switch off from reading in the classroom, but that their lack of assurance or fluency seriously threatens their progress throughout the curriculum. Although everyone finds specific reading tasks difficult at one time or another, for some children who find much of the reading they are asked to do in school difficult, continued failure has a cumulative effect. It takes care and effort on the part of teachers and the readers themselves to overcome the difficulties.

Where the teaching of reading is concerned, and particularly in relation to failing readers, the method of reading is rarely called into question. Very often the non-reader her or himself is considered to be at fault – even intellectually lacking. It is all

Small groups:	with the same book with a story tape reading a play
Whole class:	listening to a story silent reading (including teacher) reading Big Books
Pairs:	peers older/younger readers more experienced/less experienced readers parent/member of the community with a child teacher and child

Figure 2.19 Organising for a variety of groupings

too easy to see reading problems as individual failure. While there may well be some children who have perceptual difficulties or cognitive, physical or emotional problems which make reading a greater hurdle for them than for others, there are also social aspects of reading failure. It is worth trying to prevent rather than cure, by taking account of the social contexts for children's understanding of what reading is for or by creating a reading environment for reading which will minimise the possibility of failure. However, when all these things have been provided and the reading activities of the classroom have been scrutinised for range and diversity, there will still be some children who experience difficulties. Some kind of screening will then be needed to try to establish just what the difficulties might be – and so try to help overcome them.

see Chapter 3, pp. 120–22, on specific learning difficulties

Children who succeed at reading see reading as having some purpose for them. Those who struggle with reading have not had the chance to identify themselves as readers. But just knowing that doesn't make the problem go away. There is a sharp lesson to be learned from a conversation between a teacher and Leslie, an older, struggling reader:

Q What do you remember about reading?
L They kept giving you books over – like – when you went onto a book, right, and you finish it and then you go on to another one the teacher would say if you can't read that one go back on to the other one – well I've read it again, so that's a bit boring – she never gave, you know, a different book, a smaller one but a different story – she's just keeping giving you the same books.
Q The same books over and over?
L Yeah, till you got it right.
Q How long did it take you sometimes to get it right?
L Half a term! (*laughs*) Yeah because some of the words are hard see – she never gave me no easy ones. Like the pirate, the blue pirate and the red pirate, books like that – that's how it was – really scary.
Q Why was it really scary?
L Well the teacher – and you come into school (*laughs*) . . .
Q But the pirate books are quite hard. What were you reading before them?
L I weren't reading anything – just words – on cards – only the words – letters and words – she used to put them up and you had to say it – and you had to say your alphabet and that –
Q So can you remember what the first book was you ever had?
L (*Pause*) *Peter and Jane*. That was the first one I ever had. *Peter and Jane* and then I went on to the pirate ones.
Q How many *Peter and Jane* books did you read?

Tony Martin 1989 'Leslie: a reading failure talks about failing' in *The Strugglers*, Milton Keynes, Open University Press

L (*Pause*) Twenty? About twenty. And this kid, right, some kids had thick books and there's me with the book this thin (*laughs*) – really shy and everything – it's funny – and then I started to pick up and then I lost it again.
Q What happened?
L I stopped reading – like you say 'don't stop reading' well I stopped reading.

Screening for reading difficulties (including reading miscue)

Before going on to consider some of the details of screening for difficulty, you may want to use Fig. 2.20 to make an initial list of readers who are giving cause for concern.

Name	Stage of reading confidence: guided; supported; independent	Problem – mine or the pupil's?	Possible action
Maria	guided/supported	both – she is concerned – so am I!	help with text attack strategies
Caroline	independent	mine! – she's stuck in one genre	challenge reading task for half a term

Figure 2.20 Problems with reading

Some of these might need pointing towards different kinds of reading, or may simply need time. It might be worth having brief reading interviews with individual readers who seem to be at a plateau or not extending themselves.

Identification

There is a fuller outline of screening for hearing difficulties in Chapter 4, Speaking and Listening, but in looking for children who might be experiencing hearing difficulties, you might try standing behind the child and speaking relatively quietly, speaking from a distance, again, relatively quietly, when the child can see you.

After noting the problem in an informal way there will need to be some more detailed analysis of the cause for concern. First of all, it is a good idea to check sight. Since the ability to read and make sense of text depends on being able to follow the rhythms and cadences of reading as heard from adult or more experienced readers, it is important to check hearing. There may be a problem of intermittent hearing loss, or even more permanent loss which is having an impact on reading. A note in the home/school reading book might help identify some of the common hearing difficulties many young children experience.

Sometimes a child's anxiety and refusal to read can be linked to earlier instruction. When children are asked about what helped them to read, they point out that the teacher's confidence in the reader is a key factor. In Reading Recovery procedures, much emphasis is placed on weaning the child away from dependence on the teacher for words which are 'difficult'. Not only is this relevant to teachers, but to many parents, too, who may see accuracy in reading as the most important element in making progress in reading. Understandable anxiety surrounds reading. One of the first moves in screening for reading difficulty, then, might be to try to identify home attitudes to reading and the strategies which are used to support reading at home.

Observation

Watching children's behaviour as readers can help a teacher devise a suitable programme for reading improvement. But watching them as they attempt to tackle print is not the only kind of observation which is informative. With children who are giving cause for concern, it is worth watching to see how they choose books; how – or if – they share them with others; how long a child can sustain active interest in chosen reading; whether the child reads the environmental print of the classroom. It is also a good idea to involve parents in this kind of observation. There are two reasons for this: it is a means of checking whether a child has a particular problem with school reading as opposed to reading at home (when children are asked about their attitudes to reading many of them say they prefer reading outside school); the second very good reason is that it gives the teacher a chance to explain to parents or carers that attitudes to reading – choices, preferences, involvement – are markers of progress which go alongside getting to grips with decoding the print itself. Such conversations can allay parents' fears and so, perhaps, help them to encourage engaged and satisfying reading.

Cause for concern can be usefully documented by the completion of a Screening Record with its consequent action (Fig. 2.21). Reviews of the position would be made both by the class teacher and the language support teacher and subsequent Reading Records would be made to keep a watching brief on progress.

Miscue analysis was pioneered by Kenneth and Yetta Goodman in the late 1960s. The Goodmans created the term 'miscue' after extensive research into children's reading in the United States because they wanted to signal that often the 'errors' children make when reading are positive indicators of active processing of a text rather than failures. Other educationists, notably Helen Arnold in the United Kingdom, have developed the method.The fullest explanation and examples of carrying out miscue analysis can be found in Helen Arnold 1992 *Diagnostic Reading Record*, London, Hodder & Stoughton. Also, The Primary Language Record has a clear outline of how to carry out a Miscue Analysis and a Running Record: Myra Barrs, Sue Ellis, Hilary Hester and Anne Thomas 1988 *The Primary Language Record Handbook for Teachers*, London, ILEA/Centre for Language in Primary Education.

Miscue analysis

Observations at home and school will start drawing a picture of a child's reading behaviours, but there needs to be a close analysis of the strategies any reader uses to tackle text if there is to be a useful diagnosis. Miscue analysis remains the best approach. It takes time and so should only be used as a diagnostic tool for the few individuals who give cause for concern about tackling print. The aim is to identify the strategies a reader uses so that appropriate support can be given to help develop confidence and fluency. The procedure can be used when a child is at Level B on the Scale of Reading Progression (Fig. 2.22, pp. 62–3). If a child is still at A it is best to use observation and a running record to diagnose problems. A miscue can be informative about a reader at any age – capable fluent readers as well as those who are experiencing difficulty. Its value lies in providing a clear analysis of the individual's strengths as a reader and offering a picture of how he or she might be moved on.

Diagnosis

The analysis should be carried out in a relatively quiet place where you can have a tape recorder running. You need not, of course, tape the process but you should be aware of the effect on the child if you sit there writing on a text while he or she is reading.

The following outline of a diagnostic reading analysis draws on both the Goodmans' and Helen Arnold's work on miscue analysis.

Procedure

1. Choose a text – one which the reader will enjoy but which is at the leading edge of her or his competence. Find a text which is unfamiliar to the reader and, where possible, one which includes some variety of sentence length, some dialogue as well as narrative and some familiar as well as unfamiliar vocabulary. It should certainly be of sufficient interest for the reader to want to read it! You will need at least two copies – one for you and one for the child – and perhaps

SCREENING FOR DIFFICULTIES – READING

Name: Maria **Class:** 4 **Year:** 1996/7

Languages spoken: Turkish/English **Term** 1 2 3

Cause for concern:
Cannot tackle simple text independently

Checks made on:	Date	Comments
hearing	Spring '96	Some hearing loss
sight	Spring '96	Fine
perceptual problems	Spring '96	None diagnosed
physical difficulty/impairment	—	Clumsiness observed
medical condition	—	
other		mainly Turkish spoken at home

Relevant information from home:
Older sister had problems with reading

Most recent contact with parent/carer:
Summer Parents' Evening

Record of evidence: focused observation period from: 1.10.96 **to:** half-Term

Observer(s):
Peter Griffiths (class teacher) / Gita Shah (support teacher)

Existing assessments/level of progress:
(A) on scale of progression

Summary of observations:
Sound/symbol correspondence very insecure
Doesn't know English alphabet
Over-reliance on pictorial text and random guessing

Targets set:
Shared reading & writing to practice onset and rime
Learning alphabet

Dates for review:
February 1997

Parents' comments:
Parents very keen to help with shared reading

Review and suggestions for further action:

Figure 2.21 Screening Record for children experiencing difficulties with reading (Blank provided in Appendix: A4)

another photocopied one for you to write on later if you don't want to write on the book. It is important for the reader to have the book itself, rather than photocopies so that he or she can use all available context and pictorial cues. You may find it helpful to have another couple of texts ready in case you have under- or over-estimated the reader's competence. The passage should be about 100–150 words long.

2. Explain to the reader what you are about to do and perhaps ask for help in setting up the tape. Explain that this is a way of looking closely at how the reader goes about reading so that together you can work out ways to get better at it. It is important for the child to feel that this is part of a collaborative analysis rather than 'a test'. Then there are four stages. The reader will:

- read the extract quietly to her or himself
- tell you about the extract (start taping here)
- read the extract aloud
- discuss the extract with you again more fully.

(a) Reading the extract quietly. The amount of time needed for this will vary. During this time, notice the reader's strategies – for example, the ability to sustain quiet reading; eye movements; the time taken to settle to the task; the level of involvement in the book.

(b) Telling you about the extract. This should be as near as possible to a genuine conversation about the content of the extract. Start with a prompt like: 'I'd like you to tell me what that was about' and then invite the reader to start the tape recorder. The child's recounting will give you some idea of what she or he has understood so far from the extract, but it is worth remembering that retelling is a learned activity and your chosen reader may not be confident at doing it. You will have the tape to return to so that you can listen attentively later to how the recounting goes.

(c) Reading the extract aloud. You will need to explain to the reader that you are not going to give any help unless it is absolutely necessary, because the idea is to see just what they can do on their own. Be reassuring but clear that you would like the reader to keep going without help (although you could say that if they get absolutely stuck you'll help out). It is important to give the reader as much scope for trying things out as you can. You will see when you do the analysis that this means that the reader is stretched to show the extent of strategies available to get meaning out of a text. You will use the tape recording to do the full analysis but you might want to note any observations about reading behaviour whilst the child is reading. It is a good idea to stay as low-profile as possible while the reading is going on; for one thing so that the reader forgets that you might be a convenient provider of a tricky word, for another so that your presence proves as uninhibiting as possible.

(d) Discussion of the extract. This will depend on what the reader said before and the kind of book. You might want to pick up on previous points, asking about a character, for example, if the text is a story, or about what might happen next. A more experienced reader might be able to make comments on implications in the text. It is important that you find ways of encouraging the reader to say as much as possible and to keep your prompts to open and general questions rather than asking the meanings of particular words, for example. The aim is to see how much the reader understood of the extract and how it might fit with the longer text it was taken from.

Analysis

The analysis of the taped extract may take about half an hour. When you are aware of the strategies a reader uses you are in a better position to help move her or him on. Some of these strategies might be:

- reading on in order to help work out a word by its meaning in context
- going back and repeating a word or phrase previously read in order to make the meaning or context clear
- stopping if what is read doesn't make sense and self-correcting
- using the graphophonic features of a word to help decode it
- substituting a word which means something similar
- substituting a word which looks similar to some of the letters or blends.

Listen to the tape and tick each word correctly read, marking the miscues according to the following codings:

No attempt	cross the word through with a diagonal line
Long pause, teacher gives help	mark with T
Repetition	underline the repeated word as many times as it is repeated
Omission	put a circle round the word missed out
Insertion	write the word inserted above ^
Reversal	mark the words with a continuous line
Substitution	write the word substituted above the correct word
Self-correction	mark SC after the substitution, omission, etc.
Hesitation	mark with a diagonal / before the word paused at

You may also want to note any punctuation that the reader ignores. In analysing the miscues it is important to look for positive strategies which the reader uses as well as looking for negative miscues or patterns in miscues. A positive strategy would be the substitution of 'home' for 'house', for example. It has some phonic correspondence; it fits in terms of syntax (both are nouns) and it certainly fits semantically – it means much the same. A negative miscue would be one which interferes with the sense of the extract and shows that the reader is not reading for meaning.

Example miscue analysis

with thanks to M and Phil Crossley, his teacher at Hoylake Holy Trinity primary school

The following marked extract is from M (aged 7). It is given as an example of how a miscue is carried out since M reveals most of the features which inform a teacher about positive and negative miscues. M's reading was not a significant cause for concern to his teacher.

Phil analysed the miscue:

> When M read the extract to himself he was perfectly happy to sit and read, mouthing the words to himself. He moved his eyes up and down between the verbal text and the pictures.
>
> In talking about the text he gave a good account of what was happening although he went a bit back and forwards with the sequence of some events. Throughout the reading M uses a range of strategies and self-corrects several times after reading on. His pauses show a pattern in that he hesitates before words or phrases he is not sure of, but then has a go – or just doesn't worry about the particular word – and is successful on most occasions. His substitutions show good use of phonic and semantic cueing, although it's a little difficult to decide whether his substitution of 'far' for 'fair' is positive or negative. He might be using his personal knowledge of Father Christmas's

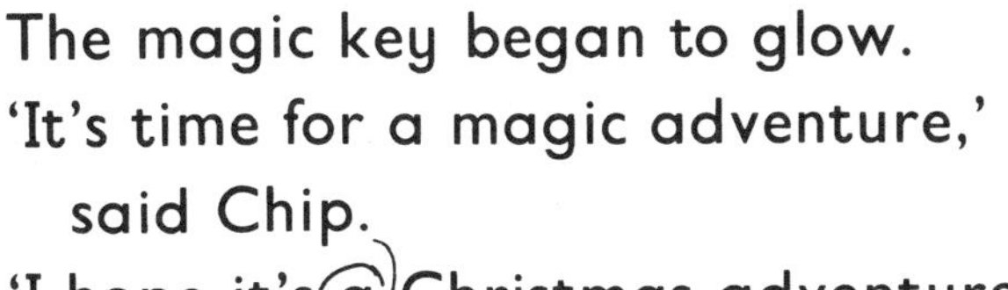

The magic key began to glow.
'It's time for a magic adventure,' said Chip.
'I hope it's a Christmas adventure.'

The magic key took the children to the land of Father Christmas.
'Hooray!' said Wilf. 'We can tell Father Christmas what to bring us.'

The children were excited.
They all wanted special presents.
'I want a new bike,' said Kipper.
'I want a new skateboard,' said Biff.

The children rang the door bell.
They rang and rang, but nobody came to the door.
'That's funny!' said Chip.

The children looked for Father Christmas, but he was not there.
There was nobody there.
'Where is everyone?' asked Wilma.

The children were disappointed.
'It's not fair,' said Chip.
'I wanted to ask Father Christmas for a computer.'

The children looked for Father Christmas.
They came to his house.
'Maybe he's in here,' said Kipper.

The children went inside.
An old man was asleep in a chair.
'It's Father Christmas,' said Wilf.
'Why is he asleep in a chair?'

Biff looked at the date.
'It's the 25th of December,' she said
'Father Christmas must be tired.
He's been at work all night.'

Suddenly, Father Christmas woke up.
'What are you doing here?' he asked
'It's Christmas Day.
Did I forget to call at your house?'

home being a long way away. The word certainly fits graphophonically and could be said to fit semantically since it makes sense as a part of the sentence although not, perhaps, in the larger context of the extract.

This last comment serves to make an important point.
Uncertainty over one miscue is not really significant in the whole of a miscue analysis; what matters is the overall picture gained. In this case the overall picture is of a reasonably confident and fluent reader who can now be pushed a little further with the kinds of material offered. This was rather a surprise to M's teacher who had not realised just how actively he could read. It might be worth reminding him about other ways of tackling unknown words – he could have had a go at 'Hooray' by the use of phonic matching and 'tired' by visual matching – both of which strategies clearly he can use. A careful miscue analysis like this can provide very valuable information to take to the screening record.

Recording and reporting progress in reading

Public concern about standards means that it is important for teachers not only to know how each child is progressing with reading but to be able to prove it. At the same time, teachers have become more and more convinced that some types of reading test do not provide adequate evidence of reading in its fullest sense. The capacity to decode is not the same as effective reading; there is more to it than that. National Curriculum levels give some detail about the text-processing strategies that pupils should acquire and some of the analytical and inferential areas of reading for understanding which readers should develop. The documentation uses the categories of accuracy, fluency, understanding and response. There is, however, little mention of the development of independent choice and discrimination, nor any reference to the importance of discussing texts.

BECOMING A READER – SCALE OF PROGRESSION	Approximation to NC Levels
A A reader in the early stages of learning: • might not yet have made the connection between meaning and print • recognises some environmental print, logos, etc. • can read pictorial text but needs others to read print aloud • can express a response to the written word • can behave like a reader: turning pages, holding book the right way up, etc. • tends to choose known texts for shared/paired reading • can identify own name, familiar signs or symbols • understands stories, rhymes and information read aloud by a more experienced reader • knows about how a book works (e.g. the cover, front, back, beginning, end of a book).	**W and Level 1**
B A reader who is gaining experience and fluency: • can read and use classroom notices, labels, captions • still needs support in reading reference or informational material • can express an opinion or preference for a particular book/story • chooses reading material with more pictorial than print text • shows greater assurance with familiar texts but still needs help with new or unknown text • may depend on one strategy more than another when reading aloud • shows evidence of drawing on several strategies when attempting to read unfamiliar material (e.g. picture cues, initial sounds, memory of similar word shapes) • reads own dictated 'emergent' text with some assurance and accuracy • can use some vocabulary to talk about books (e.g. word, letter, page, cover, title) • can predict events of stories read aloud by or shared with a more experienced reader • shows understanding of behaviour of characters in fiction • knows the difference between fiction and non-fiction.	**Level 1 to Level 2**
C A more assured reader, growing in experience: • can use some reference material with assurance • reads some texts with developing accuracy, fluency and expression • reads silently at times • browses purposefully • chooses a wider range of types of reading and some unfamiliar material but returns to the known for independent reading • uses a range of strategies when reading aloud (e.g. picture cues, shape and sound of words, one-to-one matching) • is beginning to skim/scan for familiar words or phrases • is beginning to read own text critically • shows understanding of the main points of a story/passage • usually talks appropriately about books using relevant vocabulary (e.g. author, illustrator, characters) • can discuss structure of texts with a more experienced reader • uses different reading strategies to get meaning from fiction and non-fiction.	**Level 2 to Level 3**

Figure 2.22 Reading Scale of Progression

D A more experienced and independent reader: • readily uses information and reference material • can locate information through contents, indexes, glossaries • is beginning to use inference and deduction when talking about written text • shows increasing assurance with books and with a greater range of reading activities • usually reads silently and for more sustained periods • reads for sustained periods of time and 'has a go' with more complex material • chooses books purposefully and offers opinions about types of preferred texts • reads a range of print and pictorial texts with assurance, accuracy, fluency, expression and understanding but may still occasionally need help • reads own text critically • talks readily about books and other types of text (e.g. poetry, pictorial and media) using relevant vocabulary.	**Level 3** **to** **Level 4**
E An experienced and almost independent reader: • can find information from a variety of sources for own research purposes • is beginning to draw inferences from books read independently and makes thoughtful observations about content • can distinguish fact from opinion and discuss the differences • is confident with a wide range of print and pictorial texts and reading activities • chooses material confidently and can decide whether to read silently or aloud for own purposes • can justify own opinions about texts • is prepared to persevere with complex texts • shows accuracy and some versatility in reading aloud • reads a range of texts critically • can compare and discuss different types of text using technical vocabulary (e.g. reference, narrative, informational) • can comment on structure of texts (e.g. climaxes, complications).	**Level 4** **to** **Level 5**
F A very experienced and independent reader: • can follow instructions independently from a range of procedural texts • is able to sort and classify evidence from a range of kinds of material • reads between the lines well, can sift ideas and understand inference and allusion • reads accurately, fluently, thoughtfully and with understanding for a wide range of purposes • can make choices from a wide range of reading material for pleasure and research • has established tastes in fiction or non-fiction • can give reasons for preferences in reading • shows development of a personal response to literature • can vary pace, pitch and expression when reading aloud • draws on a range of reading styles for different reading tasks • shows critical awareness of a wide range of texts • can discuss how language is used to create particular effects, using relevant terminology	**Level 5** **to** **Level 6 and** **beyond**

Figure 2.22 Reading Scale of Progression (continued)

These statements have been developed, reviewed and modified by groups of teachers in different areas over several years. The aim was to find ways of describing children's progress rather than a list of curriculum items they should have learned.

The development of these progression statements owes a debt to the Reading Scales in *The Primary Language Record* edited by Myra Barrs *et al.*

The descriptions offered in the Scale of Progression (Fig. 2.22) include the text-processing elements both at word and whole text level: investigative, analytical, evaluative and inferential skills, but take descriptions of progress further to include behaviours and the social elements of reading. The statements are arranged to coincide with the four areas of English outlined in the model for the English curriculum in Chapter 5. They cover areas of language at sentence and word level and at the level of whole texts ('accuracy' and 'fluency' in the National Curriculum), processes of getting and conveying information ('understanding' and 'response' in the National Curriculum) but these descriptions go further to include the process of developing discrimination and assurance. The statements are not hierarchically arranged within sections. They reflect what teachers might expect to see as children develop towards independence as readers. They provide a useful basis for discussion with colleagues but are intended to be open to adaptation since no single set of descriptors can fully answer to specific school circumstances. The sections have been paralleled with the National Curriculum levels as a guide, but not as a fixed programme of learning. They are not intended as watertight categories and there is likely to be some overlap with pupils showing competence in areas in two (or even more) sections and there will be gaps – which readers using this book are invited to fill.

Individual and whole-class progress

One way to use the scale is to track individual progress. Using a highlighter in October to mark the statements which reflect what a child can do at the beginning of the school year, then using a different highlighter the following June, provides an immediate visual indication of progress. Used in discussions with parents or colleagues, the descriptors can be a useful basis for talking about specific elements of the reading curriculum. Highlighting suitable descriptors for each child twice or three times a year during a Key Stage can contribute a quick and effective summary to records of progress over several years. The statements in the Scale of Progression may help focus on difficulties experienced by particular pupils. Identifying statements which genuinely reflect what a child can do with reading can provide a very clear picture of the areas which they may need help with. However, the scale can also provide a way of summarising whole-class progress. The graph in Fig. 2.23 shows progress noted by one class teacher over the year. The darker column shows the number of pupils at levels A–E in October; the lighter column shows the shift upwards recorded in the June of the following year. The teacher simply recorded on a class list (Fig. 2.24) the point on the Scale of Progress reached by each child during October, then in June of the next year. There were interim records for February, but these are not included in the graph.

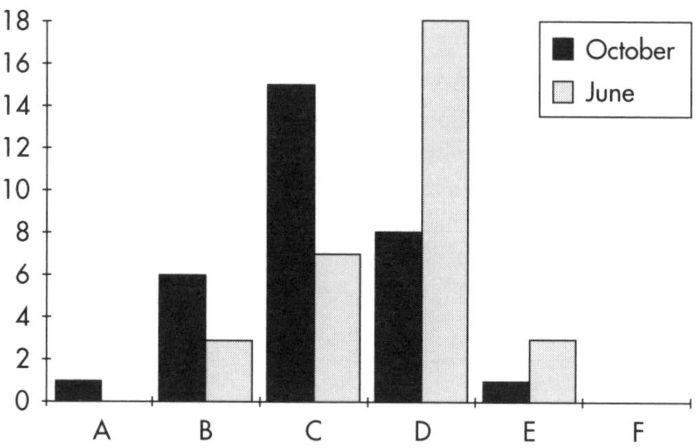

Figure 2.23 Progress made by a Year 3 class over one year

CLASS RECORD SHEET – READING

Teacher: Pat Brown

Class: 3PB

Date (year) 1996–97

Name	Age	Boy/ Girl	Languages spoken	Reading Level Term 1 (15·10·96)	Reading Level Term 2 (17·3·97)	Reading Level Term 3 (10·6·97)
Ricki A.	7·2	B	Eng.	B	B	B
Kate A	7·5	G	Eng	C	C/D	D
Khadisha B	7·3	G	Turkish/Eng	C	C/D	D
Stephen C	7·9	B	Eng	D	D	D
Billy C	7·8	B	Eng/BSL	C	C	D
Maria d'E	7·11	G	Portuguese/Eng	C	C/D	D
Deborah F	7·6	G	Eng	B	B/C	C
Sunil G	7·4	B	Urdu/Eng	D	D	E
Dijana K	7·4	G	Polish/Eng	D	D/E	E
Richard L	7·5	B	Eng	C	C/D	D
Madeleine M	7·5	G	Eng	B	B	C
Charlie M	7·3	B	Eng	C	C	D
David N	7·8	B	Eng	B	B	B
Petronella N	8·1	G	Eng	D	abs	D
Eric O	7·8	B	Eng	C	C	C
Nkechi O	7·2	G	English/?	C	C	D
Szechuan P	7·4	G	Cantonese/Eng	B	B/C	C
Robert R	7·6	B	Eng.	C	C	D
Kevin R	7·10	B	Eng.	C	C/D	D
Jilna S	7·11	G	Urdu/Eng.	D	E	E
Selma S	8·0	G	Bengali/Eng	A	A/B	B
Kevin T	7·3	B	Eng.	C	C/D	D
Peter T	7·11	B	Eng.	D	D	D
Steven T	8·1	B	Eng	C	C	D
Louise V	7·4	G	Eng	D	abs	D
Richard W	7·9	B	Eng	B	B	C
Kate W	7·8	G	Eng	C	C/D	D
Alex Y	7·3	G	Eng.	C	D	D
Leigh Z	7·5	G	Eng./Italian?	D	D	D

Figure 2.24 Grid for recording class progress in reading (Blank provided in Appendix: A5)

Termly reading records

Termly records can help track progress and be a useful focus both for the teacher and for the individual reader, helping to identify where to go next in developing reading. If the Reading Record in Fig. 2.25 is completed once a term it builds to a clear and confident teacher assessment. In completing the record the teacher carries out a running record with the reader, noting the strategies used in decoding the text. The text can be chosen either by the child or the teacher, but it must be clearly indicated whether the text presents the reader with any particular challenges. Discussion following the reading would establish the child's understanding of the text and an analysis of the running record information about accuracy in decoding.

All of this information will feed into a summary of the child's present level and the future teaching strategies needed to make further progress. If this record is completed alongside the Scale of Progression (Fig. 2.22) the conclusions will offer prompts to further action to help the child make progress.

Evaluating reading and how it is taught

Keeping careful records of progress is one of the best ways of reviewing the effectiveness of teaching and learning. There is one further way in which evaluation can inform future planning, and that is to invite the children to reflect on their own learning. Reading journals, reviews of books read, databases with comments on reading, cannot only help readers to reflect on their own choices but inform the teacher about progress. Conversations about reading are important, too. Janet Towlson had been reading *The Frog Prince*, illustrated by Jan Ormerod, with two 6-year-olds in her class. They had been paying very careful attention to the borders of each page, discovering more and more in the details of each illustration:

Janet Towlson 1995 'Up and up: young critical readers' in Eve Bearne ed. *Greater Expectations: children reading writing*, London, Cassell

> When I asked Maria and Caroline 'Do you think if you look at *The Frog Prince* again you would see things there that you didn't see first, second or even third time around, different things in the pictures?' Caroline replied, 'It's a bit like when I got on my climbing frame, I got to know more and more things – how to do it – the more I had goes on it.' I'm convinced Caroline and Maria will re-read and re-read *The Frog Prince* and more and more will be revealed and unravelled to them from childhood to adulthood. Maria's opening line when she writes about *The Frog Prince* sums it all up in a very sophisticated and succinct way: 'I think the text is telling you to keep a promise.'
>
> (p.104)

Mike Millroy found that after he introduced reading journals his Year 6 class became much more involved in their reading and keen to share ideas with him. He began using the journals because after asking the children *Do you like reading to the teacher?* he received some responses which concerned him:

Mike Millroy 1995 'I also read to Jinxy my kitten: children writing reading journals' in Bearne *Greater Expectations*

> The children expressed a variety of concerns ranging from frustration at being slowed down, to nervousness and even fear of making mistakes; one child remarked that when she read aloud she 'couldn't build up the pictures in her head as well'. I decided this was an opportune moment to introduce the reading diary as it became known.
>
> (p. 81)

Later in the year it became clear that attitudes had changed :

> After using the diaries for some time, children who were initially most reticent about reading to the teacher commented:

READING RECORD **Name:** M – **Class:** 3 **Age:** 7 **Languages spoken:** English **DATE:** 2.12.96

Text chosen: (Title) by child / (by teacher) familiar / (unfamiliar) (fiction) / non-fiction

level of difficulty for the reader: (e.g. straightforward, a challenge . . .) I thought it would be a challenge, but it wasn't!

Behaviours: Talking about / approaching text:

- assurance ✓
- involvement ✓
- book language ✓ title, author, characters
- telling the story – sequence not always clear
- commenting on likes/dislikes ✓
- cross-referring – to other Christmas stories

Reading aloud:

- self-correcting ✓
- seeking help – tends to appeal first before trying
- reading on ✓
- reviewing ✓

Strategies:

- directionality ✓
- letter/sound matching – could do with more practice
- letter shape matching – overdependent?
- word recognition ✓
- picture cues ✓ v. good use
- meaning cues ✓ good
- text structure cues ✓ good

Understanding of text:

- predicting events ✓ good (tho' this text a bit predictable)
- commenting on character and/or setting or plot – good on character
- responding to the content ✓ shows enjoyment/humour
- picking up details – partic. in pictures
- grasping inferences – not always
- asking questions – often!

Accuracy:

- number of words read accurately: 190
- number of self-corrections: 2
- number of errors/miscues: 15

Level on Scale of Progression: C

NC Level (if appropriate):

Summary and future teaching strategies:
This was very useful – I'd under-estimated M's reading ability. He has a good grasp of how texts work and uses the pictorial text very well. He needs practice with phonic strategies and seems to be a little too ready to guess at any word once he identifies a letter he recognises. He enjoys reading but could do with more help in choosing more challenging texts. (non-fiction?)

Figure 2.25 Termly reading record (Blank provided in Appendix: A6)

> I haven't been reading to you lately, I want to read to you more often. I want to tell you about *Honey I Blew Up the Kids*.
>
> (Nisa Dell)
>
> I do think I'm a better reader now, I enjoy books better than I used to, I also concentrate more. I wish I could read to you more.
>
> (Jane Kaye)
>
> I feel pretty confident about reading now, before I came into this class I used to get bored with reading I used to say to myself when are we going to stop reading but now I want to read more than we do. . . . I really enjoy reading now, I like all kinds of books like funny, adventures and lots more. (Helen Gough)
>
> (p. 86)

Mike Millroy comments:

> Reading diaries can be used to elicit a wide range of valuable information about the habits and attitudes of the children as readers, and changes in these can be more readily monitored. The written reflections mean that we can draw information from throughout the reading diaries to build up a more complete picture of children as readers: their range of reading experience, responses to particular texts and the different strategies they use. At the same time it is an ideal vehicle for self-assessment.
>
> (p. 89)

Using the reading diaries brought the cycle of planning, teaching, recording, reporting and evaluating reading full circle for this teacher and his class.

Taking it further – parents and reading

Chapter 1, p. 14, includes a checklist for considering the role of parents in supporting literacy and Chapter 7 offers some guidelines (p. 320) for developing policy about parental links to promote literacy.

This chapter has stressed the importance of taking account of reading at home. The important role of parents in contributing to their children's reading development is widely recognised. There are home–school links over reading in almost every school; in some schools parents work in the classroom with teachers in supporting children's reading and often contribute to continuing records of progress. One of the greatest contributions parents can make to the development of their children's reading is to give the school information about their children's reading experience and preferences. The next major contribution is in reading with children at home. Schools can contribute to shared understanding about how best to support children's reading by holding meetings and providing information booklets about school approaches to reading. However, it is not always possible for parents to come into school so it is necessary to find other ways of making profitable contacts to support children's reading. It is also common to find that by the time children are moving out of Key Stage 1 the involvement of parents in reading declines. Fig. 2.26 offers some suggestions for keeping links going.

Schools can make links with homes over reading by:

- providing occasional information leaflets to highlight aspects of school policy or give clear guidance in response to current issues, for example, media reports of falling standards; SAT results and their implications;
- lending videos, books or magazines about reading at home. Lending books and reading games;
- making up information packs and suggestions of reading games which can be made easily at home;
- asking parents to read and comment on drafts of the school information booklet about reading;
- providing booklists to help choice in the bookshop, supermarket, newsagent or library;
- asking families to make books together – about the family's reading preferences, or books they liked when young or stories compiled through contributions from other children, parents, grandparents, friends and relatives. Families can also make very useful information books about particular interests or family histories;
- encouraging parents or older brothers and sisters to make tapes of stories, perhaps in home languages. These might be told or read from dual language books, or even versions of the English texts which the children take home;
- giving guideline suggestions for the ways that brothers and sisters or other relatives can help support reading;
- asking parents to help research information for topic work.
- asking parents to help research information for topic work.

Figure 2.26 Taking it further: involving parents in supporting reading development

Writing

Chapter Three

In outlining how to ensure progress in writing, this chapter covers:

- recent theories about writing
- writing in the early years
- the relationship between writing and learning
- planning for writing – the range and repertoire
- teaching writing
- creating a productive writing environment
- collaborating over writing
- responding to writing
- recording, reporting and assessing progress in writing
- diagnosing difficulties and planning for support
- evaluating writing and how it is taught
- taking it further: writing at home.

Introduction to writing

Teaching writing has not been the subject of such open, public debate as teaching reading. Nevertheless, there is a similar opposition of views about what matters most in writing in schools. Comments about standards of literacy often focus on the secretarial aspects of writing – spelling and punctuation – rather than the organisational aspects of longer texts or, perhaps more importantly, than the content or meaning of any piece of writing. Writing in school has traditionally been seen as the means of demonstrating that learning has happened – the 'do-it-then-write-about-it' kind of approach. Research from the National Writing Project revealed that a great deal of time in classrooms was spent in writing which seemed to have no purpose other than demonstrating that the child had been taught something. This might be copying material from one source to another (board to book; textbook to exercise book), writing short answers to questions about what has been read or writing more lengthy pieces in one go without expecting that a longer piece may need editing and redrafting. Much less attention was given to the wider range of writing which features in people's everyday lives. As Chapter 1 makes clear, much of the writing people do outside school is not to check that they have learned something but is very much to do with shaping, noting or communicating ideas. Shopping lists help us to hold thoughts which could otherwise go astray, notes remind people of important tasks or appointments, letters communicate experiences, reflective diaries help the writer to think things through. The National Writing Project research into classroom writing also identified a narrow understanding of readership (audience). Where in everyday writing there will be various readers who read for the content and meaning of the note, list or letter, classroom writing was often only read by the teacher as a means of checking that children had taken in specific information and could spell and punctuate. Writing, then, was often seen as a proof of learning facts; accuracy in secretarial skills was most valued, neglecting content and meaning.

The National Writing Project was set up by the School Curriculum Development Committee. Its three-year development phase (1985–1988) directly involved twenty-four local authorities. In 1988 the National Curriculum Council took responsibility for the Project's final implementation year. The teachers involved worked on investigations into writing in their own classrooms which they had identified as important. Their work was extensively written up and is mentioned later in this chapter.

What is writing development?

Since the National Writing Project's work, there have been some changes. The National Curriculum for English includes ideas like 'writing for a range of purposes and audiences' and specifies the inclusion of drafting as an essential part of writing. At the same time, however, there is a tendency to make judgements about children's progress in writing by concentrating largely on the technical features of texts since these have been the basis of judgements for so long. There is a sense, in the UK at least, that accuracy in spelling is a virtue; those who find the technical aspects of transcription difficult are either pitied or blamed. This runs counter not only to common sense – how can a transcription error be a 'sin'? – but also creates tensions in classroom provision for writing. While it is important to be able to present a finished piece of work which is accurately spelt and punctuated, it is equally important that writing should convey the message the writer wants it to – content and fluency matter just as much as accuracy. The teacher's job is to try to ensure that both progress side by side.

To lose accuracy for the sake of fluency does the young writer no favours. Similarly, all teachers have witnessed (or even experienced themselves) the agony of a writer who is anxious and fears making mistakes. Such anxieties don't just have their impact on the child's emotions, however, but also seriously impede progress in all other areas of school work.

This chapter focuses on the tricky job of fostering classroom writing so as to encourage the development of writing which is both accurate and fluent. But it isn't just a matter of developing the craft or techniques of writing. It is important to recognise the contribution which writing makes to learning throughout the primary curriculum. This chapter outlines some of the key elements in providing for the range and repertoire of texts and in establishing the kind of classroom environment which will best support developing writers. It invites you to consider such questions as:

- What does developing writing involve?
- How can I plan for the progress of all the writers in my classroom?
- What are my responsibilities as a teacher of writing?

In considering writing and children's progress, then, it is necessary not just to look at what 'getting better at writing' might mean, but to look at the role which writing plays in structuring thought and developing concepts. Also, since it is now clear that home uses of literacy play an important part in future learning, it is important to consider the link between home and school uses of writing. In the same way that new versions of literacy – media, computer texts of all kinds – contribute to children's reading development, it is equally important to see how these new literacies make demands on the writing curriculum on offer to children. The traditional view of classroom writing is no longer adequate for developing fluent, confident and independent writers. Writing opportunities offered in the classroom need to build on a diverse range of pupil experience of literacy. These heavy demands mean that it is critically important for teachers to be confident about how to assess, report and record progress and to be able to use both teachers' and pupils' reflective evaluations to plan for further development.

The experienced writer

In the first chapter you were invited to think about your own writing experience and the everyday demands made on you as a developed writer. It became clear that all decisions which a developed writer makes about how and when to write something are influenced by the social context in which the text is written and in which it will be read. In other words, writing is not simply a matter of getting words down accurately and neatly on the page, it is deeply embedded in social and cultural practices. A letter to friends or family may well include incomplete sentences; when I write a shopping list I don't redraft it or even bother about the neatness of the handwriting; if I leave a note on the kitchen table I include only the minimal amount of information because I know the reader shares the same social contexts as me and does not need me to be more explicit. On the other hand, a letter asking a bank manager for a loan or an application for a job will need careful redrafting, someone else to help proofread it, and will probably be word-processed. The developed and experienced writer makes decisions about how to write according to the social circumstances surrounding the writing. Generally, a proficient writer needs to have a broad and flexible enough writing repertoire to make choices about:

- the purpose and readership of a text
- the most appropriate form of text for the occasion
- the level of formality needed
- the amount of explicit detail required

- the format and organisation of the material
- the technical features of syntax, vocabulary, spelling and punctuation suited to the particular text.

All of these judgements will be shaped by an understanding of the context within which the piece of writing is to be read. What implications does this have for classroom writing where the context is very clearly defined? An experienced and fluent writer uses writing for a range of purposes – to help shape thoughts; to capture ideas; to reflect on experience; to communicate. How might these purposes match the kinds of writing on offer in the classroom? And if the list above is indicative of what a fully proficient writer can do, how can this variety, diversity and flexibility be introduced to the developing writer?

Purposes for writing

One very good starting point is to ask the pupils themselves about writing or the purposes of writing. In a survey carried out in Sheffield the teachers first of all noted their own purposes in asking the children to write, then asked the children for their views of what the writing was for. Fig. 3.1 shows the teachers' and children's responses.

Keith Stallard 1988 *Encouraging Confidence in Writers*, Sheffield Writing at the Transition Project, National Writing Project

The teachers identified the following purposes:	The children thought that they were writing because:
• confidence building • to help recall of facts • practice in building sentences • to enable them to write creatively • to gather, record and pass on information • to aid fluency in reading and writing • comprehension • handwriting practice • to think logically/to encourage reasoning	• it's good for me • it helps us • it's easy • we practise words • we're learning about Indians (work on Native American nations) • we learn handwriting • so she knows what I've been doing • so that the teacher knows how I am with my spelling • we learn about God and animals • I don't know • she can mark it.

Figure 3.1 Teachers' and children's views about the purposes for writing

These examples indicate that not only did the teachers have a wide range of different purposes for the kinds of writing they asked the children to do, but the children themselves perceived an even wider (and less clearly understood) set of purposes. There is little understanding of the idea of being able to make personal meaning through imaginative writing nor is there much sense that writing helps in communicating ideas. The only person who was being communicated to was the teacher – but even that wasn't clear to all the children. There were areas of overlap between teachers' and pupils' views but these focused on practising handwriting and showing that you've learned facts. These children felt that writing was good for them but had to resort to general comments about why the writing tasks had been set. This might either be because they had no idea why they were writing or because they lacked the vocabulary through which to describe what writing can do for them. The teachers who asked the questions were taking their responsibilities very seriously and used the children's comments as a basis for looking carefully and critically at their own approaches to writing in the classroom.

Writing was viewed as an isolated exercise rather than as a tool for communication or for getting things done. Further investigation of the types of writing the pupils were asked to do revealed that two-thirds of the writing done during the week consisted of formal exercises. These included answering questions, filling gaps and matching words. When children were given the chance to write more freely there still seemed to be a great deal of teacher control, particularly over getting the technicalities right. The teachers involved in this investigation also found that much of the children's writing was done at the end of an activity and that this was often in the form of a recounting experience – the do-it-then-write-about-it syndrome. There was little evidence that children were having experience of note-making, planning or drafting. Given the level of teacher control over the writing, there was little opportunity for pupils to express their own feelings, interests or opinions, or reflect on what they were doing. The overall picture of writing showed a restricted range and limited purposes for writing. The pupils had little chance to choose or to exercise much control over their writing.

When the teachers reviewed these findings, drawn honestly from their own classrooms, they decided first of all to tackle the issue of purposes for writing. Writing outside the classroom has purposes for the writer such as reminding or noting, and most writing is intended to convey a message to a reader. After discussion it was agreed to create opportunities in the classroom for pupils to write for people other than the teacher. This did not necessarily mean going outside the school context to find readers and in the first stage of the work the range of texts produced for readers in the same classroom or school included a school guide for new children, a recipe book to be sold at the School Fayre, a board game with instructions for the children in the class next door, a treasure hunt for another class and a class newspaper. In reviewing all the work done the teachers felt that they had begun to tackle the questions which they had originally posed about the children as writers, their lack of confidence and their need for challenge and success. They felt that they had established some new insights into writing.

Children's perceptions of writing

The views in Fig. 3.2 indicate that young writers can have quite sophisticated views of what writing is like and what it can do for them. There are also the realists and pragmatists amongst them. Perhaps more troubling are those children who have negative views of writing in school – for example, for punishment – and those who seem to be confused about why they are writing at all. One clear feature is that writing in schools attracted negative comments; all the statements about writing for personal purposes at home are favourable. This can pose some difficulties in making decisions about the kinds of writing asked of children in the classroom. Certainly, it would be wise to bring the range of home and school uses of writing closer together. There is no doubt that for many people, writing in school seems much more of an 'exercise' than the real purposes perceived for writing to friends or keeping personal writing for pleasure. The range of readers for out-of-school writing is broader and the formats more varied. Also, writing at home is usually done by choice and with none of the necessary time constraints of school. However, it is important not to become too alarmist. These comments are second-hand experiences. What responses might you get if you asked a few of your own class some of the questions in Fig. 3.3?

5- & 6-year-olds' responses:

Why do we learn to write?
So we can read
To write stories for teachers
To fill in forms
Helps us to spell
My mum puts the writing on the wall
To write letters when you grow up
It makes you feel happy

Are you a good writer?
Bad – my spellings are wrong
Nearly. I would be much better if I was faster
No – untidy!
I get the right words in my head and spell them wrong.
Yes – I can spell hard words
Yes because I use more than one piece of paper when writing stories

What is the most difficult part?
Thinking about it
Making up your own stories
Getting ideas
Writing with a small pencil. That makes your hand ache
Doing very hard words

7- & 8-year-olds
Why do you write?
To tell people the ideas I have
I like to write in my secret diary
I write to my Gran to keep in contact
Teacher says so
Punishment
If we didn't write we would waste paper
Writing helps you to learn

9-, 10- & 11-year-olds
What is writing?
Writing is a sort of code – I think it is
Writing is like a lot of scribbles and each scribble means something
I like writing when bored because it gives you something to do
I write to remember things. I also write for pleasure
People write so they can get a job. We also write to help us learn and get a job so we can make money
Sometimes we write so the teacher knows what we are thinking
If you are at home what you write is up to you but if you are school it is up to the teacher what you write

Figure 3.2 What children think about writing

- What sorts of writing do grown-ups have to do?
- Why do you need to be able to write?
- Are you a good writer? Why/Why not?
- Think about all the writing you have done. Which kinds of writing do you enjoy most?
- What do you find the hardest thing about writing?
- Think about the best pieces of writing you have done. What made them good?
- Can you find me the piece of writing you're most proud of?
- Are there times when you find writing boring? When are they?
- Do you sometimes like other children to read your writing? Why/Why not?
- What can teachers do to help children get better at writing?
- What do you like to happen to your writing when it is finished?

Figure 3.3 Questions about writing

Finding a theory about writing

It is clear from the history of writing that people began to make marks to record things because they felt they needed to. As societies developed, speech was captured in written symbols to answer a variety of practical and personal needs. Although there are complex social groups throughout the world who use oral language as the main, and perfectly satisfying, means of communication, in many societies writing is seen as the primary means of communication. The importance and value attached to it have become historically developed and enshrined in social practice. Writing also has political significance. It can be dangerous. Published writers have been imprisoned for their writing and controversies still continue about censorship or freedom of expression in writing. At a more domestic level, anyone who has tried to capture thoughts on paper knows the immediately hazardous feeling which accompanies first putting words on that blank sheet. Put briefly, writing matters. It matters inside school and outside. It matters as a means of individual expression and as it reflects the diverse cultures and communities from which our children come. It matters because of the way it is understood in the larger social organisation of the country. Those who can write have power to persuade, explain, argue and enchant. In terms of how writing is approached in the classroom it is important because of its potential in allowing or inhibiting learning in all areas of the curriculum. What children bring to learning – their past personal, cultural and literacy experiences – combines with present classroom experience and suggests future possibilities for literacy and learning.

Writing in the early years

The understandings that children bring to school about writing, both from what they observe as script in their environment and in their own early attempts at mark making, contribute to their progress in writing. Yetta Goodman outlines three principles of writing development – the functional, linguistic and relational. Children learn very quickly that writing can do things for them – that it has a function: notes and greetings cards carry messages, for example. They are also fascinated by the patterns of language as they learn to write, noticing phonic links or the shapes and length of

Yetta Goodman 1986 'Writing development in young children' *Gnosis* 8 March 1986, Birmingham, Questions Publishing Company

functional principle: the idea that writing can serve a purpose, has a function and that a writer can do things by writing – for example, putting up a notice saying *Keep out of Jo's room!*; **linguistic** principle: the idea that writing is a system which is organised into letters and words; even before writing recognisable words children can be seen to separate their letter strings into chunks corresponding to what a word looks like on the page; **relational** principle: the connection between what is written on the page (or published print) and spoken words, the realisation that the written system carries meaning

see p. 78

words. Perhaps the clinching moment of beginning to be writers and readers comes when they see a relationship between the symbols they write down and the words which people say. These are all represented in the (often under-acknowledged) amount of writing which children participate in before they come to school, the extensive playing with writing which they engage in before they have any knowledge of the orthodox transcription elements of their own language – be it Hindi, Greek or English – and the messages which they assume their writing will carry. In outlining the development of these principles, Yetta Goodman points to the complexity of the systems children are developing in this early experience of making and seeing texts:

> Their learning occurs in a complex social cultural environment through a complex array of written forms for a variety of complex purposes. It is from this morass of complexity that the beginning writer evolves the functional purposes for writing, the organisation of the writing (linguistic principles) and the ways these relate to meaning.
>
> (p. 3)

Children actively make hypotheses about the ways in which written language is ordered and patterned and, most importantly, of the contexts in which written texts are made and read. Goodman goes on to argue that teachers need to understand and respect the developmental aspects of writing in young children and to organise for activities which build on and expand what children already know. Her analysis of the process of writing development echoes the complexity of parallel processing as a description of the process of reading. As children put together the functional, relational and linguistic principles of language through their experiments with writing, they are engaging in highly complex cognitive operations. The teacher's role is to support this process and create the conditions in which more explicit instruction will work with the child's developing written system rather than blocking it or causing anxieties. This is critical in the early stages of schooling since written language forms an important part of the whole curriculum.

Writing and learning

Writing helps us to learn. We can work out ideas and reflect on them, record observations, capture and concentrate thoughts and so generate new ideas. Often we don't acknowledge what we know until someone points it out to us. 'Thinking on paper' is one of the most effective ways for a learner to get to grips with what is to be learned. The development of concepts is, of course, fundamental to children's learning and very much part of a teacher's classroom responsibility. That is why it is important to have a clear view of the relationship between writing and learning. It isn't just that writing demonstrates learning, but that it actively contributes to learning. This has important implications for classroom practices about writing.

If writing is to be recognised as an important means of learning in all areas of the curriculum, then any theory of development will need to take account of a range of factors. One complexity is that development does not happen in a straight upward trajectory; as we learn anything, and get better at it through practice, we suffer reversals and plateaux. There are times when nothing seems to be happening, and then ability shows itself by sudden spurts of confidence or productivity. A technique learned in one context can be revisited and improved in another. In other words, development follows a looping, recursive pattern and this can make it difficult when trying to pin down descriptions of what progress looks like in any simple way. Writing development is rather too complex to be dealt with by simple checklists of skills. To see progress in writing as a matter of simply being able to spell correctly, write in sentences and form handwriting elegantly misses out large and significant areas of what genuinely contributes to children's writing development – and indeed to their learning as a whole.

Writing as process and product

transcription: the process of putting the text on the page correctly; **composition:** the process of developing ideas through writing

Not only is it important to find a balance between the transcription or secretarial aspects of writing and the compositional and content elements; it is equally important to see the relationship between writing seen as a finished product and writing as a process. For many years writing has been seen as a noun – a thing which represents the end point of an activity. This is characterised by the teacherly phrase 'give in your writing'. More recently, however, and now as part of National Curriculum requirements, writing is seen as a verb – a process, perhaps represented by phrases such as 'writing to develop ideas'. One of the major influences on writing as a process is the American educator Donald Graves. He stresses the importance of observing and aiding children as they compose, review and revise their writing. It is particularly important to recognise a 'pre-writing' phase where children think their way into what they want to write. One of Graves' central assertions is that children want to write but that school approaches to writing take control away from children and put obstacles in the way of their progress. He advocates methods of helping children take greater control over their own writing. His studies are explained through carefully documented case studies and exemplify his view that 'the teaching of writing demands control of two crafts, teaching and writing' (p. 5). However, although Graves' work has had its critics, the approach has been widely recognised as influential in both the UK and the USA. One criticism has been that emphasis on the process might lead to a sense that written end-products should be considered less important than the process. Quite clearly, the most balanced view would be to recognise the variety of types of writing which children need to experience and practise and to see writing as a process of production of the whole range of texts. Some will need to be taken through to final proofread and edited form; some – notes, jottings, reflective comments, for example – will not.

Graves' most influential work was published in 1983: *Writing, Children and Teachers at Work*, Portsmouth, N.H., Heinemann Educational Books.

Perhaps it is more helpful to think about 'outcomes' of writing. The idea of seeing writing as a process has led to a greater understanding of the role which writing plays in learning – getting ideas going, capturing newly developed thoughts, organising disparate items of memory. This realisation is sometimes taken into account in classroom practice at the outset of a set of activities, but often the end-point is still the written account or the story. However, the product or outcome of thought is more than that. Writing is not just a matter of transcribing language which is somehow already 'in the head' waiting to be made permanent by marks on paper. The process of writing can help in shaping ideas, realising in print what we think of in the act of writing. In writing, we struggle to find ways of saying what we want to say, and so stretch our thoughts further. The activity of composition is a powerful mental process and the product or outcome involves making meaning which we had not realised (in both senses – made real *and* understood) until the act of writing. The role of writing as a means of helping us make our meanings clear, both to ourselves and to others, is just as important when we use jottings, notes and aids to memory as it is when we elaborate ideas in more extended writing. And its accompanying product or outcome is both a text – something tangible – and an extension of learning.

New insights about writing

It is important, then, before starting out on any set of activities involving writing to have clear ideas about what the outcomes of the activity might be. They may be tangible products in written form, or they may be intangible outcomes such as the children expressing opinions more clearly, learning how to find out information, or developing strategies for editing their writing. The crucial point is not only being sure of the purpose of the work but being able to explain to the children the purpose, potential readership and form of any writing involved. In this way, both partners in learning should be able to avoid some of the misconceptions and misperceptions outlined earlier.

Greater attention to writing has led to specific requirements being included in the National Curriculum document which represent important aspects of writing development. There is greater emphasis on purpose and readership (audience) and the process of writing is seen as central to improving writing. These are welcome moves, but recent research has also emphasised the importance of aspects of writing which cannot be easily captured in a generalised document. It has become increasingly clear that in the early stages of becoming writers children interact with the print environment which surrounds them and use that knowledge to make their own meanings in marks on the page. This indicates that children are engaged in a complex set of processes as they 'play' at writing. Another linked and equally important point is related to readership and the role of instruction as children move from their own emergent writing to take on the conventions of written language. Reading writing for its meaning is now just as important as helping children form their letters and handwriting correctly; indeed the compositional, communicative and secretarial aspects all should go hand in hand. There have been significant moves in looking closely at the processes used by individual writers, and the social, cultural and behavioural aspects of writing. These have important implications for the teacher of writing. Fig. 3.4 lists some of these.

New insights into the teaching and learning of writing suggest that if teachers are to support and extend developing writers they need to attend to several areas at once. Any theory which seeks to inform practice must be able to:

- articulate ideas about early writing development and how children's own knowledge of texts can best be built on
- offer a useful analysis of how the process of writing is best supported in the classroom
- take into account the behavioural, social and cultural factors which influence successful writing
- help develop shared practices in supporting writing development and responding to writing across a whole school.

Planning for writing

Children are surrounded by writing in the street, the shops and at home and use writing extensively for their own purposes and pleasure in their own time. However, the process of developing writing is rarely given attention outside school and it is perhaps in the classroom environment that it can best be supported and extended. New strategies for encouraging children to take on responsibility for their own writing will mean establishing different ways of working. You may already have looked at your own classroom as a supportive environment for literacy and noted that organising the classroom for writing can involve arrangements for:

- special times and places for writing
- making available a range of writing implements and materials
- developing collaborative practices
- providing for choice and diversity
- involving other people as readers of the children's writing (or sometimes as co-writers)
- key experiences in writing for your class during any week.

You might also have noted gaps in your own organisation for writing, matters of concern and questions you still want to address.

Individual development of concepts and strategies

1. As children watch adults write they observe and work out their own systems and rules. They also notice the value adults place on writing in different forms. Some young writers will describe writing as pleasurable and will 'write' fluently and enthusiastically before being able to use orthodox spelling conventions. Others come to writing with concerns about neatness and accuracy.

2. Children discover a great deal about written language long before they come to school, particularly if they have the chance to experiment with writing. They hypothesise about the organisation and uses of the writing system as they make their own early attempts at meaning.

3. The act of composing a piece of writing is a powerful and complex mental process. In a similar way to the parallel processing of reading, developing writers are grappling with handling the functional, linguistic and relational elements of language as well as learning how to manage a writing implement and holding thoughts in their heads as they write.

4. A developed writer needs to make fast and flexible choices about several elements of composition, communication and secretarial skills all at once: the purpose or intention of a piece of writing, the level of explicit detail needed to satisfy the needs of the reader, the tone, form and format of writing.

5. An essential element in developing writing is to help writers become attentive and critical readers of their own writing.

Behavioural, social and cultural factors

6. Writing is not only a complex cognitive process, it is a complex social practice. It includes a number of different types of behaviour: sorting out ideas, talking with others, deciding what to say and how to say it, physically writing drafting and redrafting, revising, editing and perhaps publishing and finding out what others think about the writing.

7. The involvement of parents and the community in the writing curriculum can establish valuable partnerships and provide a rich learning ground for children as writers.

The teacher's role in promoting writing

8. Children's writing develops most effectively when they themselves have responsibility for their learning: making decisions about what, how and when to write; understanding about reasons for writing; learning to comment on and discuss their own and other people's writing. The teacher's role is to make this possible by providing appropriate opportunities.

9. A teaching emphasis on literacy skills alone seriously underestimates the significance of the implicit understandings about literacy that children bring to school.

10. Young writers learn the most valuable lessons about writing when their teacher is a writer, too.

Figure 3.4 Ten things we know about writers and writing

The range and repertoire of writing

If you have asked your own pupils about their perceptions of writing in school and at home, it will have become clear that there are many different views of what writing is, what it can do and what individual writers feel they can do with writing. Individual predilection and personal experience mean that there are diverse writers in any classroom with a diverse range of needs. This means that, while it is possible to provide some common starting points for writing, the pathways taken from those beginnings may have to be varied; for some there will be more stops by the way while others will forge ahead steadily. The teacher's role therefore has to be flexible and responsive, considering the *who*, *what*, *how* and *where* of classroom writing.

In any Key Stage 1 or 2 classroom, at any time there may be writers who:

- always finish first
- confuse quantity with quality
- can't keep up with their own thoughts (and need a scribe?)
- draw on their reading for ideas, forms and expressions for writing
- like to write in a particular genre
- need practice to help fluency
- use the writing area as a means of getting their own meanings on paper
- don't know what to write
- always know what they want to write or who they want to write for

or who are:

- painstaking perfectionists
- enthusiastic and fluent (even before learning the conventions)
- persistent and practised delayers
- writing refusers (perhaps insecure spellers)
- prolific and accomplished
- anxious to get things right
- at the transition between emergent and conventional writing
- self-motivated
- proud of their work
- independent and confident.

In order to provide for differentiation, you will need to identify the strengths and difficulties of the writers in your classroom and ensure that you cater for the range. But differentiation doesn't just mean making distinctions between the writers, but providing a flexible enough writing curriculum for all of them to make progress. To start this off, you need to find out about what your writers know.

What writers know

E. Ferreiro and A. Teberosky 1979 *Literacy before Schooling*, London, Heinemann

Various researchers have observed that children have rules about writing. Ferreiro and Teberosky write about a child who wrote OIA for cat. When asked to write 'kittens' he produced OIAOIAOIA. This might not be the way that most languages have decided to represent plurals (although there are some cultures where plurals are made up in this way) but it certainly seems a possible and sensible solution when you are trying to make up rules to help you make sense through writing. So it seems that children bring a great deal of experience and knowledge of literacy with them to school. In a highly literate culture such as the UK, children are surrounded by print: posters, signs, letters, forms, books, menus, newspapers as well as print on T-shirts, toys and television. They are also surrounded by writers: of cheques, shopping lists, birthday cards, tax forms, letters, etc. The print will be from different languages and in many scripts and sizes. These serve as useful models for children's developing writing as they attempt to write for specific readers in particular forms. Often, however, children's knowledge of texts is implicit; if they are to be able to extend their writing repertoires then teachers have to help them get their implicit understandings out into the open – to examine them and make them explicit. This means that teachers have to be attentive and vigilant in recognising the kinds of knowledge children bring to their writing.

Fig. 3.5 shows a writer who is fascinated with the shapes of letters and with her own experiment. She didn't want to read this, she just wanted to play with the letters. In the same nursery classroom, another writer shows a robust sense of the sound of words and how they relate to his experiments with writing: *when I get angry I'm like a tiger and rush upstairs* (Fig. 3.6). The example from Darryl (Fig. 3.7), aged 6, gives an insight into how home reading can provide children with valuable models for writing. Darryl is an avid comic reader; the class had listened to *Peter and the Wolf* and were writing in response to the music when Darryl asked his teacher *What do you call those curly things? I've seen them in my comic.* His writing reveals that he was asking the name for brackets which he has used appropriately in his text.

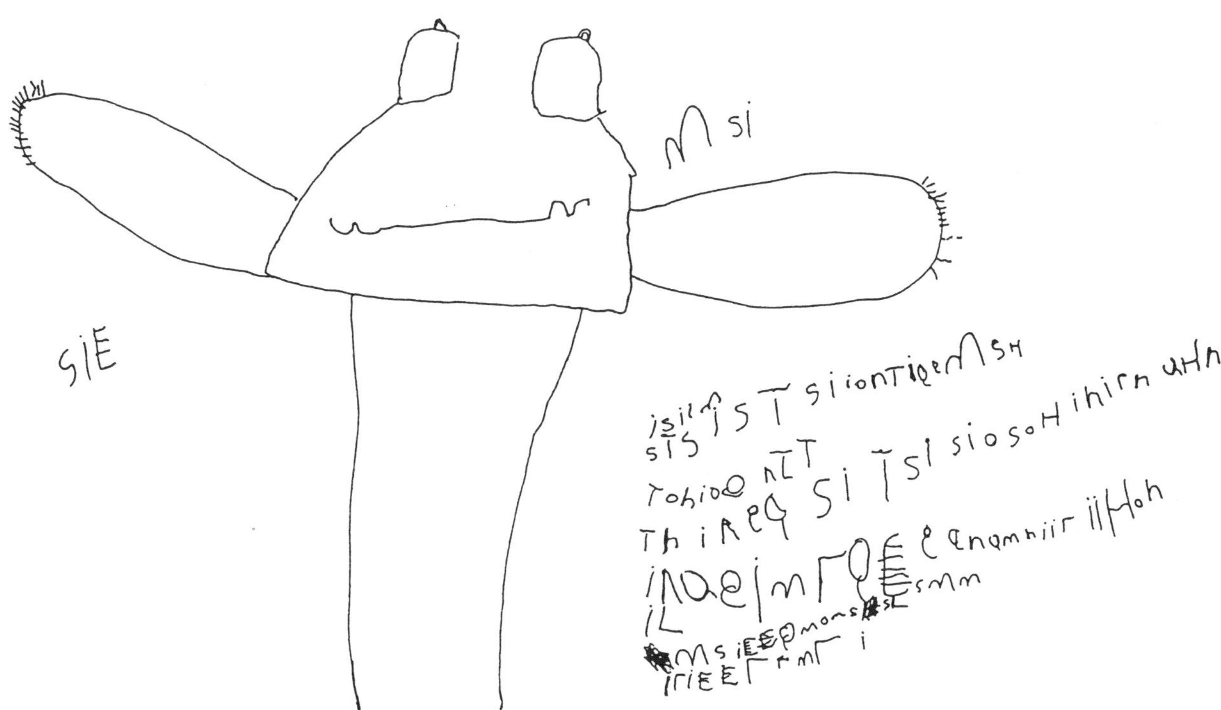

Figure 3.5 A 4-year-old experimenting with writing

The important aspects of the exchange with his teacher, Sally Wilkinson, about this writing was that she had recognised the value of his preferred home reading – comics – and that he knew that she was a good listener. If school experience is genuinely going to build on what children know about texts, then it is important to give genuine attention to the knowledge and experience that they bring into the classroom. This is where your knowledge of your pupils' reading tastes, particularly those at home, can be helpful, since when children write, they draw on their reading experience. If you have not already asked them the questions on p. 77, this might be a good place to start.

Sally Wilkinson, who taught in Ipswich and is now advisory teacher for Primary English in Suffolk, provided all these examples. Her work on home literacy is described in more detail in Chapter 2, pp. 10–11

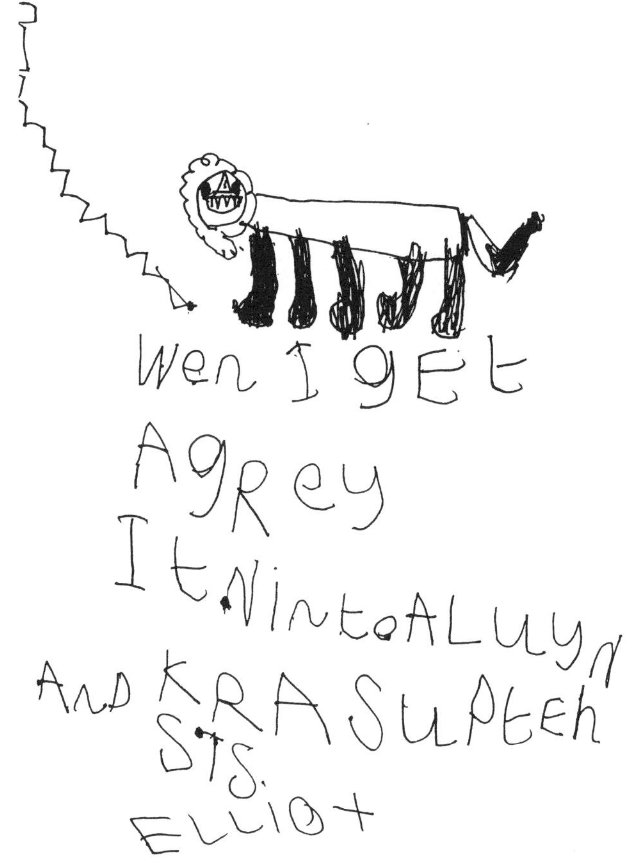

Figure 3.6 Drawing on oral experience in early writing

I'm a Wolf and I'm
hungry I'm walking trough the
meadow Ive seen a tasty duck
I'm chasing it now. Emmmmm tasty
but · it went down to quickly
I fancy my chances with
that boy. Oh no hes seen me
Hes got a rope whats he going
to do with it? when he comes out
Ill rush him! But the boy (whos
name was peter) threw his rope
around my neck and some hunters
took me to the circus.

Figure 3.7 Using language knowledge drawn from home reading

Teaching writing

The single most potent resource and model for developing language in the classroom is the teacher. When it comes to writing, there are many ways in which the daily requirements of classroom routines show the teacher writing the register, on the board, on slips of paper in letters home, in comments on children's work. Sometimes, the teacher will also write poetry, reflective journal entries and stories. All of these activities serve as very useful reminders to children that the classroom is a context for everyone to be a writer. If the processes of writing are explained and made clear to the younger members of the writing community, then the modelling is even more useful. The teacher's role extends beyond acting as a model or example, however. Cath Farrow sees the teacher as providing important supports for developing writers:

Cath Farrow 1991 'The writing environment' in Eve Bearne and Cath Farrow *Writing Policy in Action*, Milton Keynes, Open University Press

> - models
> - an atmosphere where risks can be taken without fear of reproach or recrimination
> - audiences who treat their writing seriously
> - the feeling that they are apprentices working alongside other apprentices
> - the chance for them to discuss their writing during the composing stage with other interested people – adults or peers
> - the insight to appraise their own and each other's writing
> - the vocabulary with which to do this.
>
> (p. 61)

She sees these elements as essential in promoting a sense of purpose in writing, stressing the need for the teacher to be seen as a genuine reader of a child's writing:

> resisting the temptation to comment only on the presentation or technical accuracy and reading instead for meaning: commenting, praising, giving constructive criticism. Any child's text should be taken seriously, taking into account the writer's intentions, the way it is composed, the success with which meaning is communicated and the sense of audience shown by the writer. The teacher needs to make it clear that any suggestions she makes are only suggestions and that the writer has the right to accept or reject the proposed changes. This is difficult to do, since it seems natural to a child to do what the teacher says, but it is a vital part of the teacher's role if the atmosphere of apprenticeship is to be maintained.
>
> (p. 62)

These aspects of the environment of expectation and opportunity are critical in developing fluent, confident and accurate writers.

The writing environment

The ability to initiate writing, to re-read, revise, edit, and proofread – the capacity to become an attentive and critical reader of one's own writing – can only come about if a developing writer can begin to take responsibility and charge of the process of writing. You might like to check out your classroom as an organised environment for writing:

Classroom organisation for writing can mean:

An important part of the writing environment of any classroom should be access to Information and Communications Technology. This used to be referred to as Information Technology (IT) but is now more precisely called ICT.

- pupils starting and writing tasks at different times
- using folders (and other formats) as well as exercise books
- structuring ways in which writers can collaborate
- creating specific places and specific times for peaceful individual writing

- having a range of writing materials easily available
- extending the range of reading material in the classroom
- making the purpose and outcomes of learning explicit
- demonstrating how to revise, edit and proofread
- providing experience of brainstorming, planning, making diagrams or 'learning maps'.

Teachers sometimes fear that more flexible arrangements for writing can result in even more correcting or marking or pupils not having enough guidance about the organisation or technical accuracy of their writing. Time is always a pressure and there are sometimes concerns about sustaining the enthusiasm of less fluent or experienced writers. Some ways of dealing with such concerns include:

- outlining the programme of work with specific points at which discussion and evaluation can take place between pupils or between pupil and teacher
- framing questions to guide pairs of pupils in scrutinising the content, organisation and technical accuracy of their work
- showing stages of drafting which have been used to reach a finished piece of writing
- using journals or learning logs for dialogue between pupil and teacher
- asking pupils regularly to choose a piece of their own writing (in draft or final form) as a basis for a timetabled discussion with the teacher
- inviting pupils to ask their own questions about a topic or about the problems they think they have with their work
- explaining the use of editing symbols in revising writing
- offering a range of different writing tasks using the same materials/starting point (for example, a poem)
- using other pupils or adults as scribes or co-writers
- displaying reference charts made by the teacher or pupils giving guidelines about editing techniques, brainstorming and planning strategies
- explaining and publicly displaying programmes of work including points at which activities or outcomes should be completed (the time scale could be within the day or several weeks)
- explaining to parents (by letter from children or teacher or by personal contact) the purpose and use of, for example, drafting or journals
- teacher and pupils bringing into the classroom a range of everyday publications: pamphlets, advertising material, magazines, letters, newspapers, instruction manuals.

Once pupils have grasped strategies for reading and evaluating their own work, they can often suggest ways of organising work for themselves. Response and intervention can become shared responsibilities between you and your pupils and can help focus on particular areas of difficulty or potential for development. These issues are explored in detail in the case study which follows.

The developmental writing programme

Ian Eyres describes how he introduced developmental writing to his class of Years 3 and 4 children in the September of the new school year.

On the second day of the autumn term I began the writing lesson by giving each child two sheets of paper – one lined and one rough. Taking a piece for myself, I explained that I was going to write down on the rough paper four subjects that I thought I might write about and that the children should do likewise. They were free to discuss topics with neighbours if they wished. Some seemed very confused by this, so after I had chosen two topics I said a few words about each and also asked a few children to say what they had written. Despite this help, after ten minutes there were still some children with only one idea and a few with none at all. I felt that the more hesitant ones would not benefit from being pressured, so I decided to move on to the next step.

I gave the class a few moments to choose one of their subjects to write about (again I allowed discussion with a neighbour) before announcing that for my part I would write about my one and only fishing trip. Maybe, I added, the writing would help me see why I never went again. I said that I, like them, would not want to be disturbed while writing. It is worth noting here that a prominent feature of the previous day's *What I did in the holidays* session had been a long queue of children asking for spellings. This time they were told to circle any words which they thought might not be spelt correctly and carry on writing. I then began to write, half the class wrote with me and the other half quietly began to panic. After about ten (very calm) minutes I began to wander around the classroom and, without intervening, looked at what the children were writing. After visiting a few of those who had made a start, I talked individually to those with blank sheets and in each case managed at least to unearth one topic they felt comfortable with. By the end of the session (which was concluded with a general discussion of 'how it went') every child had at least begun to write. Everyone was in a position to get started straight away the next day.

This initial lesson set the pattern for subsequent writing sessions. Two important principles had been established: that writing time is *for writing* (no more queuing!) and that writers always have the opportunity of continuing their drafts in the next session, which means that every piece can be developed as far as the author wishes. (Goodbye to *I woke up and it was a dream.*) Over the coming weeks the class came to see that as authors they had complete ownership of their work and that this independence was in part made possible by an interested and supportive writing community.

The most visible sign of this sharing aspect of the approach is the classroom publication of finished work. The children's simple books are among the most frequently read and discussed by class members. Drafts in progress can be discussed at whole-class sharing sessions where listeners are able to ask supportive questions.

Children learn techniques for discussing work in individual conferences with me. In any conference it is the writer who does most of the talking and provides all the information. As teacher my job is to ask questions which will bring out what the child knows and wants to say about a subject. In conferences children feel free (not pressured) to add, delete, or remove material. One thing which surprised me at first was how often they would choose to start a piece afresh so as to incorporate all their changes legibly. I must emphasise that all decisions are the author's – the teacher raises problems for the writer to solve. I think that the fact that the children see me as a fellow writer (I often write with them and when I give advice it is always in personal terms: *I just put a line and make up the names later*) makes them more likely to accept my advice, whether it is implicit or explicit.

Conferences affirm the primacy of meaning. Children come to master the conventions of spelling, punctuation and so on because they find them to be essential servants of their

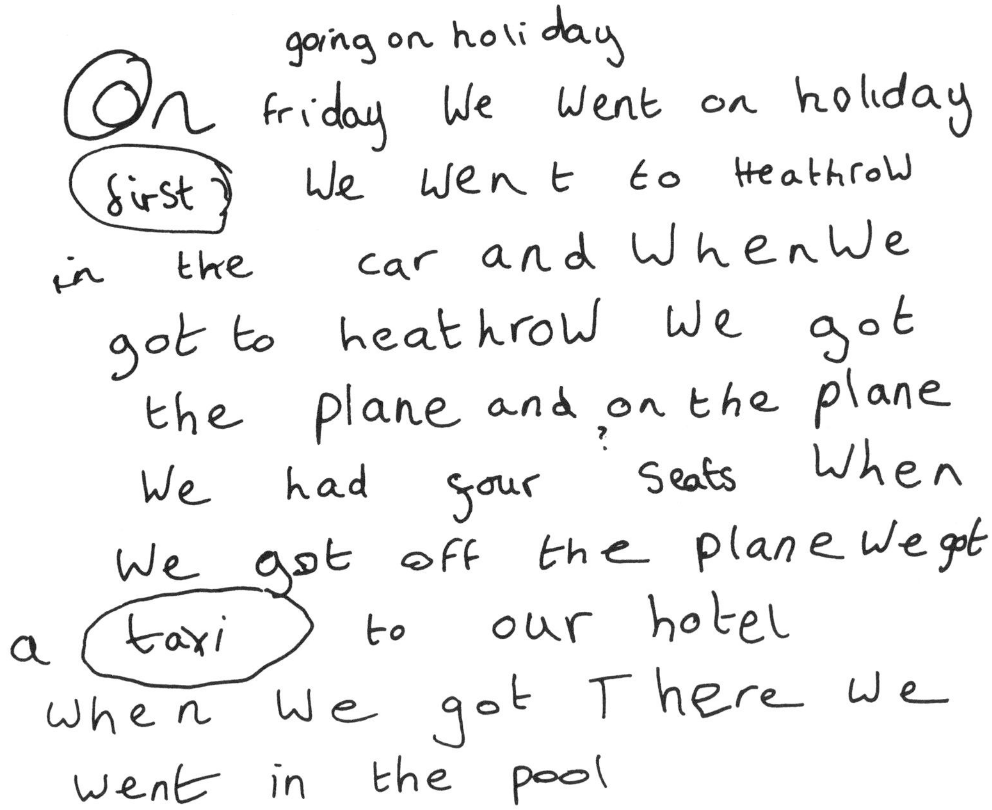

going on holi day

On friday We Went on holiday
first We Wen t to Heathrow
in the car and When We
got to heathrow We got
the plane and on the plane
We had four Seats When
We got off the plane We got
a taxi to our hotel
when We got There we
went in the pool

Figure 3.8 Draft 1 *Going on Holiday* – the writer does not mark sentences

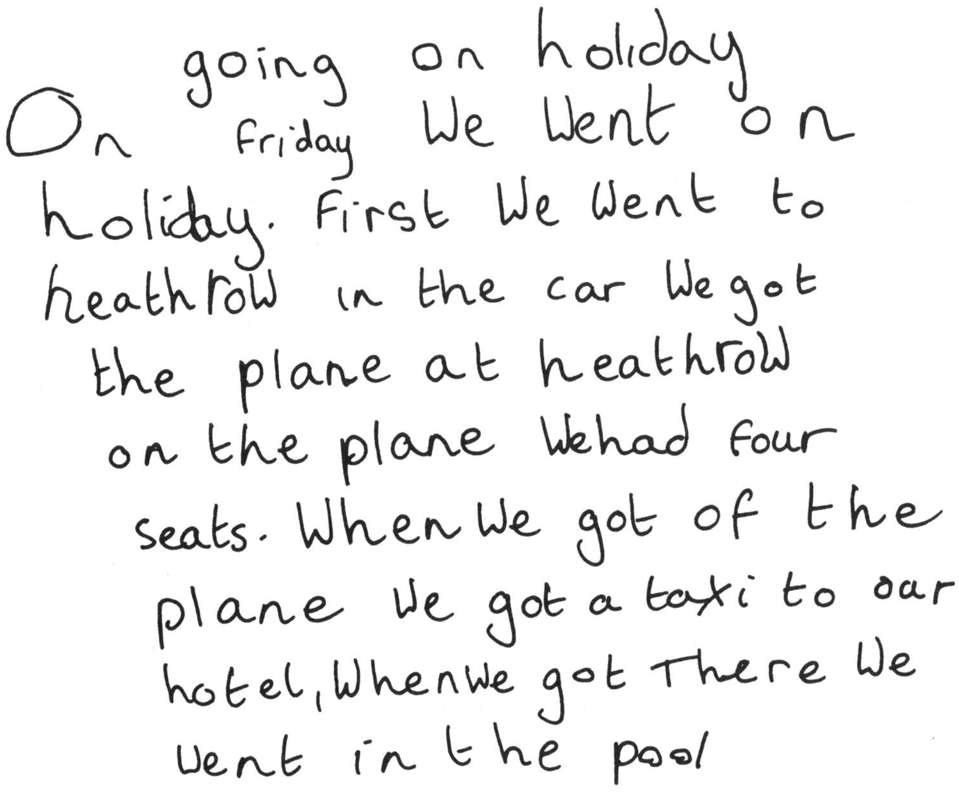

going on holiday

On friday We Went on
holiday. First We Went to
heathrow in the car We got
the plane at heathrow
on the plane We had four
seats. When We got of the
plane We got a taxi to oar
hotel, When We got There We
Went in the pool

Figure 3.9 Draft 2 *Going on Holiday* – she inserts some full stops and deletes two *ands* the duk Who codnot swim

ther Was a duk But he codnot
swim. So he just licked,foting
a rownd and stying owt of thub.
then own day he we nt swiming
practice. and he nilly drowned
then he thowt to go on a adventure.
he packed his bag and said, bye. he, saw
a frog he said Wher der you going
on a adventure. oh be ceafall
owt ther

Figure 3.10 Draft 1 *The Duck Who Could Not Swim* outline story

The Duke Who Codnot Swim

ther Was a duk But he, cod not swim. So
he just licked floting a rownd and stying
owt of thu ball. His nam Was doneld.
Then own day he went to swiming
practice. And he nilly drowned then
hes Mother calld can you tidi yor bedge
room. Yes when he was tiding his bedge
room he fownd his ruksack. then he
thowt to go on a adventure. he
packed his bag and said good,
bi. he saw a frog he said wher
are you going. on a adventure.
oh be ceafull owt ther

Figure 3.11 Draft 2 *The Duck Who Could Not Swim* elaborated with details and explanations

metalinguistic terms: vocabulary with which to talk about texts – a language about language

developing meanings. Conferences are simple and predictable, so that children quickly learn how to ask characteristically open questions, a skill put to use (together with a battery of metalinguistic terms – *edit, draft, paragraph, capital letter*, etc. – introduced and rehearsed in conferences) when they came to working in pairs on each other's drafts.

Every child has an appointed conference day. This ensures that I make personal (albeit sometimes very brief) contact with every writer at least once a week. Conferences may also be triggered by my reading of drafts (something I do after every writing session) and although my aim might be to address a problem (from writer's block to absence of full stops) just as often it will be to affirm some positive feature – an emerging spelling pattern or an especially effective opening, for example. Finally, there is a blank sheet of paper on the wall where children can sign up for an unscheduled conference.

A conference always precedes publication. At this point I am able, without taking control away from the author, to make demands about technical and editorial standards. I never require perfection, but I expect each piece of work to be as good as the author can make it and to have developed significantly since its first draft. I then give it a final edit myself (I offer this as a service, pointing out that all published writers need editors) and pass the final draft to a team of parents who come in voluntarily to type the work.

Whole-class activities can assist in raising awareness of the writing process. 'Writing together', where I act as scribe for the construction of a text on a familiar theme, for example some aspect of the class topic, gives me the chance to model many techniques and in particular emphasises the notion that drafts may be changed many times before they are 'finished'. I find that if I resist the temptation to 'tidy things up' as we go along and simply accept the words I am given, in time the necessary changes are proposed by the children themselves.

Another whole-class activity is the discussion of published literature. The books which children publish are stored and displayed alongside commercially produced books. The children are encouraged to view their own work and that of professional authors as alike, and consequently they are inclined to ask similar questions about each type of book. Often these involve questions an author has raised without giving an explicit answer: *Why did the heroes run away? Why did Jim so badly want to win?* On one occasion the class decided that so many loose ends had been left by one author that the publisher should have sent it back for redrafting! Far from approaching stories negatively, however, these children are reading as writers. They enjoy stories enormously and often use themes from their reading in their own writing.

It might be helpful to describe the children's equipment. Each writer has a folder which contains all their drafts, an editing card on which I write the words they have circled, a sheet headed *Contents of this folder* and another headed *Ideas for future pieces*. The classroom enables uninterrupted writing through free access to paper and a good supply of pencils, sharpeners and pens on each table.

In summary, the principles which guide the writing programme are as follows. First, children are considered to be writers. Their writing is taken seriously, and they are given the time and support necessary for the full development of their work. Writing remains the property of its author, who must make all decisions, including whether to publish a piece or not. Second, support for writing derives from the establishment of a writing community in which all class members, including the teacher, are fellow writers and in which they feel secure enough to take the risks necessary to becoming an independent writer. Third, whole-class activities and individual conferences are used to foster a questioning attitude which results in writing becoming a dialogue with the text and this in turn raises awareness of writing's power to clarify and elaborate meanings under construction. The ideas that writing is a process and that its function is to express meanings as well as they can be expressed, are principles essential to a developmental approach to writing.

One of the key points Ian Eyres makes is about the kinds of interventions which teachers should – and, importantly, shouldn't – make. In a more traditional approach to writing, intervention has often been seen as teacher with pencil/pen, perhaps with child, perhaps not, making marks on the child's text. Ian Eyres has shown that not only is this not necessary if you set up an atmosphere of a community of writers, it can restrict children's efforts and not result in the kinds of development you most wish for. Fig. 3.12 shows guidelines compiled by groups of teachers showing just how intervention can genuinely lead to progress. Their suggestions follow the National Curriculum list: Plan, Draft, Revise, Proofread, Present. In many of the instances they give, teacher intervention is in spoken form. The chart describes ways of developing drafting as a progression from Reception to Year 6 gradually moving towards greater independence in writing. Some strategies are, of course, repeated with each year group – discussion before composing, for example. This list should be seen as a starting point which can be added to or expanded to suit individual schools and classrooms. Whilst the computer is mentioned a couple of times, it is worth remembering that using word processing or desktop publishing is appropriate for any stage of the planning to final presentation process.

Setting up a writing area

A writing area that is seen as an important part of the classroom environment, and is well equipped and integrated into everyday classroom work, gives very powerful messages about the value you place on writing – both the children's independent work and general class activities. It is intended as an area where the pupils have some independence and responsibility. It gives them the space to choose their own writing activities. Depending on age and taste this might be jotting down ideas and illustrating them, writing letters, cards and other messages, making posters or leaflets, copying out a favourite poem, etc. It is one way in which classroom experience of writing can most closely replicate home uses of writing. However, it should not be seen just as a free-for-all zone! A writing area needs to be planned for and to fulfil your objectives for the children to learn more about texts. Whilst it may be seen as a place where the pupils are in control, your intervention as a teacher of writing will be made in the examples of text you supply for the walls, showing different languages, scripts and formats. You might have post-it pads for a notice board, lists, captions or the children's poster of 'rules for the writing area'. You might provide A4 paper folded in a concertina shape and an invitation to 'make a concerntina book about . . . ' or you might ask children to contribute to a class anthology of poetry, either a poem of their own or one they like. You will need to keep an eye on the supplies in the area and it is often a good idea to get the children involved so that they see it as an important one for them. They are often the ones who have the best ideas for stimulating writing – and you might even ask them to devise a 'writing challenge' for the week (or fortnight).

There might be some organisational problems, however, so it's as well to think about them beforehand. What if no one wants to use the area or if they all want to use it at once? Or, there might be a few children who always use the area and others who never do. These problems can only be solved by your knowledge of the children and the work you're doing. It may be a good idea to 'timetable' use of the area (without losing some sense of spontaneity and children's choice!) or to organise tasks which need some work in the area – perhaps the big thesaurus or dictionary is in there or the child has written a poem which deserves putting in the anthology. It is also a very good idea for you to use the area occasionally as a writing place for yourself, as this offers a good model. Writing areas can be messy. Rotas for clearing up or a big reminder notice about picking up your own mess can help. One of the most effective ways of keeping the area clean and tidy is to negotiate rules with the children – and make sure they are kept. You might need occasionally to remove post-it pads, sticky tape or scissors temporarily if they are causing a problem.

STRATEGIES FOR SUCCESS How we help children to:	RECEPTION
Plan: note and develop ideas	Before any class writing activity, make it clear what the finished product will be. Children would be working individually (probably emergent writing), in pairs or in groups with teacher as scribe, modelling the process. • start with oral work – brainstorming: talk and discussion as a whole class/group, using brainstorm diagram as prompt • read stories and poems, discussing structure – beginning middle and end • use storyboards • sometimes decide on and discuss a particular focus e.g. starting or ending the story • use story tapes as starting points or puppets to create a story
Draft: develop ideas from the plan into structured written text	Continue modelling the process until the children are gaining experience and fluency. Individual story writing may also be part of a range of different literacy activities. • encourage children to have a go at writing • remind children to refer to brainstorm (or other) prompt • provide concertina books, small books, other formats (in the writing area or writing box for group work) • record oral stories on tape – individual pairs or small groups • give reminders about structure/focus e.g. beginning and end • have recently learned words in different places in the classroom as resources for writing
Revise: alter and improve the draft	At first, teacher models revising the group/class story on flipchart/easel, making changes after discussion or from the children's suggestions. Individual work may be carried out alongside group or class work. • remind the children what they want the writing to say • encourage individual writers to re-read before coming to show the teacher • replay tapes asking the children to use prompt questions: *Is there anything missed out? What happened in the end?* • select one sentence to go on display accompanied by a (scribed) speech bubble: 'I like this sentence because . . .'
Proofread: check for errors, omissions or repetitions	• In group scribed story the teacher demonstrates by emphasising punctuation, reading aloud asking children *Is this right?* proof-reading for individual writing may not be appropriate for emergent writers • refer children to classroom display of sentences, punctuation and words • remind the children of punctuation noticed during group/class Big Book reading sessions • use the occasion as a chance to consolidate sounds/blends learned or particular points about layout and punctuation
Present: prepare a neat, correct and final copy	Teacher scribed work can appear as Big Books, typed or word-processed and illustrated by the children. • individual books or concertina books become part of the class library • poems as wall display • drama/puppet plays are performed • any of the stories can be read to the class by the teacher or the writer • stories can be read at school or class assembly

Figure 3.12 Progression in strategies to help drafting

STRATEGIES FOR SUCCESS	YEARS 1 & 2
How we help children to:	
Plan: note and develop ideas	Before any class writing activity, make it clear what the finished product will be. Discuss final presentation and method of work. • whole class/group discussion of story structure (beginning, middle, end) discussing, exploring and expanding on the children's ideas • brainstorm from initial stimulus e.g. familiar story, in groups, class or pairs • use talk partners to get ideas going • key words/key points written on board/flipchart for consultation • use storyboards
Draft: develop ideas from the plan into structured written text	Teacher models class example of story, focusing on e.g. setting or character. Use individual ideas from volunteers and add detail through discussion. Emphasise at this stage that ideas are more important than spelling, but remind about punctuation. • individual work supported by storyboards or other pictures, planning sheets or class prompt • paired work with writing/talk partner • occasional focus on one aspect e.g. character • some groups working with teacher support as part of routine literacy activities • remind children to use class word displays
Revise: alter and improve the draft	Teacher models by using class story or own story/poem to show how to improve draft, teaching about using arrows, numbering points, highlighting and/or changing words. • show/remind children about final layout • individual or paired work focused to add more detail in one particular area e.g. at beginning or to describe character • partners to help talk about how to revise • read to teacher/with teacher to check for sense; teacher guiding, e.g. with more adventurous vocabulary, or asking if the child wants to make any improvements
Proofread: check for errors, omissions or repetitions	With class draft, teacher guides children to supply suggestions about any words which need checking for spelling or any punctuation which could be used for effect. • children read paired work aloud to talk/writing partner to check for punctuation and missing words • prompts on board/flipchart for the week's word/letter string focus and for punctuation • teacher reads piece back to individual child, asking about punctuation and focusing on selected spellings • more fluent and assured writers can underline their own doubtful spellings and check for spacing • refer children to class dictionaries, personal word books, computer lists or wall displays for independent spell-checking • teacher sees all writing (put in folder on desk) to confirm accuracy
Present: prepare a neat, correct and final copy	All stages of group work displayed to show drafting process. • individual work (small books or contributions to Big Books) put in reading area • use pens, special paper, guidelines . . . • volunteers might read their work aloud to the class and choose two people to say what they like about it • print on computer • display in general school area - library/corridor/entrance hall • take home to show parents

Figure 3.12 Progression in strategies to help drafting (continued)

STRATEGIES FOR SUCCESS How we help children to:	YEARS 3 & 4
Plan: note and develop ideas	Before any class writing activity, make it clear what the finished product will be. Class discussion and reminders about structure, ways of working, stages of drafting. • relate planning to final product or presentation • model ways of writing based on current reading or on extracts from other books, plays . . . • individuals, pairs or groups brainstorm ideas in rough • use planning sheets e.g. beginning, setting, main characters, plot line . . . • occasionally give title and opening sentence for individuals/pairs to continue
Draft: develop ideas from the plan into structured written text	Children will be working individually or with drafting partners (sometimes on personally chosen topics) with the teacher giving support to those needing it. As part of other literacy activities the teacher may be working with a group, supporting their writing through any stages of the drafting process. • reminders about using extracts from books as models • sometimes compose group stories – continue where someone left off • select sections to plan in detail in rough, using ideas sheet/planning sheet • prompts about structure, paragraphing, punctuation, use of vocabulary • partners consult each other as necessary • make arrangements for teacher consultation clear
Revise: alter and improve the draft	Children continue to work individually or with partners whilst teacher systematically sees work at specific times in order to guide revision • emphasise that the children should be reading for content and structure • individuals read own work or read to each other to discuss flow of ideas and consistency using prompt questions e.g. *What are the most interesting parts? Is there anything missed out? Is the ending satisfying?* • children asked to evaluate and work on one section only • individuals refer to personal target sheets (personal good points and points for improvement, compiled through routine discussion with teacher) to help individual revision • remind children to use known strategies – numbering, arrows, highlighters to help revision
Proofread: check for errors, omissions or repetitions	Teacher continues process of seeing individuals/groups to guide proof reading. remind about using dictionaries, word books, computer lists, wall displays and reference to published books to check for punctuation and layout conventions. • occasionally provide wall displays with suggestions for alternative words for (e.g.) *said* • pairs read work aloud to each other to check for punctuation, repetition and omissions • individuals circle/underline words they think may need correcting and insert punctuation • teacher looks for patterns in spelling errors and selects particular pattern for correction and further attention • discuss words/phrases with individuals and suggest use of thesaurus • make arrangements for individual work to be read by teacher
Present: prepare a neat, correct and final copy	Redrafting a whole, lengthy text might be too arduous for an individual. Taking a whole piece through to final product will need to be carefully planned for either by asking the children to select a part to make perfect or by using adult typing help. • explain to the children that not all spellings need to be correct unless the work is going on public display • final copy should be on plain, clean and carefully kept paper • work can be read in groups/pairs or selectively (through children's voluntary decisions) to class or at assembly • finished books can be put in class reading areas or taken to younger classes to be shared/lent to them

Figure 3.12 Progression in strategies to help drafting (continued)

STRATEGIES FOR SUCCESS	YEARS 5 & 6
How we help children to:	
Plan: note and develop ideas	Make it clear what the final product will be. Remind about text structures, setting, characters, narrative devices like flashback technique, use of sub-plots . . . • read excerpts from published text for focus on character, setting, descriptions • encourage individual use of storyboards or planning sheets • use varied stimuli – events, objects, pictures, drama – as starting points at times • teacher and/or children compile lists of key words, useful vocabulary on board, computer or wall display • after some time planning, ask for volunteers to tell class about their ideas, or do this in pairs/groups
Draft: develop ideas from the plan into structured written text	The children will mostly be writing individually and independently by now, using drafting partners by choice or by teacher suggestion. The teacher may decide to write at the same time as the pupils to model the process. Teacher intervention can be on a group/individual basis as part of planned literacy activities. • verbal/display reminders about paragraph structure, punctuation, use of language to create effect and/or refer children to personal targets • sometimes children may be asked just to draft part of a story as a focus for (e.g.) endings or as part of a group story where one child provides the setting, another two provide characters etc. • during drafting sessions, occasionally stop to hear individual extracts read by writer or teacher
Revise: alter and improve the draft	The teacher's writing can be used to model constructive criticism for revision, deliberately developing the vocabulary of analysis and criticism. • remind about strategies for marking up text for revision – numbers, highlighters etc. • pairs/groups read work aloud to each other and follow model of constructive comment, using prompts specifically geared towards setting, character, complication, resolution, where appropriate • individuals revise work seeking help where necessary and referring to personal targets • plan layout and illustrations (if necessary) for final publication • make arrangements for teacher to see individual work where needed
Proofread: check for errors, omissions or repetitions	Teacher's text continues to be a focus. There may need to be some 'deliberate mistakes' to model proof-reading. • individuals self-correct for punctuation, paragraphs, speech marks, spelling, vocabulary, using word books, dictionaries, thesauruses, reference books, published fiction (as models for paragraphing or speech punctuation layout, for example) • children use proof-reading partners to help • spell-check if written on computer • make arrangements for teacher finally to read and offer editing comments
Present: prepare a neat, correct and final copy	Presentation may be in a range of forms, spoken, for display or for identified readers. • individuals choose how to present their work and how to illustrate • class books of extracts or anthologies of short stories • individual books for specified readers • plays performed for class or assembly • stories used as a basis for class telling or reading aloud • shared with families

Figure 3.12 Progression in strategies to help drafting (continued)

Some classrooms aren't big enough for writing areas, however, so you may want to arrange writing boxes which could include:

- plastic folders of paper of different sizes and colours
- cards, post-it pads, envelopes
- message pads, small notebooks or blocks of small memo paper
- line guides, stencils
- felt pens, biros, pencils, highlighter pens, rubbers, a stapler, rubber stamps, glue, labels, sticky tape, paper clips, scissors.

Alternatively, the writing area might be a role play area – as a newspaper or book publisher's office with different roles assigned to particular individuals or groups – editor-in-chief, sub-editors, features writers, word-processing typists, proofreaders, designers – and bring into the area relevant models and examples of text. Or, for a while, the whole classroom could become such a writing area. Role play can be a very valuable way of supporting and extending writing. Fig. 3.13 is an example of

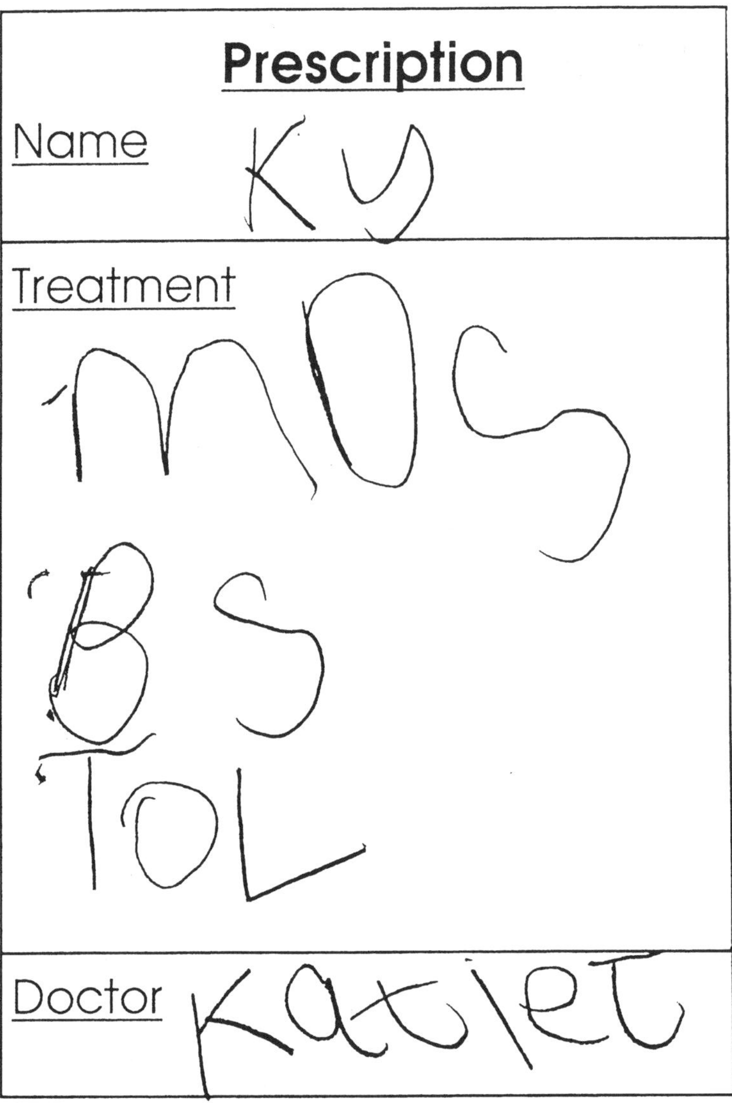

Figure 3.13 Writing in Reception: role play prescription for medicine, bandages and tablets

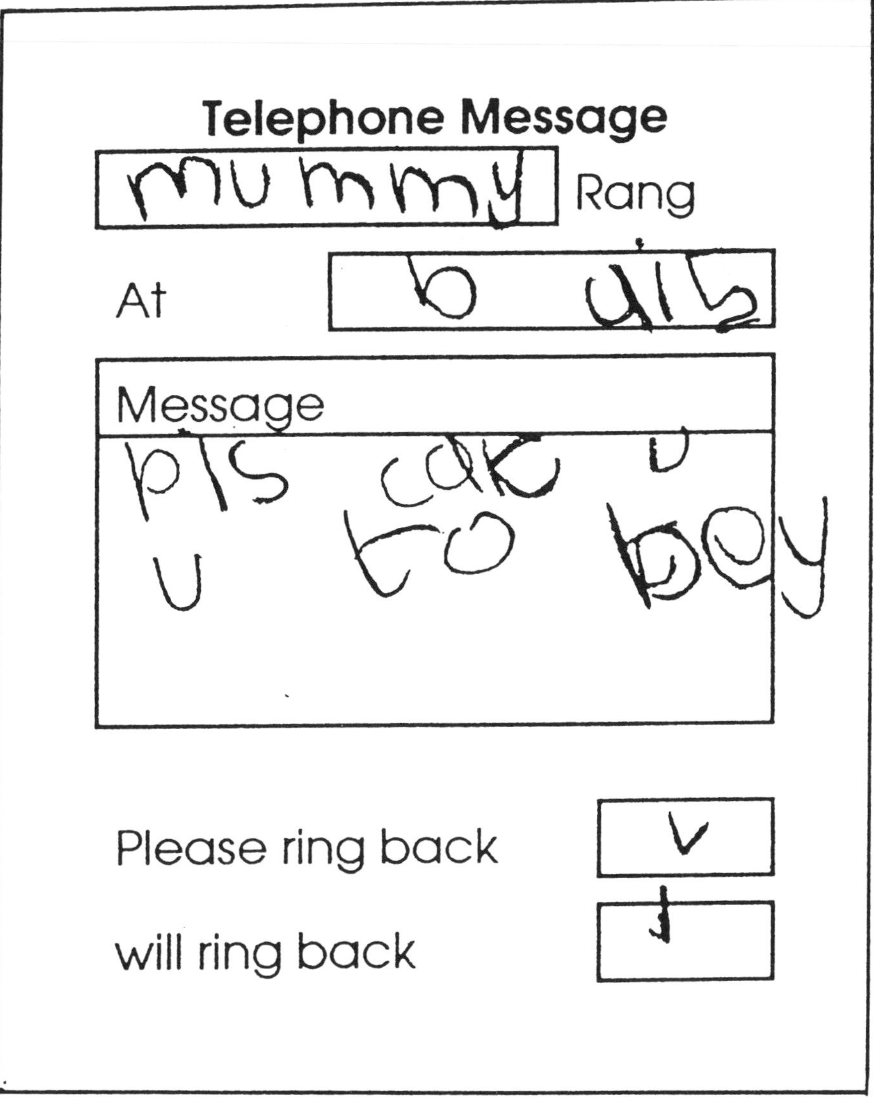

Figure 3.14 Clare wrote down the phone message 'Please call you today'

a prescription written by Katy in a Reception class role play clinic. It says *medicine bandages tablets*. By the telephone in the classroom, Clare wrote *Please call you today* (Fig. 3.14). Fig. 3.15 gives a checklist for evaluating the writing environment of the classroom.

thanks to Sue Bailey and children from Town Lane infants' school, Wirral

Audiences for writing

One of the points which the teachers who compiled Strategies for Success (Fig. 3.12) emphasised was the importance of the children knowing the purpose for the writing. Equally important is the need for children to know who is going to read their writing. Whilst teachers often acknowledge the value of a responsive and genuine readership for writing, it is sometimes difficult to think up yet another audience. Fig. 3.16 gives a range of suggestions, but it is worth remembering that the classroom itself holds a very useful set of responsive readers.

The National Writing Project theme pack *Audiences for Writing* (1990), Walton-on-Thames, Nelson, is an invaluable resource for teachers wanting to think about the readership of writing. It contains a series of classroom case studies describing different approaches with the whole age range of Key Stages 1, 2, 3 and 4.

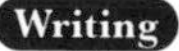

What opportunities are offered for children to:

Use their existing language (and other) experience?	
Write in different ways:	for personal and communicative purposes briefly and more extensively to keep or to throw away?
Write for a variety of readers:	in the class in the school outside the school?
Read a variety of texts:	informational, persuasive, explanatory, narrative, plays, poetry, novels, factual, by children, by adults?
See writing in a variety of formats:	handwritten, typed, desktop published in folders, books, scripts, comics, leaflets?
Talk about writing with	other children in the class other children in the school adults in school and out?
Talk about reading with	other children in the class other children in the school adults in school and out?
Develop a vocabulary through which they can express ideas about texts?	
Collaborate over writing with others	in the class in the school outside the school – children/adults?
Develop self-editing, drafting and revising techniques?	
See adults writing?	
Choose how and when to use writing in particular ways?	

Figure 3.15 Reviewing the environment for writing

Writing to learn

While learning to write is an accepted part of the writing curriculum, there is another sometimes neglected area of the writing repertoire – writing to learn. The assessment of what a pupil has learned often depends upon writing as evidence. As has been pointed out earlier, this has in the past been end-product one-shot writing which is not necessarily a reliable measure of learning. Alongside developing techniques to help pupils to draft their writing towards final product there has been an equally important move to see the value of preparatory writing, exploring, hypothesising, predicting, asking – and answering – questions developed by the writers themselves. This has been in response to one of teachers' most perennial concerns – how to encourage pupils to make ideas their own rather than copying chunks out of reference material. How can learners be encouraged to select relevant material, relate new information to what they already know and write it in a form which clearly shows that

Figure 3.16 (opposite) is based on a diagram included in the National Writing Project Inservice Materials *Making Changes* (1991), Walton-on-Thames, Nelson

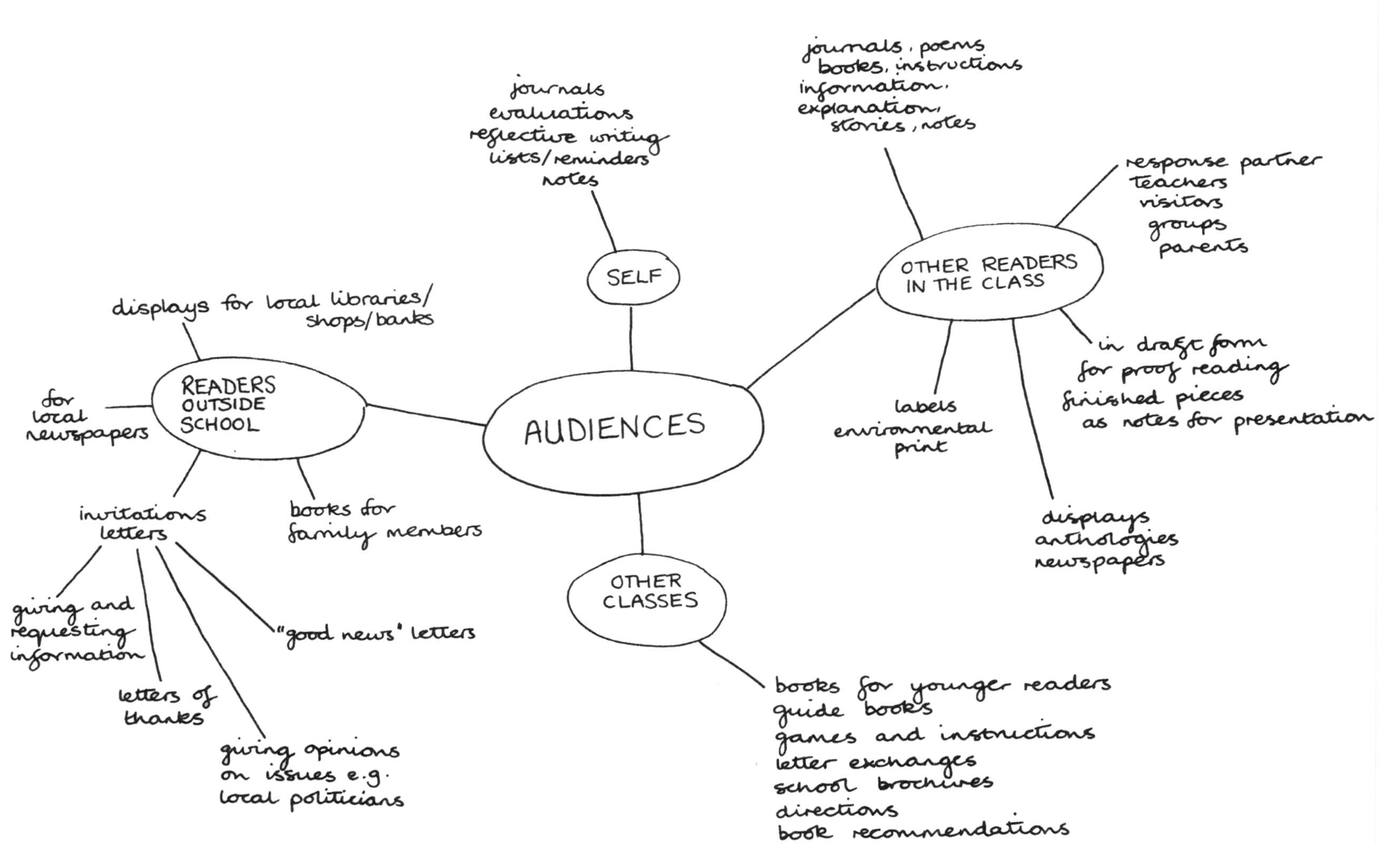

Figure 3.16 Possible audiences for writing

RAS... ...RY
UNIVERSITY O... ...FAIRBANKS

Sketch notes

Question: ....?

What equipment did you use?	What was the first stage of the experiment?	What happened?

What was the next stage of the experiment?	What was the end result?

What is the answer to the question? ....

Why did the experiment turn out as it did? ....

How did you check that this was a fair test? ....

Figure 3.17 Sketch notes for recording science investigations they understand concepts or facts? Not easy, but much easier than formerly since now there is a more clearly understood role for tentative, even disposable writing which can be discarded when it has helped the process of thought and knowledge gathering. Writing can help make explicit and visible what the writer already knows and what remains to be investigated. Jottings, brainstorming, diagrams, lists, questions all help to confirm knowledge or to reveal gaps; these techniques can help get ideas out into the open for scrutiny. Establishing what is known can help frame questions about what remains to be discovered and different forms of presentation can make knowledge even more available for teacher and pupil to evaluate what has been learned and what remains to be clarified.

Frameworks for writing

The teacher's role in helping pupils use writing for learning is often to provide frameworks or 'scaffolding' for learning or in offering opportunities for speculation, prediction and reflection. Planning work helps pupils to sort out their ideas, get an overview and have some sense of where their learning – and writing – may be going. Planning sheets can guide the early stages of investigation or research and help give shape to later writing. They can offer the kind of support which, once used and understood, need not necessarily be offered again – the writer will have learned the strategies and techniques to help get ideas together and re-present them. Many teachers are used to the idea of storyboards or picture planning for narrative. What is not so familiar is the idea of picture planning for information work. Using a storyboard as a basis for planning and then evaluating a science experiment or investigation can provide opportunities for later oral presentation or for summary of the whole process by giving a label to each of the parts of the storyboard. The advantage of this kind of approach is that it offers a good vehicle for differentiated outcomes from a single starting point. It also does not penalise enthusiastic and knowledgeable scientists who may not be quite so confident as writers. A science storyboard or sketch notes could be offered as a set of frames but might benefit from questions under each frame, as in Fig. 3.17, for example:

Scaffolding is used by Jerome Bruner, the American cognitive psychologist, drawing on ideas by Vygotsky. It suggests the ways in which support can be offered for learning. Most importantly, Bruner sees language as 'providing a framework for the child's thinking and experience' (p. 21). Jerome Bruner and Helen Haste eds 1987 *Making Sense: the child's construction of the world*, London, Routledge

What equipment did you use?
What was the first stage of the experiment?
What happened?
What was the next stage of the experiment?
What was the end result?

Planning diagrams can be equally helpful, with guide questions. Fig. 3.18 can be used for any kind of research task.

Figure 3.18 Guide questions for research tasks

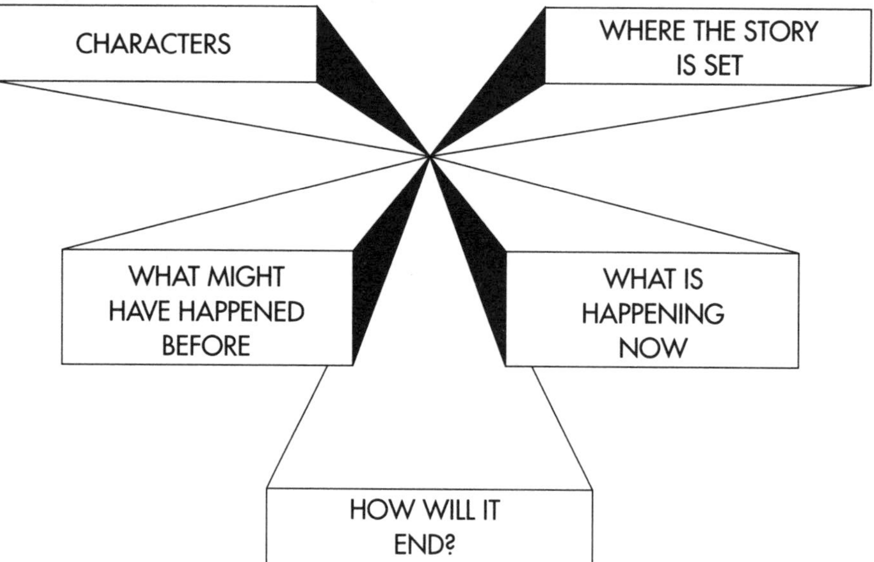

Figure 3.19 Prompts for storymaking

A great deal of work on writing frames has been done by the Maureen Lewis and David Wray 1994 EXEL Project, University of Exeter. See Maureen Lewis and David Wray 1997 *Extending Literacy: developing approaches to non-fiction*, London, Routledge.

Fig. 3.19 provides useful story prompts. One important area for writing to learn is the opportunity for pupils to ask their own questions. Many teachers are now familiar with the 'What I know'/'What I need to find out' format. Devices such as these can be extended to guide the final writing of a piece of text but such frameworks need to be carefully handled so that they don't lead writers into formulaic writing. Some materials use 'starter' phrases like: 'In order to explain . . . I shall first have to give some facts about'. These give children a model for constructing their own sentences, for example: '*In order to explain* why the plague spread so rapidly *I shall first have to give some facts about* the way trade was carried out in those days.' These starters can easily be adapted, for example: '*In order to explain* why we designed our model like this *I shall first have to describe* the other ideas we tried out.' Starter phrases can also introduce alternative points of view: '*I shall first outline what x said then I shall give the other point of view*.' They might offer vocabulary which can only be used to present differing sides of a question, like 'however', 'on the other hand' or 'nevertheless', as in Fig. 3.20. Or offer frameworks for getting details down as a basis for further writing. Fig. 3.21 gives an example of one way to start opinion writing.

Other ways of helping children get information from source material and 'make it their own' include alternative representations like drawing maps from prose texts or photographs, using sketches as notes (see Fig. 3.22) or putting material on to a computer database. All of these techniques and strategies ensure that what has been read or heard must be understood before it is represented as evidence of learning. One of the greatest advantages of these approaches which use writing for learning is that they can also involve a great deal of talk if they are carried out in collaboration with others – and this enhances the quality and durability of the learning.

Collaborating over writing

Collaboration can help children develop the capacity to become attentive readers of their own and other people's writing. However, developing collaborative practices can be tricky. Teachers often fear that children will not offer supportive responses and, at

What do you think?

I think that . . . . I don't think that . . . .

I agree that . . . . I disagree because . . . .

I feel strongly about . . . . because . . . .

It's true that . . . . but . . . .

Some people believe . . . . but I think . . . .

On the one hand I think that . . . . but then you could argue . . . .

There is evidence that . . . . however . . . .

I still think . . . . although . . . .

I've come to the conclusion that . . . . because . . . .

I feel strongly about the council closing down our playground because it's the only one near to our estate. It might be better if

I still think that the professional foul is wrong although lots of footballers do it. It's because

On the one hand you could say that there are too many soaps on television although everyone in the class enjoys watching them. So . . . .

Figure 3.20 Beginning to express different points of view

Different opinions

You can sum up different points of view on charts like this:

For	Against

Then you can think about how to answer some of the points made:

On the one hand	On the other hand

If I say . . .	They'll say . . .

For example:

If I say there aren't enough television programmes about wildlife . . .

They'll say they're very expensive to make.

If I say they could ask children like us to make videos about our own animals . . .

They'll say that there wouldn't be enough people interested in watching them.

Figure 3.21 Starting points for opinion writing

There are many different kinds and sizes of fruit. Some fruit is smooth and some is prickly.

A fruit forms on a plant after the flower has died. The centre of the dead flower becomes a seed. Soft, fleshy fruit grows round the seed to protect it.

Some fruit has thick skin which you peel off before you eat it. Other fruit has thin skin. You do not need to peel this off before eating but you should wash the fruit first.

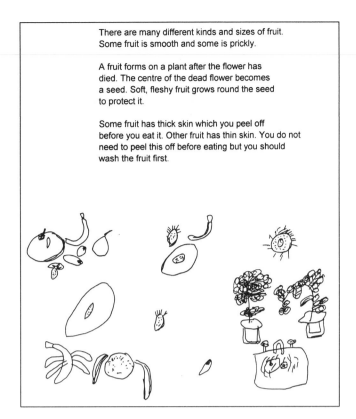

Figure 3.22 Note making using sketches

worst, make negative comments which are harmful and hurtful. Nevertheless, it is clear that collaboration is important and valuable in the process of learning.

There are good educational reasons in terms of conceptual development which support the notion of collaboration, but there are other organisational and social benefits. However, effective and harmonious collaboration cannot just be achieved by putting children together in groups. They need to learn how to collaborate and what the benefits are for them. Fig. 3.23 outlines the advantages and disadvantages of setting up collaborative practices in the classroom. Working together can be used in a range of writing – and other – activities. You might like to consider how collaboration could help and how it could be organised when children are asked to:

- write the draft of a story
- express a point of view about an issue
- sort out headings for a topic
- plan, carry out and interpret the outcomes of an experiment
- produce instructions for an activity
- make a presentation of research findings
- recount a recent experience.

You might also consider at what point in the process of writing collaboration might be most effective. Before setting up opportunities for collaboration it might be useful to decide on:

- with whom?
- for what?
- how?
- when?
- for how long?
- with what expected result?
- and what kind of follow-up?

These statements were made by teachers who had reflected on the value of collaborative writing both to themselves and to their pupils. You might like to discuss these with colleagues and put them in order of importance to you as a group.

It encourages self-evaluation through discussion of ideas with peers.
It gives pupils a chance to clarify and order their ideas.
It gives the teacher greater flexibility.
It gives pupils greater independence and responsibility.
It encourages exploration and investigation.
It provides pupils with a range of ideas and opinions to consider.
It provides pupils with opportunities to support each other.
It provides pupils with opportunities to learn from each other.
It provides pupils with opportunities to review their ideas or their completed work.
It provides pupils with immediate feedback.
It provides pupils with feedback which they are likely to act upon.
It encourages revision, redrafting and editing.
It emphasises discussion to marshal and focus ideas.

These statements were made by teachers who were keen to establish collaboration as a common way of working but looked realistically at the possible problems. Choose one or two which might be true of your class. What strategies or approaches might help to lessen or overcome these difficulties?

Some pupils tend to dominate.
Some pupils don't want to work with others.
It is more time-consuming.
It is difficult to organise.
It is difficult to monitor what is happening.
Less able pupils find it difficult.
Some pupils tend to do all the work.
Some pupils don't see the value of working in this way.

Figure 3.23 The benefits and drawbacks of collaboration

Responding to writing

Everyday writing tasks generally receive a response by which we judge their success. The shopping list prompts us to buy those things which ensure that we can run the home for the next few days; the note on the kitchen table makes sure that the cat is fed; the letter to a member of the family conveys our concern and affection. In the classroom, writing tasks may not have this immediate or satisfying pay-off. Also, while it would be most unlikely that we would redraft and correct our own shopping list or that the person feeding the cat would mark the spellings on the note on the kitchen table or our friends would send our letters back to be neatly redrafted, in the classroom it is the teacher's role to make sure that children get better at writing and so there is an instructional element missing in everyday writing. Unfortunately, however, that responsibility for helping children improve their writing has often resulted in over-emphasis on the surface technicalities of writing. Sometimes this is necessary but at other times the task may require a different kind of response. In planning for writing it is worth considering a range of factors which will help guide the kinds of response which will best help the writer. If pupils are to become able to evaluate their own writing, they can only do this through practising strategies for independence. Fig. 3.24 outlines some key questions.

You might like to look back over some of the comments you have made to children's writing recently. What impression might your pupils have formed of what you think is important about writing? Do you offer a different kind of response when you speak to a writer and when you write a comment?

You could discuss some of the following questions with your colleagues:

- What different ways do we respond to children's writing?
- What is the response meant to do?
- In what circumstances do we respond?
- How effective are our responses?
- Could the time be better spent?

Or you might want to concentrate on your own response. Choose one of the pupils you teach. Look back at her/his writing over a period of time. What kinds of response have you been making? For example, have you been looking for:

- technical errors
- factual content
- structure/sequencing
- positive aspects
- anything else?

extracts from the National Writing Project material *Making Changes*, pp. 99–100

When children say 'I can't' ?

Sometimes children come to writing with fear, reluctance, refusal, a need to be convinced that 'they can . . . '. Much of the fear can be offset over time by the creation of an environment in which a young writer can feel safe and free to experiment and take risks.

Some usual classroom strategies are:

- offering the option of 'play' writing with very young writers
- setting up a writing corner/table
- including some language/literacy objects and opportunities in the role play area
- having writing partners throughout the class
- demonstrating drafting and providing strategies for checking accuracy
- setting up opportunities for collaboration – group or pair work; with parents, other adults, children in other classes, etc.
- using drama and role play as rehearsal for writing
- writing for recognised or acknowledged audiences
- using models and examples drawn from printed texts, teacher's and children's demonstrations
- carrying out whole-class activities accessible to all levels of fluency and confidence (to take the heat off individuals)
- helping children to acknowledge themselves as writers by publication and enjoyment of their efforts.

However, there may also be a need to provide specific support for an individual or group who are lacking in motivation because of fear or reluctance. In order to plan for a programme of supportive work which will help these children deal with some of their difficulties, it will be necessary to observe and note precisely what those problems are before setting targets and taking any action. In the meanwhile, some quickly available strategies could include:

see section on supporting children who experience difficulties with writing, p. 118

- scribing for a child or group of children, inviting them gradually (over a period of days or weeks) to take over some of the writing. This can help to erode lack of confidence, difficulties over effort or physical problems, but may need help to set up. Other adults in the classroom could act as scribes or you might arrange to write alongside a child when the others are writing;

This chart owes a debt to the National Writing Project Theme Pack *Responding to and Assessing Writing* 1989, Walton-on-Thames, Nelson.

WHAT?

- What is the writing intended to do?
- What/who is the intended readership?
- What form is the writing going to take?
- What kind of response will best help the writer?
- What aspects of the writing need attention – ideas? audience awareness? structure/organisation? technical features?
- What aspects of the work can be left for the moment?

WHY?
Do I want the response to:

- encourage/promote confidence?
- suggest further ideas for writing or thinking?
- point out general or recurring faults?
- give feedback about content?
- suggest additions/amendments which will help the reader make sense of the piece?
- give an indication of the level of success of the piece in achieving what it set out to do?

WHEN?
Is the response being made:

- at the beginning – to help sort out ideas?
- in the middle – to monitor progress, organisation of material, reader appeal?
- at the end – to give feedback on interest, success in getting the job done, or suggestions for next time?

HOW?
Is the response going to be:

- spoken?
- written on the work? on post-it stickers?
- in some other form – publication, sent for other people to read?

WHO?
Is the response being made by:

- the writer herself/himself?
- other children in the classroom?
- older/younger children?
- the teacher?
- other readers?

Figure 3.24 Key questions about response

- using magnetic letters or plastic letters for making words;
- word processing or using the concept keyboard. This is an acknowledged support for those who find the physical act of writing difficult and can result in some overnight success;
- using the tape recorder to capture ideas, help to re-shape writing or sometimes substitute for writing.

Reflecting on writing

Reflective uses of writing provide a powerful means for a learner to organise thought, stand back from it and review it. The benefits for learner and teacher seem to be that:

- Journals and learning logs allow learners to work out their own ideas at their own pace; to ask questions which spring from a particular need to know; to speculate about possibilities, clarifying them by the act of writing; to record successes or failures.
- Teachers have the chance to see evidence of teaming as it is happening, rather than having to rely on a written account after an activity has taken place, where writing may not reveal what has not been learned.
- The chance for dialogues with individuals can bring surprises. When freed from the constraints of fixed time limits, specific questions about a topic, or concerns about what will happen when a piece of work is marked, learners can show greater confidence and understanding.
- Reflective writing forms a continuing record which both teachers and pupils can use as a basis for discussions about progress; evaluation by both partners in learning becomes an integral part of the process and can be extended to explain and report to parents.
- The teacher's response can be a demonstration of how to tackle ideas, a means of motivation, an explanation of the purpose of any task, and particularly a way of showing children that writing is for reading – by themselves or others.

However, using journals, learning logs or diaries has implications for classroom practice:

Introducing a different kinds of writing, and perhaps a new way of dealing with children's writing, may need careful explanation – about what the writing is for, who will read it, and how it will be treated.

The teacher's response may vary according to the way reflective writing is used, and arrangements about responding may require more flexible organisation than marking a set of exercise books. Fig. 3.25 gives an example of a general learning journal.

with thanks to Belinda Kerfoot, who provided these from when she taught at Burnham Copse junior school, Tadley, Hampshire

I am enjoying the work about the eye. But it is quite hard to understand about the etina and the papil. I would be very happy if we could watch programmes in the music room about wildlife like we did in the first year. It would be good if we could have more Roald Dahl books read to us because he is a great writer and I am enjoying him. The class talks are great so far but it is funny watching ourselves teaching.

You're right Owen, the structure of the eye is quite difficult to understand but I hope the experiments we did explained a little. Do you think they helped?
I thoroughly enjoyed our Roald Dahl week too, I agree, he is a great writer. I think we'll have another author's week later in the term – have you any suggestions?

Figure 3.25 Extracts from a Year 4 learning journal

Figs 3.26 and 3.27 are examples of the use of maths journals with a Year 6 class. Both examples demonstrate the importance of the teacher's response in affirming current learning and prompting further thought.

In developing a range of strategies to respond to children's journal writing and to use the writing to move learning further forward, teachers may need to:

- give guidelines for pupils to respond to their own and other children's writing until they have become familiar and comfortable with reflective writing
- ask questions about entries and prompt ideas
- select particular points for explanation
- notice whether boys and girls use their journals differently and use that awareness for sensitive intervention
- arrange times for consultation over journal entries
- allow reflective writing at different times of the day
- write journals themselves.

Describing progress in writing

Whilst the National Curriculum gives guidance about the range and key skills for writing, it cannot provide a full picture of what progress looks like as you observe an individual writer. It isn't just a matter of being able to write for this or that audience or readership, or being able to self-correct spellings. Much of the work in this section has pointed to the importance of developing writers coming to behave like real writers, of the value of collaborative practices and the flexibility needed for any writer to put together a satisfying and satisfactory piece of writing. There is little about the development of choice and discrimination or of the ways in which writing is used to why didn't you come out – that's why I'm there!

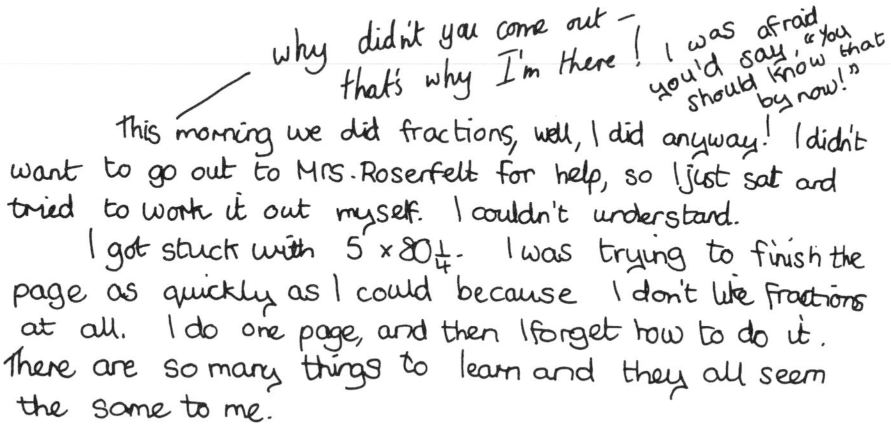

I was afraid you'd say, "You should know that by now!"

This morning we did fractions, well, I did anyway! I didn't want to go out to Mrs. Roserfelt for help, so I just sat and tried to work it out myself. I couldn't understand.

I got stuck with $5 \times 80\frac{1}{4}$. I was trying to finish the page as quickly as I could because I don't like fractions at all. I do one page, and then I forget how to do it. There are so many things to learn and they all seem the same to me.

Figure 3.26 Year 6 maths journal (i)

with thanks to Margaret Rosenfeld, who provided these when she taught at Croesty primary school, Bridgend, Mid Glamorgan

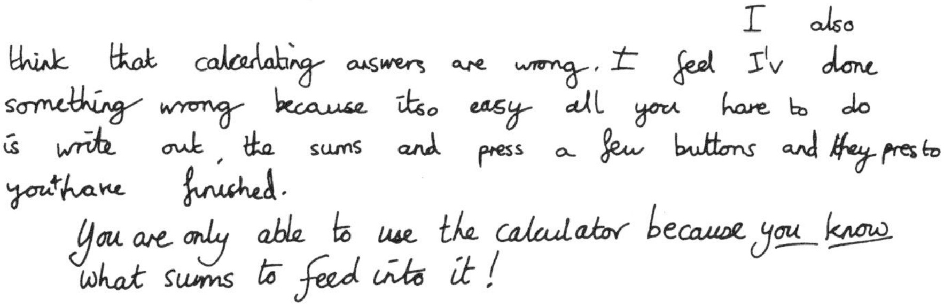

I also think that calculating answers are wrong. I feel I'v done something wrong because itso easy all you have to do is write out, the sums and press a few buttons and they presto you have finished.

You are only able to use the calculator because you know what sums to feed into it!

Figure 3.27 Year 6 maths journal (ii)

aid learning. Equally, apart from references to writing in standard English, there is little encouragement for writing dual language texts or for teachers building on the knowledge of different languages which children have access to. Inevitably so; no single document can hope to provide for the varied and diverse contexts of the schools in this country. It is, nevertheless, crucially important for teachers to be confident about describing what they think 'getting better at writing' means. It is tricky to put into words the ways in which a young writer is beginning to take account of the needs of a reader or is writing to 'hook the reader in'. It is a temptation to stick to commenting on the surface technicalities of spelling, punctuation and handwriting. But these don't tell all the story about what a developing writer can do.

Writing development happens across four broad areas which reflect any writer's increasing assurance and fluency in:

1. fulfilling her or his own intentions or purposes in writing and choosing a way of doing this to suit these intentions
2. taking account of the needs of a reader, or deliberately setting out to engage the reader in what he or she has to say
3. using a range of different forms, genres or formats for writing (the larger units of text)
4. handling the technical conventions of spelling, punctuation, syntax (the smaller units of text).

These can act as a guide to careful appraisal of children's writing in order to comment on present capabilities and, most importantly, to be able to decide on areas for further development. Teachers are used to looking carefully at children's writing in order to assess it and respond to it, but very often the emphasis is on the technical features, rather than on elements of choice and audience.

This appeared originally in Bearne and Farrow *Writing Policy*, pp. 32–3.

The analytical framework in Figs 3.28 and 3.29 shows how the four areas of development can be used as guides to more detailed comment on individual pieces of work which might then be included in a writing portfolio compiled over the course of a year or even a Key Stage. Perhaps it is important to point out here that a detailed set of comments on samples like this would only be recorded once a term for any child.

Choices/intentions

- gives explicit instructions
- statement and helpful description: *just before it, outside on the bookcase, some have got 3 on*
- abbreviates sentences; omits words not necessary for his purpose: *Go to corner, with maths on front.*

Awareness of reader

- gives explicit details of place, colour, titles, sections . . .
- remembers *please*
- directly addresses his reader: *go, look, take out* . . .
- alters original *ask* to *go to* so as not to confuse his mother or his teacher!

Go in, Go to corner with the book case. Just before it are some trays. Mine is at the top and it has my name on. inside get a yellow book with maths on front and a small blue book and a green book inside. The blue book has A day on and the green book has 8 A day on. Bring both Books please.

out side on the book case are some folders. some have got 3 on, 4 on and 5 on. Go to 5 and take out the card in side of the maths Book. look at the top: Book 5 section – and page –. go back to the folder and take out 5 and the no. on the section from the card. take out the next one card on from mine.

Text organisation

- structure fits the task; knows the whole shape of the piece before writing
- logically sequenced: follows the precise route needed to find the books, visualising exactly what his mother will need to do to find the books

Strategies and technical features
(syntax, vocabulary, spelling, punctuation)

- self-corrects for clarity and accuracy
- clear, direct sentences
- simple vocabulary appropriate to the purpose
- uses accurately: commas, colon, dashes, underlining, full stops
- spells whole piece correctly

Figure 3.28 Steven's note to his mother (Year 6)

Choices/intentions

- fulfils teacher's purpose; explains why they decided on a mixture of animals
- chooses a list for clarity in explanation
- explains choice of virtue clearly
- selects informative and straightforward tone appropriate for explanation combined with storytelling rhythms: *He gives dreams to people at night and thoughts in the day*

Awareness of reader

- speaks directly to the reader (teacher/others?)
- gives explicit details in brackets to help the reader understand
- hooks the reader in with a promise of another story
- knows that writing can be a dialogue with the teacher

God's Valuse

Our god is the god of ~~imagenation~~ imagernation. It has the head of a rabbit, the nakk of a gariffe, the body of a elephant, has the arms of a monky, no hands and legs of a kangaroo. He gives dreams to people at night and thoughts in the day - in one story, Javen (thats his name) gives an old man a ~~ctnt~~ cunning plan to warn off wild ~~commonal~~ - anamles and it saved his life.

Have you written the myth about the god Javen and the old man?

* No! we said it is in another story!

Text organisation

- knows how to organise information clearly and logically: statement in first sentence, physical description in second, qualities of character which benefit people, example of how this works in practice (the old man in the promised story)

Strategies and technical features

(syntax, vocabulary, spelling, punctuation)

- evidence (words crossed out and insertion) of re-reading and self-editing
- writes in sentences of varying structure
- uses repetition for clarity
- knows how to use capitals for proper nouns, commas for lists, insertion mark, brackets, possessive apostrophe, asterisk and exclamation mark correctly
- makes only 7 spelling errors in 73 words; visual spelling good – gets *elephant* and *kangaroo* right

Figure 3.29 Writing from collaborative work Steven and Jay (Year 6)

Fig. 3.28 is a note written by Steven (aged 10) to his mother when he had a sore throat but wanted her to collect some work from school to keep him occupied. The teacher held on to the note as she found it such an impressive set of instructions. The piece shows Steven as a confident writer who knows that he can use writing to fulfil his own intentions; he has understood exactly how important it is for instructions to be clear and explicit if they are to do the job. The text is highly geared to the reader's needs, taking account of his mother's lack of knowledge of the classroom environment. The altering of the word 'ask' on the first line to 'go to' indicates that he can adjust his writing as he envisages the classroom context. Even more importantly, perhaps, he has learned what information to omit and what is necessary for his mother to follow the instructions, and is economical with language and information. The writing shows a high level of technical competence, using punctuation which is helpful to the reader and entirely fits the intention for writing. Taken on its own this shows us quite a lot about what Steven can do in writing.

The second example is a draft written for an RE activity where the class had been studying Hinduism. They had also heard several stories and myths from India. Their teacher had asked them to make a model statue to represent a virtue and to write an explanation of why they had decided to represent their chosen moral aspect as they had. Steven and Jay had worked together, but Steven wrote the account. Fig. 3.29 shows the writing and analysis. Looking at both pieces together shows Steven's assurance in adapting his writing according to his intentions to explain and inform as well as according to his knowledge of the reader – in these two cases, his mother and his teacher. He can vary his choice of language, the tone he adopts for particular purposes, the way he organises his material and the technical strategies he uses to fulfil the different demands of each piece. However, there are some aspects of his writing capabilities which an examination of the writing alone cannot give. Most particularly, the two pieces cannot tell a reader about Steven's behaviour as a writer – the extent to which he can self-edit, or how he comments on his writing, or settles to tasks which might be more challenging. These aspects are absent, too, from the kinds of assessments required by the National Curriculum, yet they are crucial if a teacher is to be able to make decisions about how best to move a writer on.

Recording and reporting progress in writing

The Writing Record in Fig. 3.30 is one way of recording not only the features detectable in a sample of writing, but of recording the behavioural aspects of an individual writer's progress, too. It is often a good idea to complete a Writing Record like this as part of a conversation with the writer her or himself, in a similar way to the Reading Record in Chapter 2. Whatever method is preferred, there should be one sample taken for each child each term. This builds to an informative portfolio over a Key Stage. It is probably best deliberately to select a range of types of writing and if this were combined with the writer's own choice of one piece of writing a term, commented on as suggested on p. 135. A full record of a writer's repertoire can be compiled very quickly and easily. This kind of portfolio is very useful when writing progress and development are being discussed with parents.

One of the main aims of keeping records is to offer parents, children and colleagues informed and precise reports on progress. The Writing Record, used alongside the Scale of Progression in Writing (Fig. 3.31), provides the means of doing just that. The descriptions include all four of the developmental areas listed above. They include the technical and secretarial aspects of writing as well as the organisational and meaning structures. They offer ways of describing increasing fluency and independence, being able to adjust writing to the demands of what the writer wants to say and what the reader might need to know. They also include the essential elements of evaluation and discrimination. The descriptors are not arranged according to any hierarchy of skills but reflect what teachers would expect to see as children develop towards being confident, fluent, independent and discriminating writers. Whilst they can usefully prompt discussion with colleagues, they are intended to be open to adaptation. Each school will want to develop its own way of recording and describing progress. The sections have been paralleled with National Curriculum levels as a guide, but not to suggest a programme of learning. The levels are not intended as watertight categories and there is likely to be some overlap where pupils might show some of the features in two (or even more) sections, and there will be gaps – which readers are invited to fill.

The statements match the four aspects of English outlined in Chapter 5 – the knowledge about language and genre necessary for writers to construct texts and the processes of conveying information through writing and developing greater discrimination and choice.

They have been developed, evaluated and modified by teachers in different areas over several years. The teachers wanted to find ways of describing what children could do in writing rather than simply listing what they should have learned.

WRITING RECORD **Name:** Steven **Class:** 6ST **Age:** 10·4 **Languages spoken:** English **Date** 10·10·97

Title and type of writing: God's Values

Stage of completion: (draft) / notes proofread / edited by writer not proofed proofread by teacher finished piece (handwritten) / word processed

Context: (teacher directed) (collaborative work) with Jay at first part of research (self-chosen content) other (specify)

Choices made by writer about type of writing

content explains abstract concept 'virtues' quite well. Chooses appropriate tone

organisation follows logical explanation

technical features

Awareness of reader:

e.g. level of explicit detail gives helpful details in brackets

register informative for teacher

engaging the reader Direct approach to reader

Behaviours: (assurance involvement) v. good self-editing N/A here

(talking about writing) good

(handwriting fluency) good (using appropriate language) good

still a bit easily satisfied

Text organisation (e.g. does the structure fit the task? is it clear/logical/sequenced?)

Strategies: directionality ✓ attempting orthodox spelling good proofreading ✓

Syntax: variation in complexity: ✓ good

Vocabulary: variety and experimentation: ✓ good

Accuracy in spelling

number of words in piece: 73

number spelt accurately: 67

patterns in spelling errors: tends to draw on phonic cues too much

Accuracy in punctuation

number and range of punctuation marks used: • , ∧ ( ) ! ' (6)

number used accurately: 5/6

patterns in punctuation errors: possessive apostrophes need care

Level on Scale of Progression D

NC Level (if appropriate) predicted 4/5

Summary and future teaching strategies: This is a good explanatory / reflective piece showing that Steven can write clearly and accurately at first draft. I want to challenge him to write non-fiction at more length and complexity now. I'll also get him to look at possessive apostrophes in books and come up with some rules for using them.

Figure 3.30 Termly writing record (Blank provided in Appendix: A7)

BECOMING A WRITER – SCALE OF PROGRESSION	Approximation to NC Levels
A pre-writer: • is aware of adults needing to write (e.g. sees parents writing notes, shopping lists, etc.) • uses writing as communication during play • experiments with writing • shows an inclination to imitate symbols and express ideas in print • uses a variety of means/methods/media for letter formation and attempts at writing.	
A A writer in the early stages of learning: • knows that writing communicates meaning • writes for an audience but needs help with technical conventions • is keen to write and will experiment • can comment orally on own writing • writes own text (emergent) but needs adult to scribe or interpret meaning • knows about direction and orientation of writing and can form some letters correctly • can construct a simple sentence • has ideas for extended writing but needs teacher or other adult as scribe • can represent ideas pictorially, sometimes with related phrase or use of vocabulary • can tackle captions, lists, labels, greetings, other small pieces of text.	**W** **to** **Level 1**
B A writer who is gaining experience and fluency: • can compile lists/charts, organise writing into separate pages • demonstrates some enthusiasm for writing • writes some texts independently but still needs help at times • is gaining confidence in writing • can comment on own work orally and in writing • varies chosen vocabulary and experiments with newly discovered words • writes in sentences showing some use of capital letters and full stops • forms letters correctly, joining letters if appropriate • attempts spellings using some rules and phonic awareness • is beginning to write stories with a character/event; a beginning, middle and end • writes accounts of experience in chronological order.	**Level 1** **to** **Level 2**
C A more assured writer, growing in experience: • has experience of a variety of types of writing and a variety of forms, e.g. account of science experiments, observations • can tell the difference between writing a list, a report, notes, etc. • shows some confidence in experiments with content and technicalities of writing • is maintaining enthusiasm for writing and is developing sustained concentration • is beginning to comment independently on own and peers' work • drafts and redrafts with help • uses more varied connectives and description more often • uses generally accurate sentence construction • tries a wider range of punctuation more often (e.g. commas, question marks, exclamation marks) • spells more key words correctly • uses cursive writing • is increasing the complexity of events/characters in story and using models drawn from reading.	**Level 2** **to** **Level 3**

Figure 3.31 Writing Scale of Progression

D A more experienced and independent writer: • can produce non-chronological writing independently • makes notes from reference material with guidance • can use different planning formats • uses writing to organise thoughts • is learning to collaborate over writing • can write extensively and with enthusiasm at times • is developing strategies for redrafting writing independently, using thesaurus and dictionary more often • is becoming more selective about publishing and increasingly able to comment critically on own work and that of others • experiments with more varied punctuation (e.g. brackets, hyphens) • draws on a range of strategies to get spellings right and uses standard spelling more consistently • can use paragraphs • has experience of a variety of types of writing and a variety of forms • is beginning to use different genres and experimenting with developing new genres • includes character and setting in story writing.	**Level 3** **to** **Level 4**
E An experienced and almost independent writer: • can write extensive pieces of non-narrative writing • can make notes, identifying relevant key words/phrases without help • usually chooses an appropriate style for the writing purpose and readership • shows assurance and commitment in writing independently • will collaborate over writing • drafts, redrafts, revises and proofreads more independently or in collaboration with other pupils • responds helpfully to other people's writing • achieves standard spelling much of the time • uses paragraphs consistently and accurately • is becoming more discriminating about using a range of punctuation • structures lengthy narrative logically • can write direct and reported speech • can depict atmosphere, character and setting.	**Level 4** **to** **Level 5**
F A very experienced and independent writer: a writer who: • selects from a range of non-narrative writing forms for own purposes • selects from a range of appropriate models for planning • shows consistent independence in all writing tasks • gains satisfaction from writing • is able to work to deadline/set own deadlines • shows a greater range of critical comment in writing, e.g. in response to books • uses a wide range of vocabulary for specific effect • looks more for content/style/vocabulary when redrafting, rather than technical features alone • sets out direct speech correctly after opportunities to self-edit • can achieve standard spelling and accurate punctuation most of the time • uses a range of narrative sequencing (e.g. starting at end and using flashback; fracturing a narrative for effect; leaving a story hanging) • chooses and sustains an appropriate register for writing • uses a variety of genres showing awareness of elements involved • draws on a wide range of reading in order to explore other writers' techniques.	**Level 5** **to** **Level 6** **and beyond**

Figure 3.31 Writing Scale of Progression (continued)

Individual and whole class progress

see Chapter 2, p. 64

The Writing Progress Scale can be used in exactly the same way as the scale for reading. The graph in Fig. 3.32 shows progress noted by one class teacher over the year. The darker columns show the number of pupils at levels A–E in October; the lighter columns show the shift upwards recorded in the June of the following year. The teacher simply recorded on a class list (Fig. 3.33) the point on the Scale of Progress reached by each child during October, then in June of the next year. The teacher also recorded their level in the spring term but decided that it was not necessary to use this for the purpose of demonstrating progress over almost a whole school year.

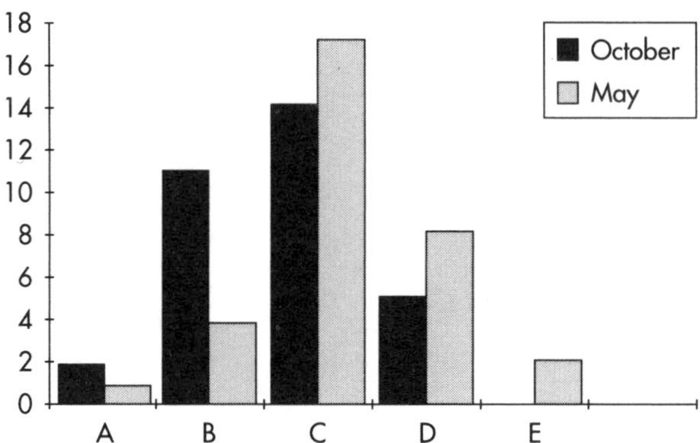

Figure 3.32 Progress made in writing by one class between October and June of the following year

Diagnosing difficulties (including miscue analysis)

When children are experiencing difficulties with getting words down on paper, or show that they are having problems with the technical elements of writing, there will need to be a screening process to pinpoint just what might help. This can lead to a plan which is individually tailored for the needs of the particular child. Other questions can arise about the correct but dull, the fluent but disorganised writer or the complacent fluent writer: how do we get fluent writers to become more critical and attentive readers of their own work? For example, it may be that the 'flowing story' syndrome has reduced the perceived importance (for some writers) of getting the technicalities right. This may just be a phase of development in writing, but nevertheless there is evidence that there are some highly competent writers who appear to be too easily satisfied.

Planned and undisturbed conversations with individual writers can often be helpful, but raise questions of classroom management, particularly the perennial problem of how to make time for everything. Group work – reading aloud, collaborative editing, word processing – can sometimes allow space for individually timed discussions about writing. Sometimes the writer sees no point in revising. Sometimes the writing may not need it. Poetry, for example, may need different revising techniques in comparison with a book written over a period of weeks. It is important for writers to experience the challenge of sustaining a piece of writing over a period of time. This, linked with a public readership, can be the motivator for careful critical reading of own writing. However, there will be individuals who are still unwilling to take their own writing as far as they might. Once you have confirmed satisfactorily that you have tried all sorts of approaches to push a fluent writer to the leading edge of her or his competence, then it becomes necessary to carry out some individual screening.

CLASS RECORD SHEET – WRITING

Teacher: Pat Brown

Class: 3PB

Date (year): 1996–97

Name	Age	Boy/ Girl	Languages spoken	Writing Level Term 1 (22.10.96)	Writing Level Term 2 (21.3.97)	Writing Level Term 3 (19.6.97)
Rieki A	7.2	B	Eng.	A	A/B	B
Kate A	7.5	G	Eng.	C	C	D
Khadisha B	7.3	G	Turkish/Eng.	B	B/C	C
Stephen C	7.9	B	Eng.	D	D	D
Billy C	7.8	B	Eng/BSL	B	B	C
Maria d'E	7.11	G	Portuguese/Eng	B	B/C	C
Deborah F	7.6	G	Eng.	B	B/C	C
Sunil G	7.4	B	Urdu/Eng	D	D	E
Dijana K	7.4	G	Polish/Eng.	D	D	E
Richard L	7.5	B	Eng.	C	C	D
Madeleine M	7.5	G	Eng.	B	B	B
Charlie M	7.3	B	Eng.	C	C/D	D
David N	7.8	B	Eng.	B	B	C
Petronella N	8.1	G	Eng.	D	abs.	D
Eric O	7.8	B	Eng.	B	B	C
Nkechi O	7.2	G	Eng/?	C	C	D
Szechuan P	7.4	G	Cantonese/Eng	B	B	B
Robert R	7.6	B	Eng	B	B/C	C
Kevin R	7.10	B	Eng.	C	C	C
Jilna S	7.11	G	Urdu/Eng.	D	E	E
Selma S	8.0	G	Bengali/Eng.	A	A	A
Kevin T	7.3	B	Eng.	C	C	C
Peter T	7.11	B	Eng.	C	C/D	D
Steven T	8.1	B	Eng.	B	B/C	C
Louise V	7.4	G	Eng.	D	abs.	D
Richard W	7.9	B	Eng.	B	B	B
Kate W	7.8	G	Eng.	C	C	C
Alex Y	7.3	G	Eng.	C	C	C
Leigh Z	7.5	G	Eng/Italian?	C	C/D	D

Figure 3.33 Grid for recording class progress in writing (Blank provided in Appendix: A8)

One of the areas to look out for here would be the otherwise perfectly capable child who seems not to be able to express ideas in writing. It is all too easy to make the mistake of assuming that lack of assurance or fluency in literacy means an equal lack of confidence in grasping new concepts and knowledge. Every teacher has met a child whose cognitive levels are way ahead of their writing or reading. Sometimes it is best to decide to leave things for a while; to remove the spotlight and to set a timetable for later action and review.

Screening for support in writing

If a decision is made that there should be immediate action, screening needs to be carried out deliberately and carefully in order to make a proper diagnosis. The school and parents can seek help where necessary and work out an individual learning plan for the child concerned. You might like to use the chart in Fig. 3.34 to identify the children in your own class who seem to have hit a plateau in their writing. Where would your 'problem writers' fit?

Name	Stage of writing confidence: guided; supported; independent	Problem – mine or the pupil's?	Possible action
Caroline	Independent	mine – she's stuck in one genre	writing challenge – information book for younger reader
Michael	Supported	his – it's such an effort for him	using I.T. and handwriting practice

Figure 3.34 Problem writers (Blank provided in Appendix: A9)

If a child is underachieving in writing for any reason, and if all the usual – and special – kinds of support seem not to be helping find a way forward, then it is time for careful identification and diagnosis which will lead to a short- and longer-term plan of action. The process of this will follow a similar path for writing, reading and speaking and listening. Before being too definite it is worth checking the child's health and home circumstances to see if there are any clues there. Difficulties with writing may well be affected by intermittent hearing loss or difficulties with vision. About 8 per cent of children have sight problems at the age of entry to school; by the time they reach secondary school the number can be as high as 18 per cent. Visual problems are usually picked up by the health visitor or school nurse, but the frequency of testing may not be as regular in some areas as in others. In the classroom you might notice a child screwing up her or his face when trying to focus, working very close to the paper, having frequent headaches, for example, or copying or writing unevenly. Children who usually wear glasses will need these checked by the optician – probably once a year – to monitor possible deterioration. If the health records suggest that this has not been done recently, then a discussion with the parents might help to deal with some of the difficulties.

These figures are quoted in the very useful manual edited by Geoffrey Moss 1995 *The Basics of Special Needs: a Routledge/Special Children Survival Guide for the Classroom Teacher*, London, Questions Publishing Company/Routledge.

Another area to check might be for specific learning difficulties (often described as dyslexia). This remains a highly contentious area of education, but Fig. 3.35 offers a checklist to help teachers identify specific learning difficulties and it would be as well to monitor these over a period of time, having consulted the child's records for previous references to teachers' concerns about specific learning difficulties.

Moss *Basics of Special Needs*, pp. 141–2

checklists for specific learning difficulties

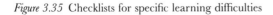

The following pattern of strengths and weaknesses may help indicate children with SpLD, but bear in mind that the pattern will vary from one child to the next:

The child

- shows mature speaking skills
- shows good spatial ability
- shows good scores on cognitive ability and oral comprehension tests
- confuses similar letters and words, either when spoken or written
- has great difficulty in producing 'appropriate' written work corresponding to perceived ability
- has difficulty in correctly pronouncing words
- has difficulty in remembering familiar words
- has difficulties in recalling facts learned by rote, e.g. multiplication tables
- will often reverse letters and numbers
- has difficulty with visual tracking, e.g. when copying from the board or reading from a book will often lose the place on the page, or omit lines
- has difficulty in sequencing events, e.g. days of the week
- experiences difficulties in understanding direction, e.g. left/right, and in spatial awareness, including layout of work
- has poor coordination and may be generally clumsy
- has difficulty in copying accurately
- reads inaccurately and at a slow rate
- produces spelling which looks bizarre
- produces work which varies in standard from day to day

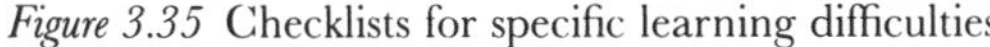

Figure 3.35 Checklists for specific learning difficulties

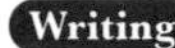

At the primary stage, children who perform certain subject tasks at a level and quality that obviously does not correspond with their performance in other areas will soon become the focus of the teacher's attention. Some characteristics to look out for at this stage are:

- progress in reading becomes very slow
- there is confusion with letters of a similar shape, e.g. b/d; p/q
- there is confusion with letters that sound the same, e.g. v/f
- there are often letter and word reversals, e.g. 'was' for 'saw'
- written language does not contain simple punctuation, e.g. capital letters
- syntax within sentences is often jumbled and simple words are often omitted
- there is confusion when and where to use lower and upper case letters
- written words become 'telescoped', e.g. 'permance' for 'permanence'
- written work is poorly presented and indicates severe spatial and organisational problems
- the child has difficulty in remembering more than two or three instructions at a time or three to four number digits
- there are difficulties in recalling the alphabet or multiplication tables
- there is confusion with his or her own body direction, e.g. left/right

The following checklist may be helpful in identifying SpLD problems in secondary school children.

- the main characteristics that they will display general knowledge, oral language and comprehension levels that are significantly better than their performance in reading and written work
- their reading performance continues to be poor: decoding (word building) is not really developed, although some simple strategies will have been learnt and are being used; words will be guessed at with their middle and end parts often causing difficulties; words will be omitted; words will be inserted; the rate of reading will be poor; phrases will be often repeated to establish meaning
- spellings will be less bizarre but still indicate that serious problems remain; spelling dictations show that they can still only retain up to three to four words at a time
- presentation is generally poor and handwriting deteriorates when rushed

Figure 3.35 Checklists for specific learning difficulties (continued)

Diagnosis

This can be made on the basis of a writing interview and writing miscue analysis, but could be supported by observations from colleagues or parents/carers. The interview and miscue analysis should lead to an agreed programme of action with specific and structured targets being offered. The key will be effortful success. There is no point in making a programme of improvement too easy for a child – they won't be fooled by that. At the same time, there should be genuine possibility of success with some (supported) effort from the child. You will need to make the targets explicit, possibly with dates for review; you will also need to make explicit to the child the parts of the curriculum where the targets might be tackled and reached. It may be necessary at this stage to involve the parents in an informal 'contract' of support for the child as he or she tries to reach the targets. Decisions about involving outside agencies will be a matter of discussion with the headteacher, SENCO and parents; there can be no general rules. Fig. 3.36 gives a suggested format for a screening process.

Writing miscue

This is intended as a diagnostic analysis and should not be seen as a summative assessment like a SAT. It has borrowed some ideas from reading miscue analysis, but since writing is more capable of individual variation, there are some significant differences. Children read the words which are printed for them; they write from their own minds. This means that the field for considering miscues (or 'developmental errors') is much wider. For example, there is no objective reference point like the passage used for reading.

The analysis covers matters of writing behaviour, the process of writing, purpose and audience as well as looking at the more technical elements of form or format, text construction, vocabulary choice, spelling and punctuation. In a similar way to a reading miscue this involves looking at the piece of writing for meaning (semantic features) at the level of the text as a whole as well as at sentence level. For syntax – sentence construction – and for graphophonic features at individual word level, a first analysis might be followed up six months later to note progress in the areas identified for development.

It is not intended that any teacher should carry out a writing miscue on every pupil. It may be helpful to carry out a writing miscue with a child whose writing is fluent but technically more faulty than might be expected at this stage; or to look at construction of longer stretches of text with a writer whose work is technically correct but underextended.

You will need to make time to observe the child at the outset of the writing and at times during the writing. After the piece has been written you will need to spend about twenty minutes hearing the child read the piece to you and discussing it with her or him. *You will need a tape recorder for this* so that you do not need to be taking notes while you are talking with the writer. This conversation may be the most revealing part of the process and is worth making time to complete undisturbed.

Procedure

The writing can take place during any usual class writing time. You simply need to ensure that you are in a position to watch the child as he/she begins to write and occasionally while the writing is in progress. If the class usually collaborates at particular stages during writing you do not need to vary their routine, but would note any points of collaboration. However, you should make it clear to the writer that you can offer no help during this particular piece of writing. It is important that the writer should not feel threatened by the procedure so that you may want to talk with the child before

SCREENING FOR DIFFICULTIES – WRITING

Name: Michael **Class:** 4 **Year:** 1996/7

Languages spoken: English **Term** 1 2 3 (1 circled)

Cause for concern:
Handwriting slow & laborious; very poor physical control yet has plenty of ideas

Checks made on:	Date	Comments
hearing	Spring 1996	Fine
sight	Spring 1996	Wears glasses
perceptual problems	—	None diagnosed
physical difficulty/impairment	—	None obvious
medical condition	—	Asthma
other		Concern about deterioration of behaviour

Relevant information from home:
Parents are very anxious about Michael's lack of progress

Most recent contact with parent/carer:
Summer Parents' Evening. Phone call last week from mother to Headteacher

Record of evidence: focused observation period from: 14·10·96 **to:** half-Term

Observer(s):
Peter Griffiths (class teacher) / Parents

Existing assessments/level of progress:
Mostly (B) on scale of progression

Summary of observations:
Contributes to discussion & demonstrates good grasp of concepts. Imaginative. At home occasionally chooses to write stories which are much more legible & fluent than classwork.

Targets set:
Using computer at home & at school when possible
Daily very brief handwriting practice

Dates for review:
Spring term

Parents' comments:
Surprised (and pleased) about the stories he wrote by choice at home

Review and suggestions for further action:

Figure 3.36 Screening record for children experiencing difficulties with writing (Blank provided in Appendix: A10)

the writing, explaining that you will be asking her/him about the writing after it is finished and looking at the piece carefully to see what they are good at doing. As far as possible, avoid the sense that this is a 'test'; it may make the child feel uneasy, and could have an adverse effect on the fluency of the writing.

Time allowed for writing will vary according to age group and the child's written fluency, but you will need to encourage an extended piece of writing in order to make a full analysis. If the writer is used to making plans before writing, these should be included in the analysis. The topic for writing can either be about something which fits with the current work of the class or you might want to choose a discrete topic – letter, personal narrative, imaginative narrative, instructions, explanation – according to your own knowledge of the writer. For a first analysis, poetry poses rather more of a challenge, so you may want to avoid that in the initial stage at least.

1 Starting off

Make sure that the child has all the necessary equipment, is comfortable, understands the task and knows that you will be discussing the writing later. Most importantly, you should make sure that the child knows that you will not be offering any help during the writing. These observations will give you some insight into *writing behaviour* and the *process of writing*.

Observe the child as he/she begins to write, making notes at specific stages:

Readiness to start – are there any signs of uneasiness or is there evidence of the writer's thoughtful engagement with the topic? Look for position of head; eye movements, posture, stillness; whether the child speaks to anyone.

The first writing – this might be a plan or the writer may go straight into writing. Note how hesitant or assured this is; look for evidence of re-reading first few words/sentences. How engaged is the writer with the task? How long does he/she take to settle to more fluent production?

During the writing – note any significant incidents: use of wordbook, dictionary, friend for consultation. As far as possible note whether discussions are about technical matters of spelling or punctuation; about coherence of the whole piece; about something else entirely!

After the writing is completed – ask the child to re-read and make any alterations he or she wishes to make.

2 Discussing the writing

This is intended to give the writer a chance to provide an insight into some of the decisions and choices made about the writing. You will be asking questions designed to elicit some comments about the *process of writing*, *audience*, *purpose/intention* and *form or format*. When the child is satisfied with the piece sit down with them and discuss it. Explain that you are taping the conversation so that you can listen to it later and note any interesting points the writer makes.

It is very important to bear in mind that you are asking for the child's responses, not pointing to places where the piece might have been improved! This section is all about finding out what the writer thinks.

The process of writing

Ask the writer:

- to read the piece to you. Then ask whether there is anything he/she has noticed and wants to change after reading it aloud;

- to tell you which parts of the writing they like best and why. If they are reticent, you may want to identify a phrase or sentence you particularly like and explain its appeal to you, but only offer one example since it is important that the child feels free to comment, and that you get a chance to see behind the scenes!;
- whether they feel satisfied with the writing; if so, why; if not, why not;
- whether they enjoy writing generally.

To a certain extent you will need to shape the following questions to fit with the type of writing.

Audience/readership

Ask the writer:

- who they think will read the writing or who they imagined the writing was intended for.

Purpose/intention

- Generally, you are trying to find out why the writer chose to write this piece and include specific details. If the writing is narrative, you may want to ask why the writer chose the subject itself, or, if you gave the subject, you might ask why he/she chose to include a particular incident or character. If it is an explanation, you may want to ask why the writer chose to include certain details.

Form or format/layout

- You are trying to find out why the writer shaped the piece as it is. If the child has written a straightforward narrative, this section may not be necessary, although you might want to ask whether the writer is pleased with the ending or with the beginning or middle. If it is a set of instructions, you might want to find out how the writer knew about how to set it out.

You should end this session by giving the writer some positive comments about the piece and telling her/him when you will be able to give full feedback.

3 The analysis

Although the analysis is divided into specific areas, it is difficult to separate them since a piece of writing is a complete entity. As you carry out the analysis you may find it difficult to decide whether a comment should be entered under, for example, purpose or structure. Do not spend too much time being concerned about this! You are seeking an overall picture of a writer's present competence and potential for development, so that one or two unclear points will not prevent you from making an adequate overview.

see pp. 112–13 (Steven's work analysed) for an example of surrounding a text with comments

You may find it helpful to put the piece of writing on top of an A3 sheet of paper so that you can jot down your ideas on that whilst still having the piece unmarked. You will make your analysis from your observational notes, the taped discussion and a careful analysis of the text.

The areas for analysis are:

- Writing behaviour
- The process of writing
- Purpose/intention
- Audience/readership
- Structure/form
- Technical features.

Writing behaviour

You will note this from your own observations, particularly at the beginning of the writing, for example how the writer settled to the task and how engaged he/she was with the task, and the taped replies to the questions about whether the writer enjoys writing and feels satisfied with this piece. What does the writer's approach to the task tell you about her/his confidence, ease with writing or sense of control? After thinking about this section, summarise your conclusions to the critical question:

How does this child see herself/himself as a writer?

The process of writing

This is analysed through:

your observations as the child wrote and redrafted. Did the writer use a plan or go straight into the writing? How often did the writer make amendments? Did he/she seek help? What amendments, if any, were made when the writer had read the piece aloud and was invited to make changes?

the writer's responses to the questions, particularly about which parts of the text he/she liked best and why. What does this tell you about the writer's ability to comment on her/his own writing?

alterations made to the writing itself. Look at the text and note all the crossings out and other editing marks. What do these tell you about the child's ability to self-correct and/or edit larger pieces of text? Were the alterations made for clarity, for spelling accuracy, for logical flow of the piece, for other reasons?

When you have considered these areas, summarise your conclusions to the following:

What does the writer's approach tell you about her/his fluency and independence in writing ?

Purpose/intention

You will mainly gather information about this from the writer's response to your questions during discussion. In looking at the text, consider how far the writer has been able to fulfil her/his intentions or purposes. What choices did he/she make in writing the piece for a specified purpose? Does the piece do the job the writer wanted it to?

Having listened to the tape and looked at the text, summarise your conclusions to the following :

What does this piece show about the writer's success in making her/his own meaning and intentions in writing clear?

Audience/readership

You will find evidence for this section in both the taped discussion and the text itself. In looking at the text, consider how far the writer shows awareness of the reader he/she talked about. If the child did not respond to that question, you will need to look for evidence in the writing that the writer is aware of the needs of a reader. For example, does the writer address the reader directly? Give explicit information to help the reader make sense of the piece? What choice has the writer made about the register of the piece for a specific readership/audience? After looking at the text in the light of the writer's comments, summarise your analysis of the following :

How does this piece show the writer's understanding of the needs of a reader?

Structure/form

Some of the analysis of this will come from the discussion with the child about structure or form, but mainly you will use the text itself for this section. In looking at the text, ask yourself some or all of the following (as appropriate):

- What form/structure has the writer chosen? – straightforward narrative or flashback technique; letter form; explanatory brochure?
- How consistent and clear is the form? For example, is there a clear beginning and conclusion suitable to the chosen type of text? Is it divided into paragraphs?
- Do the ideas link logically? Is there evidence of cause-and-effect or reasoned action by the characters? Is it a cohesive piece?

When you have looked carefully at the piece in the light of the writer's own comments, consider:

> What does this piece indicate about the writer's ability to present ideas clearly and coherently? How does the form fit with the intended task?

Technical features

This will all be carried out from the text itself. You will be looking at the text at word level and sentence level, considering spelling, vocabulary choice, punctuation and syntax.

Spelling

- Count the number of words in the whole piece, then the number of words incorrectly spelt. Note the number of errors in proportion to the whole text.
- Look at the words spelled incorrectly. Can you detect any patterns: e.g., use of double/single consonants; letter strings consistently but incorrectly used? If more than a third of the words of the whole piece are incorrectly spelled, select a proportion of the errors; if less than a third is incorrect, analyse all the spellings and look for evidence of attempts at graphophonic matching and for evidence of attempts at visual correspondence.
- Look at the words spelled *correctly* and note evidence of successful attempts at graphophonic and visual correspondence.

Vocabulary choice

What is the range of vocabulary used? Does the vocabulary seem restricted by difficulties with spelling or is the vocabulary ambitious?

Punctuation

- Note the range of punctuation marks used in the whole piece.
- Is the piece organised into sentences – whether they are marked or not?
- If direct speech is used, is this marked by punctuation or new lines?
- Overall, is punctuation used consistently? Adventurously?

Syntax

- Look for evidence of variation in sentence length and for complex sentence structures. Notice sentence openers and conjunctions particularly.
- Note any repetition used for specific effect.

After considering these four areas, summarise your technical analysis by noting:

features which show the writer's competence in handling the transcription elements of, for example, syntax, punctuation, vocabulary, spelling

how effectively the writer has varied technical features in relation to intention and readership.

This completes the analysis. Now you need to summarise your findings. Using the summary sheets (pp. 130–1), note your conclusions for each section of the analysis and add your comments about possible future action. (Blank provided in Appendix: A11)

Writing miscue – Tricia – just 7

This miscue was carried out by Beverley Long, Tricia's teacher at Downing primary school, Suffolk

The following example provides an analysis completed on a 7-year-old writer who is having some difficulty in getting to grips with literacy. The writing came from topic work on classical times where the teacher had talked about Greek gymnasts. The task was to write in role a page from a diary by an athlete competing in the ancient Olympics.

The miscue analysis revealed some significant points about Tricia's approach to writing and about how Beverley might support both Tricia's writing and that of the whole class.

Webnesbst ay 20th
Iam slepin on therasflor wiv awt at
a curu to bay is abig bae fore me
Iam actsin mI syils I hate
were a curu

Figure 3.37 Tricia's text reads: 'I am sleeping on the floor without a cover. Today is a big day for me. I am practising my skills. I am wearing a cover.'

Observation Notes:

Introduced book. Reminded Tricia about the margin and the date. A bit of rubbing out of writing to fit margin in. Wrote a sentence. Left seat, moved to other table, played with CDT work from yesterday. Returned. Carried on. Leaning on hand, tilting head, pencil in mouth, staring at nothing, finger in mouth.... similar actions between writing individual words. Saying words quietly to herself as she writes them. Continually tilting head and talking as she writes pausing momentarily. Asks Kieran if he's drawing a picture the same as the photo. She then stopped writing and drew a small picture herself.
She then told me she was drawing someone running. Stopped drawing. Resumed writing.
Finger in mouth. Stopped writing and put a circle round picture. Kieran said his picture wasn't any good - she stopped her work and said it was very good.
Went to write, stopped hand mid-air, mouthed something, pencil to mouth, eyes fixed then pencil down again briefly. Talking again to Kieran looking at pictures of Olympia. Looking round the room. Re-read what she had written. Audibly said 'skills' several times. Looked for rubber. Asked Kieran for it. Waited for it.
Knees on chair, fidgeted, looking at work. Finger in mouth said 'skills' again and 'hmmm' then back to writing saying each letter sound as she wrote. Showed Kieran her work. Suggested he did a circle round his picture to tell him how much paper he was using.

Background:
Tricia sees herself as an independent writer. Although she was told not to ask for help she seldom does anyway nearly always using her own spellings. She was quite fidgety throughout the piece - but she's very small - she genuinely seemed to be adjusting herself comfort wise - she fidgets on the carpet during instructions but gets 'lost' in a story. She paused frequently to think and consider before writing. She was confident enough to suggest adjustments to another child but also adjusted her own style of presentation in the light of someone else's approach. Tricia dived straight in initially. She and others were reminded about the date and the margin which inhibited her flow as she had to accommodate these somehow.
Tricia is too inexperienced to make a formal writing plan but her stopping, fiddling, staring seemed to indicate thinking time - she didn't really interact with other people at these times - and mouthing out what she was about to or had just written. She seems to be planning and revising here. At one point her hand stopped mid-air as she thought and mouthed her ideas. One word in particular caused a lot of thinking, rubbing out and re-writing 'til she was satisfied. The alteration was for spelling. I can't be sure but it seemed that the silent mouthing was for flow and clarity. No choice on task; they were directed to write in role. This piece could be part of a diary or could just be an account. She probably didn't have enough/any experience of diaries (bad choice by me!)

WRITING MISCUE – SUMMARY OF ANALYSIS

- **Writing behaviour**

How does this child see herself/himself as a writer?

She sees herself as a successful and competent writer. She is confident and enthusiastic and feels free to comment on and praise other children's work.

Possible future action:

Maintain that enthusiasm and find a way to include technical checks as a matter of course – part of the natural process.

- **The process of writing**

What does the writer's approach tell you about her/his fluency and independence in writing?

She needs thinking time throughout a piece – her interactions with children may be talking but are not necessarily off-task. She redrafts as she goes.

Possible future action:

Introduce discussion with her during the process; don't wait until she's finished. Help her refine her redrafting techniques.

- **Purpose/intention**

What does this piece show about the writer's success in making her/his own meaning and intentions in writing clear?

Good sense of feeling in limited piece. But probably not enough experience in writing style and genres to be able to complete task required.

Possible future action:

Give some examples of what I mean i.e. show/read diaries, letters, notes etc. at first. We do 'stories' – perhaps I need to start using different words for different kinds of writing.

- **Audience/readership**

How does this piece show the writer's understanding of the needs of a reader?

She doesn't give much indication of realising the reader's needs. Assumes everyone knows what she knows or that the reader will be me. No inclusion of time, place or reason.

Possible future action:

Not sure. Do we simply teach this or is it developmental? Talk about it making sense, maybe ask children to take the role of a reader – eg what won't the reader know? What must you include?

- **Structure/form**

What does this piece indicate about the writer's ability to present ideas clearly and coherently?

The ideas link logically – but their understanding assumes an implicit knowledge. She chose to draw and circle the picture, not asked for at this stage.
Ideas are clear and coherent provided you know the background.

How does the form fit with the intended task?

Narrative – form laid down by me. Clear – just one short episode. Task probably very restricted as far as allowing choice of form/structure is concerned and due to inexperience of particular form.

Possible future action: see above – purpose

- **Technical features**

What features show the writer's competence in handling the transcription elements of syntax, punctuation, vocabulary, spelling?

spelling: 27 words 14 spelt incorrectly (about half)
spelling patterns: double letters missed – 'ee' in sleeping and '00' in floor.
word beginnings correct – blends included ie 'sl' and 'fl' (we've done these)
syllables split into 2 words 'bae fore' (before) and 'to bay' (today) and 'd' reversed.
lots of word endings incorrect – as she says them
uses aural experience to help try spellings – 'wiv awt' (without) and 'mi' (my)

Vocabulary not restricted by spellings – eg 'practising'; use of the word 'skills' I might have used this word in the intro. but I don't think so.
Vocabulary not limited in this piece; words used are quite representative of her spoken language.
Punctuation: no demarcation, but organised into sentences.

How effectively has the writer varied technical features in relation to intention and readership?

Syntax: variation in sentence length (Four sentences: 10 words, 7, 5 and 4) and in opening phrases. First sentence complex. Clear announcement for reader: 'Today is a big day for me'

Possible future action:

Help her with endings – do some onset and rime practice with whole class or a group, perhaps. Sentence marking would be helped by reading aloud with a response partner, perhaps.

Evaluating writing and how it is taught

Keeping portfolios and records of progress can be a good way to review the effectiveness of teaching and learning. These go alongside the other important ways in which writing can help in evaluating learning – through reflective writing in journals, review sheets and learning logs. Examples of such kinds of writing show the value of reflection-in-process but there is also a place for reviewing writing after a period of time – for both teacher and pupil to check that targets have been met and learning objectives reached. Keeping files of work and comments on what children can do with writing offers useful – and usable – evidence on individual progress. But it can provide more than that. Children's own contributions to assessments can give the teacher a chance to glimpse the working of the child's mind; to see some of the perceptions held about what makes a piece of writing 'good'; to discover what the particular young writer sees as the next thing to tackle on the path to improving her or his writing. This kind of review is part and parcel of the process of planning and teaching. Conscious attention to writing – reflecting on it, evaluating its success, developing a vocabulary through which to talk and write about writing – are all essential for helping writers develop independence and discrimination. One way of building to a continuing record of work which involves the writers themselves is to develop a Portfolio or Record of Achievement in writing.

This work is written up more fully in Bearne and Farrow *Writing Policy, Chapter 5.*

Fig. 3.38 gives an example of Andrew (aged 8) in Cath Farrow's class reflecting on his writing and includes her comments. This shows not only Andrew's ability to reflect on the process of writing, but indicates some teacher strategies used to help children become more attentive readers. The comments offer a model for the writer to take on in reflecting on his own writing.

If a teacher gradually introduces the vocabulary of reflection and evaluation, then pupils have a chance to use that language as a model for their own developing evaluative terminology. Helen Maguire had a class of 8- and 9-year-olds, many of whom had significant difficulties with literacy. Their confidence in reading and writing was not in line with their ability to talk about ideas. Helen introduced Writing Record Sheets, which had been developed by her colleague Cath Farrow, as part of a planned strategy intended to help the class build on their keenness to talk. She wanted to extend the vocabulary available to them so that they could comment more effectively on writing – their own and other people's. About once a fortnight in the first half of the summer term Helen asked the children to choose a piece of work and complete a Writing Record Sheet for it. These sheets would then be added to the selection of writing which she made as part of the regular gathering of material for each child's portfolio. The children were encouraged to select writing from different curriculum areas. Very quickly the children got the basic idea:

5 May	I'd like to do the ending better
17 May	I would like to do more of the story (Cymone)
5 May	a better beginning (Neil)
5 May	I was pleased with the middle (Sarah)

Karen's awareness of the structure of her writing ripens as the weeks pass to a confident statement of what she would like to do with a present piece of writing. On 5 May she notes that she was *pleased with the way it rhymes* and in response to the 'what would you like to do better?' question commented, *I changed the rhyme and it was funny*. By 9 June her comment about how she could improve a piece of factual writing shows a solid understanding of what she can do to make her writing communicate her ideas more clearly when she comments *I'd like to put the sentences in order.*

Textual features and the possibility of organising them for yourself became accepted knowledge for these children. Similarly, they demonstrated what they already knew about form and genre. Being able to select information and quote or refer to it as you write about what you read is a recognised feature of writing in academic genres. Knowing that informational text may need diagrams, or that illustration can also be text, are important steps in understanding the structures of particular genres. Graham comments that he would like to draw a picture to make his explanation clearer and Deborah says that she would have *liked to draw the spider on the web.*

Making progress in evaluation

From the early stages where they identified what they liked about their own work, after only a few weeks these children were able to comment on just how they could improve things. From general statements about 'making the ending better' they moved on to being able to say how they might go about it. They give reasons for their selections and quote from or refer closely to their own work. Marie moves from:

5 May — Title: Odd
What I was pleased with: because I liked it
What I'd like to do better: the ending

through

17 May — Title: Story start – the Big Wood
What I was pleased with: it was good because we went to the north pole
What I'd like to do better: I would like to do more of the story

to

9 June — Title: My cat
What I was pleased with: when I said that when I looked at her on the photo I started crying
What I'd like to do better: when she came back with blood all over her.

As she becomes more familiar with the idea of commenting on her own work and comes to understand that she can change things, Marie is able to be far more specific and attentive to her own writing. This is not just because she has been given the Writing Record Sheets and been asked to comment but is a direct result of the supporting talk, conversations about what the class was reading and writing and the models and examples offered by her class teacher. Other writers make different kinds of progress – learning that writing is more than inscription and secretarial skills, for example. Gillian commented on 9 June 'I liked the way I thought. I thought about the story carefully'; Graham was pleased that he got all the words right in a word search but comments 'I would have liked to write a poem'. However, one of the most valuable aspects of using review sheets like this lies in revelations about those children who are still having problems in self-evaluation, or who have not moved at all. This is important information for the teacher's evaluation of the effectiveness of the learning. What response should a teacher make to David's apparent complacency?

5 May — *What I was pleased with:* the way I made the story up
What I'd like to do better: nothing really

9 June — *What I was pleased with:* the story was very long
What I'd like to do better: I wouldn't want to do anything else to it.

Or to Karen's more obvious anxiety about accuracy?

5 May — *What I was pleased with:* the information
What I'd like to do better: look more careful

17 May — *What I was pleased with:* I got all the answers right
What I'd like to do better: to get my writing better

9 June — *What I was pleased with:* I only got 7 words wrong
What I'd like to do better: to write more.

RECORD SHEET

Title pandoras box

Name

Date May 5th

What I was pleased with the bit I was plesed with was when she the key and fidled with it opened

What I'd like to do better I wold like to make it better by putting I little bit more exting bits in

What other people said Alex said he liked the bit when pandora was shocked.

Teacher's comments The sort of opening you would expect from this kind of story. It sets the scene and tells us that the world was peaceful. Your ending is a good one which explains the point of the story. You kept the reader in mind. Two improvements: you could have described the appearance of the box. You could have put in more detail of the troubles that the insects caused. You mark your sentences correctly – most of the time! Capital 'P' sits on the line!

Figure 3.38 Writing Record Sheet

These examples suggest that there is more to the process of helping children make progress in writing than simply inviting them to fill in a framework for comment. And this brings us right back to planning for writing, providing a supportive and challenging environment and intervening to help move each individual on.

Taking it further – parents and writing

While there are often established links made with parents over reading, it is less common to find parents involved in school writing activities. Parents themselves can sometimes feel reluctant to intervene in writing because of their own inhibitions and fears about writing. Many adults carry scars from insensitive treatment of their writing when they were at school. Nevertheless, parents often treasure the first marks and drawings their children make at home and, as the comments by children at the beginning of this chapter indicated, children's writing is often highly valued by families. Children are included in writing on birthday cards, postcards from holidays or letters to friends and families. They write their own lists when they go shopping with parents and often write letters, poems, posters and diaries at home for their own interest and they show them to parents and other members of the family.

Some schools are now asking parents to bring examples of their children's early mark-making to discussions when children first enter school. These can give very useful information for Baseline assessments. Increasingly schools are producing booklets about approaches to developmental writing similar to those given to parents explaining early reading practices. Other involvement by parents in writing at school can be as scribes or typists, or even in some cases as writers themselves who come into school and talk about the process of putting texts together. Parents who work on newspapers or who help with the parish magazine are knowledgeable about how texts are constructed. However, not all parents can come into school and some might be daunted by the idea of getting involved with writing so Fig. 3.39 gives some suggestions for involving parents and the wider community in writing.

- Parents and families can contribute when children write books or stories by scribing or illustrating them.
- After a school visit parents can jot down for the child their memories of the best parts of the experience.
- Photographs from family holidays can be annotated as part of geography work.
- Parents and families who speak languages other than English might be asked to write stories or information accompanied by photographs or pictures in their home languages.
- A commercially produced scrap book can be used for a collection of reflective pieces of writing by any members of the family – brothers, sisters, grandparents, aunts, uncles, cousins – of my favourite book/film or my most enduring memory.
- Parents can be asked to contribute family documents, letters, postcards and other memorabilia for class topics on celebrations or the history of the 1960s.
- Children can write to local pensioners' clubs when researching historical material or to local companies to find out about the way businesses work so that they receive replies from adult writers.

Figure 3.39 Taking it further: involving parents and the community in writing development

Chapter Four

Speaking and listening

In outlining how to ensure progress in speaking and listening, this chapter covers:

- recent theories about oracy
- early language development
- the relationship between talking and learning
- language diversity
- bilingual learners
- planning for talk – the range and repertoire
- teaching speaking and listening
- the classroom environment for talk
- gender and talk
- organising groups for talk
- observing, reporting and recording progress in speaking and listening
- children who have difficulties with oracy
- evaluating talk and using talk to evaluate
- taking it further: involving parents.

Introduction to speaking and listening

Studying talk in the classroom can be difficult. Because those of us who can talk and hear easily spend so much time speaking and listening, it's a little tricky to identify the many strands of talk – the purposes and functions that we use it for; the different audiences for talk; the effects of contexts on the way we speak and listen. Because talk is necessarily a thing of the moment, it's difficult to capture; and when we do capture talk on tape, sometimes the very act of taping alters the context and so affects the talk itself. Then there remains the issue of how to judge progress in talk. What should teachers be doing to help children get better at talk? What does this imply? Some of the hottest educational issues are related to that question!

Andrew Wilkinson and colleagues ran the Oracy Research Unit funded by the Schools Council from 1967 to 1972.

Before going much further, however, it would be useful to look a little more closely at the terminology used about talk: oracy, talk, speaking and listening, spoken language. Oracy is a relatively new term, brought to teachers' attention by the late Andrew Wilkinson. It is intended to convey something of parallel breadth to the word 'literacy' – to signal the fundamental importance of all facets of spoken discourse, particularly in relation to education. *Talk*, used in an educational context, is usually taken to mean the everyday uses of spoken language; using this term signals, perhaps, some of the less formal elements and includes listening as a matter of implicit understanding, since listening has to be there to make talk work. *Speaking and listening* used in this chapter will generally refer to the more formalised way of regarding spoken language as represented in the National Curriculum. There is a difference in formality implied when making a distinction between *talking* and *speaking*, the second including some of the more public and perhaps performative aspects of spoken language. Finally, *spoken language*, or just *language*, denotes the full potential range of oral forms and functions. Since speech is the basis for literacy, then it is clear that the word 'language' has very wide application. It refers to the potential which every individual has to draw on a wide, diverse and flexible repertoire of all kinds of text. It returns, also, to the essentially social and cultural nature of discourse – whether spoken or written – and at the same time is a reminder of the ways in which language is bound up with individual identity. For example, the important relationship between language and how we feel about ourselves and others is keenly emphasised when *standard English* and *Received Pronunciation* are discussed.

Received Pronunciation is a version of spoken English which is not associated with any region of the United Kingdom. It is, however, often associated with particular classes of people – the upper classes of society.

Standard English and Received Pronunciation

Whereas in the past it may have been possible to link 'BBC English' with Received Pronunciation, this is no longer possible and it is difficult to pin down just what Received Pronunciation might be. Perhaps it might be as well to consider Received Pronunciation a will-o'-the-wisp and turn to the much more loaded matter of standard forms of English. Most books without dialogue – and newspapers – in the United Kingdom are written in standard English. It can be recognised as distinct from dialect writing by particular words or phrases or by uses of spelling which reflect the phonics of different, often regional, ways of speaking. Even where there is no marked dialect, informal speech can be written down and distinguished from more standard forms and this is usually referred to as using different *registers*. When it comes to spoken forms, the distinction is not so easily demarcated. Most adult speakers switch or slide from a more to less formal register according to context. A typical situation is answering the telephone in our 'best' voice, then relaxing into our more everyday way of speaking when we realise it is a friend who is calling. The implications of the standard English debate are set out in more detail on pp. 192–4. The critical point as far as classroom teaching is concerned is that while the National Curriculum requires attention to standard English it is important not to undervalue children's own language or undermine children's feelings about themselves as individuals or members of particular speech communities.

Language as social and cultural practice

This chapter will look at some of the implications of the social and cultural nature of language in considering:

- What does developing talk involve?
- What is the teacher's role in planning for and teaching speaking and listening?
- How can progress in oracy be assessed?

In considering the range and scope of talk in the classroom, it is necessary not just to examine how to help children 'get better at speaking and listening' but to look at the role which spoken language plays in developing knowledge and ideas. Since most children come to school able to talk fluently, in contrast to their experience with reading and writing, it is important to look at the early development of talk and to ponder just what 'teaching speaking and listening' might mean if children are already fluent when we meet them first in an educational setting. They don't (usually) have to be taught *how* to speak, so what do they need to be taught? Gordon Wells puts it like this:

> The importance of discourse – or conversation, as it is more commonly called – has long been recognised with respect to the pre-school years. . . . However, it is only in recent years that explicit acknowledgement has been given to the important role that spoken discourse continues to play, throughout the years of schooling and beyond in mediating the culturally valued knowledge and skills that learners encounter and are expected to master.
>
> (p. 287)

Gordon Wells 1992 'Endpiece' in Kate Norman ed. *Thinking Voices: the work of the National Oracy Project*, London, Hodder & Stoughton

Just what are the 'culturally valued skills' he mentions? Where does talk fit in? And what does this mean for classroom uses of talk? This chapter will offer ways of looking at all these questions.

Personal aspects of language

One thing is certain when reflecting on our own speech: it is perhaps the most revealing and deeply personal aspect of our language use. Also, our early experience in the language communities of our homes will have had a profound and lasting effect on us. The section on the Language Family Tree in Chapter 1 made that clear. It's not just a matter of the accent we use or the dialect words or expressions, or even the different languages we can speak. The impact of our own language is felt in the way that speech is entangled with a sense of value and being valued and how values about talk link with our cultural origins. Above all, some of the most deeply remembered experiences about personal and cultural aspects of oracy are related to school

Anne wrote this as part of Reflections on Language Histories asked for by her teacher Barbara Borland, from the Vyne School in Basingstoke. More examples are given in Barbara Borland 1987 'The history of my language experience and reading development' in *Hampshire Writing Project Newsletter*, summer 1987.

'Chris' is an invented name for this 14-year-old from Rotherham who wrote this as part of local project work of the National Oracy Project. The educational importance of talk was signalled by the setting up of the National Oracy Project which ran from 1987 to 1991 with a dissemination phase from 1991 to 1993. This chapter refers to some of the important work carried out by teachers during the course of the many local initiatives fostered by the Project.

attitudes to talk. A comment from a 14-year-old captures some of the importance of the unique quality of our own talk:

> I think accents add individuality to speech, it makes what you say unusual. I don't think that accents are just a label to say where you come from, they are special. The world would be a boring place if everyone spoke alike.
>
> (Anne)

Many teachers would agree, but there are the requirements of the National Curriculum to deal with, as well as social opinion – and prejudice:

> In school when us kids are talking to each other teachers correct us with words we say, such as when we say 'Duz tha wanna come wi us', they say 'Do you want to come with us' then they tell us to talk properly. I think people have a cheek to tell us to talk properly when people in other towns and cities speak too fast or too slow and with funny accents.
>
> (Chris)

Examining beliefs about talk

These two older pupils give some thoughtful comments about their own beliefs about spoken language and the values and attitudes which surround everyday speech. But what do younger pupils think about talk – and the ways they talk? Children often have rich and diverse language experience in their homes and communities, but how can teachers build on them if they don't know what these might be? Kath Scott, coordinator of the North Tyneside Oracy Project, and her teacher colleagues interviewed children aged from 4 to 13 in many different schools, using varied techniques – one-to-one and small group discussion and written questionnaires, asking them the questions in Fig.4.1.

- Where did you learn to talk?
- How did you learn to talk?
- Who taught you to talk?
- Do you think you are a good talker?
- Who do you know who is a good talker?
- What talking do you do in school?
- Who do you talk to in school?
- What do you talk about?
- Does your teacher like you to talk?
- When shouldn't you talk?
- What do you like talking about best?

Figure 4.1 Questions about talk

The North Tyneside teachers found that, while the young children thought they were good talkers, the response became more varied amongst older children. Even those who answered positively often indicated that being a good talker depended on how much or how loudly or clearly they spoke.

Many teachers involved in the National Oracy Project throughout England and Wales noticed that children tend to become more self-critical as they get older – often in a negative way. Other responses suggested that talk is something you do outside the classroom or at home; in school it was reported to happen when doing 'easy work', playing in the role play or home corner or when children 'were stuck' and needed help with their work.

Two classes of children in a school in Cambridge were asked their views on talk. In the Year 2 class, most of the children thought they were good talkers:

with thanks to Jane Brooks and children at St Philip's Church of England school, Cambridge

Yes, I like talking a lot

Yes, because I know some words that other people don't know

Yes, I know a lot of words

When they were asked *Does your teacher like you to talk?* they mostly felt that she did:

Sometimes she likes me to talk and answer questions

Yes. Sometimes when I'm with a partner

Not when she's talking, but yes

When we're working in groups

Yes, because it helps me to learn

The Year 5/6 class were also mostly confident that they were good talkers:

because I'm not shy

because I do talk to my friends and family a lot

because at home and in the playground I talk all the time

once I have started I can't stop

because I usually have lots to talk about

although there were occasionally less confident replies:

No, because nobody ever listens

No, because I'm shy

Their answers to the question about the teacher's attitude to talking showed a good understanding of occasions for talk:

When we're asking or answering a question

No because it can distract people from what they are doing

Yes, because she asks me things

At the right time

There is often a risk of children getting contradictory messages about school attitudes to talk. Good talkers are seen as fluent talkers who can explain things clearly but while talking loudly, clearly and fluently in public seems to be valued, when talk is conversational, personal and informal, it can be seen as less valued and valid. Yet these are the qualities which lead to successful talking-for-learning in the classroom.

Pupils' responses to questions about talk can provide useful information about classroom talk from their point of view. It might be worth finding out about what pupils in your class think about the uses of talk – and your attitude to it. Their views could help in planning for extending or developing talk in your own classroom. Figs 4.2 and 4.3 give an example of one way to begin investigating talk – by writing about it in response to questions.

SURVEY ABOUT TALKING

- **Where did you learn to talk?**

  At home and Relitives.

- **How did you learn to talk?**

  My mum and dad and my Relitives taught me to talk.

- **Who taught you to talk?**

  My Relitives and my mum and dad by using books so I can say words

- **Do you think you are a good talker?**

  Yes I do because I'm always talking at home and reading books

- **Who do you know who is a good talker?**

  Kieran Jenkins. my Nana and my little Sisster.

- **What talking do you do in school?**

  Reading

Figure 4.2 A Year 5 child reflecting on talk (i)

- **Who do you talk to in school?**

Arron, Carl. F. Richard, Clinton, Kieran, Graham, Miles, Haley

- **What sorts of things do you talk about?**

Football, Music, Food,

- **Does your teacher like you to talk?**

Yes a bit because she tells us what todo.

- **When shouldn't you talk?**

When are teacher is talking and not to talk when working.

- **What do you like talking about best?**

Football, Spice Girls, Mike and the Mechanics, Alan Shearer, Arsenal, Food, Dream teams,

Figure 4.2 A Year 5 child reflecting on talk (i) (continued)

SURVEY ABOUT TALKING

- **Where did you learn to talk?**

  At home

- **How did you learn to talk?**

  My family used to talk to me and I used to listen.

- **Who taught you to talk?**

  My family.

- **Do you think you are a good talker?**

  Yes beacause I am a Chatterbox.

- **Who do you know who is a good talker?**

  my mum + Dad and school staff because the explain things properly + my freinds

- **What talking do you do in school?**

  Talking about work
  Talking to freinds
  Talking to school staff

Figure 4.3 A Year 5 child reflecting on talk (ii)

- **Who do you talk to in school?**

Staff
freinds

- **What sorts of things do you talk about?**

Work News
music Fashion
T.V

- **Does your teacher like you to talk?**

Sometimes

- **When shouldn't you talk?**

When someone else is talking.

- **What do you like talking about best?**

I don't have a favourite because I like everything.

Figure 4.3 A Year 5 child reflecting on talk (ii) (continued)

Finding a theory about talk

There is no doubt that a wealth of talk is happening in classrooms throughout the country; what is important is to be able to identify just what the different talk experiences and opportunities might be contributing to children developing as speakers and listeners, and, indeed, as learners. Once talk has become a part of the established teaching and learning programme of the classroom it is then possible to set up methods of assessing speaking and listening. That means getting a picture of just what talk in the classroom involves and what is happening when children talk – a complex business which involves considering just what is involved in the talk curriculum. Any plans for developing children's talk will need to take into account this complexity, which starts, perhaps, by acknowledging that spoken texts, like written texts, combine four interdependent aspects:

The social aspect: the ways in which talk forms, confirms or changes personal relationships

The communicative aspect: the ways in which talk helps in shaping and sharing experiences, emotions, ideas

The cultural aspect: the ways in which talk reflects home and community experience and the kinds of oral texts available from an early age

The cognitive aspect: the ways in which talk helps concept formation and the construction of knowledge.

All of these contribute to the development of children as speakers and listeners.

Then there are the areas of: who children talk to (the audiences), what they talk about (the purposes) and where the talk takes place (the context), which have an effect on the talk itself, how it is shaped, the level of explicitness needed, and the tone or register chosen. Addressing a large gathering in an assembly hall, talking to a family gathering at home or working with friends on a technology activity in the classroom will require different ways of speaking and will combine the above aspects of talk in varying degrees. Children themselves are aware of these differences from a very early age and can switch their talk accordingly. In aiming to help children develop as speakers and listeners, it is the school's job to provide even wider and more varied opportunities for talk. This means considering a further element which influences talk – the content. What is talked about will also influence how talk is structured and carried out. So, audiences, purposes, contexts and content will all have a place in the picture of what talk involves and how children can be helped to make progress in speaking and listening. Fig. 4.4 suggests some possible situations.

Talk behaviour

To add further complexity, however, since talk (as part of language as a whole) is necessarily social and cultural in its origins, any classroom agenda for speaking and listening needs to take talk behaviours into account, too. Performance and confidence will be influenced by a wide range of factors including gender, personality, interests, culture and assurance in whatever language is used; these can affect turn-taking in conversation, fluency of explanation or the level of contribution a speaker makes. Pupils' and teachers' perceptions and expectations of particular contexts or activities also play their part; teachers can sometimes be surprised, or even shocked, by children's responses to questions like 'Do you think you are a good talker?' or 'Do I like you to talk in the classroom?' Previous knowledge or experience of activities, and how they are organised, can also influence the successful development of talk; when a new strategy – like using talk partners – is introduced, for example, previously fluent speakers can be temporarily silenced while they learn to negotiate new ways of collaborating. When new practices become part of regular classroom experience,

	Formal		Informal	
Audiences	Unknown large group, e.g. meeting of new parents to talk about school policy on oracy	Known pair or individual, e.g. interview with parent(s) about a child's difficult behaviour	Mixed group of people – some known and some unknown at a party	Unknown or known individual or pair delivering milk
Purposes	To inform and get information	To negotiate and listen	To be sociable and enjoy the company of others	Transacting business
Contexts	Large space – public gathering	Private – in head's office	Large space – public gathering	Private – at home

Figure 4.4 Some examples of the range of formal and informal talk

previously reticent contributors can find their voices. It is evident from everyday experience, too, that response and support from others is crucial in locking or unlocking our tongues. The behaviours associated with speaking and listening are critically important in describing what progress looks like. Making progress in talk isn't just a matter of practising different kinds of purposes for talk, or having experience of a greater number of audiences, or even having experience of all the types of talk text listed in the National Curriculum. It includes more socially and culturally influenced qualities like growing flexibility and the ability to choose how to speak – or not – in any specific circumstances; the increasing confidence to initiate discussion or to support opinion by reference to wider experience. All of these elements linked to talk behaviours begin in the home and add to the range of what should be included in a full and challenging talk curriculum.

Children's early language

If you have children of your own, or young relatives or friends, you will have noticed the engaging and fascinating way young children take on the language of their community. Even very young babies learn how to have conversations, 'turn-taking' with adults in gurgles and early undifferentiated speech. Gordon Wells refers to 'compelling evidence that children actively construct their own hypotheses' about the way language is patterned and used.

Gordon Wells 1986 *The Meaning Makers: children learning language and using language to learn*, London, Hodder & Stoughton

But children are not just active makers of meaning in terms of acquiring the vocabulary and syntax of their language community. In taking on the forms of language, children also take in the meanings carried by the language – the social and community principles about how life should be lived. It only takes a moment's thought about the sayings we remember from childhood at home – *sing at your meals, trouble at your heels* or *if you keep knocking, the right door will open* – to see how from very early years children learn more than just how to talk in the speech community of home. These sayings are sometimes embedded in home anecdote or story which ends with a moral: *and she never did* **that** *again* or *and that's what happens if you . . .* All of these spoken texts form the models for the kinds of texts children can use for themselves later on; they carry with them very strong flavours of the ways life is lived in home and community.

As well as these ways of absorbing the morals, precepts and life practices of the community – the culture of the home – children learn from popular oral culture – radio and television, songs, adverts, rhymes, stories. In the following extract from a much longer pre-sleep monologue, 3-year-old Simon reveals a wealth of cultural experience which feeds his talk. He had only been in England a few days, having flown from Australia when his father taped, transcribed and annotated his talk:

(*indistinct sounds*)
Oh, no you can't
Oh, yes I can
(*repeated three times*)
Oh, yes I can
Oh, no I'm not
(*repeated three times*)
That's the slip
It is the slip to go in the water
That's the water down there
and you jump
jumpy, jumpy, jumpy (*chant*)
(friends back in Australia had a swimming pool with a slippery dip)
We had a piggy
A piggy nick
(*sounds like R, rrrrr . . .*)
A piggy nick
A piggy nick?
Oh, that's another good word
Squash in
(*indistinct sounds*)
I don't know what to do
A dear, dear, dear
A dear, dear, dear (*repeated chanting*)
A dear, a dear, a do ya, you do, you do
you do ya
(*one and a half minutes' silence, then simulated sleep sounds*)
Uncle Grant had a . . .
Car, car
(*simulated sleep sounds . . . yawns*)
(Uncle Grant, back in Australia, had various nicknames for Simon, including 'car, car')
Why did you turn it back there?
Catherine, I love you
(*fifteen seconds' silence*)
(Catherine, his sister, is in the same room)
Ready to go
Fireman, Fireman, the Fireman
Bzz Bzz Bzz
Wee wee wee wee wee its
Is it a plane, is it a bird
It's a teddy bear
It's an upside down teddy bear
(obviously from the old favourite 'Is it a bird, is it a plane? No it's Superman')
Goldilocks, goldilocks
(*practised to become something like 'bawdy looks'*)
Leven, twelve, thirty, forty, fifty, sixty, seventy
eighty, ninety, seventy, eight, ninety . . .

Just before he goes to sleep:

(two minutes' silence; yawn; indistinct sounds)
Sing . . . yella
the ella sumporine *(sings)*
We all live in the ella sumporine
ella sumporine, the ella sumporine
We all live in tile ella sum . . .
(and the rest is silence)

(to the tune of 'We All Live in a Yellow Submarine')

(pp. 6–9)

Garth Boomer 1985 'Piggy nick – that's a good word' in *Fair Dinkum Teaching and Learning: reflections on literacy and power*, Upper Montclair, N.J., Boynton Cook

Simon provides a lively example of what children might know about language and what they can do with language before they ever come to school. Many of the texts he draws on are from popular culture – from films, pop songs, nursery rhymes, even pantomime verbal games, perhaps repeated by his parents – and from what he has heard from family and friends. Wisps of many oral texts interweave as he plays them over to himself before he goes to sleep. But of course, children may learn from more formal settings – from church, mosque, synagogue, temples, meeting house; from theatre or cinema; from speeches at family gatherings. But how are these related to school ways of using language?

Language at home and school

Children learn to make their meanings clear through everyday conversations with members of their family or community; talk is just an everyday act. In the classroom, however, language is not only the means by which the daily business is carried out; it is an object of study in itself. But children's experience of using language cannot easily be put into separate compartments labelled 'home' and 'school'. Although there may be significant differences between the ways talk is used in either place, children may not find it easy to see what those differences are – or what they signify. Since language is so central to a child's whole experience of learning – both at home and at school – it is important to find ways of identifying just what children can do with language when they come to school, and what they understand about language, so that teachers can build on that experience.

The patterns of thought which are available to children as they hear adults talking, reasoning, predicting, confirming and questioning are necessarily socially and culturally developed and influenced by the child's early environment. People express ideas in different ways depending on whom they are talking to and where. These different ways of using language act as models for children themselves to use as they grow up. Maggie Maclure points out that not only do children absorb the ways of using language they hear in their communities, but that adults actively induct children into the language patterns and expectations of their communities by 'the four S's'. *Shaping:* treating children's utterances as meaningful and responding to them with more conventional language and phrasing. *Sharing:* emotions, ideas, experiences and opinions through conversation. *Supporting:* providing children with enough response and input to sustain conversation without doing the talking for them. *Stretching:* in a range of everyday and unremarkable ways, adults extend children's communications, by asking genuine questions, for example, or asking children to give their opinions about what they see, want to eat, or liked on television.

Maggie Maclure 1992 'The first five years: the development of talk in the pre-school period' in Norman *Thinking Voices*, p. 107

These ideas imply that if teachers are to help children learn as efficiently as possible, attention to language is crucial. However, the child's home experiences of language are equally important because they are the bridge between home and school learning. Children work all the time to get to grips with language so that they can negotiate fully with others in their social surroundings. Their active manipulation of language becomes very clear when they invent ways of using words, as Simon does with 'piggy nick'. Similarly, when children say things like *I wented*, *goned* or *buyed* they are showing very clearly that they can make informed guesses – or hypotheses – about how to make words do what they want. When a child, using binoculars for the first time, says *I just binoculared the car* she is showing an implicit knowledge of the way language works. As children tussle with language, using it in daily conversation with people who are engaged in genuine conversation with them, they uncover rules – like the 'ed' ending of past tense regular verbs. As they practise in a speech community whose adults inevitably use the four S's, they begin to construct a much more complex inner set of rules, which means that they can generate an infinite number of sentences which follow the grammatical pattern of the language of their community.

Deficit views of language

For some years the differences between home and school uses of language were expressed by educational writers in terms of 'problems'. There were commonly held beliefs that the language used in some children's homes (particularly in working-class homes) was deficient or restricted. Barbara Tizard, Martin Hughes and Gordon Wells, amongst others, set up extensive experiments with children aged between three and a half and four and a half where they recorded and then analysed their language at home and in the nursery, including paying attention to the language of the adults who interacted with them. Their results began a move towards a much more informed way of thinking about home language – not seeing it as deficient but equally as complex and challenging as a child might meet anywhere. Indeed, these researchers found that children's home experiences of extended conversations or stories were rarely replicated in the classroom. The following extracts show Joyce in conversation first with her nursery teacher and then at home with her mother In both extracts she is struggling to put complicated concepts into words:

see Chapter 2, Reading, for discussion of deficit theory, p. 11

B. Tizard and M. Hughes 1984 *Young Children Learning*, Fontana, London; Gordon Wells 1985 *Language at Home and at School*, Cambridge, Cambridge University Press

TEACHER: What's that going to be, Joyce? (*no reply*) How are you making it?
JOYCE: Rolling it.
TEACHER: You're rolling it are you? Isn't that lovely? Oh, what's happening to it when you roll it?
JOYCE: Getting bigger.
TEACHER: Getting bigger. Is it getting fatter?
JOYCE: Yeah.
TEACHER: Is it, or is it getting longer?
JOYCE: Longer.
TEACHER: Longer. Are my hands bigger than your hands?
JOYCE: My hands are little.
TEACHER: Your hands are little, yes.
JOYCE: It's getting bigger. Getting long. And long. Look.
TEACHER: Mmm. What's happened to it, Joyce?
JOYCE: Got bigger.
TEACHER: It has. My word.

The teacher is keen to teach Joyce about shape and size, which she does by asking questions to which she already knows the answers. Joyce's responses are minimal. Before the taping, Joyce's teachers said that her language was 'poor'. A conversation at home while she is eating a sandwich lunch in the kitchen, reveals a different picture of Joyce's language use :

JOYCE: Mum, it was good to have something to eat while you was at the seaside, wasn't it? (*Mother cuts sandwich.*)
MOTHER: Was good I agree.
JOYCE: Well some people don't have something to eat at the seaside.

MOTHER: What do they do then? Go without?
JOYCE: Mm.
MOTHER: I think you'd have to have something to eat. (*Kettle boils and mother makes tea.*)
JOYCE: Yeah, otherwise you'd be (*unclear*) won't you?
MOTHER: Mmm. When we go with David's school we'll have to take something to eat; we go on the coach that time. (*They are going on an outing with the older child's school.*)
JOYCE: Mmm. To the seaside?
MOTHER: Mmm; probably go for a little stroll to the seaside.
JOYCE: Mmm? Yes, I still hungry.
MOTHER: When?
JOYCE: When we was at the seaside, wasn't I?
MOTHER: We weren't. We had sandwiches, we had apples.
JOYCE: But we . . . but when we was there we were still hungry wasn't we?
MOTHER: No, you had breakfast didn't you?
JOYCE: But, we were thirsty when we got there.
MOTHER: Yes, suppose, so; yeah, we were.
JOYCE: What happened? We wasn't thirsty or hungry.
MOTHER: Why weren't we? What happened?
JOYCE: Well, all the thirsty went away.
MOTHER: Did it?
JOYCE: Mmmm.

from Martin Hughes and Jacqui Cousins 1988 'The roots of oracy' in M. Maclure, T. Phillips and A. Wilkinson eds *Oracy Matters*, Milton Keynes, Open University Press, pp. 112–13

Although Joyce is struggling to express a sensation felt in the past, she is, nevertheless, not a child with 'poor language' as her teachers assumed. She uses complex sentence structure and vocabulary, for example *otherwise*, an interesting vocabulary choice for a 4-year-old. Also, it is equally clear that her home environment is not deficient in respect of language. On the contrary, the conversation is genuine, where each participant is interested in what the other has to say. Furthermore, it is a balanced conversation where Joyce feels confident to initiate discussion, ponder and ask questions.

Talk in the classroom

When these ideas are related to the classroom there are important implications not just for the ways in which teachers might be able to support and stretch children's own language use, but for adults' own use of language when working with children. Chapter 1 referred to work by Shirley Brice Heath on the language uses of three different communities, the ways in which these were received in school and the effects on the children's later school experiences and progress. Her research indicated no deficit in the language practices of the homes, but very complex ways of using different texts both oral and written. This became particularly apparent when teachers were asking the children questions about the stories they were reading in the classroom. These questions often asked children to identify particular features of picture and written texts – to 'label' features such as colour, shape and size. For the children from the black working-class community where stories were oral, interactive and full of inventive hyperbole, this was an unfamiliar way to deal with narrative. In their particular community people asked questions not about individual items but about whole events, how an object might be used, or to consider causes and effects; they didn't just ask children to label things. Often the answers in this community would involve telling a story or finding a comparative example – using metaphor and analogy, in fact. The ability of these children to be able to link two situations was not being fully tapped in school. Their experience was not like that of the children from the middle-class white community where a trip to the shops often involved incessant 'labelling'. It is easy to imagine such a trip – the adult keeping up a running conversation which might go something like: *Can you see the shop? It says 'Mason's'. That's where mummy buys the bread.* The children who had not experienced such home conversations were also not used to dealing with questions which were disguised commands, for example *Why don't you take that book?* The answer any of us might give to that question could be *Because I don't like the look of it.* However, it would be easy to see that children's inability to respond to such types of questions could look like slowness, refusal or lack of respect for the adult concerned.

The ease with which home uses of talk fit with school practices becomes critical for certain groups of children – not because their home language is in any way lacking, but that the social and cultural practices surrounding talk are dissimilar. Sonnyboy, from a Traveller community, at 6 years old was particularly apt at translating school types of language for other children. He and his cousin Emily have been playing with a collection of small dolls:

EMILY: I loves them little things.

SONNYBOY: Yeah . . . I loves the little sand things – that tiny wee spade. . . . And this little bucket . . .

TEACHER: Do you think it would be a good idea to ask Cathy to get some? (*Cathy runs a playgroup for the Traveller children on their site.*)

EMILY: What for?

TEACHER: So that you'd have some at home.

SONNYBOY: And who'd pay for them? Would Cathy pay?

TEACHER: No, it would be part of the kit.

EMILY: I don't know what you mean. Kit – who's Kit? Me da's called Kit – would me da have to pay?

SONNYBOY: Not your da – it's not that sort of kit, Emily. It's the sort a box with things in that you play with . . . Like toys and things for the little ones.

Hughes and Cousins 'The roots of oracy', p. 117

These examples shift the emphasis on classroom development of children's speaking and listening a little. They show very clearly that whilst teaching is often seen as adult talking and children listening there are very good reasons – linked with the development of thought – for teachers to listen rather more to children. Then the four S's – shaping, sharing, supporting and stretching – will be founded on an informed basis and will be more likely to extend, rather than deny or restrict, children's language and learning.

Talking and learning

It is now widely accepted – and made explicit in the National Curriculum – that talk helps children to learn. The Use of Language section in all documents specifies that pupils 'should be taught to express themselves clearly in both speech and writing' (National Curriculum documents). In geography, for example, reference is made to children using information and their own observations 'to ask and respond to questions about places'. It is an unquestioned assumption that talk will feed into learning in all areas of the curriculum. It is so usual that it might seem strange to emphasise the point here. However, the relationship between talking and thinking is a complex matter. It isn't just that talk is a good way for children to show what they have learned. There's more to it than that. Although the business of teachers asking questions and children answering them is part of traditional practice in classrooms, this isn't the only way – or by any means the best way – to use talk to help learning. The role of talk in learning deserves more careful analysis.

Lev Vygotsky trans. 1962 *Thought and Language*, Cambridge, Mass., MIT Press

The psychologist Vygotsky, writing in the 1930s, emphasised the centrality of language to learning. He explains that thought and language are interdependent in the formation of concepts. To Vygotsky, language is not just the clothing for thought but a tool for thinking and developing thought further. The problem-solving function of language is the aspect which is most significant for understanding the role of language in learning. Language plays a part in helping children to learn from their very early days, but it is important, according to Vygotsky, to draw a distinction between school learning and home learning; home learning is more spontaneous and unplanned and school learning is more planned and analysed. In drawing this distinction, he emphasises the importance of authentic contexts for language learning and, importantly, he stresses the value of collaboration with other children. Such collaborations and genuine conversations are necessary not only for learning to use language more flexibly and effectively, but also for using language to push learning further. The implication for any teacher, then, is to make sure that purposeful talk is planned for in the course of work throughout the curriculum.

Since talk is a social phenomenon, the social space of the classroom needs to be organised to use the existing language habits and experience of the children to extend learning. Children have heard adults talking through ideas, attempting to solve problems – even deciding what food to buy. All of these speculative, hypothesising, predictive ways of talking offer models which most children use very readily; listening to children at play can show that very clearly. One of the most impressive aspects of children's talk overheard when they are playing is the speed with which they can get into role, shift registers, and take on the phrasing and vocabulary of a range of speakers.

Language diversity

This is at one and the same time one of the most valuable resources teachers can draw on – from their own experience as well as that of the children – and one of the hottest areas of debate about oracy. Language diversity does not only suggest the existence of different languages within a classroom or community, it also includes variation between dialects, accents, registers and types of text, both written and spoken. Language diversity is also deeply involved with social and cultural judgements about what is valuable or worthy. Many adults carry scars from other people's comments about their spoken language. Judgements are often made about intelligence, social status, trustworthiness and potential for future employment on the basis of how people speak – not the content of what they say, but their accent, pronunciation, choice of vocabulary and tone of voice. Such attitudes can have an impact on later learning.

If children are to be given a chance confidently to expand their language repertoires to the full, they need first of all to know that the language which they speak every day is a valid form of expression. They are then in a more secure position to be able to compare the different ways of talking (and writing) they come across and to build on these models for a full and flexible range of language from which they can choose how and when to use particular forms. Unfortunately, though, the social values attached to particular ways of speaking can intervene, as Anne's comments show:

> I hated —— junior school; I was picked on by the pupils because I pronounced my words properly, using 'h's', 't's' and 'ings'. It was not only the pupils who picked on me at school, though, but also some of the teachers. They called me 'Lady Jane' and 'Miss ——' I don't want to disclose the second name.

This is another extract from Anne's Language and Literacy History (see also this chapter, p. 142)

What is 'bad grammar'?

One of the difficulties about any discussion of 'correctness' in personal uses of language is that there is a great deal of confusion about 'poor speech', 'bad grammar' and 'proper pronunciation'. What might 'poor speech' be? and what is 'good speech'? It is very plain that attitudes to accents and dialects are permeated by social and cultural judgements about the comparative status of speakers as suggested by their home language use. Since teaching standard forms of English is now explicitly part of every element of the National Curriculum for English it is worth clearing up some of the misconceptions here. Many of the ways of speaking which are described as 'bad grammar' are, in fact, dialect forms of speech. The National Curriculum document for English distinguishes between standard forms and 'other forms of English' and makes it clear that 'spoken standard English is not the same as Received Pronunciation and can be expressed in a variety of accents' (p. 3). However, it does not offer much more detail about the relationship between the grammar of English and standard forms. Chapter 5 deals with grammar in much more detail, particularly with its teaching, but it is important to distinguish between 'bad grammar' and anyone's home use of language. It is also important to recognise that people can speak or write in standard forms of a language and with Received Pronunciation but present their ideas ungrammatically, mixing singular nouns with plural verbs, or the reverse, for example – a very common feature of politicians' radio contributions!

The fact of the matter is that teachers and schools have always taught standard English. Indeed, children very often write in standard forms of English even when they may speak a non-standard dialect. This is true of many adult speakers, too, and suggests that the proper emphasis for teaching standard English should be placed more on writing than on speech, where it can become a focus for fruitful discussion about shifts in register, formality and grammatical patterns. Nevertheless, teachers do need to reassure themselves that children can use standard forms when speaking. This is where drama and role play can be useful – and reassuring. Asking children to take on the role of a weather forecaster or news reader will show immediately that they can switch into standard forms when they wish to – and that they know something about when such standard forms are used. If a quick experiment like this reveals a number of children who cannot switch in this way, then there needs to be some more extensive drama work in order to give them opportunities for practice. Using drama in this way avoids the suggestion that a child's own language – and so, by implication, the child herself or himself – is socially deficient.

Bilingual learners

When it comes to working in classrooms with children who have access to more than one language, teachers can sometimes feel at a loss, as Helen Savva points out: 'Bilingualism is a sensitive issue; it arouses strong emotions in teachers. They can feel defensive, threatened, guilty, they can feel they are doing their best in difficult circumstances with very little guidance or support' (p. 6). However, she makes some striking points about bilingualism:

> Operating in more than one language is normal. It is not in itself a problem and it certainly does not constitute a learning difficulty. Yet those of us who live in England live in a country in which monolingualism is still regarded as the norm. This is both a cause and an effect of official attitudes towards bilingualism and bilingual children.
> (p. 7)

Most of the world's population is bilingual or multilingual, yet there seems often to be very little knowledge about bilingualism in English classrooms. One of the dangers is to define children as bilingual first and as individuals second:

Helen Savva 1991 'Bilingual by rights' in *Language and Learning 5*, Birmingham, The Questions Publishing Company

> One of the key lessons to be learnt about bilingual children is that they are not a homogeneous group. There is a tendency to discuss them and their needs as if they were identical. Linguistically, socially, culturally, politically, the lives of bilingual children are complex and their experiences diverse.
> (p. 7)

Just as diverse as any monolingual population of children!

The advantages of bilingualism

One of the important facts which has emerged recently, however, is that bilingual children are often in a position of advantage in learning if they are encouraged to use their home language and the language of school when they want to. If a child is learning two languages simultaneously, or even learning a second language during the early years, the cognitive patterning is similar; the repeated experience of matching an already known word or expression to one in another language sets up a mental framework for other kinds of matching – the kind of analogical thinking which helps the development of mathematics, for example. It can also lead to the ability to reflect more analytically on language as Dejay, a 6-year-old talking with his teacher, explains:

DEJAY: If you're lonely you talk in your mind and talk to yourself.
MRS K: Tell me about that – you talk in your mind?
DEJAY: You talk in your mind and talk back.
MRS K: Mm . . . Mm . . .
DEJAY: And when you're lonely and stuff you talk back. When you're in bed you can think and think back – when you've got teddies you can pretend to speak to them. But, really, you speak in your mind and talk.
MRS K: What kinds of things do you think about when you're doing that?
DEJAY: I think about . . .
MRS K: Talk about . . .
DEJAY: I talk about counting backwards and counting forwards.

Later in the conversation, the teacher returns to the topic:

MRS K: Tell me something – you know when you talk in your head do you talk in English or Gujerati?
DEJAY: Gujerati and English. Different sorts.
MRS K: Sometimes in Gujerati, sometimes in English.
DEJAY: Yes.
MRS K: That's good, being able to talk in two languages in your head.
DEJAY: I speak in English then I feed back in Gujerati.
MRS K: I wish I could do that.

from Sally Barnes and Cynthia Knight 1989 'If you're alone you just talk in your mind and talk back', in *TALK: the Journal of the National Oracy Project* no. 2, autumn 1989

A comment that many teachers would echo and a telling example of the relationship between language and thought.

Helen Savva's arguments and Dejay's remarkable insights emphasise the most central and significant point about language diversity – that everyone, teachers and the children who enter their classrooms, has unique language experience. It is important to be able to recognise and identify children's language repertoire but equally important to manage linguistic diversity in practical terms every day in the classroom. The following sections on planning and teaching talk take up issues of managing classrooms for diversity in talk.

New insights about speaking and listening

Talk is essential to the development of thought and the progress of learning. Conversation which is purposeful and focused, which allows for hypothesis, prediction and questioning, is one of the most powerful means of helping children to think and to consolidate what they have come to know by other means. Many adults will testify to the ways in which talking something through helps to make clear just what the key issues are, and explaining to someone else is one of the best ways to discover whether you really know something yourself. In the classroom, then, talking and listening have become more central to the process of organising for learning.

Even though the status of talk in the classroom has been raised, there are still some reservations about children's capacity to listen attentively. This is quite a teaser for any teacher since it soon becomes obvious that, unless children are suffering temporary or permanent hearing loss, they can listen perfectly well to matters which concern them deeply. Even a whisper can catch some children's attention if it is about when they might be going out to play or having a treat of some kind. The challenge, then, is not so much to develop children's listening skills as to develop their awareness of how to pay attention (and hold their attention on what is being said) when it is important. Children have to be taught such strategies since in their out-of-school lives most listening is to what they have elected to pay attention to.

There has also been a set of theories linked to home language, particularly in relation to working-class homes. In the past it was felt that some (mostly working-class) homes were deficient because they operated a 'restricted' use of language as opposed to the 'elaborated' language of middle-class homes. Further substantial research suggests that this view is inaccurate and misleading. The problem seems to have been in the speech practices of the schools where working-class children (and other children, come to that) were being taught. Often, the teachers' ways of talking, particularly of questioning, and some of the language practices used in the early stages of learning, were unfamiliar to the children and needed explaining if their progress was not to be impeded. Parents of bilingual or multilingual children were often told that their children should not speak their home language at home because it would interfere with their learning of English. This has been disproved – indeed, the reverse has been seen to be the case.

These terms were first developed by the sociologist Basil Bernstein, writing in the 1960s: **restricted** language was taken to be incomplete sentences, brief, functional utterances; **elaborated** language was seen as nearer to written forms of language with complex sentence structures.

Emphasis on speaking and listening in the classroom has led to a recognition that spoken utterances can be regarded as texts which have purposes very like those of written texts. The similarities are not so much in sentence structure – there are usually marked differences in the construction of spoken and written sentences – but in their functions. A telephone call to a member of the family is like a personal letter; the headteacher's report at a meeting of parents may be like a newspaper report. For every spoken text there is likely to be a written parallel and referring to spoken utterances as texts makes it easier to consider just how to manage teaching speaking and listening in the classroom.

New insights into the teaching and learning of speaking and listening suggest that if teachers are to support and extend children's talk development they need to attend to several areas at once. Any theory which seeks to inform practice must be able to:

- articulate ideas about early language use and how children's own knowledge of spoken texts can best be built on
- offer a useful analysis of how talk is best supported in the classroom
- take into account the behavioural, social and cultural factors which influence speaking and listening
- develop conscious and planned activities to support the development of speaking and listening across a whole school.

Speaking and listening in the classroom

Over the recent years of attention to oracy it has become clear that helping children to extend the range of their spoken language use means careful planning and skilful intervention from teachers. Sometimes, of course, that intervention is best expressed by not interfering with children's talk, by listening and responding as part of genuine dialogue. In order to identify the kinds of intervention which will be most helpful, it is necessary to form a picture of what the possibilities might be for a teacher's role in helping children to make progress in talk.

Individual development of concepts and strategies

1. As children interact with adults, they observe, listen and work out their own systems and rules for talk. Children hypothesise about the organisation of language and try out rules and expressions as they get to grips with the grammar of the language they are learning.
2. Children learn more than the grammar and vocabulary of language as they grow up in the language environment of the home. From a very early age they learn behaviours such as turn-taking and conversational strategies; they also pick up patterns of longer stretches of spoken text – stories, jokes, moral anecdotes, rhymes, advertising jingles, etc.
3. The development of language is deeply enmeshed with the development of thought. As children learn to use their home language they are also learning to use language as a tool for further thought.
4. Even very young children can switch from one way of speaking to another, shifting codes according to the circumstances, audience and purpose of the spoken text.
5. It is now clear that children can learn even more about language if they are invited to think about it and to talk about what spoken language can do for them and other learners.

Behavioural, social and cultural factors

6. Speaking and listening are not only complex cognitive processes, but complex social practices. The way we speak reflects the culture of the community in which we learned to use language and can evoke responses which are themselves more to do with social and cultural expectations and values than to do with speech itself.
7. The language of the home is the essential bedrock of later language learning; home language practices can develop ways of perceiving the world, ways of using language and ways of learning which will have important implications for the value given to home language in school. Previously held deficit views of home language have now been superseded by more detailed research.
8. Bilingual children have advantages when taking on other concepts because of the experience they have of consciously matching words in the second or third language they are learning with existing words and ideas in their home language.

The teacher's role in promoting speaking and listening

9. A teaching emphasis on correctness at the expense of fluency can seriously underestimate and undervalue the implicit knowledge about language that children bring to school.
10. If teachers are fully to use the languages resources which children bring with them to school, it is necessary to listen to what children have to say and to avoid teacher questioning which is intended only to elicit a pre-existing answer.

Figure 4.5 Ten things we now know about speaking and listening

Planning for talk

Most primary teachers are now adept at planning for a range of outcomes in reading and writing as required by the National Curriculum. However, although the three components of English carry equal weighting there seems to be less confidence in planning, teaching and assessing speaking and listening. Although it is clear that a great deal of purposeful talk is happening in classrooms, it is still not as evident in teachers' written plans as activities to promote reading and writing. There are many reasons why this might be so. The social value of children's talk has only recently come to be appreciated. Children are inclined to regard talk as an alternative to 'work'. Teachers and other adults listening to children in classrooms often view exploratory talk as being off-task talk, giving greater weight to the more performative aspects of speaking and listening. Although it is important to acknowledge that talk is a complicated business, there is no need to organise separate activities to provide for the extension of talk experience. It isn't always necessary, for example, to prove that children have learned something by having written evidence; talk can reveal learning just as convincingly.

Incorporating talk activities into work plans means considering from the outset what kinds of talk to expect from pupils as they work together. For example, during a science task, pupils will use different words and phrases from the kinds of talk they might use when describing their thoughts on the images of a poem. Different talk texts require specific ways of talking. A considered approach to planning for speaking and listening will not only attune the ear to noticing these variations in talk but will ensure that planning can incorporate a range of talk outcomes.

The range of speakers and listeners

Planning will need to take account of such factors as personality, interests, gender, cultural experience, fluency in the dominant language of the classroom. This means moving away from seeing talk as a matter of performance alone, towards an awareness of variations within contexts. Silences might be important productive times or signals of confusion. Or in one type of grouping an individual might appear assured, insightful, able to converse considerately, while in another – even on the same day – he or she might show reticence, lack of confidence, confusion or unhelpful domination.

An important question, as for writing and reading, is *What kinds of speakers and listeners do we have in our classrooms?* They might be those who:

- are assured, fluent and know when to contribute
- are usually unwilling to contribute to discussion even in small groups or pairs
- help other children by explaining things to them
- catch on to ideas quickly
- find processing heard information difficult
- 'can't find the words'
- are selective listeners!
- can sustain active listening for extended periods of time
- find learning generally difficult and do not orally communicate their ideas with assurance
- are naturally reflective
- only comment when they want to
- have intermittent hearing difficulties
- can speak more than one language
- use a local/regional dialect
- are very voluble without seeming to have any control over their talk
- can summarise group talk concisely

- find narrating easier than fact-giving
- are used to interacting on equal terms in conversation as adults
- have speech impairments
- frequently elect to be silent when upset
- are accomplished storytellers
- have physical or medical conditions which make speech difficult (cerebral palsy, for example)
- do not seem to know about changes in register according to audience
- are persuasive and convincing – or charming!

It is certainly a challenge to provide for the range and the following sections suggest ways of providing for the diversity of speakers and listeners in the classroom.

What children know about talk

If you have already asked the children some of the questions on p. 142 you may already have gained some important information about what they know about spoken language. Analysing children's knowledge about language may involve looking at a range of aspects:

- children learning language
- children learning about language
- children learning through language
- children learning to talk about language
- children showing through language what they have learned.

Certainly, teachers can often be surprised when they have listened attentively to children's language use:

> Watching children working in small groups on practical activities and talk tasks has made me rethink my ideas about who is able and who isn't.
>
> One little girl just made two mounds of sand, but what I heard was a wonderful story about a ship, a princess and a parrot.
>
> A group of boys sorted out their science problem in Gujerati.
>
> I overheard the children playing out a theme we had done months earlier.
>
> I never realised they bothered so much about world issues.
>
> (p.13)

from Kate Norman ed. 1990 *Teaching Talking and Learning in Key Stage 1*, York, National Curriculum Council/National Oracy Project

Careful attention to children's conversations can reveal what they have learned in any area of the curriculum. Judith Allen, a teacher in Lowestoft, tape recorded a group of Year 2 children as they went for a walk around the school grounds. They had already talked about the effects of sun and the need for soil and water to help plants grow:

LIZZIE: Plants are growing where there is soil and damp places and on the garden. Plants can get water and it's safe. They wouldn't grow in concrete.
ANDREW: Plants can't grow on paths because it's too hard.
KAYLEIGH: Whitton Wood there's loads of soil. The sun can always get to it 'cos it's in an open field.
LAURA: Soil needs water so it soaks in.
GRACIE: No-one will tread on the flower beds at the side.
DANIEL: A good place for the daffodils because it's sunny.
AARON: The daisies are coming up. Why are the daisies closed up?
DANIEL: It's cold.
TEACHER: When will they open?

DANIEL: When it's sunny.
GRACIE: Flowers only come open in the summer because it's warm.
MATTHEW: Rain makes everything grow – and sun.
KAYLEIGH: Flowers need water and food. Plants can grow up fences.
LAURA: There's a dead sunflower. There are seeds still in there. There are places for seeds.
MATTHEW: If you put them in the ground you can have new plants.
LAURA: Plants need space to grow.

One of the most useful sources of suggestions for language study is Mike Raleigh 1981 *The Languages Book*, London, ILEA Languages Centre (still very good although published some time ago) and also Richard Bain 1991 *Reflections: talking about language*, Sheffield, National Association for the Teaching of English.

Judith Allen notes that Matthew, Aaron and Daniel have difficulty with writing, yet it is very clear that they are perfectly capable of discussing the concepts of plant growth in an informed way and that they have a good level of knowledge about plants. All the children listen to each other and respond as the discussion progresses.

Opportunities for learning through language – and expressing what has been learned – can be introduced into planning for areas of the curriculum other than English. In specifically timetabled English lessons, however, there are chances to study language itself – to find out what children know and can do with language. There are many language awareness projects which can reveal what children know about their own and other people's languages. This can often be carried out in a class, for example, by examining language family trees, but needs to be done with sensitivity, since some children may not feel comfortable revealing their own cultural linguistic roots in public.

Case Study 4

Planning for storytelling

Sally Elding explains how a class of Year 5 pupils were helped to create oral stories for themselves. It required the pupils to work in a variety of groupings and drew on a range of aspects of speaking and listening. Fig. 4.6 shows her plan for the activity.

I began with a demonstration of 'twinning', using the services of a willing Learning Support Assistant. We sat facing each other with the class in a circle around us. I had already explained that between us we were going to try to create a story or at least part of a story one word at a time with the story bouncing like a tennis ball between us. I began and my partner responded.

One
dark
and
windy
November
morning
Clarence
awoke
to
the
sound
of
something
snuffling
and
sniffling
outside
the . . .

Activity Planning Sheet

Activity Title	Year/Group
Storymaking	Yr. 5

Activity Details	Planned Learning	Organisation Resources	P of S	Assessment Opportunities
Twinning activity Adult demonstration of how to create a story one word at a time ↓ Repeat with a child	Listen/learn how to create a story	Whole class	1a – tell, develop, share	Use of story lang. Incorporating elements of known stories
↓ Pairs try this together Reflect on this – invite comments ↓ Change partners and try again	Collaborate with a partner	Pairs	1b 1c	Lang. of negotiation
↓ Pairs join to make fours. Tell/retell their stories to each other ↓ Share some stories with everyone	Recall/retell story to new audience ↓	Fours Whole class (Tape record ?)	2a – recall, represent Listen to others	Retell using increased choice of words and more adventurous words/phrases. Evidence of ideas being developed and improved

Evaluation and Extension

Use Talking Together sheet to reflect on activity with partner.

Figure 4.6 Planning for assessment of speaking and listening – storymaking (Blank provided in Appendix: A12)

It was a predictable tale of a solitary creature who befriends another. Although unfinished by us, it sparked a whole range of ideas from the children about how it could end. Furthermore, as we at times during the telling struggled to find the next word, a range of suggestions were always being offered from the listeners which, on reflection, would have taken the story off into many different directions.

Next, two volunteers demonstrated as we listened to the story of a large and terrifying dragon who was beaten into submission by a clever princess. It was clear that the pair were drawing on their knowledge of stories, of how characters behaved and how the events rounded to a satisfying climax.

The rest of the class were eager to have a go for themselves by now. With a partner they were to create a story in the same way with no talk or planning beforehand. I allowed about ten minutes and then helped the children to reflect on both the stories and the twinning experience, with some questions:

- Did you create a whole or a part of a story?
- Were you satisfied with the story?
- Was it okay? good? excellent?
- How could it have been better?

- Did one of you seem to have more control over the story line than the other?
- Did some words seem to fit naturally after particular words? Which?
- Thinking about it now, how would you change the story in order to improve it?
- What genre of story would you say you had just told between you?

Summarise your story in as few words as possible.

The children commented that, while one of them might know how he or she wanted the story to proceed, their partner was not always of a similar mind and said something unexpected, which meant a readjustment of ideas. Few of them said that they would change their created texts substantially. Although nobody felt that a partner had controlled the story, some developed strategies for passing decisions about moving the action forward across to their partners, so avoiding some responsibility; the use of adjectives was an effective way of handing over the storyline to a partner!

After this period of reflection, one person in each pair was then asked to stand and move clockwise to team up with a new partner. The whole process was repeated in these new pairs. It was noticeable this time that little to no time was wasted negotiating who was going to go first. The fun of discovering what sort of story it was going to be, how the characters were going to react and who was going to speak the 'best' words, guided the task along. Now that the children knew what was expected of them the stories were longer, funnier, more daring, and it was clear that the pupils were using structures and knowledge from known stories to help them through.

Here are just a few snatched excerpts from some of the emerging stories:

> Once long ago there lived a really bad king who terrified everyone in the land. One day one of his soldiers . . .
>
> Once there was an animal and this animal was a cheetah and the cheetah was very hungry because all the other animals in the forest hid when he came along . . .
>
> . . . The next day Mr Smith went out of his back door and unlocked his lorry. He put the key in the ignition and turned it, but nothing happened and then he saw a long furry thing sticking out of the bonnet . . .
>
> . . . The people decided that the giant had to be killed so they had a meeting . . .

Again, once a story had been created, pupils were asked to use the questions help them to reflect and summarise. Pairs joined together to make groups of four and between them each pair re-told their story to the new audience. This oral redraft was a good first opportunity for pupils to really feel and behave like storytellers (this class had previously had experience of being storytellers to a younger age group) rather than story creators. Hands and eyes were used more in the telling now as well as tone of voice. The stories became more 'polished'.

Finally, the class were asked to nominate stories for the whole class to listen to and to say why everyone should hear a particular story. As Ciaron said of the story he had heard: *It's good, it could be written in a book and sold – I'd do the pictures!*

The school and classroom as hospitable environments for talk

All the people who enter the school or classroom are potential resources for learning. They act as models and examples and, in terms of language diversity, making contact with families can begin to bring in some useful information about what language resources are available just beyond the doors of the classroom. However, the classroom itself is the most critical resource base and environment for development of language. The organisation of furniture, the layout of the classroom and the groupings used contribute to making a classroom environment hospitable to diversity. Equally important, and strongly tied up with the physical environment, will be the environment within the teacher's head about what will promote successful talk – signalled by the expectations, approaches and opportunities offered. The following checklist offers a way of reviewing the classroom as a supportive environment for speaking and listening:

- What do I value about the children's talk?
- What are the key features in my classroom which support speaking and listening?
- How do I provide experience for a range of:

    groupings and audiences for talk
    different purposes for speaking and listening
    different types of talk
    levels of formality/register
    levels of fluency and assurance?

- How do I cater for the diverse speakers and listeners in my class?

The answers to some of these questions might lead to some reorganisation or reappraisal. It is often easiest to start any development in practice by concentrating on the physical environment. Many classrooms have reading corners and even writing areas, but what about talk corners? How might rearranging the layout of the classroom encourage more productive talk? It is easier to organise for talk if the furniture is arranged in a way that can accommodate to different groupings. However, this isn't always possible so it is probably even more important to establish procedures where the pupils know the ground rules about moving to an appropriate setting for a talk activity. This might need explicit discussion, as careful as discussions about behaviour and consideration in group talk. Fig. 4.7 suggests some supportive strategies for talk.

It might be difficult to ensure a quiet area for tape recording so arrangements have to be made for taping to take place during quiet times or in other places in the school. There should be an area agreed by all staff as a suitable place to send pairs or groups of children who want to tape an extended spoken text (and reserved as far as possible). Headphones are usually sufficient to ensure reasonable quiet for listening. One

The Talk Corner

might have:

- a noticeboard where the teacher (or any of the children) regularly posts up interesting things for the children to discuss
- a discussion box where the children put in written suggestions of things they want to discuss (it is important to emphasise anonymity here since some discussion topics might include requests for help in dealing with *people who are picking on me*, for example)
- cassette recorders and blank tapes
- tape players and story or song tapes (these can be put together by the pupils themselves or the parents and can include stories in community languages)
- headphones
- a quotation board and a supply of empty speech bubbles for *things we have said, things people say to us*
- telephones – with message pad and telephone book with the numbers of familiar story-book or nursery rhyme characters to ring up
- games
- pictures with questions like *What happened next?*
- stories in pictures, with gaps in the narrative for *What happened in the middle?* or *What happened at the end?*
- intriguing newspaper pictures/stories.

Figure 4.7 Supporting talk in the classroom

teacher turned her stockroom into a 'recording studio' which became so popular that the children had to invent a booking system and a notice to show when it was engaged.

Younger children explore different forms and uses of talk as they enact a range of roles. The role play areas suggested in Chapter 2 can provide opportunities for a wide repertoire of types of speaking and listening, as Fig. 4.8 shows.

ROLE PLAY AREAS

Post Office: Asking questions, explaining, conversations in the queue, reading letters aloud, talking on the telephone, etc.

Café: Ordering food, taking orders, reading items from the menu in other languages, conversations at the table, etc.

Doctor's or Vet's: (waiting room or clinic) conversations relevant to babies, animals, medical matters, reading aloud labels, health advice posters (some in community languages), advertisements for proprietary products, explaining symptoms to the doctor or vet, etc.

Home corner: all kinds of made up conversations, extended stories, soap opera-type dialogue, telephone conversations, baby and parent talk, etc.

Shops, supermarkets, travel agents, airport, railway station, toy emporium, computer stores – all of them offer infinite opportunities for role play talk.

Figure 4.8 Opportunities for talk in role play areas

Teaching speaking and listening

One of the most difficult decisions teachers have to take is the perennial one about when it is useful to intervene and when it is better to stand back. In the words of the school hymn:

from 'Lord, dismiss us with thy blessing' – a hymn often sung at the end of term in English schools

> When to speak and when be silent
> When to do and when forbear.

When it comes to teaching speaking and listening such decisions are even more critical. The extract showing Joyce with her teacher is a sharp example, but any teacher who has transcribed a tape where he or she is talking with a group of children may well have winced at the urge to intervene too much in children's discussions. It is no wonder, of course; there is the curriculum (ever more loaded) to get through; a colleague sees group discussion as a lapse in discipline; we need to get on! The recognised fact that talk helps children to learn can sometimes lose its force when time is pressing and SATs are looming. There are also organisational and assessment issues to be taken into account. Many of these concerns can be dealt with by thoughtful planning and clear delineation of just what is going to be learned. Ensuring that they are going to be learned (as far as possible) is the next hurdle. This is where careful management of learning – the content and the groupings – comes in.

As far as English is concerned, the content can be very wide indeed. And just what is a group? It's rather like asking *How long is a piece of string?* Even more challenging is the question *What is effective group work?* in other words, *What will really get the learning done?* These questions might have myriad answers, depending on the context, the task, the individual teacher and so on. The whole subject of group work is complex and diffuse, but certainly bears scrutiny if organising for learning is to be as effective as possible. Just putting learners into groups doesn't guarantee learning happening; there has to be rather more focus than simply rearranging the furniture! Also, roles within groups can be different or can vary during the process of a group's work; the person who is an information giver in one grouping, or at one stage in a group's work, may be the scribe or a silent appreciator in another group or at another stage of the group's work.

see Chapter 5, p. 194, for a model of the content of the English curriculum

- What kinds of groupings do you use?
- How much do you vary them?

Gender and talk

While it can be easy to slip into routines about who works with whom, there are distinct advantages to varying groupings. One of these is related to gender. The Ofsted report *Boys and English* noted that 'There were no obvious differences in the performance of boys and girls in spoken English, although girls were sometimes more reticent and took less part in class discussion. In low-attaining groups in particular, boys dominated oral work.'

Office for Standards in Education 1993 *Boys and English*, London, Department for Education

There are obvious dangers in assuming that boys are noisy and dominant and that girls are put into the shade. Not only can every teacher find opposite examples, but it is unhelpful anyway to stereotype behaviours too readily. Nevertheless, evidence does suggest that it is worth paying attention to gender, particularly in the oracy part of the curriculum. There are two (at least) reasons for this in terms of teaching speaking and listening. The first is that although the National Curriculum focuses on the range and key skills within English, it is clear that behaviours, attitudes and social practices about literacy and oracy have an important impact on children's future learning potential. If talk behaviour is unequally weighted towards any group, then it needs to be carefully monitored and adjusted where necessary so as not to impede learning. Second, although Ofsted found equal performance between boys and girls in English, they do not comment on the impact which dominant talk habits might have on the learning opportunities in other subjects. However, just noticing such practices and habits won't make them go away – and teachers themselves have found that even if they are aware of different demands on them by boys and girls they are not always able to balance them. A key feature for every classroom is first of all to notice what is actually happening.

It is worth observing and listening to the pupils before thinking about how you might want to alter things to ensure more or less equal access to talk for all of them. This might mean talking with colleagues and beginning to forge a policy about talk and gender; it could mean some alteration in your own practices to avoid stereotyping. It might be useful to discuss rules about using equipment in the classroom – toys, constructional materials or the computer – or to discuss with the children their views about the books on offer. Other organisational strategies might be to look at the groupings you use and make some adjustments. The following strategies for inclusion apply equally well for any individual or group who are 'silenced' in the regular run of classroom activities.

see Chapter 2, pp. 30–3, for a discussion of boys and reading

Organising groups for talk

Single-sex grouping: This can be useful, particularly in areas where boys might traditionally be seen to dominate, such as technology or science. However, it is worth deliberately mixing groups at times for these activities; this might be done at a second stage of the work when the boys and girls have had a chance to develop some expertise or knowledge which can be shared. This strategy is also useful for a group of children who share the same community language; they can work together first to establish their knowledge, then change groups to share that knowledge with others.

Organising roles within groups: Identifying a group chairperson, a scribe, a listener/reporter can be a very effective way of sharing roles. Equally, giving specially assigned roles ensures that all have a chance to contribute. This might also be a chance to subvert traditional stereotyping by deliberately assigning specific roles to particular individuals.

Listening triangles: In groups of three, children take on the roles of speaker, questioner and note-maker. This can be done with almost any activity but may need to be demonstrated first. The speaker explains to the others about the topic decided on; the questioner finds two areas which might need clarification or prompting for further detail; the note-maker reports back briefly at the end. (It is sometimes useful to give time limits, and to practise keeping to them.) The next time round, the roles change and so on.

Group observers: One member of the group, using prompt questions devised beforehand, acts as the observer to reflect back to the group the way it has been working. The observer watches, listens and notes as the group works. This information is then fed back to the group to be discussed.

Pair building: One of the most automatic groupings in the classroom is the idea of working with a partner. It is always useful to build on children's established ways of collaborative working, but pairs can also be the basis for more extended mixing and varying groups. They might join up in fours or sixes according to the kinds of science experiments they have been doing – to compare or contrast findings; they might have been working on the same maths investigation or have read similar books or poems. The content of the mixed paired discussions can be managed by the teacher, of course, deliberately to get children working together for particular reasons.

Jigsawing: This will need careful explanation, tight timing and management of resources. *Home groups* of about six pupils research a topic over a specified period of time. The teacher decides on six (or other appropriate number) areas within the topic which can be researched with supporting materials. Each child is assigned a particular area within the topic with the aim that he or she is to become the *expert* in that area. During the work of the Home groups, time is allocated for each of the experts to share their findings with the whole group. Children then re-form into Expert groups made up of all those from the Home groups who had the same topic. After the Expert groups have met, they return to their Home groups to recount the additional information they have picked up and to plan any final display or presentation for the whole class.

This idea and envoying, which follows, was first explained widely by the National Oracy Project. The Project books *Teaching Talking and Learning at Key Stage 1* and *Teaching Talking and Learning at Key Stage 2* are a mine of useful and practical information.

Envoying: This can ease the teacher's load of always having to be the expert and consultant. One member of the group may be sent to the library, to another group, teacher or individual to find out or check a particular fact, detail or procedure. It is wise to limit the number of envoys to be sent on research jobs at any one time! An envoy can also be sent to explain a group's findings to another group.

There are, of course, many other ways in which groups can be organised effectively. The key point is to consider the range and extent of variation you want to provide over a specified period of time. Once children get into the way of working with flexible groupings, of course, the management can be much more relaxed.

The teacher's role

When groups are working more independently in the classroom, then the teacher is freed to be able to manage teaching and learning in a more focused way. This is particularly true when it comes to observation. When groups are engaged actively in their own work, it is possible to target one group to observe for a few minutes. This can give valuable information to feed forward into future planning and can be the time when routine observations for termly assessments of talk can take place. Another good opportunity for observation and recording which can feed forward to assessment is in work around the computer.

Information and communications technology needs to be introduced into all aspects of work in the classroom. It is an ideal way of promoting and developing explanatory, predictive and hypothesising talk as well as encouraging negotiation and collaborative practices. Also, of course, it allows for individuals to find pleasure in their own expertise. Computers provide very good opportunities for children to work independently of the teacher and, although you may need to manage the timetabling of use (and to monitor boy/girl use), once routines have been established it can be a site for fruitful observation of collaborative talk. Word processing can give a chance for pupils to draft, revise, edit and proofread writing together. Databases involve a great deal of discussion about what should be entered and how it can best be entered. CD-ROMs offer opportunities for explanations, questions and the display of a pupil's knowledge which the teacher may not have known about. The discussions might not even have to take place around the computer; work for databases can be discussed in groups before entering the information on the machine, as in the following example. This group of Year 4/5 pupils have just read together *The Iron Man* by Ted Hughes. As part of their normal classroom routine they have been asked to review the book by completing a datafile sheet at the computer. After filling in details of title, author, publisher and illustrator, the datafile asks them to respond to various aspects of the text such as the narrative voice, the characters, the setting, when the story takes place plus any themes and messages suggested in the text. Here, the group of eight – two boys and six girls – are trying to decide what the genre of the book is. A list of suggestions is on the screen in front of them. In this lively discussion, everyone joins in, sometimes all talking at the same time:

LAURA:	. . . and the genre is . . .
STACEY:	Genre . . . What's the genre? Adventure?
CHLOE:	Fantasy.
GILLIAN:	Horror.
PHILIP:	I'm just taking time to think which is the best 'cause we're arguing.
GILLIAN:	Yes.
TOM:	Right, what do you think?
PHILIP:	I think probably . . . probably adventure or fantasy.
CHLOE & VICKY:	Adventure or fantasy . . . fantasy.
STACEY & OTHERS:	I think it should be science fiction 'cause there isn't such a thing as an iron man.
TOM:	Anything else?
GILLIAN:	Adventure.
LAURA & VICKY:	Horror and fantasy.
GILLIAN:	Fantasy.
TOM:	I think it's fantasy 'cause it's not real.
VICKY:	Definitely adventure though.
TOM:	It is a bit of horror because . . .
VICKY:	It's adventure, though.
PHILIP:	Probably is . . . No I think it's fantasy 'cause it's not real there's never been a monster of iron.
STACEY:	Hey you guys we're arguing again.
PHILIP:	Fantasy probably.
LAURA & TOM:	Horror as well because of the Space Bat Angel.
VICKY:	Definitely adventure though.
LAURA:	Mystery . . . mystery, why did it come down?
PHILIP:	WHY did it come down?
CATHERINE:	Yes, mystery.
LAURA:	Yeah, 'cause why did it come down, we don't know that.
PHILIP:	Yeah we did 'cause we read the book yes 'cause he heard all the wars and things.

This discussion shows that taping discussion can be a very informative experience – for pupils and teacher alike. While it may not always be necessary to transcribe fragments, a transcript can reveal aspects of pupils' talk which might otherwise go unnoticed. Silences can speak; for example, in this extract, why does Catherine only speak once? Is this representative of her classroom talk pattern? Some children, like Vicky, can emerge as tenacious. Philip gives clear evidence of using talk to hypothesise; Gillian can be seen as a summariser while Stacey shows understanding of the dynamics of group work. There is much more, too, which might be drawn from this brief transcript – and even more from a class where the teacher knows the children well.

with thanks to Jennifer Reynolds and her class at Thorndown junior school, Huntingdon, Cambs.

Reflecting on language

The group in the example above were asked to listen to the tape and evaluate their own work. Their reflections show an understanding of the purpose of group discussion for learning, how experience helps improve talk and how thoughtful evaluation can improve personal talk practices:

> I think we worked well because everybody got to share their ideas.

I think our group worked well because we weren't nervous and we've worked on the tape recorder before.

This time I wasn't very bossy like I usually am.

Not only is it possible, through transcribing what children say, to see that particular pupils show specific strengths, but transcripts also allow for more general observations. Although the group say they are arguing, they aren't coming to blows; in fact, they are arguing in the more 'academic' sense of the word. They are using each other as sounding boards, speculating through talk, justifying opinions and giving reasons for holding particular views. They also show that they know what genre means; the teacher will not need to go over that again. They are confident with each other, make thoughtful responses to the text and their discussion overall demonstrates that they have understood the book and that reading it has given them pleasure. Taped evidence can give the teacher proof of the effectiveness of learning activities.

Talking about a tape of a group's work can be an effective way of introducing some of the language awareness aspects of the curriculum; such discussions often make explicit a great deal of the children's knowledge about language. Including the pupils where possible also offers a chance to explain just what is going on as a teacher lurks near the role play area, notebook in hand! Most particularly, asking pupils to reflect on their talk can lead right back to the important aspect of talk helping learning.

Talking about talk

The following offers a list of ways in which children can be encouraged to look very closely at language and to talk about it.

Talk diaries: Children can keep notebooks of talk where they write down anything that they find interesting or important. This could be about the ways in which they or anyone in the class has used talk. If the teacher also keeps a talk diary, then this acts as a valuable model of what might be recorded. Children might be guided to research and write about family sayings or unusual words or to collect playground songs or sayings.

Making tapes and transcribing: Children can make their own tapes giving examples of different ways of talking or gathering opinions, rhymes, stories or anecdotes. These might include taping family members and are a good way to involve parents and carers in the work which goes on in school. Some valuable libraries of taped stories have been built up this way. While listening to tapes of different types of talk draws attention to the larger structures of talk texts, transcribing can be an effective way of focusing on the smaller elements of the language – at sentence and word level. Children working together transcribing a fragment of paired or group discussion can get involved in very detailed discussions about language – particularly about how best to represent words in standard or non-standard spellings and how to punctuate to capture the sense of the texts.

Discussing attitudes to talk: An ambitious way of doing this can be to have a tape exchange with a school in another geographical area, specifically aimed at discussing regional differences in speech. A more easily set up approach might be to develop a series of questions about talk and variety, such as *Can you speak more than one language? Do you know any words in a different language?* An alternative approach might be to collect – and then discuss – anecdotes which parents tell about pupils' early sayings.

Talking about the media: Television, video and radio provide an immediate and rich resource for research into language variety, types of talk, registers, opinion versus fact – almost the whole speaking and listening curriculum. Children can be invited to express their own opinions about programmes and also analyse some of the different ways people speak according to the purpose of the talk text, the content or the intended audience. This can lead into a whole range of drama and role play activities based on programmes which are familiar. Switching or combining programmes can also stretch children's talk repertoires and inventiveness – what about presenting the news as the favourite soap opera? or making a documentary in the genre of a pop music programme – a rap, perhaps?

Word focus: This can be organised to fit in with any area of the curriculum. Children might collect and display words which are relevant to a particular subject area; words with the same prefixes or suffixes, or words which are opposites; people's names and their origins – the list is extensive. A few pre-produced word bubbles can make an instant display which can then become a feature for discussion and future 'word searching' activities.

Links between speaking and writing: Word activities can often lead on to explicit discussion of the distinctions and similarities between written and spoken forms of text. Pupils might make lists of types of written texts and their spoken equivalents as well as being asked to notice in the books they read the differences between narrative and dialogue. This provides a chance to introduce specific vocabulary about language grammatical terms, descriptive terms like onomatopoeia and assonance, for example, which are often fascinating to young learners. Most importantly, it helps children develop a vocabulary through which to talk about language.

see Chapter 6, pp. 274–7, for more suggestions about drama activities

Talk and performance

Earlier in the chapter, children's comments on talk indicated that they felt that being able to speak clearly, loudly and fluently is valued in school. The other side of this coin is that children who are not assured in public settings can feel diminished. This is a perennial problem which teachers have to try to solve in classroom work. Whilst quite properly wanting to encourage fluency in speech, there is the equal responsibility to maintain the self-esteem of learners. Traditional forms of performative speech do not always allow teachers to balance the two requirements: a play performance or individual readings in public can emphasise the assurance of some children in contrast to others' shyness. In order to find ways of supporting the less and more eloquent alike, teachers have turned to group work which ends in some kind of public presentation. Drama (not plays), role play and poetry offer rich possibilities here.

With younger children (although this can work equally well with older pupils) active storytelling offers a group activity which can be organised to include everyone. This builds on the natural role play which young children slip into very easily in the classroom. Active storytelling involves the whole class (or a group if appropriate) and begins with the teacher making it clear to the children that they are going to make a story. This is important so that the children are in control of the action and don't become alarmed at any point in the narrative as they become more immersed in it. Depending on the space available, the children will be able to move about and enact the story, visiting places which are introduced as the narrative unfolds.

The teacher's role is central, taking on a role within the narrative and stimulating the action by questions. The first one to ask is *Where is our story going to take place?* The progression of the story will depend on a variety of decisions made by the group. It might proceed by the teacher asking *Who are we going to meet? What will they say to us?* As the story progresses, different children can be asked to take on different roles as characters. Since the teacher is guiding by asking questions, the narrative can go anywhere. Often active stories become journeys with a variety of adventures, near-escapes and mishaps. The children can visit caves and hilltops, or even fly on magic carpets. The land can become rocky, slippery or made of jelly. Through careful intervention (though not interference as this tends to block the children's engagement in the narrative) the teacher can make sure to include all the children to the extent of their readiness to be involved and there are immense opportunities for language development. The teacher's role allows the skilful involvement of even the least assured children, who can be prompted by thoughtful questions to take an active part.

for a fuller account of active storytelling see Lesley Hendy 1992 'The Pearl Princess and the Whale's Stomach' in Morag Styles, Eve Bearne and Victor Watson eds *After Alice: exploring children's literature*, London, Cassell

Many poems lend themselves to simple performance. Pairs or groups of children can work on existing poems or can make up their own, modelled on some of their favourites. Children take naturally to parody and composing a mock version of a poem cannot only offer the chance of public presentation from the assured position of the author, but can stretch the children's knowledge of language, challenging them to find humorous alternatives for existing versions. They might be started off by reminders of the well-known parody of 'Twinkle, twinkle, little star' or of what they do to Christmas carols or in playground versions of known songs and rhymes. As long as the warnings about keeping within the bounds of decency are maintained, the presentation of different versions can be very enjoyable and certainly valuable for language development – both in terms of performance and in content. With already published poems children can take parts to enact dialogue, take a section of the poem in pairs and learn or prepare it for group presentation (this works well with cumulative rhymes such as 'I know an old lady who swallowed a fly'), ask and answer questions, for example in the nursery rhyme 'Pussy Cat, Pussy Cat', provide background sounds for atmospheric poems, or mime actions while others speak the poem. The rhythms of poetry give children a supportive framework for remembering the words and encourage more adventurous intonation and expression. It is always a good idea to allow rehearsal time and have a few runs through before expecting a polished performance, although work on a poem need not always lead to this. More serious presentations can be made of narrative poetry, and extracts from Shakespeare are ideal for introducing children to more public presentations of poetic language in the securely rehearsed context of a group or pair performance.

for other useful ways of linking poetry with drama see Jan Balaam and Brian Merrick 1987 *Exploring Poetry 5–8*, Sheffield, National Association for the Teaching of English

Observing, recording and reporting progress in talk

Parts of the following section first appeared as a series of articles written by Eve Bearne and Sally Elding in *The Primary English Magazine* vol. 1 no. 3 and vol. 2 nos. 1 and 2 1996, Birmingham, Garth Publishing.

There are perhaps more everyday opportunities for observation and assessment than might at first be obvious – during PE, science activities, school visits, paired reading activities. Teachers automatically make informal assessments in a range of social and learning situations and jotting down 'significant moments' can help to build a fuller picture of an individual's progress with speaking and listening. Assessment enters at all stages of the planning–teaching–evaluating cycle. Throughout the process of teaching and learning, observing, assessing, recording and reporting can offer a range of benefits. Observation and assessment of talk can:

- reveal what pupils are thinking about and how they are thinking
- give information about learning across subject areas
- provide insights into what pupils understand – or misunderstand – about the task, concept or information under discussion
- offer a more complete and representative picture of a child's attainment than assessments based only in reading or writing
- be an equaliser, showing surprising quality and sensitivity of thinking from children who may otherwise be considered to be failing
- help teachers become more aware of their own use of language and the positive and negative effects of intervention
- give status in the eyes of children, colleagues and parents to a traditionally undervalued form of communication
- enable the keeping of careful records to identify progress and inform future planning

- provide evidence for reporting to parents; for summary reports and for assigning National Curriculum levels of Attainment.

Compiling records

The aim of any recording system is to build up a gradual picture of a child's repertoire and, because talk is ephemeral and the way in which people speak or listen varies, observations have to be like snapshots, building a picture of any developing speaker/listener over a period of time. A starting point would be to make a few initial observations, deciding on who to watch or listen to – this may be one child or a group of children; deciding how long the observation will last – five minutes or for a sustained period – and deciding when to carry out observations – at the beginning, middle or end of a lesson or throughout the process of an activity. Children should be made aware that someone will be listening to them and taking notes about their speaking and listening. In the main, there will be three aspects of observing and recording:

- informal jotted observations
- brief transcripts of tape-recorded talk
- more formal record sheets.

All of these might be kept in the pupil's portfolio or record of achievement. Organising for observations over a set period of time needs to capture the individual using a variety of talk texts in different contexts. Individual observers will have their own preferred methods – notebooks, file cards, post-it notes, clip boards. The frequency of observations will also depend on the arrangements and possibilities of the particular classroom. After making observation notes, the teacher will filter these and decide on significant moments which will count as evidence of a particular aspect of the talk repertoire to be noted on the Record of Evidence. Notes need to include details of the grouping, what is seen and heard – either the gist of what was said in continuous prose or the actual words spoken, together with a date and a short description of the task. The notes in Fig. 4.9 were taken during the case study storytelling activity.

see pp. 162–5

A notebook entry of pupils working on paired story-making might record interesting use of vocabulary, memory of a told story, enjoyment of the task, and it might also reveal that in one kind of pairing a pupil shows greater assurance than in another. Any one of those might be considered sufficiently significant to be captured as a snapshot of development on the more formal record sheet. Even a very short transcript can provide evidence which might otherwise go unnoticed.

Assessing talk

Assessments of children's talk can serve two (at least) purposes:

- assessing experience and assurance *of* talk in different contexts
- assessing what has been learned in any curriculum area *through* talk in different contexts.

This means that it is possible to make assessments of both kinds during any curriculum activity. But the distinction between the two is important. A child who feels confident with her or his knowledge in a particular area is more likely to be fluent, at ease, capable of communicating information, making explanations or being persuasive, than a child who has no particular expertise in that area. On the other hand, a child might know a great deal yet not wish to voice that knowledge publicly,

Storytelling — Tues. 3rd 11.00 am

Pairs – Terry & Kelly

1st go – lots of giggles, then K 'we got to have a go...... you start' T – once K – upon T – a time (giggles) K there T (pause) was – (can't keep up) They're off! v. concentrated faces. Keeping mostly to story stop once. T. looks round and K. prompts ....
(Look v. smug when finished!)

11.30 class discussion T 'it was hard but I thought about the words Miss E said' Later – K 'my tongue was flapping to do more words'....

11.45 change of partners K. w. Emma – this time Emma is i charge. K. v. hesitant, watching, fiddling..... got into it i the end but not such a good story

---

12.05 group of four K much happier now – ended 'and there was no-one i the whole world who knew about the thrilling adventure'.... (with a flourish!) T. v. confident, too.
own newly invented ending?

Figure 4.9 Notes for formative assessment of speaking and listening or show the ability to use particular talk strategies on any given occasion. It is important to record what children can do – not what they can't – and they will only show their experience and assurance if they are provided with learning contexts which allow for this.

This raises the important issue of the role of the teacher when making assessments of speaking and listening: children will only be able to provide evidence of learning what the teacher makes it possible for them to learn and demonstrate that they know. Of course, children bring significant knowledge into the classroom with them – knowledge of facts; knowledge of how to use talk for particular purposes; knowledge drawn from the experience of belonging to particular families and cultural groups. They also bring their individual preferences and characteristics into the classroom and that might include preferring to wait before voicing opinions, or vocalising throughout every activity. The teacher's role is to provide opportunities for a range of experiences for all the speakers and listeners in the class.

Realistic decisions – timetabling observations

Records and assessments need to be useful and informative, otherwise they simply take up valuable teacher time and space! When observing and recording progress, an important principle is to be honest and realistic about what can be achieved. The endpoint of observing and recording is to be able to make fair assessments at the end of the year or Key Stage. Making a termly timetable of observations helps. Organising for observing one group of children – say five or six – during any one week or fortnight works well. The Record of Evidence in Fig. 4.10 shows how the first two terms' records are formative. After the first term, specific areas may become a focus for future records of progress. In the third term, observations lead to summative assessments which carry through to the following year and are also useful for discussion with parents.

Whether the observation time for each group of children is a week or a fortnight, it will be necessary to look at plans for teaching in order to ensure some coverage of contexts and learning opportunities, for example groupings, types of task, familiarity with the task, previous experience and language preference where relevant. Observations will also cover Range and Key Skills and some elements of language awareness (Standard English and Language Study in the National Curriculum). In addition to these will be notes on fluency and assurance, including the choices made by speakers in different contexts and taking into account diversity – gender, language difficulties or disorders, cultural factors influencing ways of speaking and listening.

An important element of being realistic about what can be achieved is to focus on particular aspects, not to imagine that it will be possible to cover a wide variety of these. Trying to do too much will not give helpful information. For example, a storytelling observation might focus specifically on fluency, narrative organisation and the vocabulary of story whilst a tape of a discussion might be analysed in terms of the kinds of contributions a particular child makes – asking questions, changing views according to what others have said. The key to managing observations lies in being selective.

Children who experience difficulty with speaking and listening

Many of the problems which present themselves as part of speaking and listening may not be properly to do with the development of a child's talk repertoire. Difficulties linked to oracy might well be related to behaviour or emotional causes. Nevertheless, since the individual control and extension of oracy affects learning throughout the curriculum, the behaviours accompanying talk – for example, uncontrolled volubility

RECORD OF EVIDENCE – SPEAKING AND LISTENING

Name: Kelly T. **Class:** 5 **Languages spoken:** English

TEXTS AND CONTEXTS	Term One date: 3rd Oct Type of evidence: Observation Notes	Term Two date: 12th Feb Type of evidence: short transcript	Term Three date: 24th June Type of evidence: Observation
Learning focus:	Paired story-making	Filling in database on computer – book review	Presentation after Science practical activity (investigating the spectrum)
Groupings – indicate: • pairs/small group/large group • friendship/ability/random • child/child: child/adult: all children: children with adult • older/younger • familiar/unfamiliar • same gender/different gender	child / child started with friend (T) changed partners to work with Emma Then group of four Mostly familiar boys & girls	group - familiar, mixed gender, all children	Individual to assembly
Range of purposes: e.g. exploring ideas; investigating; reporting; discussing; narrating; presenting	After a shaky start, K narrated fluently and coherently with T. Not so fluent with Emma. She can tell stories and engage others' interest.	V. capable of speculating and giving opinions. Took time to reflect. Discussed ideas thoughtfully.	Presented and summarised the group's work clearly, using evidence and examples. I was surprised at the level of clear explanation in communicating
Key skills: e.g. organising and communicating ideas; taking different views into account; listening attentively and responding accordingly; qualifying or justifying ideas	Listened well and responded suitably. Took turns in story-making very smoothly after practice. Can sustain concentration.	Delightful way of justifying ideas and giving reasons. Listens carefully to others and modifies views accordingly.	Organised ideas well. Used notes enough – not too dependent. Obviously prepared, but made it look 'natural'. Used scientific vocab. well & gave explanations.
Language awareness: e.g. reflection on own use of language; self-evaluation of key skills; use of particular register or vocabulary	In evaluation K. was very sure that she had become more fluent. Story-type vocabulary developed significantly as the task went on.	When they read the transcript, K. made very sensible comments about how they had reached decisions. Lots of KAL! Used 'lit-crit' vocab.	When we talked about it afterwards, K. mentioned how she knew she had to 'talk sensibly' to the assembly.
Fluency and assurance: speaking and listening behaviours according to context	Is confident with friends, but less sure when works with others. Not gender-related.	Showed conviction in advancing own views. Works well in groups – asks other people questions to help them.	Projected clearly to such a large audience and space. Selected suitable information.

Summary Kelly has developed splendidly in sp. & listening during the year. She has gained assurance and has benefited from the regular work with her talk partner. Although she is generally quite willing to contribute ideas, at the beginning of the year she was overfaced by the more vocal children. She can now adapt to almost any talk context. Her greatest strength is that she is a good and positive listener. With me she reveals a perky sense of humour. Future development; more story-making. She's more confident with fact and opinions than making up imaginative narratives.

Figure 4.10 A year's evidence of talk

– may well become causes for concern and it is important to act on them for the sake of the individual and the group.

Dealing with problems associated with talk raises some tricky issues, however. As outlined earlier, the way we speak is closely bound up with our personal and cultural identity, so that when a teacher wants to tackle a cause for concern in the area of speaking and listening, it needs very sensitive handling. While maintaining cultural and personal courtesy, some aspects of a child's talk repertoire may need attention. A common cause for concern is the child who does not seem to contribute much orally in any circumstances. This is difficult, since any teacher would want to respect the pupil's right to her or his own personality and if the child is naturally reflective and diffident, then this needs to be valued. However, a decision may need to be taken about the point at which this reserve is likely to affect the child's learning. This is where close observation and consultations with parents come into their own. A child may seem not to be relating socially to the other children yet reveal on systematic observation some solid and companionable collaborations with others. Or, a child may seem very quiet at school yet boisterous at home.

Before considering the kinds of actions which might be taken to help children who experience difficulties with speaking and listening, it may be worth noting on the chart in Fig. 4.11 those who present problems in the classroom.

Name	Stage of speaking and listening confidence: guided; supported; independent	Problem – mine or the pupil's?	Possible action
Phillip	supported	both – he lacks confidence and needs plenty of encouragement	small group work paired talk
Tim	independent	mine – he talks incessantly	structured turn-taking in groups, circle time

Figure 4.11 Problem speakers and listeners

Identification

A very good reason for careful identification is the effect that hearing loss, whether it is intermittent or permanent, can have on behaviour. It is estimated that up to 20 per cent of children may suffer from middle ear problems in their primary years; these are most frequently conductive hearing loss because of fluid in the middle ear which prevents the ear-drum and ossicles vibrating in response to sound waves. One manifestation of conductive hearing loss is often called 'glue ear'. These problems are different from sensori-neural hearing loss, which is permanent and usually rather more severe in its impairment. A child who has sensori-neural hearing loss may also, of course, be subject to additional conductive deafness through infection. Although school medical services and general practitioners might be able to detect some individual cases of hearing loss, the intermittent nature of conductive deafness often means that there are children whose hearing loss may go undetected until there are some other – often learning – difficulties. One important identification procedure is to make some initial observations to check a child's hearing.

A child suffering from hearing loss may show some of the following:

- ability to hear noticeably worse during and after a cold
- becoming easily tired
- not responding when called from behind
- showing untypical aggression or irritability
- speaking very softly, sometimes with nasal sound
- tendency to shout and be noisy without being aware of it
- indistinct speech, perhaps missing final consonants in speech
- apparently day-dreaming, or not concentrating particularly at listening times
- unsure about instructions
- seeking individual help much more frequently than others/than usual
- acting on some requests or instructions and not others.

At the stage of identification of a potential problem with hearing or speech behaviours, both health records and conversations with parents may reveal important information. An initial consultation with parents might also help in setting up an observation schedule at home and at school. When a child sees parents or carers and teachers working together, particularly if the child is involved at some stage in the discussions, it is likely to give greater confidence and security – or warning! – that the problem is being seriously tackled.

Observing children who experience difficulties

The schedule of observation may need to be over several weeks and will certainly need to take place during a range of classroom and school activities. Frances Lockwood, herself a teacher who has hearing impairment, stresses the effects of hearing loss in school: 'Isolation in a learning environment is the quickest way to demotivate a child, giving opportunity for a valid excuse to find distraction' (p. 114).

She points out that good organisation for learning will necessarily support children who experience permanent, intermittent or temporary hearing loss. She stresses, however, that the whole school environment can be difficult for a child experiencing hearing impairment:

> The classroom is only one area of the school in which the child is expected to learn. The library (how difficult to understand whispered instructions on how to find the coveted book; how distressing to whisper back without hearing the sound of your own voice!), playing field (the wind and a hearing aid are sworn enemies with painful effects!), and hall (I don't think I have ever understood what assemblies are for!) are all taxing on the hearing impaired child's listening skills. Classroom noises might seem innocent enough, but placing a tape recorder by a hearing aid wearer will demonstrate on playback just what is being amplified.
>
> (p. 114)

Frances Lockwood 1996 'Hearing impaired children in the classroom' in Eve Bearne ed. *Differentiation and Diversity in the Primary School*, London, Routledge

Diagnosis

Step 1: Focused observation

Observations need to be carried out in a variety of settings, during classroom learning, physical and creative activities and at playtimes. The observation record sheet in Fig. 4.12 summarises the range of talk texts, contexts and behaviours which need to be observed over a period of time. The kind of evidence used for diagnosis is also relevant, since talk is fleeting. This sheet would be completed during a period of focused observation and used to complete a full screening record (see Fig. 4.13).

Speaking and Listening screening – Observation Sheet

Name: Phillip **Class:** 4 **Year:** 1996/7

Focused observation period from: 18/9/96 **to:** 25/9/96

Observer:

Date:	**Talk texts:** e.g. narrating, asking, explaining, clarifying, describing, reporting	**Talk contexts:** e.g. collaborative learning, role play; playground grouping: pair/small group/large group friendship/ability/random familiar/unfamiliar gender	**Talk behaviours:** e.g. face and body language; eye movements and contact; does child initiate? are responses appropriate?	**Evidence:** note words spoken; evidence of learning; does talk match task? other observations
18/9 lunchtime	observed asking another child if he could play football	playground pair familiar	Phillip initiated Eye contact made	said 'can I play?'
18/9 classroom junk modelling	while other children were talking about their models P. remained quiet and detached	small group familiar all boys (irrelevant?)	Eyes downcast Body language quite relaxed; absorbed in task	None
20/9 classroom whole class reading with big book	narrating – joined in with whole class repeating phrases from book	large group teacher controlled setting	watched others' behaviour Quite animated Enjoyed story	As text of book
21/9 library	observed asking teacher how to find books on dinosaurs – led to brief discussion	one-to-one child/adult	Eyes downcast at first then more relaxed as discussion developed	offered information & talked about personal preferences with animation

Figure 4.12 Screening for difficulties with speaking and listening Step 1: focused observation (Blank provided in Appendix: A14)

SCREENING FOR DIFFICULTIES – SPEAKING AND LISTENING

Name: Phillip **Class:** 4 **Year:** 1996/7
Languages spoken: English **Term** (1) 2 3
Cause for concern: Doesn't volunteer spoken contribution in lessons. Reticent even in small groups. Other children beginning to talk for him.

Checks made on:	**Date**	**Comments**
hearing	Spring 1996	Intermittent hearing loss – glue ear
sight	N	Fine
perceptual problems		None diagnosed
physical difficulty/impairment		None apparent
medical condition		Hearing loss linked to frequent colds
other		Flushes easily when spoken to by adults

Relevant information from home:
Parents report that he is communicative at home

Most recent contact with parent/carer:
Summer Parents' Evening

Record of evidence: focused observation period from: 18·9·96 **to:** 25·9·96

Observer(s):
Peter Griffiths (class teacher) & Anne Symes (midday assistant)

Existing assessments/level of progress:
(B) on scale of progression with some significant gaps

Summary of observations:
Noisy environments don't suit Phillip – he's better in one-to-one or very controlled settings

Targets set:
Teacher to be aware of limited hearing. Encourage to ask questions when confused about tasks. Structured paired oral work.

Dates for review:
Next Term

Parents' comments:
Will re-visit G.P. re. hearing

Review and suggestions for further action:

Figure 4.13 Screening for difficulties with speaking and listening Step 2: taking action (Blank provided in Appendix: A15)

The rigour of this type of observation schedule matches the diagnostic rigour of a miscue for reading or writing. It is sensible to have more than one person observing the child over this period of time, since talk behaviour is often a reflection of the person with whom we are talking. Although the observer may not directly interact with a child during an observation period, there may be personal dynamics which influence the child's behaviour. A systematic observation schedule might be organised like this:

- Identify two or three colleagues – class teacher, SENCO, lunchtime supervisor/ teaching assistant – who will carry out observations.
- Involve the parents at this stage if it seems useful to them, the child and to you.
- Agree on the contexts in which you will observe the child – avoid duplication if you can.
- Decide on the time scale for covering a range of situations, groupings and areas of the school.
- Discuss the kinds of evidence each of you will be able to provide – try to arrange for some taped material as well as notes.
- Agree on a time for review of evidence so far (a fortnight, perhaps).

Once you have collected this initial evidence, meet again to discuss what the picture seems to be. At this stage you may want to carry out some rather more focused observations to confirm ideas for which you don't yet have enough evidence. If you think you have enough evidence the next stage is to decide what action will be taken and what targets set. This will involve a meeting with the child herself or himself and the parents. At this stage you would complete most of the screening Record of Evidence and fix a time for further review.

Step 2: Taking action

Careful observation will lead to greater information and so help in the process of deciding what action to take. If the problem seems to be medical or physical, then there may be some practical rearrangements which can be made quite quickly while further professional help is being sought. The best advice for general classroom practice is to make sure that children with hearing loss are facing the teacher, within two metres of their usual vocal range, and that the teacher uses natural rhythms of speech and volume. Sometimes, 'peer adoption' can be helpful so long as it is not bossy or intrusive; a helpful (hearing) friend can interpret or explain for those children who find gaining access to instructions difficult; this may not be those with hearing loss, of course, but children who experience other difficulties.

Often, the everyday provision in the classroom for a variety of learning styles can be the most effective way of ensuring access to the talk curriculum for all pupils. Tape recording opportunities, private and shared; talk around the computer; mixed- and single-sex groupings; visual approaches to activities; tasks which allow for different paces; chances for uninterrupted conversations with an adult; role play and spontaneous play – all of these can effectively support a range of learning needs related to speaking and listening.

Sometimes, however, focused observation identifies difficulties which the school alone, or even the school with parental support, cannot provide for. There are children, for example, who have disorders which impair their learning. There may be children who have cognitive disorders which prevent processing of spoken texts. Children who seem not to respond to the usual efforts of the class teacher and parents after careful and sensitive observation may well need referring for experienced professional diagnosis. This needs to be done as soon as possible – another reason why rigorous and systematic observations are necessary. Whilst there may be reluctance to label children, if an individual child seems to need specialised help, then the stages of

see Geoff Moss *The Basics of Special Needs* for descriptions of semantic pragmatic disorder, Attention Deficit Disorder, autism, Asperger's syndrome

referral need to be activated quickly. Fig. 4.13 gives an example of a completed screening record including proposals for action. Review after an appropriate period of time should lead to decisions about when or whether to call in other support agencies.

Describing progress in speaking and listening

Since talk is the everyday currency of the classroom, it is sometimes difficult to describe progress accurately. Changes can be almost imperceptible in the daily conversations and classroom exchanges. Talk is closely bound up with personal qualities: some people are more garrulous – or reflective – than others. It is rather too easy to judge the individual child rather than judging the child's ability to use speaking and listening effectively and sometimes our perceptions of a child's behaviour can stand in the way of accurate assessment. Also, talk can only be assessed when it is heard. This can skew judgements in favour of the apparently confident child who speaks (and listens) readily. To combat these difficulties teachers need to establish their own confident judgements about describing progress. This involves developing a vocabulary through which to describe children's competence in tackling the range of talk texts, contexts and activities which build towards fluency and assurance as a speaker and listener.

The Scale of Progression

The scale in Fig. 4.14 is the result of discussions with teachers who wanted to establish record keeping systems which supplement National Curriculum level descriptors. Most particularly, they wanted statements which describe the child's progress rather than a set of statements about what should have been taught. The Scale of Progression reflects what teachers might expect to see as children develop experience and assurance in talk. It is best seen as a basis for discussion with colleagues and, since the descriptors may not always reflect particular school circumstances, is intended to be open to adaptation. The sections have been paralleled with National Curriculum levels as a guide, but not as a programme of learning. They are not fixed categories and there is likely to be some overlap, with any individual pupil showing competence in areas in two sections. For example, in October, Kelly (whose records were shown earlier in Fig. 4.10) demonstrated all the features of section C and some of D. By June of the following year her teacher recorded her as firmly fulfilling all of section D. In National Curriculum terms she had certainly progressed from Level 3 to Level 4 and was well on the way to Level 5. Using the scales and keeping records had given her teacher a sense of where to focus to help Kelly improve.

Making progress towards fluent, assured and independent oracy begins at home. Children will enter their first nursery or school environment with greater awareness, and usually greater experience, of the spoken word than they usually bring about writing or reading. The descriptions in section A of the Scale of Progression include some which most children will have achieved before they come to school. Since there are, however, a few children whose spoken language has not developed as fast as others', or who might have language disorders, the descriptive statements in A are intended to help describe progress from very inexperienced beginnings.

The National Curriculum Exemplification of Standards in Speaking and Listening at Key Stages 1 and 2 gives broad lines of progression in the NC level descriptions as: confidence in adapting talk, using standard English when appropriate; listening with understanding; participation in discussion. The statements in the Scale of Progression are loosely grouped according to these areas, but include other aspects of talk experience as well. The descriptions within each section are not hierarchically arranged. Generally, these statements are meant to be neither all-inclusive nor

BECOMING AN EXPERIENCED SPEAKER AND LISTENER – SCALE OF PROGRESSION	Approximation to NC Levels
A Beginner speaker/listener: • indicates a range of simple needs using a range of methods of communication • anticipates a known pattern in a familiar or repetitive story • communicates enjoyment of familiar stories read aloud to a group/individual • uses simple rhythms (e.g. clapping the syllables of own name) • shows understanding of the difference between role play and real life • understands an instruction to carry a message and returns with an answer (written, verbal or signed; a single word is appropriate) • answers simple questions about themselves • listens to teacher instructions in a one-to-one situation when asked to do so • joins in familiar action songs/rhymes in a group situation.	**Moving towards Level 1**
B A speaker/listener who is gaining experience: • tells a story from given pictures and picture books in a simple sequence • plays in role for lengthy periods • talks about parts of books read and enjoyed • conveys a simple or familiar message or a written message which requires remembering a straightforward verbal answer • remembers, tells and answers questions about an area of personal knowledge or experience • listens to teacher instructions when asked to • asks for things or gets friends to ask • uses rhythmic/rhymed patterns to help read aloud • joins in a whole class group story led by the teacher • talks with others spontaneously (during play, for example) but might not genuinely converse • begins to ask other people questions.	**Level 1 to Level 2**
C A more assured speaker/listener, growing in experience: • tells a story from own pictures or recounts an event with a beginning, middle and end • structures situations in role play activities • joins in a whole class/group story without adult prompting • conveys a verbal message and brings a verbal reply independently • listens to instructions without being reminded • remembers, and tells in sequence, an event of personal significance • shows a sense of audience – waiting for quiet, speaking to be heard • talks with enthusiasm/conviction about books read, commenting beyond the literal • creates a rhythm and notices rhyme when reading aloud • explains own work to another (adult) • asks own questions in response to other people's ideas • gives reasons for opinions in discussion • listens and responds in conversation with a friend • discusses familiar issues (e.g. classroom rules) with a known group.	**Level 2 to Level 3**
D A more experienced speaker/listener: • explains an extended storyboard sequence • asks and responds to questions with some assurance • makes up questionnaires or questions	**Level 4**

Figure 4.14 Speaking and Listening Scale of Progression

• gives attention to rhyme and rhythm in discussion and performance • explains personal preferences for reading material • retells events selecting significant points with detail for a group/class audience • uses different forms of talk for different people (e.g. teacher, friend, doctor, visitor) and different situations (inc. use of standard English) • uses different and specific language and registers and/or vocabulary relating to interests or activities • with support or collaboration, presents and explains work/ideas to a large audience (e.g. assembly) • copes (verbally) with peers who present awkward behaviour in discussion groups • listens to and is tolerant of others' points of view • has an established concept of turn-taking (even if not always doing it) • organises group activities and delegates tasks.	**to** **Level 5**
E An experienced speaker/listener: • explains ideas/tells stories in clear sequence • talks about own work and partner's or collaborative work, using specific vocabulary and giving adequate explanation and reasons • re-tells someone else's ideas accurately • uses role play to create different characters, genres, situations and talk about *how* and *why* (inc. use of standard English) • gives opinions about experiences, things known or learned about • discusses books (films, TV, video, poetry) giving reasons for choice, enjoyment or dissatisfaction • talks about dialect, languages, rhythm and rhyme • gives a sustained talk to the class/group • acts as enabler as well as contributor in group discussion • debates and discusses ideas found in research materials • makes appropriate and relevant (brief) comments in large group/whole class discussion • shows empathy with others' points of view • indicates awareness of others' conversational needs.	**Level 6** **to** **Level 7**
F A very experienced speaker/listener: • makes sustained (or brief, as appropriate) contributions to large group/whole class discussions • confidently (or apparently so) initiates questions and makes contributions or offers opinions in a range of contexts • describes, presents and evaluates a piece of work or activity to a group • takes on character, creates atmosphere, sustains suspense in drama/role play • varies tone and formality according to context and subject (inc. use of standard English) • discusses literature, music, ideas with balance and conviction • listens actively and attentively, responding perceptively to ideas • understands complex ideas presented orally (e.g. when read aloud or in a lecture) and shows this understanding in the responses made • initiates and leads discussion, extending and elaborating on others' ideas when necessary • engages in discussion as a contributor and listens autonomously without reminders about turn-taking • empathises and sees the points of view of others and articulates them in a range of settings (familiar/unfamiliar, pairs/groups/whole class; with peers/adults; known/unknown).	**Level 8** **and** **beyond**

Figure 4.14 Speaking and Listening Scale of Progression (continued)

exclusive, but to indicate the experience of teachers as they have paid close attention to their pupils' speaking and listening. The use of the scale is intended to be a matter of adaptation and variation.

The progress of bilingual or multilingual learners

One important point to be made here, of course, is that any of the descriptive statements can apply to a child's home or preferred language. This is critically important in the early years, or for children who enter school later with little or no experience of English. Whilst the National Curriculum suggests that teachers should begin to assume spoken standard English at around Level 4 of the National Curriculum, it is still possible for speakers of languages other than English to be assessed as speakers and listeners in their preferred language by another speaker of that language. This is particularly relevant when one bears in mind that assessing talk is often bound up with assessing what pupils show they know about other subjects through talk. Language support teachers, parents, community leaders and siblings can play an important part here. The descriptors allow anyone (including the pupils at times) to consider how the statements describe what an individual can do in speaking and listening.

Evaluating talk and using talk to evaluate

Jerome Bruner 1986 *Actual Minds: possible worlds*, London, Harvard Educational Press

> Much of the process of education consists of being able to distance oneself in some way from what one knows by being able to reflect on one's knowledge.
>
> (p. 127)

Jerome Bruner succinctly points to the value of reflection as a means of realising – 'making real' and 'understanding' – what we know. Talk, of course, is an invaluable way of doing this; talking things over with a friend can so often result in clarifying a problem, not necessarily because the friend has offered solutions but that the very act of externalising our thoughts and feelings helps us to make decisions and come to realise what we already think. This use of talk for reflecting on and acknowledging new understanding becomes even more powerful when the subject matter of the learning is language itself. Talking about talk can open up new areas of possibility for future learning. Pupils' knowledge of language is deepened and extended by discussion and analysis of their own use of language. One of the greatest strengths of increased attention to children's talk is the opportunity for greater awareness of the ways in which language is structured.

One way of saving time when observing and assessing is to involve the pupils themselves. Apart from the pragmatic matter of sharing the load, it is useful to the children to contribute to observations, records and assessments. Such opportunities give them a chance to stand back and look at their own learning whilst discussions with the teacher about the observations help pupils to develop a vocabulary with which they can comment on their own talk and their own learning. The use of a few pointers before an activity, for example: *When you listen to each other, think about the organisation of what your partner is saying – is the opening clear, does the ending sum up ideas?* cannot only help the children respond helpfully and clearly to each other, but gives them some pointers about how talk texts are put together.

These questions were devised by Sally Elding and first appeared in *The Primary English Magazine* vol. 2.1, September/October 1996, pp. 13–16.

Guide questions about Talking Together and Learning Together (see Figs. 4.15 and 4.16) not only consolidate learning for the pupils but reveal to the teacher where any gaps need to be filled or where everyone can be assured that a particular aspect of teaching and learning has been successful.

Talking Together – What Happened?

Talk with a partner or other members of your group about the following:

How well did you listen to each other?

Was there an opportunity for everyone to say something?

Were there times when you did not keep to the point?

How did talk help you to complete the task?

Did you achieve what you were asked to do?

Did anyone dominate the talk?
Was this helpful or not?

What did anyone say that was really interesting or important?

Were there disagreements?
How were these resolved?

Did you reject any ideas? Why?

What would you say or do differently next time?

Figure 4.15 Reflecting on the dynamics of talk

Learning Together – What Happened?

Think about the activity you have just done.

Talk with a partner or other members of your group about some of the following:

What did you know before you started?

What have you learned?

Did anyone say or do something that helped you to understand?

Did anyone say or do something that you didn't understand?

What more would you like to do?

What more would you like to show?

Is there anything that still puzzles you?

Do you need to repeat this work?

If you did repeat the work, what would you do or say differently?

Figure 4.16 Reflecting on the content of talk

Taking it further – parents and talk

Because talk is taken for granted as part of everyday life, its role in learning can sometimes be misunderstood. When children are asked *What did you do at school today?* it is not unusual for them to reply *Oh we just talked*, suggesting that talk is not work. This can be one area where parents might need reassurance, particularly if their own experience of school is of silent (or supposedly silent) classrooms. Meetings and curriculum discussions in school can allay some fears and explain school practices but not all parents can manage to get into school and some find the idea of curriculum discussions daunting, fearing perhaps that they might have to speak. In meetings with parents in the early years, they can be asked to recall some of their children's sayings or the songs, rhymes and stories the children like to repeat. This information is very valuable for Baseline assessments. As children grow older, however, the fact that talk is taken for granted may mean that the only contact with parents over a child's development in speaking and listening happens when there are difficulties. It is rare for schools to hold meetings at Key Stage 2 to talk about talk; the most common public meetings relating to oracy are performances of school plays, celebrations and concerts.

see Chapter 7, pp. 316–19, for a fuller discussion of Baseline assessment

Throughout this chapter it has been emphasised that the way we talk is very much bound up with the way we feel about ourselves; other people's negative attitudes can be very damaging. It is important to encourage parents to feel confident about their children's development in speaking and listening and to explain the value and importance of talk and language study. This is particularly critical if families speak languages other than English. Parents need to be reassured about school attitudes to community languages as well as all parents being made to feel valued for their own – and their children's – ways of speaking. Whilst conveying the value given to home uses of language, however, the school has also to signal that standard forms of English are covered in the curriculum. One of the most effective and low-key ways of doing this is by asking for help from home. Fig. 4.17 gives some suggestions.

Many of the suggestions for home activities for reading and writing can be adapted to include attention to talk. See Chapter 2, pp. 68–9 and Chapter 3, pp. 136–7.

- Parents and families might be asked to help children answer language study questionnaires about their own family language histories and to contribute dialect or regional words and sayings.
- All families have favourite reminiscences about children's amusing sayings. Children might be asked to gather some of these, whilst having the right to veto any that they don't want disclosed!
- Parents, brothers, sisters, grandparents, aunts, uncles might be asked to make tapes of story books to be put in the reading area or if they are storytellers themselves, to make tapes of told stories. This can be particularly valuable if the family speaks another language or has a distinctive dialect.
- Nursery rhyme collecting often draws on a range of buried knowledge. Children studying traditional rhymes might be asked to gather as many titles as they can by asking for their parents' help.
- Some parents might be involved in public speaking of different kinds – at places of worship or in their jobs. They might be asked to come in and tell the children how they prepare for public occasions.
- Children's surveys of the range of talk contexts they encounter during a day can explicitly involve parents, too. The class might draw up a chart of the purposes, audiences and contexts for talk which they meet in a day at home (over the weekend, perhaps) and in a day at school. Taking home a survey questionnaire can signal to parents the variety of talk opportunities they offer to the children.
- Many parents work outside the home. They might be asked to contribute to a similar survey of the kinds of talk experienced in the workplace.
- Television and video are often a focus for family gatherings. If children are asked to list the number of different accents or dialects they hear during an evening's television viewing or to focus on the language of a few television advertisements, families are bound to be drawn in and encouraged to see the value of language diversity.
- Similarly, a close study of weather forecasters' or news presenters' language contrasted with the dialogue of a soap opera can be a clear signal about the importance of being able to switch between standard and non-standard forms. Or a close study of apparently standard forms might reveal greater diversity than might be imagined.

Figure 4.17 Taking it further: involving parents and the community in the development of speaking and listening

Knowledge about language: the technical features of language

Chapter Five

Language is a system of sounds, meanings and structures with which we make sense of the world around us. It functions as a tool of thought; as a means of social organisation; as the repository and means of transmission of knowledge; as the raw material of literature, and as the creator and sustainer – or destroyer – of human relationships. It changes inevitably over time and, as change is not uniform, from place to place.

Department of Education and Science 1989 The Cox Report, London, HMSO, paragraph 6.18

In outlining current theory and practice in knowledge about language, this chapter includes:

- **language as a systematic means of communication**
- **what teachers know about language**
- **a model of the English curriculum**
- **what children know about language**
- **teaching grammar**
  - **lexical knowledge and terminology**
  - **structuring writing**
  - **language variation**
  - **language used for particular effects**
- **progression in grammar**
- **teaching punctuation**
- **progression in punctuation**
- **teaching spelling**
- **progression in spelling**
- **working on spelling at home.**

Language as a system

Language is a fascinating subject. As Chapter 4 showed, everybody has opinions about how people should express themselves and each of us is unique in the way we make meaning through language. Social groups create their own language, from expressions used within families to the cultural language of young people which is ever changing and deliberately designed to separate them off from the adults who surround them. Traced through a few generations this language has included *super*, *smashing*, *brill* and *wicked*, each of them inappropriate to the next generation's cultural language. The continuing evolution of language is worth studying in its own right as a rich example of human behaviour. It is also important to study language for its linguistic patterning, too. Texts, both spoken and written, are made up of systematic patterns of language, each part having a specific relationship to others – the adjective to the noun, for example. It is important to recognise, however, that language is both social and cultural as well as a system with technical features and that the texts which can be studied as part of Knowledge About Language have to be seen in context. People learn language first of all in social contexts – in the home, in the community – and children's early language is used readily and fluently without their needing to be overtly taught the rules of its use. As Chapter 4 described, children actively generate the rules of language as they tussle to make their meanings clear. Making meaning lies at the centre of language use. However, it is also true that reflection and analysis are important processes of learning. If children are to extend their knowledge of language so as to be able to make meaning in increasingly complex ways, then studying language as a system becomes an important feature of learning and teaching.

The Language in the National Curriculum Project ran from 1989 to 1992. It was funded by the then Department of Education and Science under an Educational Support Grant. The main aim of the project was to produce materials and conduct activities to support implementation of English in line with the model of English proposed by the Kingman Report (1988) and the Cox Report (1989).

Ronald Carter ed. 1991 *Knowledge About Language and the Curriculum: the LINC Reader*, London, Hodder & Stoughton

Teaching knowledge about language

This presents a challenge to classroom teachers: how can children be helped to know more about the structures and systems of language without separating the system from its use – in other words, without taking the texts out of context? The Language in the National Curriculum (LINC) Project offers guidance: 'Language study should start from what children can do, from their positive achievements in language and from the remarkable resources of implicit knowledge about language which all children possess' (p. 4).

But at the same time, it is important to be aware of the complexities of language and the ways in which it is used. The constantly shifting nature of language means that the systems which seem to govern its use are not always fixed. In other words, it is difficult to provide hard and fast rules for language use. It is important for both teachers and children to understand the dynamic quality of language. Teaching rules or definitions of parts of language is not the best way to help children study language, although it is essential that they learn how to talk about language. This means developing a vocabulary of terminology (a metalanguage) which will enable them to extend their understanding of how language can be used to make more – and more complex

– meaning. Besides this, they need to develop ways of talking about language which can take account of its social and cultural use. The LINC project lists a possible set of headings for language study:

- variety in and between languages;
- history of languages;
- language and power in society;
- acquisition and development of language;
- language as a system shared by its users.

metalanguage: a language through which to talk or write about language. This would include terminology such as 'register', 'dialect', 'rhyme' as well as concepts such as language for reflection or persuasion

John Richmond 'What do we mean by knowledge about language?' in Carter *Knowledge About Language*, p. 38

The first three elements have been touched on in earlier chapters. Chapter 4 considered some issues of language diversity; the acquisition of language – both written and spoken – has been discussed in Chapters 3 and 4. John Richmond's last heading will be the focus for this chapter, whilst the importance of the first four areas of knowledge about language is nevertheless recognised.

What teachers know about language

There is one further important point to be considered before looking at the classroom applications of language study – the teacher's own knowledge about language. Teachers, like children, have a store of valuable knowledge about language, derived from their experience as people living in social settings. The question arises as to how they can best use this knowledge to help their pupils further their understanding of the structures and systems of language. It has been stressed in all the other chapters of this book that teachers create the environment in which children will succeed (or not) as learners. This environment is both abstract and physical – within the teacher's own head and expressed in the classroom as a physical environment. A large part of a teacher's contribution to developing language knowledge, then, will be in the opportunities and contexts offered for learning about language. This will include a recognition of the value and importance of community uses of language as well as providing classroom resources which reflect language variety. It will take into account shifts of register according to social and linguistic contexts; rather than referring to 'sloppy' or 'incorrect' speech, classroom opportunities will be provided to study the differences between spoken and written texts, between formal and informal uses of language.

The assumptions held about language, and the opportunities offered in the classroom, are the fundamental contributions teachers make based on their own knowledge about language. The next moves are to plan for deliberate and thoughtful intervention to help move the children's (and possibly their own) language study forward. This will include studying language as the *content* of particular lessons or activities, to consider its structure and workings. This often happens in informal ways where, for example, there might be a brief excursion into 'thinking about all the words we can which have the prefix *super*' or where a teacher invites children to predict the ending of a traditional story. Language study pays attention to both the large and the small shapes of text – sentence and word level as well as at the level of genres or forms of language.

English as a subject

In the National Curriculum, the details of language study are mostly included in the English curriculum. However, English as a subject is peculiar because it doesn't have the same body of knowledge as the other subjects. The emphasis is not so much on facts and concepts (although they are important to English) as texts and processes. However, the processes of English occur throughout the whole curriculum because

Texts: any pieces of language, spoken or written, from one-word utterances or notes to whole lectures or books. The **processes** of language discussed here are: ways of using language to get and convey information and learning to make discriminating choices in using language.

language is both a medium of learning as well as an object of learning in its own right. We learn through language and we learn about language. Many elements of the National Curriculum for English can be reached through other subject areas, but there are areas specific to English: Study of Language and Study of Texts. Fig. 5.1 is not intended to suggest that there are watertight categories, but represents both the texts and processes associated with teaching English. The processes on the right-hand side of the chart take place throughout the curriculum – including English lessons – but the categories on the left – the texts – are the fundamental content of the English curriculum itself.

Texts	Processes
Study of language (includes standard English): small shapes – sentences, words, phonemes, parts of speech, grammatical organisation, spelling and handwriting	**Getting and conveying information and ideas:** reading for understanding and inference, responding to reading, writing to explain, persuade, inform, entertain, awareness of readership (audience), listening and speaking for the same purposes
Study of texts (includes media texts, spoken texts and aspects of standard English): structures of texts, forms and formats, different genres, poetry, plays	**Developing discrimination:** becoming independent, choosing what to read and what not to read, commenting on own and other people's writing (including published authors), using different registers in speaking

Figure 5.1 A model of the English curriculum

Developing a vocabulary to talk about language

Reflection on language is important. In many areas of the curriculum language is transparent – it is used as the medium of teaching and learning but not looked at for its own sake very often. Yet the language associated with mathematics, or art, or physical education is important in helping children grasp essential concepts in those areas of the curriculum. For example, what does 'figure' indicate in mathematics and what does it mean in art? There are many examples where language is used specifically in different curriculum areas and it is important to consider the vocabulary of the subject. In English, the specific vocabulary is to do with texts or words and teachers use a wide variety of technical terms in the course of a teaching day or week. For example:

letter, word, phrase, sentence, noun, verb, adjective, adverb, capital letter, full stop, comma, hyphen/dash, question mark, speech marks, exclamation mark, colon, semi-colon, apostrophe, paragraph, punctuation, plural, connective, upper case, lower case, consonant, vowel, brackets, caption, heading, description, explanation, account, narrative, notes, tense, beginning/opening, middle, dramatic moment, end/conclusion, flash back, flash forward, onomatopoeia, rhyme, rhythm, alliteration, poem, dialogue, discuss, predict, etc.

And, of course, there are many more. Whether at Key Stage 1 or 2 teachers are continually teaching and reinforcing reflective language about language. In talking about reading or writing about reading; in talking about writing; in talking about talk or in writing about language in journals or reviews of work, grammatical terms are constantly in use. It might be worth spending a moment thinking about the language you have used to talk about language in the past week. How many of the above list did you use? It is often claimed that the technical aspects of language – grammar, punctuation and spelling – are no longer part of what teachers teach. If you take a moment to list the terminology you and colleagues use in the classroom, what quickly becomes clear is that, contrary to popular myth, grammar *is* being taught and language *is* being carefully studied. The issues which this chapter will focus on are related to how to develop systematic and effective ways of studying language:

- How can children's implicit knowledge about language – at both textual level and word and sentence level – be made explicit?
- How does this relate to reading and writing texts of different kinds?
- How can teachers plan for progress in developing children's Knowledge About Language?

Attitudes to grammar

Any discussion of grammar seems to create quite passionate reaction. Recent interest in knowledge about language has unearthed at least three kinds of response to the issue of why and how children should learn grammar. The traditional, almost stereotypical, response is that 'it is good for you' in some unspecified sense. There is a view that learning grammatical constructions and terminology is a healthy mental discipline. At the opposite end of the debate there are those who might say that children learn how to speak, read and write their mother tongue 'naturally' and that there is no need to teach the structural elements separately. These views are not helpful: the first because it is based on a lack of understanding about the nature of grammar as well as a view that learning is simply memorising; the second because it denies children access to an important and fascinating aspect of language study. There is, however, a third commonly held view – one of hesitancy because of lack of knowledge, or lack of confidence in knowledge. The fact of the matter is that teachers do – and must – teach grammar. The arguments arise about how best to do it. But perhaps the first obstacle to be overcome is that of teacher confidence.

Teachers need to demonstrate that their own teaching of grammar is sound, systematic and founded on an informed understanding about language. What does this imply? First of all, it involves identifying our own attitudes to grammar. Then it means recognising the implicit (and often explicit) knowledge which every teacher has about language. Whenever any part of the curriculum becomes an object of study, it is important to be able to use, and pass on to the children, the appropriate vocabulary of that subject. When you are concentrating on knowledge about language, or the standard English components of the National Curriculum, this means using the language of grammar. You can start identifying what you know about grammar by asking yourself whether you are confident about grammatical terms. And if you are confident, why is that? If not, why not? Much depends on the ways in which teachers themselves were introduced to the language of grammar. It would be worth taking a moment or two to recall how you were taught grammar. What memories do you have?:

- Were you taught grammar at school?
- Primary or secondary? Or at college/university?
- In which lessons?
- What can you remember from those lessons?

- How difficult or easy did you find learning grammar?
- Why do you think that was?
- What have you learned about grammar since leaving school/college?

Looking back on it now, what do you think was the purpose of teaching you grammar? And how effective was it? How do you use that knowledge in your own teaching?

Attitudes towards dealing with grammar in the classroom are also very often influenced by people's reactions towards our own ways of speaking. Negative comments about our language may well lead to negative views about teaching or studying grammar. As Chapter 4 made clear, comments about 'poor grammar' are very often nothing to do with grammar at all but judgements about the perceived value of different ways of speaking – particularly about people's accents. Whilst it is important to have a responsible view of teaching children standard forms of English – particularly written English – it is equally important to separate judgements made about individuals on the basis of social or cultural opinion (perhaps prejudice) and judgements about the linguistic organisation of how people speak and write.

A very simple definition of 'grammar' is that it describes the set of patterned possibilities through which the speakers (or writers) of a language communicate meaning to other speakers, writers, listeners and readers in their own speech community. In short, it describes the syntax of a language. In English, I might say *I'm going to London today*; in German I would say *Heute soll ich nach London fahren* (Today, shall I to London travel). Those are the distinctly different grammars of the two languages. If someone says *I ain't goin'* or *She be fair mithered*, they are not speaking ungrammatically since the syntax is recognisably that of English. The first is an example of colloquial speech with dialect use of 'ain't' and the second is an example of dialect use with a specifically regional way of using a personal pronoun and vocabulary. In each case the speaker may well be able to speak a more standard form of English at will. If a speaker said *Grass green is* or missed out all the verbs in sentences, then those would be examples of incorrect grammar. However, with native speakers of a language this is so rare as to be unknown except where a speaker might have a language disorder. Studying grammar in the classroom means looking closely at the patterned ways in which language is used to make meanings in different kinds of texts.

Planning for grammar teaching

A good starting point for planning would be to ask: what do children need to know about grammar? Answers to this might include:

- *lexical knowledge:* knowledge of word meanings, structures and derivations (morphology); also knowledge of the alphabetic system (graphology) and the sound system of spoken words (phonology) and how these two systems are related;
- *terminology:* knowledge of some of the language of grammar – terms needed for commenting on language, for example: adjective, noun, paragraph, dialogue;
- *how to structure writing:* knowledge of the different ways in which texts are put together for different purposes or intentions and how and when to use standard English or non-standard forms. This would include different genres of writing, for example: a letter to a friend, a newspaper sports report, an advertisement. It would also include being able to use the word endings and transformations appropriate to the written form to show tenses and singular/plural, for example: came, helped, thought, sheep, ladies, monkeys, children;
- *language variation:* knowledge of the flexibility of language. This would include differences between spoken and written forms of language used in different contexts with different people, for different reasons: dialect and standard forms,

informal and formal ways of speaking and writing, different kinds (or genres) of spoken texts, for example: a prepared talk, a conversation, a reprimand;

- *language used for particular effects:* knowledge of the ways in which writers make grammatical choices in order to put across a message. This means developing a critical sense of written or spoken language and the ways in which it can be used to persuade, gain sympathy, include or exclude others, for example the verbs used in reporting or commentating on a football match, or the culturally exclusive language of experts in different types of pop music.

A second question might be: what terminology is important for the age-group you teach? Before listing these terms, however, it might be worth looking back at the vocabulary you already identified (p. 195). A group of colleagues could very quickly develop a progressive programme of knowledge about language by answering the following questions, first of all individually, then looking across the Key Stage or across the whole phase:

- What grammatical terminology do you already use with your class?
- What terms do you hear the children use?
- What other terms do you think could be included?

A prompt for the last question might be to look in the National Curriculum for English and note the kinds of terminology used there for your particular Key Stage. Assembling each teacher's list from Nursery/Reception through to Year 6 will give you a basis for considering unnecessary repetition, the kinds of repetition needed for consolidation, as well as any gaps. Fig. 5.2 shows a format for recording uses of grammatical terminology.

	Terms introduced
R	letter, word, vowel, sentence, consonant, story, author, illustrator
Yr 1	rhyme, rhythm, intonation, caption, dedication, beginning, middle, end
Yr 2	phrase, joining words, verbs, explanation, headings, index, contents, paragraphs, chapters
Yr 3	section, statement, adjectives, nouns, headlines, plural and singular
Yr 4	tenses of verbs, agreements, synonyms, antonyms, homophones, homonyms
Yr 5	negative/affirmative, adverbs, idiom, text structure, flashback, connectives, dialogue, direct/reported speech
Yr 6	genre, register, simile, metaphor, anthology, standard English, argument & persuasion

Figure 5.2 Current use of grammatical terminology – a Year 3 class

Children's knowledge about language

see Fig. 5.1, the model of the English curriculum on p. 194

Before going on to discuss how grammar is (or could be) taught, it is important to discover what your pupils already know about language – about the smaller units and the larger grammars of whole-text organisation. A first step would be to have a notepad in the classroom and during the course of a few days note down any terminology about language which you hear the children using. This gives a view of their explicit knowledge about language. However, there is also the reservoir of implicit knowledge which is worth tapping. Children's writing is a good indicator of their implicit knowledge of language, revealed through the ways in which they structure sentences and longer stretches of text. The following case study offers a chance to examine a 6-year-old's writing for what it reveals of her knowledge about language.

What does Anna reveal she knows about the large and small text structures of English?

Case Study 5

Anna's knowledge about language

A very close look at both the process and the end result of one child's story writing reveals the extent of knowledge brought to just one act of composition. This analysis of her writing is based on the writing miscue procedure explained in Chapter 3.

pp. 123–32

Anna was 6 years 4 months old when she wrote this story. She decided on the title for herself and when invited to begin writing settled straight away. When she had written her title she re-read it. She wrote one line then drew the first of the small pictures. As she continued to write she was re-reading. Occasionally she would gaze upwards then get back to writing with gusto. At one point she repeated *shut the door* several times (she later altered the spelling of 'door'), gazed into mid-space, then got back to the writing. After about ten minutes when she was asked if she had nearly finished, she said *I'm getting to an exciting bit.* After about twelve minutes she drew another picture and re-read her work. She then added another sentence and repeated it to herself. She was invited to re-read and she altered a word round about line 5 ('shut'). She read the piece aloud quietly to herself before reading it to the teacher.

Anna talked to herself throughout the writing, sometimes sub-vocalising the story as she wrote it, but also commentating on what she was doing. During the writing she seemed very much at ease. When she was asked to read the piece aloud immediately after writing it she read without much expression and rather haltingly. The piece is annotated to indicate how she read:

> The Princess and the Unicorn
>
> One day a princess said to the king [*I* self-corrected] Am I old en-ough to go into the woods yes said the king you are see she put her coat and shut the door and crossed the road and went down the little passage that led to the little wood, suddenly she heard a rattle she saw a white thing it was a unicorn wow she said she got on it she rode it to the king. Here. The king was cross he sent her away so he could have the horse she ran to the pond and wished for the mermaid and the mermaid came at [repeated *at*] the [*what's that?* Teacher supplied *out of the water*] out of the water she said [*I wish* self-corrected] I will make your father send you back. The end.

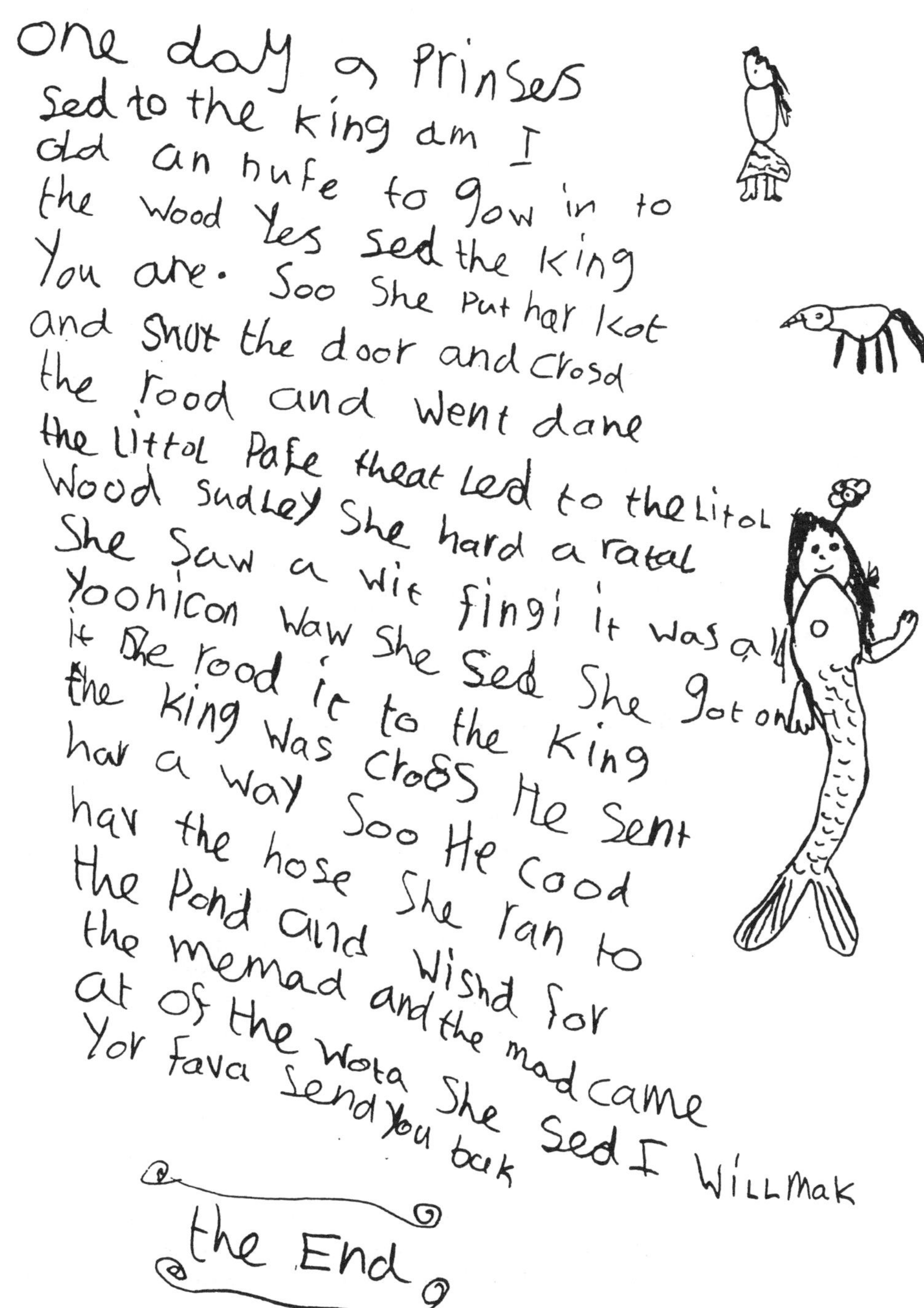

the Prinses and the Yoonicon

One day a Prinses
sed to the king am I
old an nufe to gow in to
the Wood Yes sed the King
You are. Soo She Put har kot
and Shut the door and Crosd
the rood and went dane
the littol Pafe theat led to the Litol
Wood sudley She hard a ratal
She Saw a wit fingi it was a
Yoonicon waw She sed She got on
it She rood it to the King
the King Was cross He sent
har a way Soo He cood
har the hose She ran to
the Pond and Wishd for
the memad and the mad came
at of the Wota She Sed I WiLLMak
Yor fava Send You bak

the End

Figure 5.3 Anna's story *The Princess and the Unicorn*

What Anna knows about reading and writing

In conversation afterwards, Anna said that she liked the bit she had written about the mermaid best *because she comes and gives you a wish*. When asked if she usually writes stories like this she said *Mmmm mostly fairy stories about fairies and stuff*. She had no hesitation in identifying the piece of writing she had done recently that she was most pleased with: *The Treasure Box – it's one I've done pages and pages of – lots of writing. There's three girls and they're all poor and they go on a journey and they go underneath the sea and find the treasure box and they come rich*. She writes it mostly at home although she did bring it into school once.

Anna likes reading stories and poems to herself and prefers it when her dad reads to her because he reads more than her mum. *In 'Charlie and the Chocolate Factory' if I ask mummy she only does one chapter but if I ask daddy he does two or three*. In reply to the question *How did you know how to write the story like that? – to write 'one day . . . ?*, Anna replied, *I just usually put 'one day' but Daddy usually puts 'once upon a time' – he thinks once upon a time is better*. She said that her father tells her which bits he likes best when he reads the stories she has written.

Anna is a child who emphatically sees herself as a writer. She is comfortable with the act of writing and knows the pleasure to be gained from writing lengthy stories. She also knows what she likes about her own work and something about the process going on in her own head as she writes. Much of this is based on her own experience of stories being told and read to her at home and at school. She has a well-developed strategy for re-reading to ensure that she is keeping the flow of her story. Her comments indicate that she has no shortage of ideas for imaginative narrative. She made two alterations and got them right.

What Anna knows about text structure

She knows the shape of the whole piece and it unwinds as she writes. She has a good sense of what makes a story interesting – the mermaid's magic – and develops character – the greedy king and the resourceful princess. She also develops setting and uses all sorts of intertextual references to create her own story – *Am I old enough to go into the wood?* (like Red Riding Hood) – as well as the video and traditional tale characters of the little mermaid and the unicorn. In structuring the piece of writing she indicates in the text that she knows that a reader needs detail. She creates character immediately before setting the scene, then gives delightful detail of the actions of the princess in a narrative rhythm – *put on her coat, shut the door and crossed the road and went down the little path that led to the little wood*. She uses this to build to a climax for the complication of the plot *and suddenly* . . . and introduces the magic mysteriously – *she heard a rattle and saw a white thing* – she certainly knows how to hook the reader in!

Anna uses narrative structure very surely to unfold a complicated story. She is aware of different ways to start stories, and is not afraid to plunge straight into the dialogue before leading the reader carefully through the setting towards the problem the princess has to deal with. The resolution to the story is also sophisticated since she leaves us knowing that all will be well, but doesn't feel the need to give us a scene where the mermaid makes the king give back the unicorn. She has been able to work within time constraints to make a complete narrative. She not only uses known story structures but moulds them into new ideas for her own purposes. The illustrations follow the form of the story, echoing the introduction of the characters.

What Anna knows about language

Anna very effectively varies technical features. She knows how to invite and hold the reader's attention by carefully balancing sentences. This comes from her developed capacity to hear the rhythms of narrative in her head. Although she does not mark sentence boundaries consistently, when she read the piece aloud she showed that her implicit knowledge of syntax was sound and consistent. The syntax she uses is complex and varied. A quick look at the sentence openers alone shows how remarkably sophisticated the syntax is. It follows the rhythms of told and heard story, using repetition and contrast between long and short sentences as, for example, in the first two sentences, the second of which is particularly delightful. She builds tension with short sentences: *Suddenly she heard a rattle. She saw a white thing. It was a unicorn* and balances these with *He sent her away so he could have the horse* and *She ran to the pond and wished for the mermaid and the mermaid came out of the water*. She also shows that she can distinguish between different transformations of both regular and irregular verb endings for tenses and can use the modal 'will' appropriately.

Although there are only two full stops in the piece, when Anna read it aloud she stopped at the end of sentences. The title indicates that she also knows where to put capital letters. Her vocabulary is varied. Although she uses the language of fairy tale she also uses everyday language – *a white thing; the king was cross; wow she said*. Nevertheless, her chosen vocabulary is well suited to the piece. Her repetition of 'little' is deliberate and enhances the build-up to the complication in the narrative. In 127 words she spells 85 conventionally. There are clear patterns to Anna's attempts at conventional spelling:

- She draws on her knowledge of the sound system to attempt to relate this to the graphic system, using phonetically convincing words – *prinses, yoonicon, crosd*.
- She is able to use phonic knowledge successfully for *king, cross, send*, etc.
- She uses a simple 'd' instead of 'ed' for past participles and 'ol' instead of 'le' consistently.
- In reading the piece aloud she split words like *enough* and *away*, and in attempting to spell them she divides them again by using her phonic knowledge and an awareness of morphology, as well as a sense of the relationship between graphology and phonology.

morphology: word meanings, structure and derivations; **phonology:** the sound system of spoken words; **graphology:** the alphabetic spelling system

Moving Anna's writing forward

Since Anna is so good at intuitively structuring stories, a move towards helping her make further progress would be to talk to her about story structure so that she can get even better at it, perhaps trying flashbacks eventually. She might also be encouraged to discuss the differences between the structure of stories and, for example, instructions or poems. She would have some interesting things to say! It would be worth looking closely at her other writing to see if she is equally successful with poetry, instructions, explanations. She may need some structured help to shift her away from constant stories about magic and princesses, without preventing her from continuing to choose to write such stories at times.

She should be helped to build on her ability to re-read by learning strategies for attempting to put in full stops and beginning to identify a few words which she thinks may not be correctly spelt. Her awareness of punctuation could be developed by asking her to read her own work aloud more often. Her spelling can be built on through her phonic knowledge and noticing and practising some patterns of word endings, although she needs more attention to word shape recognition.

All in all, this piece of text shows a high level of literary and structural knowledge as well as a sure grasp of grammatical conventions. At a little more than 6 years old, Anna has a fund of knowledge about language in its large and smaller shapes which she draws on

Eve Bearne with thanks to Anna from St Philip's Church of England primary school, Cambridge

freely. When she is invited to reflect on her own writing she has some interesting things to say. She can succinctly tell a story with a complex narrative structure (*The Treasure Box*) as well as being able to talk about the choices she might have made in opening her story. She is also aware that there are different ways you could do it and that she has the right to hold a different view from an adult. In terms of progress in developing knowledge about language, it is clear that Anna can be invited to reflect – and act – on her writing with the promise of further success.

Anna's immense reservoir of knowledge about language raises the question about how that implicit knowledge can be made explicit. It also prompts questions about how she can be moved on in her knowledge and how the other children in the class might similarly be helped to recognise and expand their knowledge about language. Helping children to reflect on language is essential if they are to develop new and more ambitious ways of using language to make meaning. However, if children are to be encouraged to think and talk about language through the medium of specific terminology, there remains the matter of how these terms are taught. Whilst they might be introduced and consolidated by specially developed activities, many of them arise from the everyday reading, writing, speaking and listening which is part of continuing English teaching. Most particularly, the kinds of texts used for reading – individually, as groups and as whole classes – are the most usual and fruitful resource. Classroom reading can help in developing knowledge about the larger textual structures as well as the more usual sentence level constructions usually associated with grammar.

Text grammars – or genres

The notion of a grammar – patterned possibilities of language which are recognised and used by all members of a particular speech community – can also help in thinking about the structures of longer texts. 'Story grammars' in particular have become a focus for some linguists who have traced recurrent patterns in the ways in which narratives of different kinds are put together. Children know about, and can be helped to make explicit, structures of language which are longer than the basic and most usual unit of grammar – the sentence. They very often enter school able to predict how a story which begins *Once upon a time* or *In a far off land* might continue. They can often talk about the kinds of characters that might be involved in a story like that, and even suggest a possible ending – *And they all lived happily ever after*. It is often through narrative that children enter the world of language study.

Particularly in the early years of schooling, narrative is a useful way of identifying what children know about texts of all different kinds – including non-narrative. It is also an effective way of promoting and extending that knowledge. Much of social life is entwined with narratives – from the conversations we have when we get home about *How has your day been?* to the ways we encourage particular kinds of behaviour in younger members of the community. Many religious texts have narratives as the essential vehicle for teaching principles and religious beliefs. The parables of the Bible or the teaching stories of the Sufis or any other cultural or religious group bear witness to the primacy of narrative in any culture's meaning-making activities. Since narrative is a powerful way of teaching in families and communities, it is an ideal bridge from home-based learning to school-based study. Knowing the patterns (or grammars) of told stories leads into constructing written texts.

In everyday terms, narrative texts can be organised to explain, persuade, hypothesise, argue and entertain (and a lot more). Children's narratives can often be seen as making hypotheses as they explore the possible worlds allowed by story: *What if I could fly to the moon?* or *What if teddy could speak?* In constructing stories about going to the moon or teddy talking to other toys, children test the boundaries of imagination, checking out the real worlds against the imaginary – and they have abundant models to help them try on different ideas for size. Very often, young children combine ideas from other texts in their own narratives and show that they have literacy knowledge drawn from a variety of sources.

Using literature to develop knowledge about language

Even very young children can reveal that they know a lot about language and how it is used. This often comes from the stories and other books which have been read with them and to them. Sonnyboy and his cousin Emily, Traveller children, show their knowledge about text in a conversation while they are 'reading'. He is telling her his version of the story *The Avocado Baby* while he turns the pages of the book to show her the pictures:

SONNYBOY: You know this 'un – it's about that strong kid – the one that ate that pear thingy . . .
EMILY: What kid?
SONNYBOY: You remember the one – the poor babby boy as weak as a floppy dolly – that poor little boy, a poor weak little babby. His mam and his da fretted an' fretted about him being that weak. Then they buyed him this pear thingy – not a pear like on an ordinary tree – a great big magic pear that hung in a magic place. A' his mam cut it and mashed it an' he ate it all up an' from that minute he got stronger and stronger, an' – till he could break his bed to bits.
EMILY: He never done that – you jus' made that bit up.
SONNYBOY: An' that's just what you do with stories. You can make 'em up all you like, all you wants to.
EMILY: You cannot, Sonnyboy. You got to read them words.
SONNYBOY: Nah – I knows that story. I know about him gettin' strong wid pear – and his mam buyed a lot o' them so's he'd get the strongest in the whole world, stronger than the thief what came in the night and all the wild devils who creep round the house and bit his dog to death. . .
EMILY: That's a real creepy story. It never says it like that.
SONNYBOY: *My* story does – how 'ould you know?

Hughes and Cousins, 'The roots of oracy', p. 119

Sonnyboy is 6 years old and is just starting to get to grips with literacy. But even though he is not at the stage of reading the words on the page, he demonstrates a sophisticated knowledge about texts and draws on a range of linguistic resources. His storytelling has the rhythms of an accomplished narrator – repetition for effect, asides, metaphor, hyperbole. He draws on book language, or at least the ornate language of practised story making, to enhance the effect of his telling: *a great big magic pear that hung in a magic place* and *the strongest in the whole world, stronger than* . . . He also knows how to manipulate his audience, evoking sympathy with the image *the poor babby boy as weak as a floppy dolly*. But it is even more impressive that he can make explicit some of the things he knows about text – that stories can be changed, that they are constructs made up to entertain and, importantly, that he can be an independent story maker. It is also clear that although Sonnyboy uses his home dialect 'buyed' instead of the standard form 'bought' he is, quite clearly, using grammatically conventional sentence structures. It would be easy to think that Emily's role in this conversation is only as the responder, but she, too, reveals that she knows things about texts – different things from Sonnyboy's knowledge. Emily knows that books have words which can be read to take the meaning from the page; she knows that you can check what is said against what is printed. She also knows the difference between a told story and a written one.

Picture books as reservoirs of knowledge about language

Picture books can often be powerful ways to release children's knowledge about how language works. Pictorial narrative can help children develop their knowledge about the larger shapes of text organisation and picture sequences can often be starting points for children's own spoken or written narratives. Further than that, they can be vehicles for non-narrative writing. Fig. 5.4 shows a piece of explanatory writing by Imelda (aged 8) which came from a familiar type of activity after the children had looked at *Dr Xargle's Book of Earthlets* by Jeanne Willis and Tony Ross. The children had been asked to write about a familiar object as if explaining it to Doctor Xargle's class. Imelda not only had to think carefully about descriptive explanation using language which does not give away too many clues, she also adopted the kind of familiar communicative tone which is much more like speech written down than written language alone. This echoes the tone of the book which had been used as a stimulus and model. However, it is not enough simply to note the implicit knowledge about language that Imelda, or any other writer, reveals. If narrative is to be used as a means of releasing and increasing children's knowledge about language, it is important to identify the kinds of interventions teachers might make to move children forward.

I am an Alien from outer Space and I've Come
down to discover new things on the plant
earth I've seen loads and loads of weird
Objects including something called a hou
which was very peculiar I also Came
across a very weird thing I dont no
what it was Called but it is Certain
a very funny object. The shape of it
was well I'm not quite sure of the
shape but it was about as tall as
a humanbeing and it has a hole
which people feed square thing's throu
with squiggly lines on. And every morn
a man with a hat on Comes and op
its tummy empties it and then he dr
away again

Answer post box

Figure 5.4 A mystery object described after reading *Dr Xargle's Book of Earthlets*

Teaching grammar

Classroom experience and thoughtful observation make it clear that isolated grammar exercises are not the most efficient way to help children develop their knowledge about language. However, there is still a need to help children get to grips with the way language works and to learn how to use an increasingly full vocabulary to describe what they know about the way language works. Page 196 set out some categories for the kinds of knowledge children ought to have: *lexical knowledge and terminology, how to structure writing, language variation and language used for particular effects.* The following suggestions for activities are grouped within those categories.

Lexical knowledge is dealt with more fully in the section on spelling, pp. 224–34.

Lexical knowledge and terminology

Using stories

Figure 5.5 Collecting adjectives from familiar stories

Storytelling can be used as a basis for talking about character and beginning to collect adjectives, verbs, nouns, adverbs, prepositions, pronouns, etc. Traditional stories often use repetition and lists, so that re-tellings can be used to put the spotlight on almost any part of speech, for example prepositions in: *over* the stile, *through* the wood, *under* the trees, *across* the stream, or even to have fun with alphabetical order by giving each person who stuck to the golden goose, for example, a name beginning with A, B, C, etc. Told stories can be the basis for discussing conjunctions, past, present and future tenses, for talking about flashback and prediction.

Story books are also a rich resource for activities from consolidating lexical knowledge to considering whole structures of text. Fig. 5.6 gives some examples.

Children's books can also offer useful models for children making their own alphabet books or stories emphasising particular parts of speech. Graeme Base's *Animalia* is a good model for this. A whole class could make a big alphabet book or display, based on alliterative sentences featuring adjectives or verbs: *Angry Anna, Big Benjamin, Careful Carrie* . . . or *anteaters amble along the plain, bees buzz about the trees, crocodiles creep into the river* . . .

Harmondsworth, Picture Puffin

Older readers can make thesauruses or dictionaries based on interesting language drawn from their novel reading. In order to give each individual, pair or group some

Verbs

Princess Smartypants **by Babette Cole (Young Lions)**

An alternative version of a common theme in fairy tales with an unhappy outcome for the persistent prince. Contains verbs for 'ways of telling': she ***asked, challenged, invited, called on . . . to, sent, suggested, told, commanded***. The capable Prince Swashbuckle finally ***fed*** the pets, ***roller-discoed, rode, rescued, found*** and ***retrieved*** the magic ring. He still got ***turned*** into a gigantic warty toad for his pains!

Travelling to Tondo **(a Tale of Nkundo of Zaire) retold by Verna Aardema (Bodley Head)**

The journey of a pigeon, a python and a tortoise to the wedding of their friend, the civet cat, in Tondo. Verbs for animal movements: ***running, flying, streaking, scurrying, walking, flapping, slithering, waddling.***

We Went to the Park **by Shirley Hughes (Walker Books)**

A counting book about what a little girl sees on her trip to the park with her Grandpa, for example three ladies ***chatting***, five children ***playing***, six runners ***running***, seven dogs ***chasing***, eight boys ***kicking***, nine ducks ***swimming***, ten birds ***swooping***.

Adjectives

Dr Xargle's Book of Earthlets **(an alien's view of earth babies) translated into human by Jeanne Willis and Tony Ross (Red Fox)**

Highly amusing lessons on human babies delivered by an alien professor not well versed in Earth language descriptive words. Lovely basis for work on appropriate/ inappropriate adjectives.

Good Days, Bad Days **by Catherine Anholt (Orchard Picture Books)**

Picture book with simple labelling text. Words to describe days, e.g. ***dull*** days, ***rainy*** days, ***sunny*** days, ***sad*** days.

Two Tiny Mice **by Alan Baker (Kingfisher)**

Beautiful life-like illustrations in a picture book of countryside animals. Simple large print text including descriptive words of each animal: ***tiny*** harvest mice, ***soft furry*** rabbit, ***shuffling, snuffling*** mole, ***shy little*** hedge sparrow.

Figure 5.6 Using story books to teach grammar

responsibility, the alphabet can be shared between a group or pairs of children in a class and word meanings or derivations discussed in groups and with the whole class.

Language games

These are an inevitable part of any teacher's repertoire. Most of these are cumulative and alphabetic, for example, *When I went on my holiday I packed an apple, . . . a bingo game,*

. . . *a comb*, . . . but they could equally well be focused on specific parts of speech, particularly for older pupils. For example, adverbs and verbs: *I went on my holiday and I anxiously awaited the aeroplane, bashfully boarded the bus, carefully carried my cases* . . . Connectives/conjunctions can be used for language games: *I went to the shops and bought a pumpkin* BUT (and here someone else takes over and has to add to the game) *it was too big to carry* SO . . . A useful model for this kind of activity is the picture book *Michael* by Tony Bradman and Tony Ross. Michael's teachers think he will come to no good but Michael is secretly planning and building a rocket. He eventually escapes by blasting off into space. It has repeated sentences for modelling *but* as a connective, e.g. *He liked numbers* **but** *not the sort of sums they did in school. He liked art* **but** *not the sort of drawing they did in school.*

published by Andersen

Reading and writing poetry

Poetry can be used to talk about all aspects of language. It is one of the most useful resources for attention to spelling and punctuation as well as grammatical terminology. Children can be asked to identify particular parts of language – verbs, for instance – in a given poem and then write their own poem modelled on the original. As an example, Walter de la Mare's poem 'Silver' not only gives the chance to look at rhyme, but to examine adjectives, adverbs, and verbs as well as how language changes over time:

Slowly, silently, now the moon
Walks the night in her silver shoon.
This way, and that, she peers and sees
Silver fruit upon silver trees;
One by one the casements catch
Her beams beneath the silvery thatch;
Couched in his kennel like a log,
With paws of silver sleeps the dog;
From the shadowy cote the white breasts peep
Of doves in a silver-feathered sleep;
The harvest mouse goes scampering by,
With silver claws, and silver eye;
And moveless fish in the water gleam,
By silver reeds in a silver stream.

Children might be asked to start each line of a poem with two adverbs, or to use one adjective throughout as the poet has done. Acrostics are possibly the most familiar kinds of 'formula' or pattern poetry, but other patterns – for example:

noun	night
adjective, adjective	dark, gloomy
verb	creeping
adverb	cautiously
preposition	towards
noun	morning

cannot only produce effective, pared down, language, but act as a visual reminder of the kinds of words used. 'Formulae' like this can also be used for alliterative writing.

Collections and displays

These are also part of the teacher's existing repertoire, but can be given a grammatical twist by the kinds of words or phrases collected. Homophones – *told/tolled* and

homophones: words which sound the same but are spelt differently; **homonyms:** words which are spelt the same but pronounced differently

homonyms *bow/bow* can be cumulatively assembled. Words which can be two parts of speech, e. g. verbs which are also nouns: ***roll** down the hill* and ***roll** of carpet* are also good for list-gathering, particularly if their pronunciation makes a difference: *I am pleased to **present** you with this **present**.* Newspaper headlines and advertisements are a very rich source of such dual meanings and a clippings board might be a feature for display. Jokes are perhaps the most fertile area of all, depending as they do on word play and pun. Children who understand and can tell jokes are demonstrating some very sophisticated implicit knowledge about language.

Structuring writing

Story and information books

Story books are part of the staple diet when teaching about language structure. When children hear the rhythms of texts read aloud their 'mental ears' become attuned to how to read texts aloud, and then how they sound inside their heads. Repeated sentences as in Jill Murphy's *Peace At Last!* or *Lullabyhullaballoo* by Mick Inkpen, for example, give young children very clear models for making their own sentence-based books using different nouns or verbs, for example, from the original: *The **princess** is **sleeping**, the **knights** are **clanking**, the **ghosts** are **oo ooing**.*

London, Macmillan

London, Hodder & Stoughton 1993

A variation on this would be to have sets of cards with different parts of speech for each set. Nouns might be on blue card, verbs on green, prepositions on red, for example, so that children could learn the pattern of simple sentences by making their own. The game would be to make blue, green, blue (the cat drinks the milk) or blue, green, red, blue (the cat sits on the mat) sentences. The backs of the cards are named noun, verb, preposition so that the children learn the names of the parts of speech. This can be adapted to include adjectives (yellow, perhaps) and adverbs (purple) or any other part of speech which you want to focus on at that time. Similarly, pronouns (on pale blue) can be introduced as substitutes for the (blue) nouns. There are many variations on this and it encourages very young children to become involved in naming parts of speech in contexts which make sense to them even before they can write extensive sentences themselves.

Comparing texts

This can be a useful way to help children pay close attention to both the larger elements of text construction and the smaller features. At the level of whole text organisation as well as at sentence and vocabulary level, children can be asked to compare different versions of the same story. What language differences are there between a modern version of *Cinderella* and a traditional version? How much dialogue is used, how much descriptive detail? If you listed the verbs, what might they tell about the different versions? And what about the endings, the characters, the incidents which have to be in the story or which can be omitted? How might the story be told as a newspaper article? What difference would that make to the 'beginning, middle, end' structure?

Comparison is often used in looking at the differences between two different newspaper versions of the same story but how often are children invited to compare information given in a range of information books? And how often are they specifically asked to look at the language which is used? Older pupils can be asked to focus on particular kinds of language, like explanations of processes: how do two different books explain about the Viking invasions or the working of the four-stroke engine? Younger children might be asked to look at captions and headings – what are the differences? Which is more helpful or informative? They might also be asked to consider how the pictorial text adds to information.

Chapter 6, pp. 284–92, has a section on structuring information texts.

Poetry is another rich area for discussing comparative structures of texts and why they might be different, for example the differences between haiku and narrative poetry, or the different effects of rhyming and non-rhyming poems. Then there are valuable areas to discuss in the differences between poetry and prose.

Language variation

Narratives, poetry with dialogue, or plays themselves offer useful ways into discussing the differences between regional or geographical dialects and standard English, or between formal and informal ways of speaking and writing.

A very rich resource for language variation, however, is the television and the kinds of videos the children are familiar with. Snippets from advertisements, extracts from a range of children's programmes or from news reports and weather forecasts, all provide useful material for discussion of – and practice in – language variation. Role play will quickly establish whether children can intuitively detect differences between standard spoken forms of English and more everyday colloquial usage. Presenting a weather forecast and fronting a pop music show are excellent role play contrasts which can then be discussed in terms of language variation.

Collecting the range of regional and geographical dialects and accents represented in any one evening's viewing can be fun for homework! Can anyone in the class distinguish between different accents or dialects from the USA, for example?

Another comparison might be between a wild life programme and an information book about the same topic. What order is the information presented in? Does the voice-over in the wildlife programme offer different kinds of comment from an information book? Often there is an evaluative element in a voice-over which information books don't have. A newspaper report of a football match and the experts' reflections in the television studio can focus on both the larger structures of text – what do they comment on first? How does the studio discussion about the goals differ from or echo the newspaper report? – and on the smaller units. What about the verbs used? What differences or similarities might you find if you listed verbs from the television and compared them with the newspaper report?

Language used for effects

Messages are transmitted in all media, so that books of all kinds, newspapers and television are all fruitful areas for investigation. Perhaps one of the most easily researched, however, is advertising or promotion of products. A readily obtained resource for this kind of language study is to collect, and ask the children to collect, all the junk mail that comes to your house during a week or is inserted into your newspapers and magazines. These offer a range of ways of using language for effect – including matters of layout and visual grammar – which can be scrutinised and become the basis for studying persuasive language. Perhaps the classic text in this kind of study is the house agent's blurb!

Younger children can look at environmental print and television adverts for toys as a way into thinking about how language can be structured for particular effects. Role play can again offer opportunities for practising such uses of language so as to develop a more critical sense of how language is put together for different communicative purposes.

Newspapers and headlines are again a very important area for examining bias or slanted language, and television also offers some good examples. What language is used in trailers for programmes? What do advertisements *not* tell you? Older pupils might be familiar with certain genres of drama which have a high persuasive element – courtroom drama, for example. Their implicit knowledge drawn from their viewing can become explicit with a little guidance.

Progression in knowledge about language

It is important to make sure that there is a coherent and systematic programme of teaching grammar in all its aspects, including the National Curriculum requirement for teaching standard English. The grid in Fig. 5.7 is one way of locating when and where particular aspects of grammar are being introduced throughout a child's experience of primary schooling. Colleagues' notes on Fig. 5.2 could be a good starting point. The emphasis should be on teaching and learning grammar in context so that it is likely that these aspects of grammar will be linked to the study of texts.

What gaps might there be, or what overlaps (some of them necessary) if you filled in the grid with a group of colleagues?

see Chapter 7, p. 313

How do these relate to your planning for Units of Work?

Teaching punctuation

The fundamental idea that anyone needs to grasp about punctuation is that it tells us how to read something – aloud or silently. It indicates when to pause, when to raise the intonation for a question, when to emphasise words, when to do different voices. These features prompted by punctuation are not very often made explicit when children are asked to read aloud to the teacher. The emphasis is often on decoding individual words. It is essential, however, for children to learn the rhythms of language read aloud, the pauses, the emphases, because that is how they get to be able to read silently and fluently. Much can be done in the early stages of a child's school experience by the use of shared Big Books, where attention can be drawn to the use of punctuation, directionality and spelling. However, the area of school experience where punctuation often becomes a problem for teachers is in children's own writing, most particularly in their lack of punctuation or over-use of particular marks.

pp. 198–202

Anna's writing was an example of this. Although she wrote in sentences, she did not mark them consistently. It should be remembered, however, that this was a single draft and she had not been specifically invited to go through and put in the full stops after re-reading. If Anna had been reading a book with her teacher, however, she might have been able to name punctuation marks which she did not use for that particular piece of writing.

A starting point for teaching punctuation would be to take a similar approach to establishing knowledge about grammar: What do you know about punctuation? Are you confident about using a range of punctuation? And if you are confident, why is that? If not, why not? Again, much depends on the ways in which teachers themselves were introduced to using punctuation. It would be worth taking a moment or two to recall how you were taught. What memories do you have?

- What were you taught about punctuation at school?
- In which lessons?
- How difficult or easy did you find using different kinds of punctuation marks?
- Why do you think that was?
- What have you learned about punctuation since leaving school/college?

A second question might be: what punctuation is important for the age-group you teach? Before listing these terms, however, it might be worth listing the punctuation marks you know about or can use. How would this compare with a colleague's list? A group of colleagues could very quickly develop a progressive programme of teaching about punctuation by answering the following questions, first of all individually, then looking across the Key Stage or across the whole phase:

- What punctuation have you already discussed with your class?

Progression in Knowledge About Language 1 – Grammar				
	lexical knowledge and terminology	structuring writing	language variation	using language for effect
Nursery/Reception	letter word vowel consonant	sentence story author illustrator	speech	
Year 1	question	caption dedication beginning middle end diary	differences between speech & writing	rhyme rhythm
Year 2	phrase joining words verbs	headings paragraphs chapters index contents advertisement	"slang" accents (American)	explanation Onomatopoeia
Year 3	adjectives nouns	section headlines plural & singular news report	dialect	statement alliteration
Year 4	tenses of verbs agreements synonyms antonyms	conclusion	character & dialogue ↓	homophones homonyms
Year 5	connectives adverbs	text structure flashback	↓	negatives/ affirmatives idiom debate
Year 6	prepositions	genre	register Standard English	simile metaphor argument persuasion

Figure 5.7 Grid for compiling a progressive scheme for teaching grammar (Blank provided in Appendix: A16)

- What punctuation marks do the children use?
- What other punctuation would you like to introduce?

You could use a similar grid to Fig. 5.2 to record your current use of punctuation with your class.

One way of discovering children's knowledge about punctuation is to ask them about it. The following comments were made by a Year 3/4 class who were asked: *What is punctuation?* and *Why do we use punctuation?*

These comments were noted by Noelle Hunt, whose case study on punctuation follows on pp. 215–20.

Some of the replies to the first question were:

Year 4 pupils:

> I think it is things like exclamation marks and question marks.
>
> It's when somebody starts to talk you put . . . er . . . a punctuation that looks like 66.
>
> It's kind of things like them [pointing to speech marks in a book].

One Year 3 pupil said:

> It's like speech marks and apostrophes and all the marks you put in your book not including writing.

These children quite clearly know that punctuation is distinct from alphabetic text on a page. Some may have internalised concepts about punctuation but not be able to verbalise them. Replies to the second question provoked more varied responses:

Year 4:

> If you never used them it wouldn't make an exciting story.
>
> If you never had nothing, they wouldn't know the sentence stopped. They might just read on without stopping. You need punctuation 'cos you need a little time not reading.
>
> 'cos it's easier to read . . . 'cos then you know when they're speaking an' you know when the author's speaking.
>
> I think we use it to give things more detail. Like if you were writing 'Where are we going?' and you put a question mark at the end, or if the person you were writing about was very surprised you might put an exclamation mark at the end of the sentence. [Pause] It makes it more interesting if you do use it. [Pause] It would look awful without it. You can't pause. You just have to go on and on.

Year 3:

> To make the story a bit interesting. Without punctuation, it wouldn't make sense.
>
> So you don't get muddled up what sentence you're in. You won't know if it's another day or not if you don't use paragraphs.

These children offer articulate responses to difficult questions. It is quite clear that they know a lot about using punctuation, about its role in making text easier to understand because it tells a reader how to read something. However, the range of understanding certainly calls into question the practice of whole-class teaching for explicit language use. A Year 3 pupil can talk knowledgeably about apostrophes while a Year 4 pupil still sees punctuation as largely marking sentence boundaries. A further complication is that when children talk about punctuation they clearly know a great deal, but their written work may not, in first draft form at any rate, reflect this.

Fig. 5.8 shows that Andrew, at 8 years old, is confident in his use of exclamation marks, full stops, trailing full stops and capital letters in a first draft. He seems to overuse capitals until it becomes clear that he is using them for effect and emphasis; he could be encouraged to be a little more sparing with the exclamations, too. But his enthusiastic use of them clearly indicates that he is beginning to experiment with a range of punctuation. He does not yet mark speech although he includes it in his writing.

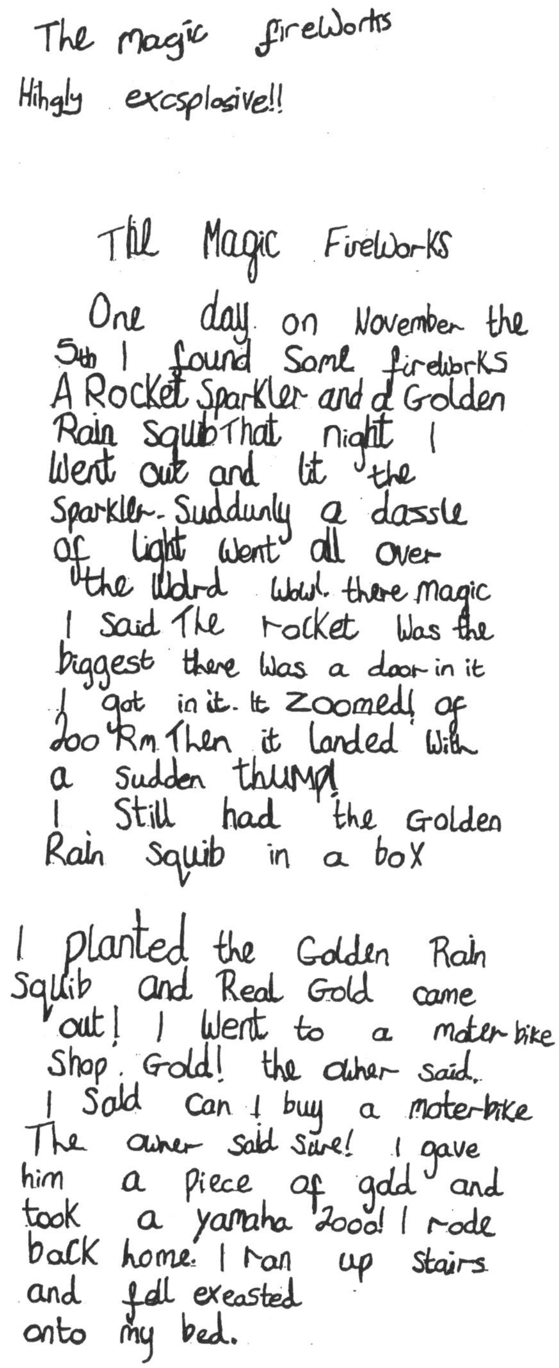

The magic fireWorks
Hihgly excsplosive!!

The Magic FireWorKS
One day. on November the
5th I found Some fireWorKS
A Rocket Sparkler and a Golden
Rain Squib That night I
Went out and lit the
Sparkler. Suddunly a dassle
of light Went all over
the Wolrd Wow. there magic
I Said The rocket Was the
biggest there Was a door in it
I got in it. It Zoomed! of
200 Km Then it landed With
a sudden thump!
I Still had the Golden
Rain Squib in a box

I planted the Golden Rain
Squib and Real Gold came
out! I Went to a moter bike
Shop. Gold! the owner said.
I Said can I buy a moter-bike
The owner said Sure! I gave
him a piece of gold and
took a yamaha 2000! I rode
back home. I ran up stairs
and fell exeasted
onto my bed.

Figure 5.8 Andrew (aged 8) is confident in using a range of punctuation for effect

Np [As she stared at me her face turned red. I quickly stood up, my heart was beating fast. "I'm sorry" I said "It just don't want to go". Mrs Bryce turned round and ~~said~~ snapped "It seems to me that it's you who dos'nt want to go this morning my girl!" She then picked up a wet rag and threw it at my feet, and shouted "get that fire lit and then scrub this floor and if it dosn't shine by the time the mistriss comes down you'll be looking for another job" I bent down and once again I tried to light the fire. At last it lit and I moved onto my next task ~~now I had the job~~ of scrubbin the floor. So I filled up a bucket of cold water fetched some sand and my hard scrubbing brush and set to work. I ~~got~~ fell down on my hands and knees and worked my way across the floor. [I kept sighing everynow and again as my nails scraped ~~across the floor~~ on the boards. They were black rimmed from cleaning out the grate and now they were starting to split, but a least they ~~will~~ would be clean when I'~~d~~ had finshed this ~~cleaning~~ dreadful task. "Oh no!" I shrieked", the floor had started to turn white from all the soap. I dipped the brush into the water and scrubbed the floor harder then ~~ever~~ until at last the soap disapeared, but I still had the rest of the floor to clean. I looked at

'll the clock*. Mrs Bryce would be back any minute now and I hadn't finshed.

Figure 5.9 Gina (aged 11) needs help in proofreading for accurate punctuation

Gina, on the other hand (Fig. 5.9), does include speech punctuation in her first draft although the punctuation is incomplete and the introductory commas for speech misplaced. She also uses apostrophes for omission, one correctly used, one misplaced. However, she correctly – and sparingly! – uses an exclamation mark. In redrafting her work she is paying attention to the paragraph structure and her use of vocabulary for effect. How might she be helped to proofread for punctuation? What strategies could be offered? The following case study gives some useful examples.

Using story books for teaching speech punctuation

Noelle Hunt is a language and curriculum support teacher, working across the primary age range supporting developing bilingual children in learning English. The case study was carried out in collaboration with Caroline Luck, a class teacher with whom Noelle has a long-standing teaching partnership. In this case study she describes some activities which arose from Year 4 children looking critically at pictorial texts.

During the past year I have planned and taught collaboratively with the teacher of a Year 4 class. My timetable allowed for two and a half hours a week with the group. By the summer term we had done some work on role play and writing dialogues, and a great deal on extending readers using a wide variety of children's literature. We decided that this would all serve as a good foundation for teaching speech marks using story books as a resource. Of course, a few children were already competent in using speech marks when writing whereas others had no experience of doing so at all. A significant middle group had noticed them in texts but were not yet punctuating direct speech when writing.

In planning an activity which focused on this feature of punctuation we wanted to combine challenge, purpose and enjoyment. As a baseline for achievement we hoped to raise children's awareness of speech marks in texts and to link their use firmly with direct speech as written. More confident writers could be expected both to follow the conventions of use and to develop a descriptive vocabulary for speech which moved beyond a 'he said' 'she said' approach. Most certainly we did not want to impose rules on children who had not yet gained sufficient knowledge about language to understand why they should follow them. Children need to know what they want to say, and be aware that it could be misunderstood, before they can pay deliberate attention to punctuating their work to make it say what they want to say.

Using a familiar story

In discussing the use of speech marks with the class, we particularly focused on the potential for misunderstanding without them. A new speaker for every line makes sense in this context. Caroline (the class teacher) had been reading to the children from *The Julian Stories* by Ann Cameron. Julian and his brother Huey are at the centre of these stories about a West Indian family. The writing has a lyrical quality, a gentle humour and rich imagery. Dialogue is another strong feature of this book and so we decided to base our teaching on one of these stories. Reading it through, I found it a good model for children to practise writing direct speech. In one chapter, the boys help their father to make a lemon pudding ready for when mother comes home from work. Once the pudding is prepared, father tells them not to touch it while he goes to have a nap. Left to their own devices, the temptation proves irresistible. Slowly but surely, and talking all the while, the boys eat the pudding completely. They then fear the consequences of doing so and rush away to hide. Using this extract as a model I prepared a sheet with an introductory passage about a mother and children making a cherry cake and the child (by implication, the author) being left alone with a younger brother. I started the ensuing conversation by writing what one child said and leaving punctuated spaces for replies. After a few lines, the sheet was left blank for pupils to complete in their own way.

Caroline and I introduced this to the class by telling them that we were going to do some work on speech marks. We showed the children what they looked like, why they were used, and pointed out examples from the text. We explained their purpose as enclosing the words someone is actually saying and that, to avoid confusion, a new line is given to each new speaker. We also talked a little about the conventions of print types; how single or double marks are sometimes used but that they serve the same purpose. We referred to the capital letter at the start of direct speech and, for the benefit of more confident children, the siting of commas, full stops and other incidental punctuation. We showed pages from the book and examples on the board to illustrate all these points.

Modelling dialogue

Having discussed the place of speech marks in written dialogue, Caroline and I acted the parts of Huey and Julian from the chapter we had chosen. Familiar with what goes before the story and what was still to come, the children thoroughly enjoyed this description of naughty behaviour. We emphasised that we found the passage easier to understand because of the way the speech is set out. As they went away to write their own conversations, some children were clearly inspired by memories of similar naughty stories from home; others let either imagination run riot and one or two modelled conversations closely on the book.

While the children were writing, Caroline and I circulated, observing how they were working. One boy, after looking at a friend's writing, noticed that he had put speech marks in the wrong place. He asked for help to correct them. Another had written a conversation very similar to the one between Julian and Huey, including details such as a spoon to smooth over the pudding. Some children, in the structured part of the sheet, had written appropriate responses to speech descriptors like 'whispered', 'shouted' and 'agreed'. At the end, nearly every pupil wanted to share their work by reading it out to the class. Caroline later collected the conversations into a book called *Will You Take Just One Cherry?* which became a popular choice during shared reading sessions. The examples in Figs 5.10 and 5.11 show generally correct punctuation and lively narrative related through dialogue. Very few children attempted any interlinking text. The varied response reflects the open-ended nature of the task. By contrast, restrictive sentence completion exercises can only be judged right or wrong. They do not allow children to express their developing knowledge about language.

Moving towards independence

We decided to reinforce this work a couple of weeks later by collecting a number of books, familiar and new, where dialogue is a strong language feature. We briefly introduced these books to the class, put the children in pairs (our choice, to prompt best support through collaboration) and asked each pair to choose one of the books. In each, a page, or pages, had been marked for the children to read and to discuss the use of punctuation in written dialogue. We allowed several minutes for this in order to give children the opportunity to look through the rest of the book too. They were then asked to write part of a story, including conversation, and to use the published text for reference in checking any punctuation. Time was short in that session and most pairs reverted to straightforward dialogue structure. However, the use of story books as a resource for reference proved a successful strategy and one that will be pursued in the future. Another positive spin-off was the interest shown by some children in wanting to continue reading books chosen for the activity.

Caroline and I evaluated the two sessions, and apart from challenging and reminding children to include conversation in their writing generally, we decided we should give speech marks a rest for the time being. We had highlighted and encouraged their use in writing and perhaps given a nudge to the intuitive process of language learning

Carry on the conversation. Remember to use speech marks and a new line for each speaker.

My mother had made a beautiful cake for tea. It had chocolate icing with cherries on top. She told me not to touch it while she went upstairs to have a rest. The trouble was my little brother and I felt very hungry.

"Shall we just take one cherry?" he asked.

" No" ," I said.

"I want to try some icing," he said.

" "OK Just a little bit Bite" ," I agreed.

"Look! You've made a hole now!" he shouted.

"Only Because you did," I whispered.

my own conversation.

NoW look What you did"!he said

dont (Sniff) Blame it on (sniff) me,"!I Cried

Quick Quik run up Stairs and Hide and pretend We Haven't done any thing."!he Said

"We are in Big, no deep trouBle,"!I said

"you're right,"| He said

A wonderful conversation. I love your (sniff) sound effects!

Figure 5.10 A Year 4 child using a model to help punctuate speech (i)

Carry on the conversation. Remember to use speech marks and a new line for each speaker.

My ~~mother~~ father had made a beautiful cake for tea. It had chocolate icing with cherries on top. SHe told me not to touch it while she went upstairs to have a rest. The trouble was my little brother and I felt very hungry.

"Shall we just take one cherry?" he asked.

"He said we cant touch it," I said.

"I want to try some icing," he said.

"Ok then if you have to," I agreed.

"Look! You've made a hole now!" he shouted.

"dont shout. dad will hear," I whispered.

"If you cantake a bit I can," He said.

"By the time weve finished there will be nothing left

I said.

" ~~Carful~~ Careful you nealy pushed me in there. he shouted

"It's going to fall off it's going to fall off!" He shouted again.

Splosh!

~~Mum~~ Dad woke up immediatly

"Whats that noise boys?"

This conversation made me laugh, especially when your little brother nearly fell in the cake, and when it fell off the table. As you talk about dad and he, I have changed the other words to make it fit.

Figure 5.11 A Year 4 child using a model to help punctuate speech (ii)

experienced by each child in the class. In blunt terms I suppose this is what we mean when we talk about 'leaving it to sink in'. Next year, explicit teaching may focus on speech marks again, and, in the meantime, individual support will be given where relevant.

Using books to teach punctuation

A natural progression in my thinking was to consider researching story books which have particular features of language as strengths and then to look for opportunities to make use of these when planning language work. When doing this there were some important points I kept in mind:

- Good quality story books, including the deceptively simple picture book, can serve as a learning resource for language development.
- Children develop knowledge about language, including that which is written, from a very young age. Even very young children may comment on the use of punctuation in picture books.
- In promoting language development in school, teachers should recognise that children already have a foundation of language experience from home and maybe from languages other than English.

Dialogue

Lulu and the Flying Babies **by Posy Simmonds (Picture Puffins)**

Lulu, feeling bad tempered, goes on a trip to the museum with her parents. Almost exclusively speech bubbles supported by simple text describing how Lulu felt.

The Cinderella Show **by Janet and Allan Ahlberg (Viking Kestrel)**

Front of house and backstage scenes from a primary school production of *Cinderella*. Pocket sized book. All speech bubbles.

Bet You Can't **by Penny Dale (Walker Books)**

A brother and sister tidying up at bedtime and daring each other to lift the heavy basket. All in speech bubbles, a simple text reflecting the title. A well-illustrated picture book.

Punctuation

A Lion in the Night **by Pamela Allen (Picture Puffin)**

A fearsome lion steals the royal baby and is pursued by the king, queen and entourage. The lion, though, is merely playful and beats them back to the castle where he invites them in to breakfast. Use of commas for listing people and series of events.

Hurrah for Ethelyn **by Babette Cole (Little Mammoth)**

Hoping to be a brain surgeon, Ethelyn, an ambitious rat, wins a scholarship to Cheddar Gables College for Richer Ratlettes. Peppered with exclamations and therefore exclamation marks!

Figure 5.12 Useful books for teaching speech punctuation

- Books chosen for classroom resources should contain realistic language as presented in a range of genres and not language which is contrived for teaching purposes.
- The content of the books should reflect the cultural diversity of the class (or the nation).
- A varied collection will include published texts by famous authors but it is equally valid to include those produced by individual children and class groups.

The work which Caroline and I did made us aware that children may be at different stages in their knowledge about language and that some of their knowledge will be intuitive and implicit rather than conscious. This means that teachers need to plan and provide open-ended activities based on relevant frameworks in order to help children confidently develop their knowledge about language in a purposeful way. It is also important to provide good quality, relevant resources which encourage children to be creative with language and to develop their understanding about its rules and conventions. Most of all, perhaps, we came to understand the value of collaboration and discussion between teachers when planning, carrying out and evaluating language teaching. Fig. 5.12 lists some picture books which we identified as offering useful examples of particular language structures.

Catering for the range of learners

One of the difficulties in teaching any aspect of language structure is that children come to understand and explore constructions at different times and according to their different interests. In noting progression in the kinds of punctuation children might be expected to recognise and use as they move through primary schooling, it is clear that by the time they are in Years 5 and 6 there is likely to be a wide variation in use of punctuation by individuals. What is needed is some way of helping each child to pay close attention to punctuation, both in their own writing and in the books and other texts they read. Fig. 5.13 shows an *I know about* sheet for younger writers and readers. Any punctuation marks can be added in the left-hand column when the child recognises them and wants to add them to the list. The 'sentence' column can be filled in with a sentence found in a book which uses the punctuation mark and a sentence made up by the child following the model.

Fig. 5.14 is an accuracy challenge designed to help older pupils get to grips with a range of punctuation. The idea is that once the children have focused closely on one aspect of language, they will have developed strategies which will become more or less part of the regular proofreading process.

Progression in punctuation

p. 223

The grid in Fig. 5.15 can be used in the same way as the grammar grid – as a means of discussing and agreeing with colleagues the progressive introduction of punctuation. Again, it is important to remember that exercises out of context do little to help children get to grips with punctuation. Encouraging them to be careful and attentive readers of their own and other people's writing is far more effective. Using tapes that they have made of spoken stories can be a good way for the teacher to model how to punctuate. An example lesson in transcribing just a brief fragment of tape can show the importance of all kinds of punctuation, including pauses for effect and underlining for emphasis. Older children can try this out for themselves.

A useful way to focus on the type of punctuation marks being taught is to photocopy a section from a book that the children are familiar with and stick it in the centre of a large piece of paper with questions which the children respond to. It is important that the extract is familiar because the children will then be working with

I Know About – Punctuation	Name:	
Punctuation mark	**What it's called**	**Sentence**
.	full stop	From a book: The cat sat on the mat. My own: I like cats.
C	Capital letter	From a book: I've been to London to see the Queen. My own: My cat is called Charlie.
?	Question Mark	From a book: Where have you been? My own: What is your cat called?
' '	Speech Marks	From a book: 'I've been to London.' My own: 'So have I!'

Figure 5.13 Catering for individual progress in punctuation (i) (Blank provided in Appendix: A17)

something which has meaning for them – a context of understanding. Useful questions might be: *How many capital letters are there in this extract? Circle them.* The same question can be asked about full stops, semi-colons, speech punctuation, exclamation marks, etc. On the same sheet there might be a question inviting the children to *Make up a rule about using capital letters* (or full stops, exclamation marks, etc.). Another question might be *How many different punctuation marks can you spot in this extract? Name them.* Alternatively, a photocopied section from a book might have certain punctuation marks blanked out with the question *Can you decide where this? (or ! or ') mark goes?* Once the children have decided, either individually or as a paired/group activity, they can check with the original text to see if they were right. Any discrepancies can then be discussed. This provides a very good opportunity for talking about the fact that punctuation can be varied according to the effect the individual writer wants to make. There are many ways in which extracts can be used to help children identify a range of punctuation marks and get to grips with the conventions which govern their use. Such activities are more effective than exercises done out of context because the children will be working on texts which are familiar to them and which have meaning for them.

The following guidelines might help colleagues when developing agreed and systematic ways of introducing and consolidating punctuation:

- Punctuation shows us how to read. It is one of the technical aspects of writing and should be treated as part of effective communication.
- Punctuation is most effectively learned when children want to make their own meanings clear and can see that it serves their own purposes.
- Punctuation is best introduced naturally as a part of reading and writing activities.
- Books and other printed materials are the best references for finding out how punctuation is used.

Accuracy Challenge – Punctuation

You have six weeks to complete this challenge. You will need to find a partner who is also doing the punctuation challenge.

You are going to choose three punctuation marks from the list to work on first. Circle the three you feel least sure about using:

Full stop . (F)	Comma , (C)	Capital letter (Cap)
Question mark ? (Q)	Exclamation mark ! (E)	Speech marks ' ' (S)

If you are doubtful about how to use any of them, look in the books in the classroom and see how they are used. For three weeks you will read every piece of writing you do very carefully and make a note in the margin, if you think you have missed something out. Use the code in the brackets to show which punctuation mark it should be. Then you should check it with your partner.

From your reading, find three more punctuation marks that you would like to try using. Write them in the grid below and give them a code.

Write down what you think the rules for using these punctuation marks are. Start trying to use them in your written work and check them out with your punctuation partner.

1 Rule:

2 Rule:

3 Rule:

After three weeks you can work on the other three punctuation marks from the grid at the top of the page which you didn't circle and find three more from your reading.

When you and your partner are sure about how to use one of the new punctuation marks, you can make a poster about it to show the rest of the class what you have discovered.

Figure 5.14 Catering for individual progress in punctuation (ii)

Progression in Knowledge About Language 2 – Punctuation		
	Punctuation marks	**How they will be introduced**
Nursery/ Reception	full stops	reading teacher input
Year 1	capitals exclamation marks question marks	look at big books classroom environment emphasised when reading individually
Year 2	italics commas speech marks	noticed in reading books talked about in drama speech bubbles activities to find punctuation marks in books
Year 3	apostrophes for common abbreviations brackets	noticed in reading books and own writing word games oral games (class activities)
Year 4	possessive apostrophes (only for those who are ready) quotations	from own writing (teacher intervention) from reading
Year 5	colons + semi-colons dashes hyphens (only for those who are ready)	from reading + own writing (reading + writing groups)
Year 6	commas for parenthesis	(ditto)

Figure 5.15 Grid for compiling a progressive scheme for teaching punctuation (Blank provided in Appendix: A18)

- The teacher is the other major resource for demonstrating the difference punctuation makes when you read something aloud and for showing how to use punctuation in the context of writing which says what you want it to say.
- Children's grasp of different kinds of punctuation varies. Introducing aspects of punctuation to everyone at the same time will mean that some get the idea quickly while others need to be given time to understand and use a new form of punctuation. Blanket teaching can lead to confusion for some learners and produce adults who fear and misuse punctuation.
- Exercises out of a context of meaning are likely to be counter-effective; skills learned in this way rarely transfer to everyday work. Whilst it may be useful occasionally to encourage practice of certain kinds of punctuation, this should follow contextualised introduction of how the specific point is used to communicate meaning.
- The children themselves may be the most effective way of helping each other get to grips with new ways of using punctuation.

Teaching spelling

One of the greatest myths associated with recent public interest in education is the one which says that 'teachers don't teach spelling any more'. Nothing could be further from the truth. However, since this does seem to be such a prevalent view, it is essential that teachers make it very clear just what they are doing to help children develop their spelling. The whole area of spelling is complicated and people who have not spent time in classrooms or in discussions with teachers can very easily think that all you need to do to teach spelling is to give children lists of words to learn and then to test them. If only it were that simple! That would ensure that every adult in the land would be able to spell conventionally. They can't – and this is part of the basis for concern. However, many adults know that if they are unsure of how to spell something they can ask someone else, use the computer spell checker, look up a word in a dictionary. They know that if you are writing a shopping list or a note left on the table for a member of the family, conventional spelling matters less than if you are writing a formal letter. Further than that, they also know that spelling is not the same as intelligence or ability; many directors of companies – and politicians – depend on someone else to make sure that their spelling is accurate. Yet negative judgements are often made about people who find conventional spelling difficult. There is a sense that a person is somehow diminished, less worthy as a human being, if they can't spell. Once more, language can be seen to have become imbued with social and cultural judgements.

This makes it all the more important for teachers to have a clear view of what they think is important about helping children to learn how to use accurate spelling in their written work. Tests and examinations measure spelling ability; work which is threaded with spelling errors can be difficult to understand or the content may be disregarded because of a focus on the accuracy of the spelling; children who are not confident spellers may avoid using complex vocabulary – although they may use it in speech – because they fear getting it wrong. Spelling matters for a variety of reasons and if children are to gain confidence and competence, their teachers need to be aware of the complexities of spelling. Most importantly, spelling (and handwriting which is associated with it) should be seen as the servants of writing, not as dominant in the writing process. One of the saddest sights in a classroom is to see a child furiously rubbing out words over and over again, or gripping the pen or pencil in a desperate fear that they will get a spelling wrong. Such fears stand in the way of fluency and fluency in writing is one of the keys to successful spelling. At the same time, it is not safe to assume that a fluent reader will be an accurate speller. There are many fluent readers who are unsure about conventional spelling.

At this point it might be worth considering your own experience and confidence about spelling:

- How good a speller are you?
- What were you taught at school about spelling? Did it help?
- How did your teachers correct your spelling? Did it help?
- What have you learned about spelling since you left school?

A group of colleagues answering those questions might find some very different answers, but there is one common factor – attitudes towards spelling have an effect on success.

How do we learn to spell?

One of the complicating factors about spelling is that not all children learn – anything – in the same way. Where one child will have a tendency to draw on aural experience, another may be better at using visual evidence for learning. And, of course, there are all the others in between. One important fact to bear in mind is that good spellers become good spellers by making mistakes. Learning to spell is a gradual process through which learners have to get a grasp of a system of rules for spelling through looking closely at written language and through trying things out in their own writing. Ian Forsyth worked for three years on a research project where teachers gathered and analysed children's spelling mistakes. He emphasises that:

This was at the Centre for Language in Primary Education, London Borough of Southwark, and is written up in 'Understanding children's spelling' in *The English Curriculum: writing*, ILEA English Centre, 1987.

> Where spelling is concerned, learners need to make mistakes and they need their teachers to help them make sense of these. Even more important, they need to know what they *can* do. The chances are that they are much more likely to be aware of what they don't know or can't do. Instead of forever drawing attention to mistakes, teachers would be much more profitably engaged in helping children to formulate what they *do* know about words and written language as a whole. Children talking with each other and with their teachers about words is far more valuable than, say, copying lists of unfamiliar words for which they have no use.

This comes right back to the idea that for children to develop careful and focused attention on language, they need a way of talking about it. One of the most fascinating and perplexing aspects of language is the set of rules which govern the spelling system of English and the pronunciation which goes with it. The following extract from an anonymous but widely known verse captures precisely that feature of English:

> Just compare heart, beard and heard,
> Dies and diet, lord and word,
> Sword and sward, retain and Britain.
> (Mind the latter, how it's written.)
> Now I surely will not plague you
> With such words as plaque and ague.
> But be careful how you speak:
> Say break and steak, but bleak and streak;
> Cloven, oven, how and low,
> Script, receipt, show poem and toe.

this version found in the *Dartmoor Town and Village News* in 1994

Linking speech and writing

The extract makes a fundamental point about the English spelling system and how we learn to use it. Spelling is learned through the eyes (and the hand in the act of writing). While children in the early stages of learning to write may draw on their aural knowledge, an important shift in their understanding comes when they see that spelling is not spoken language written down, but a special way of capturing what we say and think – a symbolic system, in fact. This is similar to the shift in children's understanding which comes in learning about number when they recognise that 5 is a way of expressing (icon for five). Children have to make the link between the sound system of speech (phonology) and the alphabetic spelling system (graphology) of English. It is very clear that trying to teach spelling based on phonic approaches alone is likely to mislead and confuse children. If children are asked to look at words to find their patterns in a context where the words make sense they are far more likely to understand and retain spelling patterns. Often, experienced spellers try writing out two or more versions of words to see which one looks right.

In the early stages of becoming writers children do draw on their aural knowledge. But they also demonstrate that they are actively seeking the rules which might help them to spell things they haven't seen before. Very early mark-making may simply signal that a developing writer knows that writing has a communicative purpose, but does not indicate that the writer is making any connection between what we say and what we write (Fig. 5.16). In the early developmental stages of writing, children often use initial and ending consonants to capture their meaning; if they use vowels they are often those which are strongly sounded. Later they introduce features from their observation of written text. Fig. 5.17 shows Christopher's labelling of 'tiny bear', 'Daddy bear' and 'Goldilocks' where he has drawn on both phonic and graphic knowledge for his writing. As children's written fluency develops they still draw on their ears as well as their eyes in attempting spellings of unfamiliar words. Anna's writing (pp. 198–202) showed that she was actively trying to follow regularities in spelling, but that she used her aural knowledge to try out words for which she didn't have any background experience – 'yoonican', for example, for unicorn. In just one word she combines aural and visual knowledge as she tries to get the word right; she knows that the written pattern 'oo' makes the kind of sound she wants but that it needs the 'y' sound to make the 'u' as it is pronounced in 'unicorn'. Similarly, she draws on her own speech patterns when she writes 'fingi' for 'thing'. The teachers working with Ian Forsyth came to the conclusion that many of the errors made by children were the result of over-generalisations of some kind – where children were seeking rules and patterns – and more often than not, the errors showed careful attention to the sounds of language. A very great number of errors were attempts at spelling as phonemic – on the assumption that one letter equals one speech sound.

This has important implications for teaching – and not just for teaching writing or spelling; it makes an important point about teaching reading, too. Relying solely on the sounds of the alphabet to help children tackle reading through phonic cues can lead to misunderstandings and some of the over-generalisations which Ian Forsyth identified. Children who are beginning to understand sound–symbol relationships, even if they do not spell well at the moment, are on the way to being confident spellers. Encouraging developing writers to look at some of the patterns in their own spelling can quite quickly help them to find ways of standardising some of their errors. At the very least, close attention to some of their own writing helps to establish an interest in the way words are put together. The more interested children are in what they write, the more attention they are prepared to give to its appearance, including spelling. Once children have developed fluency in writing, then they can begin to learn when and how to proofread for spelling errors and to develop strategies to get their spellings right. A critical factor at this stage is to do with the reasons children are being asked to write. When children recognise that their writing is going to be read for its interest, in the same way as a printed book is read, then they can see the point of being careful about spelling. Similarly, if children are occasionally asked to write for a readership outside the classroom, then they can see the importance of learning how to proofread for spelling and to get it right.

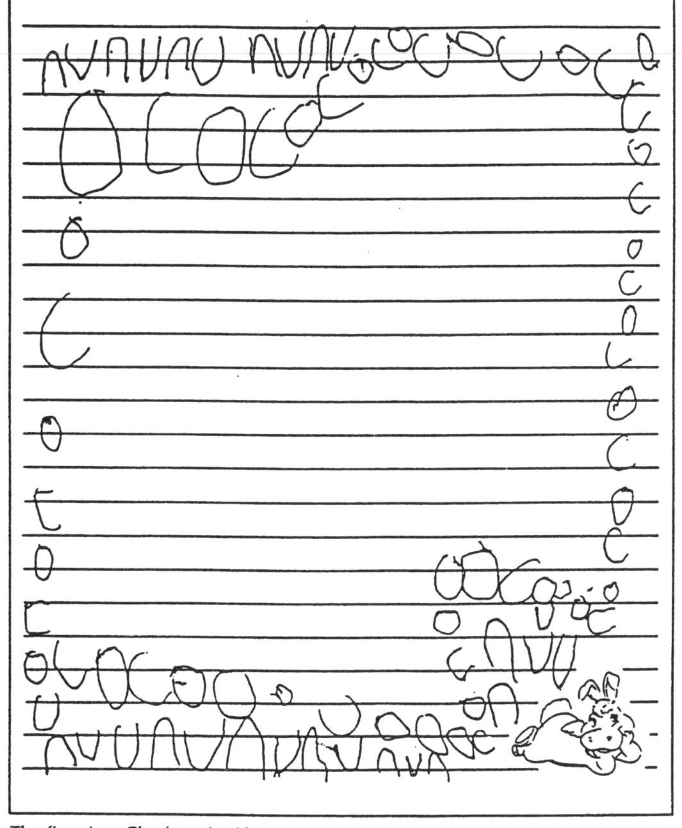

The first time Charlotte had been given lined paper

Figure 5.16 Charlotte's letter (aged 4) – the beginnings of writing to communicate

Charlotte's writing first appeared in the National Writing Project materials *Making Changes: resources for curriculum development*, Walton-on-Thames, Nelson 1991.

Figure 5.17 Christopher (aged 5) uses phonic and graphic knowledge for writing

Christopher's development as a writer is described in the National Writing Project theme pack *Becoming a Writer*, Walton-on-Thames, Nelson 1989.

Methods of improving spelling

While spelling in context is, of course, important, there are times when developing lexical knowledge needs to be the focus of particular lessons aimed at helping children develop the kinds of strategies they need for independent proofreading. Spelling does not just depend on recognising shapes of words, however. Fluent and confident writers are very often good spellers – or become so. There is a residual recognition of the link between writing and spelling in the practice of getting children to write words out several times if they have spelled them incorrectly. The link between handwriting and spelling is related to kinaesthetic memory. A technique focusing on kinaesthetic memory would be to encourage a child to try out the written word, perhaps by finger writing it in the air or on the table or to use the index finger to rub out chalked (correct) writing. Asking children to write out spellings a number of times is an implicit acknowledgement of kinaesthetic techniques to help internalise the shapes of words. As a practice, however, it has its drawbacks:

kinaesthetic memory: the way we remember things through repeated movements

- It is asking the child to write the word isolated from the context in which it was used and so does not offer help for future use.
- It associates spelling with routines, or even 'punishment'.
- The importance of the word to be corrected is often decided by the teacher and it may not have the same priority for the child. If the aim is for the child to remember how to spell the word next time they need it, a teacher-selected word may have little relevance.

Added to this is the knowledge that children have different learning styles. If they are genuinely to take over responsibility for their own spelling, then they need to be provided with a set of familiar strategies to draw on. Many teachers now believe that introducing joined handwriting from the start can help children to develop accuracy in spelling. This emphasises letter clusters and builds on the kinds of letter clusters which Christopher's developmental writing shows (see Fig. 5.17). Charles Cripps, one of the most informed advocates of this approach, argues that joined writing helps both handwriting and spelling because writing groups of letters in a connected form is necessary when writing a word.

see Charles Cripps and R. Cox 1989 *Joining the ABC*, Learning Development Aids

Look, cover, write, check – is this enough?

'Muscle memory' contributes strongly to internalising spelling patterns, but visual memory is equally important. However, simply inviting children to 'look' at a word may not be enough. What we really mean is that we want them to take in a sense of the shape of the word, the ways in which the letters are ordered. However, psychological tests of visualising have shown significant variety between ways of visualising. Some people will simply 'photograph' a word or a series of numbers so that they can read off their mental image; others see some parts of a mental image as more prominent than others; some visualise with colour as indicating significant parts of what is to be remembered; others make patterns within visual images. Some report that they do not use visual imaging very much in memorising; others depend on a visual approach to learning almost everything. Nevertheless, people can generally be helped to improve their visualising by practice. In helping children to become more proficient spellers, it is worth asking them to practise holding the image of a word in their mind's eye. Can you do it? If you asked colleagues to do the same, what different kinds of visual imaging do you find? The next question would be *Can you see the letters?* then *Can you read them out?* This is important in helping you and the child to check whether they can use visual imaging to help them learn letter patterns. It may

S. V. Thompson 1990 'Visual imagery: a discussion' in *Educational Psychology* vol. 10, no. 2 pp. 141–67

need practice and certainly offers a chance for a bit of fun as you and they describe the ways you see the images. *What kinds of letters are they? How big? Any colour?*

This can lead to an expanded version of 'Look, cover, write, check':

- Look at the word in context.
- Say the word silently.
- Think of the meaning.
- Try to see the word in your mind's eye.
- Cover it over, still trying to see the word.
- Write the word.
- Check against correct version.

One common way of using visual memory is to help children to recognise particular word endings, for example: 'ive' as in 'five' and 'dive' and in 'give' and 'live'. However, this is where the link between pronunciation (phonology) and writing clusters of letters (graphology) becomes critical. It is very clear by looking at the word ending 'ive' that spelling does not reflect speech written down, but that clusters of symbols can be said in different ways. This underlines the importance of helping children to spell by visual means. Another effective strategy is to help children see words within words: 'arm' in 'farmer', for example, or 'cove' in 'discovery'. It is important, though, to make it clear that if a child does not find visual imaging easy, this is not a failure; it simply means that they may need other, perhaps auditory, means of memorising shapes and patterns of words.

Using your ears

The most straightforward way of using auditory representations of words is to ask children to say the sequence of letters out loud. Rhythm and intonation are very useful and you might even be able to pick up the rhythms of raps, sports supporters' chants or jingles which the children are familiar with. Another way of using auditory cueing is to pronounce the word as it looks – for example, 'comb' pronounced as the first syllable of 'combination', 'That is land' for 'island', 'to get her' for 'together' or the very common 'Wed-nes-day'. If this strategy is used it needs to be made very clear that this is a way of learning and not the way you would read something aloud! Similarly, mnemonic devices can help in retaining certain spellings. 'In the end, she's my *friend*' helps to sort out the 'ie' or 'because' can be remembered by 'big elephants can always use some energy'. For children whose auditory powers predominate, SOS (simultaneous oral spelling) provides an alternative to looking at and visualising a word:

- teacher says the word; child listens
- child repeats the word
- child spells the word using the letter names
- child writes the word naming the letters as he or she writes
- child reads the word he or she has written.

Whole-class and individual strategies

In helping children develop individual strategies for correct spelling, the 'Look, cover, write, check' approach may need to be expanded to 'Look, visualise, cover, say aloud/chant/sing, write and check'. It is perhaps best summarised as 'Look, remember, cover, repeat, write, check'. Not such a neat formulation but one which emphasises some of the provision for varied strategies needed for a diverse group of learners. SOS is one of these and computers now offer special programs for consolidation of word shape recognition as well as spell checkers which offer (sometimes amusing) alternatives. A key to the successful use of any of these strategies is an enthusiasm for language. An interest in words, their meaning, shapes, history and sound, generates improved spelling. For example, as part of a history topic, gathering words which come from Latin, Greek, Norman or Viking roots can generate interest in studying language and offers practice in paying close attention to letter clusters. Part of that language study might be to recognise that spelling is changing all the time, even though this is slow. What one generation finds appalling, the next generation accepts. For example, 'program' is generally used in relation to computers, 'adviser' and 'advisor' are often alternatives and 'ize' endings have been almost totally replaced by 'ise'.

Helping children to get better at spelling means developing procedures for whole-class and individual interest and attention to words. There may be nothing wrong with a whole-class spelling test, but it can run the risk of wasting time for accurate spellers and consolidating failure for those who find spelling more tricky. Individual diagnosis of children's errors is an important first step in helping children improve their spelling. Taking a couple of pieces of writing and asking the following questions can help in setting individual targets:

- What pattern is there in the errors?
- Is the writer using generally standard English forms but making occasional errors?
- Is the writer relying too heavily on phonic knowledge, e.g. drawing on dialect forms of speech?
- Is the writer relying too heavily on graphic knowledge doubling letters unnecessarily; adding a 'magic e' at the end of words?
- Is the writer including all or most of the letters but mixing up the order?

In terms of whole-class support for spelling, the classroom environment will be one of the most useful resources for helping children to get their spellings right. What resources do you have in your classroom? Fig. 5.18 makes some suggestions.

One of the most important resources for spelling in the classroom is the teacher. Not in the sense of being a walking dictionary – teachers can offer much more than that. The environment of the classroom will be influenced by your own expectations of the children.

- How do you create an atmosphere of confidence and readiness to have a go at spellings?
- How do you minimise anxiety as far as possible?
- How do you promote an interest in words?
- How do you increasingly encourage independence in first attempts and in proof-reading?

While the classroom environment is important, systematic teaching of spelling and agreed procedures for dealing with spelling throughout the school are essential if children are to develop as confident spellers.

A summary of strategies:

- Making spelling a shared activity using spelling partners; encouraging looking at, collecting and studying words as paired or group activities; testing each other on individually selected spellings; joint attempts at finding unfamiliar words in the dictionary;
- finding patterns in error and helping children to identify patterns in their own spelling errors, then guiding them in listing and remembering their own spelling needs;

The Environment for Spelling

might include:

- word banks
- key words on display
- dictionaries – and the knowledge of how to use them
- alphabet books/ posters
- labels and instructions
- children's own made word books or dictionaries
- spelling games
- computer programs for spelling
- reminders about strategies (Look, Remember, Cover, Repeat, Write, Check or Listen, Say, Spell, Write, Read)
- word matching activities
- posters of commonly mis-spelt words (compiled by the children)
- books/posters about words
- crosswords and word searches
- words related to particular topics or subjects – displayed or in folders
- word of the week – inviting the children to add words with identical letter clusters to the list.

Figure 5.18 Resources to help children improve their spelling

- showing children patterns in words in printed material and asking them to find similar patterns;
- developing lexical knowledge by talking with the whole class about the derivation of words, their histories and countries of origin, prefixes, suffixes, etc.;
- playing with words – through poetry, mnemonics, games and drama;
- having regular surveys of the children's writing to identify their spelling of common words and to offer extra help and practice where necessary;
- developing proofreading practices, for example underlining or circling words which they are unsure of and then checking them with the help of their spelling partners;
- having regular spelling practice – of new words, of the children's own selected words or of words which just have to be learned individually, for example, 'library';
- offering challenges about spelling which can be taken home, discussed with the family and added to;
- talking about words and spelling in shared reading and writing times;
- letting parents or carers know what you do to help children get better at spelling.

Working on spellings at home

Parents and families can be involved in helping children to consolidate spelling. Teachers might set spelling challenges or suggest games for developing spelling which can be easily played at home.

Spelling challenge 1 (suitable for children at Key Stage 1)

Each week each child takes home a list of ten words to learn. These are either collected from their own writing during the week or, if they haven't made ten identified errors, words with the same letter clusters to learn: e.g. 'able' in table, cable, fable. For each word the child (or parent) should write the number of letters and whether there are any small words inside the word they have chosen. They should practise them with the family and check them out using the 'Look, remember, cover, repeat, write, check' approach (or the preferred classroom method). On Monday morning each pair of spelling partners tests their ten words in turn and keeps a weekly score of their accuracy rate. Parents can also keep a score.

Word	Number of letters	Words inside words
Table	5	able

Spelling challenge 2 (suitable for children at Key Stage 2)

This follows much the same procedure as spelling challenge 1. Each week the child works on ten words which he or she has found difficult to spell or unfamiliar when reading. For each word they will be asked to find two or more which have some identical letter clusters. If they cannot find ten incorrectly spelt words in their week's writing in school, they should identify words which they find interesting in their reading or when browsing through thesauruses or dictionaries. These can be tested by spelling partners and scores kept in the same way as for spelling challenge 1.

Word	Number of letters	Similar words
Promise	7	precise practise

Whole-class challenge – prefixes and suffixes

Each week, for a set period of time (perhaps six weeks), the class chooses three prefixes or suffixes. Each pupil has to assemble as many of these as possible, using parents, dictionaries, thesauruses, their reading and television viewing. When the words are brought in, children check the spellings in pairs or groups and make sure that they know what the words mean – not just by looking them up in the dictionary, but by explaining them to the group or class.

Spelling games

The shape game

Every word has its own shape, e.g. Monday

Draw some word shapes and give them to your child. Give them the words that the shapes represent separately and ask them to match the word to the shape.

e.g. lot

girl

holiday

Word pairs (this is like the card game sometimes known as *pelmanism*)

You need quite a large number of cards or paper squares with words written on one side. You will need to make two cards for each word.

Spread the cards out face downwards. Taking turns, each person turns over two cards. When they find a matching pair, they keep them. If the pair don't match you turn the cards face down again, keeping them in the same place. The winner is the person who has the most cards at the end of the game.

Spelling snakes and ladders

Before playing this game you need to get a notebook and write down several words for each letter of the alphabet. It is important to choose words which the players of the game will be able to spell with a little thought. The oldest person playing is in charge of the spelling notebook until it is her or his turn, when another player will be in charge of the book.

This uses a snakes and ladders game and a dice, and is played by the usual rules with the one exception that you can go up and down both the snakes and the ladders if you spell a word correctly or incorrectly. Before the game, a letter is chosen. Every time a player reaches a snake or a ladder they have to spell a word from the appropriate page of the spelling list notebook. If they get it right they go up the snake or ladder; if they spell it wrong they go down the snake or ladder.

There are a lot more spelling games listed in the LINC Project book *Spelling – how it works and how to help children get better at it*, Language Development Centre, The School of Education, Sheffield Hallam University.

Other useful reading: Margaret L. Peters and Brigid Smith 1993 *Spelling in Context*, Windsor, NFER–Nelson; C. Cripps and M. A. Peters 1996 *Catchwords: ideas for teaching spelling*, London, Harcourt Brace Jovanovitch; M. Peters 1985 *Spelling: caught or taught? A new look*, London, Routledge; B. Smith 1994 *Teaching Spelling*, United Kingdom Reading Association, Trowbridge, Blackwell

Letter steps

Starting with one word, the players have to make steps:

This can be done with an agreed number of letters – three, four, or five, or for real stretching, it can be done by expecting a longer word at each step, e.g. lip

or by finding words which begin and end with the same letter.

Study of texts

Chapter Six

Effective teaching of English in Key Stages 1 and 2 shared some characteristics. The most important were:

- a systematic requirement for the pupils to talk for a variety of purposes and at some length;
- regular provision of tasks which demanded independent reading and sustained, extended writing;
- provision of varied reading material;
- systematic and rigorous appraisal of written work, which addressed not only the surface features of spelling, layout, etc., but also structural and syntactic features and quality of content and organisation.

(p. 9)

Ofsted *English Key Stages 1, 2, 3 and 4 Fourth Year 1992–93*, Her Majesty's Stationery Office 1993

In outlining aspects of teaching about texts, this chapter includes:

- **studying text structures**
- **extending the range of texts taught in the classroom**
- **auditing current practice**
- **teaching from texts and teaching about texts**
- **fiction, including media:**
  - **narrative organisation**
  - **theme and setting**
  - **dialogue, character and action**
- **knowledge of genre**
- **extending the range of fluent readers**
- **poetry**
- **drama**
- **non-fiction texts, including media:**
  - **organisation, layout and presentation**
  - **getting information from texts**
  - **constructing information texts**
- **progression in teaching about texts.**

A model of English teaching

see Fig. 5.1 for the model of the English curriculum used as a basis for this chapter

These have been covered in some detail in Chapters 2, 3 and 4.

see the suggested framework for planning schemes of work offered by SCAA and the work of the National Literacy Project

Teaching English involves a complex mix of language study, the communicative expertise to get and convey information from texts, the development of discrimination and independence in using language, and, most crucially, studying texts themselves and how they are structured. As Chapter 5 made clear, English as a subject can seem tricky because it doesn't have the same body of knowledge as the other subjects. The content is not so much facts and concepts as texts and processes – though there are facts and concepts, too. The processes of English happen throughout the whole curriculum because language is a medium of learning as well as an object of learning in its own right. We learn through language and we learn about language. Then there are areas specific to English as a subject and these have to be planned for separately. Those areas are study of language and study of texts. Development in English will include all four components, but a major part of specifically focused English teaching will be aimed at increasing children's fluency and versatility in producing and responding to both written and spoken texts.

The Ofsted comments about effective teaching represent the kind of good practice which every teacher would want to achieve. However, there are often problems associated with resourcing and managing activities which will extend the most fluent and assured readers, writers, speakers and listeners, whilst supporting and encouraging those who are not moving so fast. This chapter offers some suggestions about extending the range – both for the whole class and for individuals. The National Curriculum for English places a great deal of emphasis on the study of texts and response to literature. Teaching from texts is the most effective means of developing knowledge about texts – both the larger organisational features of whole texts and the smaller structures of language at sentence and word level.

There are both theoretical and practical reasons for using literature – poetry, plays, novels, short stories, media and non-fiction texts – as a basis for teaching the technical elements of language, as outlined in Chapter 5. In the first place, children gain the clearest understanding of language when it appears in a form which has a context and so makes sense. The second, practical, reason is that books of 'comprehension exercises' or other kinds of language practice exercises can cost a great deal and have limited use. Even the most attractively presented books cannot make up for a teacher's careful interventions in explaining and instructing about how texts are put together. Many teachers are familiar with the experience of children being able to do exercises which focus on a particular aspect of technique, yet not being able to transfer that skill when it comes to using it in everyday writing or reading. This is often because the exercises have been done as comforting – or perhaps tedious – routines, divorced from the context of exciting, interesting or challenging reading and writing; they simply don't stick in the child's memory because they have not made any connection with the child's own urge to communicate. Very often the things which do stay in our memories are those which have been achieved through effort. In looking at how texts might be used to support more extensive and demanding learning, two important elements feature largely:

- the value of challenge and effortful success
- the structured and thoughtful interventions which will make this possible.

Texts themselves are a great support in trying to get these two elements embedded into regular classroom practice. Another important strength comes from the existing expertise and experience of teachers themselves. A teacher is an irreplaceable example and model of what an active and engaged reader, writer, speaker and listener does in communicating ideas, making choices and exercising discrimination.

Covering the range

How does the pattern of teaching from texts contribute to a child's experience of texts throughout the Key Stage or throughout primary school experience? An important first principle when deciding how best to extend children's literacy experience is to decide just what development in literacy means. Part of development will be the ability to handle the secretarial aspects of writing or the decoding elements of reading. Being able to recognise and use more complex words and phrases, being able to read for longer periods or to write more extended pieces, being able to vary tone of voice when reading or use a wider range of punctuation in writing – all of these are important parts of development. But it would be too simple – and inaccurate – to think that development meant just getting used to reading or writing longer stretches of text. One way of extending children's horizons in reading, writing, speaking and listening is to broaden the repertoire that they have available for making meaning. But how can you ensure progression in children's understanding of texts and how they are made? What does that involve in terms of teaching from texts? What different experiences should children have as they become more adept at making and responding to texts? The following sections offer suggestions about enlarging the repertoire for individuals and whole classes as well as progressively offering greater challenges to children to help them become more discriminating readers, writers, speakers and listeners.

Although Reading, Writing, Speaking and Listening are treated separately in the National Curriculum, it is now clear that whilst making distinctions between the different components which need to be covered in each attainment target, effective literacy development depends on the four modes being interrelated. To be a good reader you have to be a good writer – and vice versa – and to be an appreciative and critical reader and writer you have to be able to talk about texts and you need the experience of hearing a range of texts read aloud. Part of the process of becoming discriminating about literacy is to be given opportunities to comment on and respond to whatever we have read.

This chapter takes as a basis for considering a range of ways into teaching about texts and teaching from texts, the importance of:

- the value of challenge and effortful success
- structures, interventions and models for responding to texts
- the relationship between reading and writing
- speaking and listening in studying texts.

It provides frameworks and suggested activities for:

- whole-class and individual approaches to texts: fiction (including media, poetry and drama) and non-fiction (including media)
- looking at progression in teaching from and about texts.

What texts do I use?

As a starting point, it would be worth carrying out an audit of all the ways in which you and your colleagues use texts of different kinds in the classroom. Fig. 6.1 gives a list of some of the features which might be included as part of your text teaching audit.

Select three or four texts which you have used over a reasonable period of time with the class, either fiction or non-fiction. For example, the class reader, a book re-read as a favourite with younger classes, information books used as resources and perhaps models for the children's writing, an anthology of poetry or a Big Book used to teach particular aspects of reading. Then, referring to the list in Fig. 6.1 make a note on the chart in Fig. 6.2 of the teaching opportunities offered.

It might be useful to complete one of these for each term to check that you have covered a range of fiction and non-fiction during the year. Auditing your teaching across a whole year will soon show up any gaps in practice. An audit like this, carried out together by a group of colleagues, allows you to judge whether the children are getting wide enough experience of a range of texts as they move through the school (Fig. 6.3).

This audit will be useful for looking at Range and Repertoire in Chapter 7.

Developing a critical eye: extending literacy

Text teaching audits show how important it is to continue teaching reading beyond the initial stages of fluency. Not only is there a need to continue focused teaching to the end of Key Stage 2 and to structure opportunities for response to reading, but it

Developing a critical eye: how children can become attentive and discriminating readers of their own and other people's writing

Fiction, including media, offers opportunities for teaching about:

- narrative organisation: plots, time sequences and action
- comparing versions
- theme and setting
- making summaries
- dialogue and character
- reviewing and recommending texts
- authors
- genre: knowledge and analysis of different forms of text.

Poetry also offers opportunities for group and individual reading and writing.

Drama can also lead to investigating, experimenting, presenting and responding to improvised and written text.

Non-fiction, including media, offers opportunities for teaching about:

- organisation, layout and presentation of different types of texts – persuasion and information – including visual elements as in advertising
- environmental print and texts
- comparing texts – news, information, biography, etc.
- strategies for getting information from texts.

All of these can be used as a basis for children writing and talking about texts.

Figure 6.1 Teaching about and from texts

Text teaching audit	
Which texts have you used over a period of time with the class?	What teaching opportunities did they offer?
1 Sir Quenton Quest hunts the Yeti	– juxtaposition of text and pictures – diaries, journal entries – 'translating' into standard English
2 The Clothes Horse The Ahlbergs	– metaphor, similes, literal meanings – intertextuality (explicit) – compound words
3 Sky in the Pie Roger McGough	– comparing poems – diff. poetry and prose – making personal choices – imagery – vocab. – poetic license
4 Dorling Kindersley Egyptian Book	– discussion – appreciation and understanding of artefact Terminology – drama

Figure 6.2 Text teaching audit – over a term (Blank provided in Appendix: A19)

Year	
Types of text/genre (e.g. traditional stories, narrative poems, plays, big books, classic stories, contemporary novels)	**Teaching opportunities**
Term 1 Newspapers	- Differences between fact and opinion - Direct and reported speech - sentence structure - Use of language for persuasion / other effects - Headlines - skimming & scanning for info. - Structure of info. text - interviewing techniques - Note-taking
Term 2 Horror / Ghost	- Comparing authors & techniques (author studies) - Comparing versions (film & book) - language used for effect - Building suspense / writing own cliffhangers / horror stories - Creating atmosphere - Discussion of reality and fantasy (news reports and fiction)
Term 3 Myths and legends	- Using original sources (Homer) - Subverting genre - Alternative forms eg films, radio plays, puppet show & picture books - Cultural variation - Discussion of character e.g. heroes in myths & everyday heroes - Storytelling - Comparing versions e.g. Victorian & modern comic book

Figure 6.3 The range of text experience – over a year (Blank provided in Appendix: A20)

QUESTIONS ABOUT READING

Reading at home. Do you like reading:

- comics? (which ones?)
- magazines? (which ones?)
- books? (think of one or two that you've enjoyed recently and write down the title, or the author or what it was about)
- any other kinds of reading? (e.g. manuals, information books, newspapers, maps, diagrams)

How do you know what to choose? Does anyone help?

Television viewing

Which programmes do you watch every day?

Which programmes do you watch every week?

What other programmes do you like to watch if they are on the television?

What films or videos have you enjoyed watching recently?

Using the computer

Do you have a computer?

Do you play games on it? (say which ones)

Do you have a CD-ROM? What do you read on it?

What else do you use the computer for?

Reading at school

What book have you chosen to read for yourself at the moment?

What is it about?

What book have you enjoyed reading most during the past few months?

Why did you enjoy it so much?

Who helps you choose the books you read in school?

Your reading history

Make a list of the books you liked to read when you were very young:

Figure 6.4 Establishing children's experience of texts

is equally important to cater for the diversity of readers in the classroom. Before planning a range of activities specifically designed to help children learn more about language and texts, it is worth establishing just what experience the children have already. You will need to know something about the preferences of your readers if you are to tailor your teaching to develop their knowledge further. Chapter 2 offers some questions which increase your knowledge of the children's attitudes to reading but the questionnaire (Fig. 6.4) will help to establish a clearer picture of their experience of written and media texts both at home and at school. Depending on the age of your pupils, it might be worth talking through the questions first.

p. 24

Fiction

Once you have gained a clearer picture of your pupils' reading experience, it is easier to cater for individual progress. Differentiation can be carried out through specifically allocated tasks for different readers using a class text, personally chosen texts or through assessing the outcomes of whole-class activities. For personally chosen books, fluent readers might be asked to focus on a particular character, the beginning of the books, a favourite part, or particular vocabulary to write or talk about afterwards. Developing readers might be asked to write or talk about their favourite part or simply give a personal response to the text, while less fluent readers might be asked only to give a personal response to the text. Other activities can be carried out by groups or pairs or the whole class, regardless of reading fluency or experience.

Narrative organisation

Although children regularly read, write, tell and hear stories, there still seems to be evidence that there is room for improvement in the level of discrimination in children's comments on narrative or the complexity of their written narratives. Although children experience stories, it seems that they are not challenged enough about their response to texts. One problem may lie in the extent of written text which a child can read independently, particularly in the early years. It is assumed that if they can't read lengthy narrative, they can't make a critical comment on a text, yet this flies in the face of daily experience inside and outside school. Anyone who has listened to children's discussions about their favourite television programmes will know that they are indeed very demanding critical audiences. They do not need to be fluent readers of verbal text before they can start on the road to analysis and comment about the structure, characters, themes and settings of narratives. They can also deal with rather more complex ideas of story structure than the traditional 'beginning, middle and end'; many of the programmes they watch – particularly soap operas – have several plots and sub-plots developing at the same time, all of which children can hold in their minds and talk about afterwards. Children can predict plot structures and talk about character when they have made the choice to watch or read something for their own interest. The teacher's expertise comes in using those critical abilities in the classroom.

A study by Sally Wilkinson about children's video experience bears out the ability of pre-school children to become involved and discriminating 'readers' of moving text on a screen. The children she writes about are 4 years old, observed watching and analysing videos in their own homes:

> Jonathan had chosen to watch one of his favourite *Thomas the Tank Engine* stories from the video he and his mother had borrowed from the library. . . . As Jonathan's mother set up the video for the story Jonathan had chosen, *Fish*, which was towards the end of the tape, Jonathan told me: 'I like it when he crashes into the back of Percy's train. Nobody's hurt, but a smelly bit of fish gets in Duck's boiler.'
>
> He continued to anticipate the storyline all the way through the story, punctuating his narrative with direct quotes from the video. These phrases were also anticipated, such as 'Push hard. Push hard.' Some of the phrases he anticipated were ones which were common to many of the *Thomas the Tank Engine* stories, such as 'Then there was trouble!'.
>
> Sometimes the children's anticipation would go beyond simply narrating the action that was to follow and would include speculation, opinions and insights, such as when Michelle said of Bambi: 'He's going to slip in a minute (*pause*) on the ice. I expect he's a bit nervous. It's freezing cold water.'
>
> (p. 50)

Sally Wilkinson's careful study details the ways in which parents and siblings model ways of talking about plot, character, event, setting and atmosphere. She emphasises that discussion about videos contributes to children's development of opinion and critical analysis. This study echoes work done by Helen Bromley, who has also studied young children and their video literacy. Her interest lies in the early years of schooling:

unpublished dissertation for the MA in Language and Literature in Education at the University of London Institute of Education

> Hannah is sitting on the classroom floor, leafing through the Dorling Kindersley book of *Amazing Snakes*. She pauses at the page showing the cobra: 'Mrs Bromley, I've found Jafahl's snake,' she says. She is correct.
>
> I am reading the book *The Whale's Song* by Diane Sheldon to the reception class when Jodie points out the similarity between the imagery on its cover and pictures from Walt Disney's *The Lion King*.
>
> A parent has brought two kittens into school for us to look at. Someone wants to know if the kittens can swim. One boy replies, 'Cats can't swim, I know. I've got *Homeward Bound*, the cat couldn't swim in *Homeward Bound*.'
>
> Remarks like these happen on a daily basis, evidence of children relating knowledge gained from watching videos to everyday school life. Videos provide a wealth of experiences from which children can construct new meanings.
>
> (p. 90)

from Disney's *Aladdin*

Helen Bromley 1996 'Video narratives in the early years' in Mary Hilton ed. *Potent Fictions*, London, Routledge

Helen Bromley is aware, however, of the criticisms directed at video watching:

> If you still regard viewing as a passive activity, reflect on the last few experiences you have had with videos. You will have laughed, cried, been frightened or provoked and almost certainly you will have had a discussion with someone about it. Through discussion you may have come to a greater understanding of what you have seen or enjoyed. . . .
>
> I am not suggesting that teachers appropriate the children's out-of-school pleasures for school use, rather that we look closely at how we can provide opportunities for children to demonstrate their knowledge to us. However, demonstration alone is not enough. It is critically important that children are allowed to use what they have already learned in the joint creation of new meanings.
>
> (p. 90)

Plots, time sequences and action

Through their knowledge of video and television texts, children have vast resources of information, not only about the stories themselves or facts about other countries and cultures; they also have a wide experience of plot structure. They know, for example, about flashbacks and 'meanwhile'. They can predict complications in the plot and guess resolutions: *I know what's going to happen.* In doing this they are engaged in a kind of dialogue with the narrative, becoming involved, active and critical readers. In an increasingly visual environment, the encouragement and development of such critical discrimination is essential. Films and videos won't go away. If children are genuinely to be able to resist some of the more alarming features of television and film depictions they need to be given the credit for having some critical sense and encouraged to extend this through discussion in school about a wider range of texts, including their video libraries.

Responses from the Year 5/6 class who answered the reading questionnaire on p. 241 included 58 different videos that the children had enjoyed recently. Very few of these were PG videos; most were in the U category. This compares with 73 books they had enjoyed reading at home during the same period. The experience of this one class suggests that interest in videos does not lessen interest in books. Unprecedented sales of books which are adapted as television versions – for adults and children – also bears this out. What might the questionnaire reveal about your own class and their tastes and experience in video and book reading?

Comparing versions

An effective way of developing critical and analytical faculties is to invite comparisons between different versions of the same story. For example, looking at aspects of the Disney version of *Snow White* and a written version, Shakespeare's Animated Tales and extracts from the original plays, or the film musical of *A Christmas Carol* by Dickens, the old George C. Scott film and the original book. This is the kind of activity adults often do when talking about television adaptations of stories – and debate can be very hot indeed! Using either an extract from different versions, or referring to whole texts, children can be encouraged to work in groups or pairs to answer some guide questions (as at the top of Fig. 6.5) before feedback to the whole class. Older children can work on these questions independently but younger classes might answer them orally, or just take one aspect at a time. If groups are working independently you might want them to share their ideas through jigsawing (see Chapter 4, pp. 168–9) or to decide on who is chairing the group, who will record the group's views and who will offer feedback. The following examples could be adapted to any comparison between book and film/television version: Roald Dahl's stories – *Danny*, *Matilda*, *The BFG*; 'classics' like *The Railway Children* or *The Secret Garden*; plays like *Macbeth* as animated versions or extracts from major films and the play texts, *Peter Pan* and the film *Hook*; and Disney versions of *Beauty and the Beast*, *Pinocchio*, *Aladdin* or *Alice in Wonderland* or the television versions of the Narnia stories, *Goggle Eyes* (by Anne Fine) or *Buddy* (by Nigel Hinton).

For younger children this would be best done orally first, modelled by the teacher scribing on a flip chart or the board and selecting only one area to compare. Once the children have a grasp of the process, they can be asked to fill in sheets, as in Fig. 6.5, for specific questions.

Comparisons can also focus in closely on particular events. Towards the end of Disney's *Snow White*, for example, where the stepmother disguised as an old woman gives Snow White the apple and encourages her to eat it, the film has a series of cuts between the animals and the dwarfs racing towards the cottage in a bid to save Snow White from the old woman's efforts to kill her. This is quite different from the written story, although some versions may use 'meanwhile'. This kind of extract gives children a very good opportunity to discuss narrative structure and to consider whether a written version with so many cuts back and forth would be a good idea. They might try:

- taking one minute of the video version, write it then read it aloud to see if it works to create the same effect
- listing the ways in which the film makers build up tension and fear then listing how this is done through words in the written version
- looking at the way Disney uses humour even in the most fearful moments and reading the text extract carefully to see whether there are any humorous elements; what does the humour do for the story?

The visit of the last ghost in *A Christmas Carol* and the Christmas dinner at the end of the narrative are useful comparative extracts. Children might be asked to compare the two extracts from the film and the same two from the book to look at how character is depicted (Fig. 6.6). This can often lead to the use of quotations to support conclusions. The message of the story is very clear in both book and film – whether the old black-and-white version or the musical. The children might be asked to comment on the moral resolution of the tale in each case, for example by listing the ways in which the book and the film depict the character of Scrooge in each extract (Fig. 6.7).

Comparing versions

- Were there any differences between what happened (the plot) in the film and in the book?
- Were the characters any different? Choose one or two to compare.
- Do you think the setting shown in the film was what you had expected from the book (or the other way round, depending on which was read first)?
- How did the book and the film create atmosphere?
- What did you think about the ending (resolution) in each version?
- Which version did you prefer? Why?

Book: Mrs Frisby and the rats of NIMH   Film: The secret of NIMH

	Different	The same
Plot	Film: Not much about the laboratory. In the film Mrs. Frisby is given a magic jewel. The endings are different.	The beginning where Mrs. Frisby meets Mr. Ages and the Owl and when she meets the rats.
Characters	None	Mrs. Frisby, Mr. Ages, Jeremy, Nicodemus, Justin, Jenner
Atmosphere	Some bits are much funnier in the film-like Jeremy. The fights are more exciting in the film.	When Mrs. Frisby gets caught its very tense in the book and the film-and frightening when she goes to meet the owl.
Resolution (ending)	In the film the magic jewel sent out rays to move the stone.	It all ends happily for Mrs. Frisby and Timothy is all right.

Which version do you prefer and why:

I like the book but I prefer the film because Jeremy is funny and I liked the exciting bits when the tractor was coming and the fight at the end. The book tells you more about the laboratory, which was interesting.

Figure 6.5 Comparing video and book versions (Blank provided in Appendix: A21)

What is the character like?

Book extract 1	Film extract 1
Book extract 2	Film extract 2

Figure 6.6 Analysing character in books and films/TV

Book	Film

Figure 6.7 Similarities and differences between versions

Theme and setting

Other questions might be related to the themes of the book and film/TV version or the setting:

- What do you think the author's message is? How was this conveyed in the book and the film(s)?
- Where did the story take place? Was it modern or historical? How could you tell? Describe the similarities and differences.

Reading extracts from texts to children can help them learn about setting the scene or creating atmosphere. Judith Allen read her Year 2 class the episode from *Great Expectations* where Pip visits Miss Havisham, then asked them to write their own atmospheric pieces (Fig 6.8(i) and (ii).

Making summaries

Children use their reading experience in their writing; this is equally true of readers of television and video. Even very young children can be asked to make concertina books or contribute a page to a Big Book based on their knowledge of story from film. Older children might learn how to summarise the plot of a video in a short space of

The old house
on Sunday 8th September
I Went to the Woods. In
the Midel of the woods.
I found a house I nocked
on the door. nobody ansed
So I just went in. It was
all dark. I found a candel
I walked a long way. Then
I Saw some stars I
Went up them. I Saw a
room. I nocked on the dor
something Said enter the room,
So I enterd the room that
was full of cobwebs.
There was a bed that was
full of cobwebs. There was a old
lady.. She was in her
wedding dress. Spiders
were running around It was
horbell. I hated it.

The End

Figure 6.8 Year 2 children writing after hearing an extract from *Great Expectations* (i)

The old house
Today we are going to a old house.
we are there now its dark in here.
Theres a candele over there. Then
I went up a stair case theres a cobb
webb. At the top of the sarts there
was a door. So we all went into the
room. In the room there was a girl.
The girl was wearing a white dress a
vale open her head one shoe off one
shoe one. It looked like a wedding dress
The other shoe was on her dressing
tabble There were lots of candeles
In that room. She hadnt got her nekless
on earings on what. The dressing tabble
was mad of glass. downstairs some
Windows were blocked some had
bars in front of them. I wiped
away the cobb webbs. Then I went
home I told mum about it.

Figure 6.8 Year 2 children writing after hearing an extract from *Great Expectations* (ii)

Chapter 3 includes a case study by Tatiana Wilson about teaching narrative structure and making summaries of the plot of a story.

time. In teaching summary it is important to ask children to note only a restricted number of incidents and an example should be modelled by the teacher. After they have been shown how to do it, the basis for a summary might be compiled as in Fig. 6.9. This can be a paired activity, with the children telling each other five important things about the story before they note them down. This activity is equally useful whether the children are summarising the same story or different stories. The same strategy can be used for summarising written stories, of course.

Once the children have selected the events they want to include, they can use these either as a prompt for re-telling or as the basis for writing a first draft. Again, teacher modelling is one of the best ways of showing how to do this. One of the problems of summarising, however, is that it can become a list of 'ands' or 'thens'. Younger children could be asked to use only one 'then' in their writing and to write quite short sentences and older pupils might find a list of alternative connectives useful: *meanwhile, although, however*. If using this as a strategy for book reviewing, the children can be asked only to include points 1–3 of their notes so as not to give away the whole plot.

Dialogue and character

Children can be encouraged to focus on dialogue and character through taking a brief film extract and noting what people have said which reveals something about their character. The grid in Fig. 6.10 can be used with younger children with the teacher scribing the information. It can also, of course, be used as a basis for noting quotations from books. Older pupils might be asked to use the grid as a prompt for writing dialogue as speech bubbles, punctuated speech or as a play script. This might then be used as a model for developing their own dialogues, but rather than simply concentrating on the formal technicalities of speech punctuation, children can be asked to comment on how the speeches of each character tell us what they are like. Depending on the purpose of the activity and how it relates to other work, they may not need to transcribe dialogue, but could simply note important points or quotations as they watch the video. This can be very usefully done at home where they can replay passages to check up on dialogue. At first it might be best to restrict the number of characters, but two pupils working together might be able to deal with more than one or two.

A development of this would be to discuss how characters' actions and other people's comments, including the narrator's, also tell us things about characters. Pupils could use a different grid like the one in Fig. 6.11 to build up a rounded picture of character. This can lead to writing character sketches or can be used as a basis for planning when they are depicting characters in their own narratives or plays.

Reviewing and recommending texts

Another effective strategy is to transform an extract into a film storyboard, including notes about sound effects and music, camera angles and close-up/medium/distant shots. This can be a useful close reading activity because the children will need to look very carefully at detail in the original in order to complete the storyboard. The end products can be used as 'trailers' to encourage others to read the book. The extract might be from a book which is in the class or school library or which has been read at home. The passage selected should be no more than a couple of paragraphs so that the activity is manageable (Fig. 6.12).

This activity can lead to:

- making audio tapes supported by a series of drawings in a concertina booklet
- acting out scenes
- making a cartoon-style introduction to the story, using visual sound effects rather than tapes
- making short video tapes.

What happened – five key events				
Title of film:				
1	2	3	4	5

Figure 6.9 Making summaries

Character	What they said	What this shows about them

Figure 6.10 Analysing character through dialogue

Character	What he/she says	What he/she does	What other people say about them	What this tells me about them

Figure 6.11 Analysing character through action and commentary

Have you read this?

Choose an extract of about two paragraphs from a book you have enjoyed and plan a 'trailer' to encourage other people to read it:

Storyboard – extract from: **by:**				
Shot 1 Camera: Sound:	Shot 2 Camera: Sound:	Shot 3 Camera: Sound:	Shot 4 Camera: Sound:	Shot 5 Camera: Sound:
Shot 6 Camera: Sound:	Shot 7 Camera: Sound:	Shot 8 Camera: Sound:	Shot 9 Camera: Sound:	Shot 10 Camera: Sound:

Figure 6.12 Planning a trailer to recommend a book

Studying authors

Many readers latch on to the work of one particular writer and enjoy finding more and more books written by the same author. This is equally as true of children in the early years as it is for adult readers. Many Reception and Year 1 or 2 children can talk knowledgeably about their favourite picture book maker – the Ahlbergs, Anthony Browne, Shirley Hughes, Tony Ross, for example – and explain what they like about them. Older readers get hooked on series reading or everything they can lay their hands on written by Judy Blume, Roald Dahl, Jan Mark or Robert Swindells. There is great scope for both whole-class and individual study of specific authors, both familiar authors and new writers recommended by teachers. Comparisons of different books might focus on the types of characters, the ideas presented or the style of illustrations or text. The experience of reading several books by the same author encourages the ability to generalise and to make connections between texts, given some kind of guidance. This is where developing a vocabulary to talk about texts becomes important. Younger readers might be asked to choose one illustration from each book that they particularly like and this can be used as a basis for comparison of style. Older readers could be asked to select a descriptive passage from each book and compare the descriptive language used, picking out effective phrases and sentences. In considering characters, younger readers could draw pictures of their favourite characters from each story and attach words to them describing what they are like; this can lead to a class discussion about similarities in the way the author depicts characters. For fluent and more independent readers, a set of questions to guide thought about setting, characters, action, event or themes can be a good starting point for making general comments about an author's work (see Fig. 6.13). The questions might be used as part of group or general class discussion or individually.

Author study – question cards

Read three books (at least) by the same author.

If the characters were the same in each of the books you read, choose Card One.

If they were different, take Card Two.

Card One **Setting, character, action and theme**

1. Where was each of the stories set? Write a sentence for each book, describing the setting. Were there any similarities between the settings for each of the stories?

2. Name the main character (or characters) in each book.

3. Did they behave the same in each of the books? Give a few examples.

4. What about the action and events? Write a brief summary (no more than 3 sentences) of the events in each book. Can you find any similarities between the action in each of the books?

5. Write a sentence for each book, explaining what you think the author's message was. Are there any similarities between the three (or more) books that you've read?

Card Two **Setting, character, action and theme**

1. Where was each of the stories set? Write a sentence for each book, describing the setting. Were there any similarities between the settings for each of the stories?
2. Name the main character(s) in each book.
3. Were there any similarities between them? What were the differences? Give a few examples.
4. You may have found some similarities between the characters in each book, or you may not. What about the action and events? Write a brief summary (no more than 3 sentences) of the events in each book. Can you find any similarities between the action in each of the books?
5. Write a sentence for each book, explaining what you think the author's message was. Are there any similarities between the three (or more) books that you've read?

Figure 6.13 Questions to guide fluent and independent readers in studying authors

Genre: knowledge of different forms of text

The examples (Figures 6.14 and 6.15) are from Anna Lofthouse's Year 2 class at the Queen's School, Richmond.

Book reviews are a familiar way for children to recommend texts to each other and so many young children have good experience of video watching, they are also in a good position to recommend videos to each other. Like book reviewing, this can lead to the development of a more discriminating critical sense of what is valuable about a particular narrative. Besides this, of course, there is a great deal of print on a video pack so that children at the very early stages of reading can begin to notice and talk about the different kinds of print on the pack and to comment on design.

A Year 2 class were being introduced to genre categories through their knowledge of video. Their teacher asked them to bring in videos they would recommend to others and to talk about them. They began to use vocabulary about animal stories, fairy stories, real-life stories, funny stories, scary stories. They could talk about character, plot and theme. After a great deal of discussion the children were asked to write reviews of their chosen videos using some questions to guide their comments. They were asked to give background details drawn from the video packs, to mention aspects of the film they liked, to mention favourite characters and suggest the age group that the video would interest most. This activity is very like the more familiar book review. However, 'doing book reviews' can be problematic. Very often, the routine read-it-then-write-about-it can be stultifying and tend towards less enthusiasm for reading rather than more. Chapter 2, pp. 66–7, suggests ways in which children can be encouraged to reflect more profitably on their reading, but this is not to suggest that reviewing books is unhelpful or a waste of children's time. Used properly reviews can develop an extensive knowledge of genre.

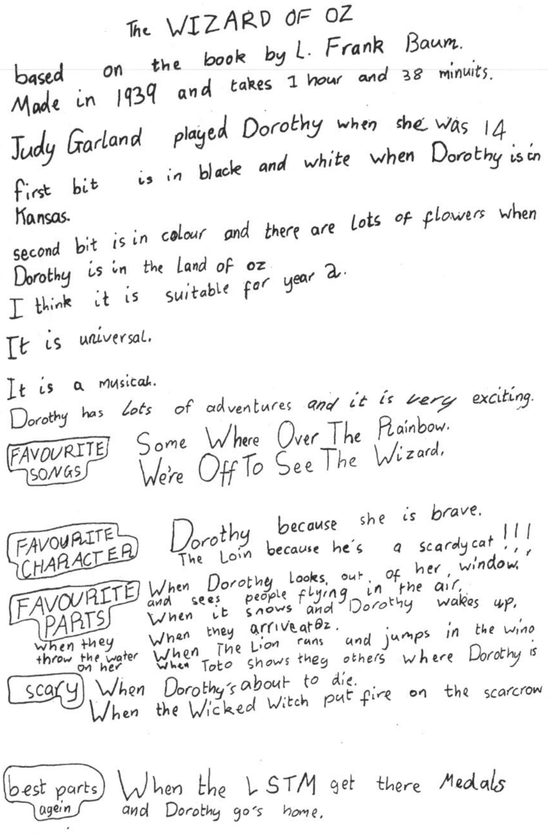

The WIZARD OF OZ
based on the book by L. Frank Baum.
Made in 1939 and takes 1 hour and 38 minuits.
Judy Garland played Dorothy when she was 14
first bit is in black and white when Dorothy is in Kansas.
second bit is in colour and there are lots of flowers when Dorothy is in the Land of oz
I think it is suitable for year 2.
It is universal.
It is a musical.
Dorothy has lots of adventures and it is very exciting.

FAVOURITE SONGS: Some Where Over The Rainbow. We're Off To See The Wizard.

FAVOURITE CHARACTER: Dorothy because she is brave. The Loin because he's a scardy cat!!!

FAVOURITE PARTS: When Dorothy looks out of her window and sees people flying in the air. When it snows and Dorothy wakes up. When they arrive at Oz. When The Lion runs and jumps in the wino. When Toto shows they others where Dorothy is. when they throw the water on her

scary: When Dorothy's about to die. When the Wicked Witch put fire on the scarcrow

best parts agein: When the LSTM get there Medals and Dorothy go's home.

Figure 6.14 A video review written by a Year 2 child (i)

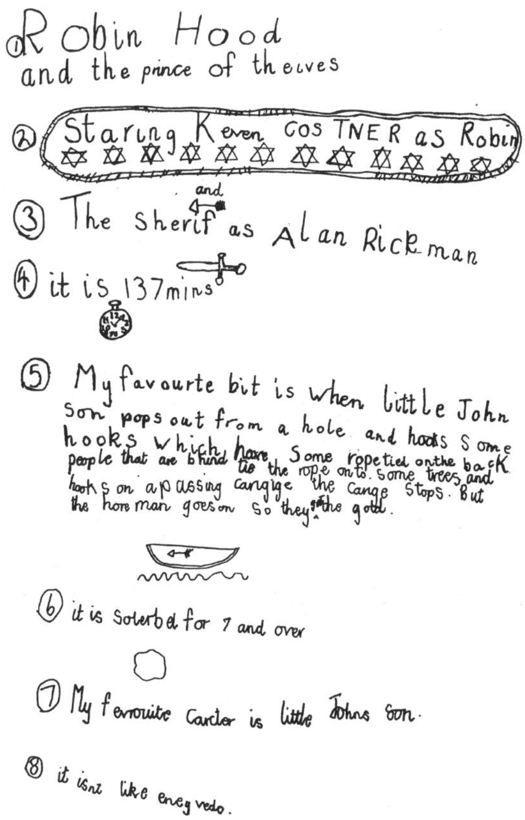

(1) Robin Hood and the prince of theives

(2) Staring Keven COSTNER as Robin

(3) The sherif as and Alan Rickman

(4) it is 137 mins

(5) My favourte bit is when little John son pops out from a hole and hooks which have Some people that are bhind the rope onto. Some tied the rope onthe back hooks on a passing carrige the carrige stops. But the horsman goes on so they got the gold.

(6) it is sotorbel for 7 and over

(7) My favouite carcter is little Johns son.

(8) it isnt like eney vedo.

Figure 6.15 A video review written by a Year 2 child (ii)

Storysearch: a database for identifying genre

As the result of over a year's discussions with children in Years 3, 4, 5 and 6, Sally Elding and Jennifer Reynolds have created Storysearch, a database which asks young readers to respond to a range of features in a text and to record their responses on the computer. The categories have been suggested by children as they discuss their responses to the texts they read. The database grows as the year progresses and as the children continually input their opinions and critical analyses of the texts they have read. After reading a book, the children are asked to record information on a sheet as a starting point for adding to the database. The growing database can be searched for particular titles, books with certain types of character or set in a specific time or place so that any child who has an interest in mystery stories with female main characters, for example, or traditional tales involving animals or funny books with illustrations, can find suggested titles with comments by their peers. The following case study captures the conversation of two children as they work on the computer recording their views on a book they have read. Their teacher, Jenny Reynolds, comments on their discussions.

Two Year 4 children, Alice and Shaun, used Storysearch to interpret *The Hidden House* by Martin Waddell. The reading group which Alice and Shaun belonged to had read the book twice with me. Afterwards they discussed the text and the pictures but were deliberately steered clear of the Storysearch structure of interpretation and mainly stuck to personal responses to the text. The children had enjoyed the book and were keen to complete a Storysearch on the computer without adult supervision.

Alice has a statement of special educational need. She has problems retaining knowledge, cannot remember events which happen at home or at school and she finds it difficult to formulate sentences in her head. Alice elects out of large group discussions and has to be coaxed into joining in with small group discussions. She has fifteen hours of Learning Support Assistance each week and since September her LSA has concentrated on involving her in group tasks to help her spoken language develop.

Shaun is a bright child, who has a wealth of general knowledge. He finds reading aloud difficult but he has a sound understanding of what he can read and of texts read to him. He is able to respond and interpret texts to a good level. Shaun, too, often elects out of group discussions if he is not working with his friends.

They both knew that they were being taped and were happy for this to happen. If anything, it implied to them that they were expected to talk and share ideas. Both children are familiar with the software and they have worked in groups inputting data. They have also completed sheets but they have never gone 'cold' to the computer before. Their taped conversation provides examples of them supporting each other's reading skills. Not only have they had to read the text of the book in order to understand and interpret the story, but they are having to read the text on the computer screen to complete the task of filling in the data sheet. The text on the Storysearch data sheet is not daunting to the children but as they come across unfamiliar words they help each other to understand them. The following extracts from a transcript of their conversation illustrate the language and literacy skills the children are developing as they complete the Storysearch sheet on screen.

Identifying the narrative voice

Alice and Shaun have completed the information at the top of the sheet and now have to make some informed decisions about the literary features of the book. They read through the list in the 'Narrator' box on the sheet. Neither of them at first understands

Storysearch

Name __________ **Boy or Girl** ____

Title __________

Year published ____

Author __________

Illustrator/Animator __________

Have you read this story? ☐ Yes ☐ No

Have you seen this story? ☐ Yes ☐ No

Have you heard this story? ☐ Yes ☐ No

Narrator

- ☐ adult
- ☐ child
- ☐ animal
- ☐ storyteller
- ☐ god-like
- ☐ other

Characters

- ☐ animal
- ☐ object
- ☐ orphaned children
- ☐ adult baddies
- ☐ wizard/witch
- ☐ adult (male)
- ☐ adult (female)
- ☐ child (female)
- ☐ child (male)
- ☐ monster

Genre

- ☐ picture book
- ☐ adventure
- ☐ fantasy
- ☐ science fiction
- ☐ supernatural
- ☐ mystery
- ☐ horror
- ☐ school
- ☐ historical
- ☐ animal/nature
- ☐ autobiography
- ☐ journal
- ☐ romance
- ☐ true-life
- ☐ humour
- ☐ other

Times	**Places**
______	______
______	______
______	______
______	______
______	______

Themes

- ☐ jealousy
- ☐ love
- ☐ loss
- ☐ change
- ☐ sorrow
- ☐ humour
- ☐ rich and poor
- ☐ war
- ☐ growing up
- ☐ relationships
- ☐ coping with problems
- ☐ conflict
- ☐ other

Other images of this text?

- ☐ music
- ☐ computer game
- ☐ games/toys/objects
- ☐ other

Messages from the text __________

Figure 6.16 Storysearch sheet

the meaning of the word 'narrator' and yet once reminded that it means the person who is telling the story, they are able to act upon this knowledge. Alice tells Shaun that the old man is telling the story. In fact, the narrator of *The Hidden House* is quite difficult to identify.

SHAUN: She says who's telling the story? (*repeats this twice*)
ALICE: The old man.
SHAUN: Is he?
ALICE: Us two – we told the story.
SHAUN: The little man. . . . God-like – yeah god-like.
ALICE: GOD-LIKE ????? It's an adult telling the story. It's an adult.
SHAUN: It's god-like.
ALICE: OK, OK, it's god-like – right let's go on to the next one.

Alice and Shaun see the narrator initially as the old man in the story, but soon, after reading the possible options on the Storysearch sheet, Shaun decides that the narrator is definitely a god-like narrator. Alice gives in to his decision; she doesn't seem to understand fully the meaning of god-like narrator and maybe she just decides to agree for an easy life. When both children become more experienced with using Storysearch and they fully understand the meaning of a narrator, I would expect them to support their opinions with examples from the text. Alice has good reason for thinking that the narrator is the old man, but if adults were analysing the text they might be led to the decision that the house is telling the story.

Understanding genre

On tape there are examples of both children substituting their own language for the language on the data sheet. Although they struggle to pronounce the word 'genre' correctly, they are able to complete the section about the text genre with little difficulty. Alice is convinced that the book should belong to the family (genre) of picture books. They have an interesting discussion about it and ask another child's advice as Alice tries to persuade Shaun to agree with her.

ALICE: It's a picture book.
SHAUN: Alice, can you do it? Look, swap places. Can you do the mouse? ALICE . . . you do the mouse control.
ALICE: I don't know what to do.
SHAUN: OK . . . what is it? . . . It is an adventure book.
ALICE: I told you it's not. . . . Oh God.
SHAUN: Picture book? Is it a picture book? No.
ALICE: Yes it is.
SHAUN: It's got pictures in, but it's not just. . . . It's not just . . . adventure book?
ALICE: You're supposed to put every single one.
SHAUN: You're not.
ALICE: Right I've done this before. . . . I did. . . . Right . . . IS IT A PICTURE BOOK?
SHAUN: No because it's got writing in too.
ALICE: I'll click it.
SHAUN: NO . . . because . . . William, Alice thinks it's a picture book.
ALICE: It is a picture book.
SHAUN: A picture book is just plain pictures.
ALICE: Click it to say 'yes'.

Apart from the literacy knowledge the children are using to think about the genre of the book, Alice is actually talking far more than I have ever heard her talk in a small group activity. She is struggling to justify why she thinks the book is a picture book but is convinced that she is correct. The children's language is purely their own. Not once do they refer to the word 'genre'. They are only one step away from linking the word to its meaning as they already understand implicitly what it means and with teacher intervention will be able to read the word and use it in context.

Thinking about characters

Alice and Shaun try to pronounce the word 'characters':

SHAUN: What's this? Char . . . ar . . . (*sounding out*) char . . . chers . . . (*aside to friends on other computer*) What's a char . . . chers?
ALICE: Oh I know what this is, Shaun, because I've done this before. It means . . . have you . . . what . . . erm . . . what has it got in it?
SHAUN: Dolls.
ALICE: No, what is it about?
SHAUN: There's an object in it.
ALICE: Has it got a monster in?
SHAUN: No.
ALICE: Is there an adult male? Yes.
SHAUN: Adult male. Yeah. William, what is this? What does chers [characters] mean?

The children are making sense of a word which they cannot read. Alice has correctly told Shaun what the word means but he does not fully understand and is unwilling to commit himself to any decision. He even asks a friend who is working on the next computer for help. Later on in the activity, I intervened and told them the meaning of the word 'characters'. Once I had explained what the word meant, the children were able to identify the characters within the text quite easily:

ALICE: Oh, look there it is . . . Child female.
SHAUN: There's a little girl, isn't there.
ALICE: Yeah, and two little boys.
SHAUN: Adult female, yeah.
ALICE: Put cats.
SHAUN: Well, where? You can't exactly put cats.
ALICE: Animals.
SHAUN: Look, that's animals I've put down. Look, there.
ALICE: Yeah. Click on animals. What's that?
SHAUN: Objects. Is a toy an object?
ALICE: Yeah. It's an object.

Alice and Shaun demonstrate that their language is developing whilst they are learning and very quickly show evidence of their understanding. Shaun is aware that certain words group similar items together. Alice wants to include the cats as separate characters, but Shaun helps her to understand that the word 'animals' applies to cats. Later, she is able to use this knowledge of grouping when they think about the dolls in the story and she identifies them as objects.

Developing their own opinions

Alice and Shaun have to make decisions about the text and in doing so find themselves having different opinions. This is an essential part of interpreting texts in groups. Alice and Shaun need opportunities to re-read and think about texts which they have read. As both of them are less experienced readers, their previous reading has been limited to scheme books which offer few chances to develop the skills of interpreting and understanding texts. In forming their own opinions about texts and discovering that their opinions differ, they automatically justify why they hold particular views. In doing so, they refer to the text to support their opinion; when asked to identify themes, Shaun clearly justifies decisions with reference to the text. They have omitted the first three categories in the 'themes' section of the Storysearch data sheet and are discussing change:

ALICE: Yes 'cos it does change.
SHAUN: And . . . sorrow . . .
ALICE: There's not rich and poor. There's NOT loss.
SHAUN: Yeah there's loss. . . . Remember they lost Bruno.
ALICE: Oh, yeah!
SHAUN: War . . . NO.
ALICE: Growing up? . . . Relationships! . . . (*giggles*)
SHAUN: Erm . . . coping with . . . coping with problems.
ALICE: Erm . . .
SHAUN: YES. I think . . . 'cos they had bugs all over 'em, didn't they?
ALICE: Yes. Coping with problems. (*entering into computer*) Erm. CON . . . FL . . . IC . . . T. conflict?
SHAUN: I dunno. . . . Not 'other'. . . . Sorrow. There was sorrow. . . . Sorrow means they're sad.
ALICE: Yeah. They were sad.

This illustrates their comprehension. Alice and Shaun are making decisions about the text and in doing so find themselves having different opinions. As children become more able to interpret texts they find themselves arguing about the themes within a text. This is an essential part of interpreting texts in groups. Alice and Shaun show that they are capable of discussing literary features, supporting each other's understanding of the text and reminding each other of what they have read and understood.

Catering for fluent and competent readers

Working with a diverse group of readers and writers, particularly as they grow older, can sometimes pose great problems for teachers wishing to extend the range of the most fluent or to broaden the reading diet of the competent, but stuck-in-a-groove, readers. How can you continue to teach about texts when readers are fluent and competent? One way is to use a specially planned individualised programme of reading. The Reading Challenge outlined here is specifically tailored to suit the needs of the individual reader. Whilst it encourages independent reading, it is important that the teacher has a clear overview of what any child using the programme is reading. It is based on a contract between teacher and reader which aims to balance enjoyment and comfortable reading with more challenging reading tasks – to achieve a variety of satisfactions in reading. It suggests two kinds of reading: Challenging Books and Favourite Reading. While it is based on individual preferences, the children will need help from the teacher, or another adult, in making decisions. It is at the point of developing the contracts that the teacher's knowledge of the reader is critical in order to make sensitive interventions based on classroom observations. It can be equally effective with readers at Key Stages 1 and 2 who are fluent readers. The challenges can be used as a basis for home/school reading so that parents can be involved in supporting development.

Before any individual plan is provided, it is important to find out as much as possible about the current reading profile of the child. An older reader might enjoy filling in the Personal Reading Profile (Fig. 6.17) individually, but it might be better to arrange a specifically timed reading interview with younger fluent readers. Alternatively, this is something which a classroom reading helper or a parent might do. You will certainly need to discuss the answers to this profile as you begin to negotiate the reading programme with the children. While the Reading Challenge is intended for the most fluent readers, the Personal Reading Profile can be used with any reader and profiles of a whole class can give you information about areas where you need to provide more experience of texts or where you can build on existing knowledge. In terms of individual development, it gives you a chance to offer personally tailored challenges to children at different levels of fluency and assurance.

The Reading Challenge is based on the view that progress in reading doesn't just mean tackling printed text which gets smaller and denser as we grow older, although, of course, reading that kind of text is part of what a developed reader can do. Nowadays it is clear that there are many different types of text which need to be scrutinised carefully if the readers of the future are to be able to have a critical understanding of what is presented to them. One of the aims of the challenge is to ensure that the developing reader is fluent and competent at tackling all kinds of text. Breadth of reading repertoire is an important aspect of full competence. For this reason, individuals are asked to choose for themselves an area of Challenging Reading (Fig. 6.18) to widen their scope.

At the same time, it is important to maintain enthusiasm and enjoyment of the kinds of texts the reader already enjoys – their Favourite Reading (Fig. 6.19). For the reader to make progress, there needs to be some kind of activity linked to the reading, but asking for the routine book review tends to become a sterile exercise, not genuinely engaging the reader's intellect or imagination. It is necessary, therefore, to find ways for the child to read with continuing enthusiasm but to be encouraged to analyse their favourite kinds of reading in some way. However, it is deadly to the process of enjoying reading if a routine develops where a reader has to 'do something' with every book he/she reads. The suggestions on the Favourite Reading Activities sheets (Figs 6.20 and 6.21) offer choices for children at both Key Stages 1 and 2 which are designed to develop an analytical view of texts. The Favourite Reading Activities can also be introduced into regular classroom work when appropriate.

The following case study describes how Jackie Lucas used the Reading Challenge with a group of Year 6 children who were very fluent and assured readers, but who were 'quiet, methodical and quite conventional in their choice of reading material'. The school where Jackie works is in a rural area. Before they began their Reading Challenge the class had completed Personal Reading Profiles.

The Reading Challenge

Case Study 8

At the beginning of the year the children in my Year 6 class showed a distinct preference for writing brief, non-committal book reviews, with an emphasis on the story and the award of points out of ten rather than any attempt to analyse the characters and the plot from a more critical viewpoint. The school has long had a policy of USSR (Uninterrupted, Sustained, Silent Reading) for half an hour each day, immediately after lunch. This should be a welcome and challenging experience for Year 6 but for some children it had become rather routine and monotonous. Several children clung to their personal favourites, preferring to 'play safe' with genre and style despite the wide variety of books available to them. The Reading Challenge offered the perfect solution for the following reasons:

(a) **PERSONAL READING PROFILE Name: ....**

Fill in the columns to say what you think about different kinds of reading

Type of reading	Like very much	Quite like	OK	Don't really like	UGH!
Comics (say which ones)					
Magazines (say which ones)					
Newspapers (say which ones)					
Computer games (say which ones)					
CD-ROM information (give details)					
Picture books (say which ones)					
Information books (say which kind – e.g. science, animals, history)					
Stories (say which kind – e.g. adventure, horror, about animals . . . or particular authors)					
Poetry (say which kind/authors)					
Plays (say which kind)					

Figure 6.17(a) Finding out about an individual's reading preferences

(b) PERSONAL READING PROFILE – sheet 2

Answer these questions:

- When do you like to read?
- Do you need to be in a particular mood to read?
- How long do you usually read for?
- What makes reading difficult for you?
- Does anyone read aloud to you at home or do you read to anyone?
- Does anyone tell you what books to read?
- What two books have you really enjoyed reading recently?
- What did you particularly like about them?

Figure 6.17(b) Finding out about an individual's reading preferences

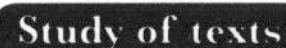

CHALLENGE READING SHEET

Reader's name .... Date ....

Type of Challenge Reading...

Agreed number of weeks for reading two books....... Ending date.........................

Title of chosen Challenge book ....

....

Author...

Agreed date for 'comments so far' ....

Comments so far (include comments on what the book is about; how long you spend reading it each day; any good points/bad points; how well you think you're tackling the challenge . . . **):**

Comments after finishing the book (What did you think about it? Would you recommend it to anyone else? Good points/bad points?**):**

Figure 6.18 Finding reading to extend the range

- The programme gave the children responsibility for their own learning and enjoyment, as they had to sign a written agreement with me to read a given number of books within a set time limit.
- Parental support could be enlisted.
- The programme was easy to administer and monitor.
- Success was inbuilt as the children have visible evidence of their progress.

FAVOURITE READING SHEET

Reader's name.. **Date** ....

Type of Favourite Reading ....

Agreed number of weeks for reading two books .... Ending date ....

Title of chosen Favourite book ....

....

Author ....

Chosen Activity ....

Agreed date for 'comments so far' ....

Comments so far (include comments on how well you think you're doing the Activity and what you think about it so far):

Questions (Are there any questions you'd like to ask about the book or the Activity?):

Comments after finishing the Activity (What did you learn? Did you enjoy the Activity?):

Figure 6.19 Comfortable kinds of reading

Starting off

We spent an entire English session of one hour and ten minutes introducing the programme, discussing how it would operate and talking through any potential difficulties. Everyone sat on the floor in a big circle, with numerous baskets of books in the middle to show the wide range of texts available. These included:

- Challenging poetry books: e.g. *The Iron Wolf* by Ted Hughes; *The Last Rabbit* (on ecological issues)
- Plays: e.g. *The Animated Tales* adaptations of Shakespeare: *Macbeth* and *Hamlet*
- Sophisticated picture books: e.g. *Rose Blanche* by Ian McEwen and Roberto Innnocenti; *Zoo* and *Kirsty Knows Best* by Anthony Browne; *The Church Mice* series
- Complex texts with an emphasis on emotional conflict: *Dicey's Song* by Cynthia Voigt, *The Diary of Anne Frank; Journey to Jo'Burg* by Beverley Naidoo
- Children's classics: *Anne of Green Gables; The Lord of the Rings; The Secret Garden*
- Multicultural texts and picture books: *Atuk; The Ice Palace; The Root Cellar*
- Fantasy books: *The Deptford Mice* series
- Science Fiction and Horror stories: *Goosebumps; Point Horror*; John Christopher titles
- Non-fiction on any chosen subject.

Everyone was quite excited at the prospect of choosing two challenging texts and much animated discussion ensued. Some children asked if they could read books from home as they had Christmas and birthday book tokens to spend. That weekend, several parents were cajoled into driving to nearby towns with big bookshops to help select suitable books. It was most heartening to hear from these parents that they had really enjoyed the experience of sharing choices with their daughters and sons. Some mothers had enjoyed remembering their first readings of *What Katy Did* and *The Children of Green Knowe* and were keen to help their children tackle the challenge.

FAVOURITE READING ACTIVITIES – Key Stage 1

Choose one of these:

Draw a picture of a character you like. Write what you like about them.

Choose two poems you like and record them on the tape which is kept with the poetry books.

Make a poster with a drawing of the cover of your favourite book and write why you liked it.

Find a friend who likes the same book as you and make a play about the characters.

With a friend, practise telling the story of your favourite book so that you can share it with the class at story time.

Choose two parts of the story you liked and read them on to the tape recorder. Explain why you liked those parts.

Find another one or two books by the same author and read them.

Write in your Reading Diary two reasons why you like your favourite book.

Figure 6.20 Activities to promote analysis of comfortable texts – KS1

FAVOURITE READING ACTIVITIES – Key Stage 2

Choose any one of these:

- If the book or magazine has illustrations, or if you are reading comics, look at the pictures carefully and decide how they fit with the words. Do the pictures give you any different information from the words? Choose two illustrations that you like, describe them and say why you like them.
- In a book with characters, or a play, decide on one character that you'd like to be. What do you like about them? Pick out a few examples from the story to show points about the character that you like. After you've finished reading the book explain what you think might happen to the character after the story has ended. Write it as if you are the character.
- If you are reading a map book, or a book with photographs or mostly illustrations, choose one and imagine what it might have looked like 100 years ago – or what it might look like in a hundred years' time. Draw what you think you would see and write a few notes to explain what you have drawn.
- If you are reading an adventure story, choose one exciting part that you like and turn it into a play script. Remember to include stage directions and sound effects. Get some friends to act it out with you. (Have a look at a play to see how to set it out.)
- If you have chosen poetry, decide on three or four poems that you particularly like. Have a look at them very carefully and decide just what it is that appeals to you about them – it might be different for each one. Write a script for a radio or television poetry programme to introduce each of your choices and explain to listeners/viewers what you enjoy about them.
- For any kind of reading, work out a plan for a television programme based on the book – it might be a documentary, a children's programme or a story. Make notes for a programme lasting about half an hour (if it is a story you will only be able to do one episode) and remember to think about background music and scenery.
- If you are reading a play, a story or a poem with a story, decide what it would look like if you put it on the stage. Design the stage set and costumes, making notes about why you have decided to set it like that. You may need to choose just one episode if you are reading a story.
- If your book appears in a different version – for example, if there is a video or television version or if there is similar information on CD-ROM – compare the book and the other version. Is one more informative/enjoyable than the other? Why?
- Write your own sequel to a story or information pack about the area you've been reading about. You may need someone to help you plan it out and read through drafts with you.

Figure 6.21 Activities to promote analysis of comfortable texts – KS2

The first two weeks

After the initial groundwork, the pupils were left to their own devices for almost two weeks. However, it was interesting to note the high levels of concentration during our reading times over the ensuing days. There was also extra reading going on at lunchtime. Overheard snippets of conversation revealed a network of recommended reading, especially among the girls. The deadline for reading and reviewing two books was two weeks. This may seem a short time for long and complex texts but the children are avid readers and many chose one long and one much shorter book. The completed reviews were given to me on a Friday afternoon and we arranged to share the outcomes on the following Monday, so that the texts would still be fresh in their minds.

The main points evident from the first reviews were that

- everyone enjoyed the challenge
- everyone had set aside a given time to read each night as well as in school each day
- the book reviews were generally longer and more detailed
- some of the most able children made lengthy analytical comments whereas the children of more average ability found this aspect of the challenge difficult to complete well
- everyone was eager to discuss choices and to recommend titles in our class discussion.

We decided to set another challenge before embarking on the Favourite Reading Activities Sheet (KS2) so that everyone had a chance to complete their selection of books. Although one or two children still found it difficult to express their reactions to the texts in more critical and analytical terms, the majority of reviews showed more reflection and maturity than their work had revealed previously. There was greater emphasis on character and plot and much more thought given to the reasons for choosing and liking a particular book.

As well as discussing their written reviews, I have had frank discussions with the group about their participation in the scheme. Somehow, empowering the children to make their own choice of challenging reading material has resulted in a greater willingness to debate in an open and honest manner:

The Animated Tales: Hamlet Shakespeare abridged by Leon Garfield (London, Heinemann 1992)
Jenny is one of the younger Year 6 children. She is an avid reader with an open mind and an engagingly honest turn of phrase:

> This book is hard to get into and understand. The language is difficult, too. I am finding the challenge hard. I don't recommend this book at all unless you're addicted to Shakespeare.

The Mousehole Cat Antonia Barber, illustrated by Nicola Bayley (London, Walker Books 1993)
Merrick's reading tends to be functional but his mother is keen for him to read more challenging texts:

> It is a lot harder than I thought it would be. I was aiming to read it in a day but it took me two because of the complex words.

Anne of Green Gables L.M. Montgomery (London, Bantam Books 1993)
Lauren is a very bright and lively girl with an astute eye for detail and a good sense of fun:

I liked Anne because she seemed very dedicated to her friends and was always happy and forgiving. Even though she was sometimes moody and sulky she usually tried to rectify the situations. I think Matt Cuthbert really enjoyed Anne's company and was always ready to listen to her.

Space Demons Gillian Rubenstein (London, Mammoth 1990)
Beth has specific difficulties with language but is a determined reader with strong opinions:

This book is brilliant! As soon as I started it I was wondering what would happen. I am so pleased I started reading this.

The Secret Garden Frances Hodgson Burnett (London, Albion Press 1991)
Gemma is a mature and quiet girl with romantic tastes:

I think I'm tackling the challenge really well and enjoying doing it, too. It's got me back into reading at home.

The Mystery of the Whale Tattoo Franklin W. Dixon, one of The Hardy Boys series (London, Armada/HarperCollins 1992)
Nick is a realist who plans to study science and adores science fiction:

Some of the jokes are a bit flat and repetitive so I think it would not be my first choice for me again.

The most striking aspect of these comments is their honesty. Before the Reading Challenge, comments tended to be rather bland but now an element of bravery is detectable as the children gain confidence in expressing their opinions.

My interview with Lauren shows the level of critical analysis:

Did you enjoy the Reading Challenge?

Yes. *Anne of Green Gables* was a book about a dream world, not realistic like I normally read. Everything was just a bit too coincidental and almost too happy. Anne was also a bit melodramatic. I thought there wasn't too much suspense. But I liked it because it was different, especially the setting of time and place.

Which types of book were you reluctant to read previously?

Picture books because I thought they were simple. Science fiction too – it's unrealistic.

Would you choose a similar book again?

I might because I admired Anne's character. She was a bit moody but she was an optimist like me.

What do you think you learned from this challenge?

I realise that reading more widely is better. It improves your skills and knowledge of words. Picture books can be just as enjoyable as thick books. Now I'll try to read more poetry especially Victorian or even earlier and lots of Scottish stuff like Robbie Burns.

The next stage

Following the success of the Reading Challenge I decided to proceed to the Favourite Reading sheets, giving the children the opportunity to revert to their favourite genre, style or author and to extend their appreciation of the text by completing a specific task relating to the selected text. We are now into the second week of fervent reading of old favourites. There is a familiar glow on the faces of the Enid Blyton fans, the Goosebumps groupies and the Roald Dahl devotees. Nick heaved a sigh of relief and said *Thank goodness I can go back to reading Alien* and *Predator* now but really I couldn't resist reminding him that it would only be for another two weeks.

Because this group has responded so positively to the Reading Challenge I have discussed the possibility of introducing it to a group of Year 5 readers who are extremely good and mature readers and who would benefit from extending their range of genre, style and author. The Year 5 teachers are enthusiastic and have been busy selecting texts from our recent Book Fair. After a trial period, we may extend the scheme to Years 3 and 4.

Poetry

As with children's knowledge and experience of video texts, their knowledge of poetic forms almost always begins before they come to school. Children will have knowledge of rhymes, jingles and songs drawn from their communities, their families, television and audio tapes. Early reading is often built on strongly rhythmic and rhyming language. The job of the teacher is to extend that experience and to help children pay conscious attention to poetic forms of all kinds – narrative, lyric, haiku, acrostic, riddles, limericks; funny poems and serious poems; funny poems which carry serious messages; poetry in standard English and colloquial speech, in different dialects and from different historical periods; poems about feelings and poems about actions; about animals, nature, machinery – every aspect of human experience. Poetry offers children – and adults – the chance to share in a range of feelings and thoughts and in composing their own poetry children can express these in a careful way which pays attention to the precise uses of language for specific effects.

Teachers are familiar with poetry which children enjoy; often the poems are the same ones which have been read with pleasure by young people for several generations. Others are poems which reflect children's contemporary cultural worlds. Some of the enduring favourites weren't written specifically for children in the first place. One of the most effective ways to encourage children to read and enjoy poetry is the enthusiasm of the teacher for old – and new – favourites. Just reading poetry aloud for the experience is a very good way to spend a few minutes in the classroom; it will have long-term beneficial effects. Morag Styles points out that 'What we have now is a positive climate for poetry. And traditional poetry is still widely available and enjoyed.' She refers to the ways in which poets of the past did – or did not – enter into the world of childhood. For example, Christina Rossetti captures the relationship between mother and child; Robert Louis Stevenson accurately reflects the world of play and Walter de la Mare 'looked at the world with the wondering, appreciative eyes of a small child'. In summarising the differences between traditional and contemporary poetry for children, Morag Styles suggests that the changes might be:

Morag Styles 'Every child may joy to hear' in Morag Styles, Eve Bearne and Victor Watson eds 1996 *Voices Off: texts, contexts and readers*, London, Cassell

- that the everyday experiences of ordinary young people have become the subject matter for a lot of poetry
- that language has changed. Standard English is still represented in contemporary poetry but dialect, patois, the vernacular have become more evident
- that poets experiment more with form. Verse forms and regular metre are still there, but there is greater evidence of free verse and variety of layout and illustration as part of the poem's text.

She also points to the diversity within contemporary poetry for young people:

- various branches of humour – parody, cautionary verse, nonsense, jokes, limericks, nursery rhymes – and extensive word play
- the continuation of the ballad tradition (e.g. Charles Causley) and narrative poetry
- poets who write in well-formed metre (e.g. Kit Wright) and others who use free verse
- exploration of children's lives through honest, realistic, sensitive poetry tackling serious issues like divorce, the environment, cruelty, death, loneliness and through light-hearted accounts of school and family life
- nature poetry in a range of guises
- poetry of magic and wonder (e.g. Richard Edwards)
- dialect poetry (John Agard, James Berry, Jackie Kay)
- translations of poetry from other cultures
- the oral tradition in poetry from all over Britain and the world
- poets who straddle different kinds of poetry – for example, how might the work of Allan Ahlberg, Libby Houston or Adrian Mitchell be characterised?

Reading poetry together

Whilst it may be thought that poetry is usually read as an individual act of reflection, there is great scope in the classroom for collaborative reading – in pairs, groups and the whole class. Helen Cook and Morag Styles explain why poetry is ideal for group reading:

1. It invites reading in unison as well as by individual voices.
2. Poetry offers close attention to sound and form. It lends itself to reading aloud: although there is much satisfaction to be gained from silent reading of the printed page, there is also a side to poetry that is inescapably oral.
3. The strong sense of rhyme and rhythm in some poetry (particularly that suitable for a younger age group) goes hand in hand with reading aloud and aids prediction.
4. As poems tend to be short, they can fit flexibly into brief as well as more sustained periods for group reading. And the pure variety of poetry accessible to young readers means there is something to suit every taste.
5. Poetry is excellent subject matter for discussions which can range through content, form, language, authorial intentions etc. and provoke shared insights, interpretations and new understandings.

(pp. 3–4)

Helen Cook and Morag Styles 1991 *The Cambridge Poetry Box*, Cambridge, Cambridge University Press. This is a set of group texts including poetry suitable for different age groups

Modelling reading is crucial in supporting group reading of poetry; in the early years each child in a group of three to six has an individual copy of the same book or booklet of poems which the teacher (or other supporting adult) reads aloud while the children follow the text. As children become more familiar with the poems and gain greater independence and fluency as readers, they take over the role of reading aloud themselves. Tapes of poems and Big Books with collections of children's favourite poems can be useful ways of introducing different kinds of poetry to very young children. When you are asking children to read (anything, including poetry) aloud, it is a good idea to allow them rehearsal time. As they grow older, groups of readers can tackle reading independently and do not need an adult with them all the time. However, it is worth the teacher joining the group occasionally to give the children experience of hearing an adult reading poetry aloud.

You might like to consider the following questions about your own favourite poems:

- What titles (or any sections) do you remember of poems which you came to love when you were a child?
- How did you meet them? Did someone read them to you? Did you read them yourself? Perhaps you didn't enjoy poetry at all. Why did you (or didn't you) like these poems?

And about the poetry you use in the classroom:

- What traditional poetry do your pupils read and enjoy?
- Which traditional poems have you read to them recently?
- Which poets are their favourites?

some popular modern anthologies:

***Where the Sidewalk Ends* Shel Silverstein 1974**
***Mind Your Own Business* Michael Rosen 1974**
***Please Mrs Butler* Allan Ahlberg 1983**
***Gargling with Jelly* Brian Patten 1985**
***Say It Again, Granny* John Agard 1986**
***The New Kid on the Block* Jack Prelutsky 1986**
***Boo to a Goose* John Mole 1987**
***When I Dance* James Berry 1988**

Other titles can be found in the *Books for Keeps Guide – Poetry 0–13* eds Chris Powling and Morag Styles 1996.

These questions could also be a good way to start discussing poetry teaching with colleagues.

Morag Styles argues that poetry for children has always addressed serious concerns, taking the view that children can be interested in and capable of understanding serious issues. However, critics of contemporary poetry for children often suggest that humour has overtaken serious concerns and that 'quality' has been sacrificed in an attempt to amuse children.

Suggested activities

Find four or five poems which represent some of the diversity outlined by Morag Styles to read with your class – try to be adventurous and choose some which you might not normally read to them.

Take a few of the traditional poems you identified as favourites and compare them with the contemporary poems you have chosen. Talk with the children about humour and serious concerns. What do they have to say about the quality of contemporary poetry?

Use the lists in Fig. 6.22 to check out the ways in which you use poetry. How might you extend the range of poetry your children experience?

Group work involving poetry need not be restricted to reading other people's poems. In the following case study, Anthony Wilson, a Section 11 teacher, explains how he worked with two Year 3 classes who wrote group poems.

Case Study 9

Carnival Week: 'Where we can talk freely'

Each term at Sir James Barrie primary school in Battersea, South London, there is a special week-long focus on one part of the curriculum. In the autumn, there is a Book Week and in the spring a Science Week. Each summer the school has a Carnival Day (a Saturday) which explicitly sets out to celebrate the diversity and the richness of the different cultures represented in the school. Leading up to Carnival Day is Carnival Week where, as with Book Week and Science Week, the children take part in a range of specially prepared activities relating to that week's theme.

Last July, a literature focus was added to the Carnival Week timetable for the first time. As we both have a strong interest in poetry, the English coordinator and I set up two programmes of events focusing on poetry reading and writing. The first comprised two twenty-minute readings each morning, taking in all the classes in the school over the week. These took place in the library. We read a range of poetry from around the world – lyrical verse and nonsense rhymes; jingles and spells; riddles and interactive performance pieces. The aim of these readings was simply for the children to enjoy listening to poetry being read aloud. There was no pressure for them to produce any written work in response to the readings and they were free to join in with the parts they knew.

Using poetry in the classroom

How do you use poetry?

- As a basis for close and careful reading
- Reading several poems by the same poet and discussing common features or themes
- Using funny poems as models for writing
- Using narrative poems for other activities which show comprehension:
  - mapping *The Lady of Shalott* by Tennyson or *Hiawatha* by Longfellow: What are the features of the landscape mentioned in the poem?
  - discussing moral questions like the piper luring the children away in Browning's *The Pied Piper of Hamelin* or Beowulf killing Grendel
  - creating new stories; explaining just what happened on *Flannan Isle* by Wilfred Gibson or what happened when the family got home after *The Car Trip* by Michael Rosen
- Group reading
- Poem of the Day – poems selected by children read aloud either by the chooser or the teacher
- Drama work – any poem can lead to enactment or newly imagined events
- To provoke debate about specific issues
- To enjoy for the sound of the words or the sentiments expressed
- To talk about alliteration, onomatopoeia, syllables, metaphor, metre, refrain, simile . . .
- To study language used for particular effects or compare older language use with modern expression
- Comparison between the same subject matter written about by different poets – cat poems, poems about brothers and sisters, etc.

How does poetry appear in your classroom?

- As displays of poems recommended by children – *poems you might like to read*
- A board of favourite expressions, images, extracts from poems
- Tapes of poems – commercially produced or made by the children
- Collected as anthologies of favourites – families can join in this, too
- Collected as anthologies of children's own poetry
- As part of cross-curricular work

Figure 6.22 Checklist of poetry activities

The second programme comprised two forty-five-minute writing workshops, spread over four mornings, with two Year 3 classes. The aim of these sessions was to re-read some of the poems from the readings, discuss any issues and feelings which arose from them and to try and shape these into poems which stood on their own. Key poems in these sessions were James Berry's 'Isn't My Name Magical?', Eve Merriam's 'Thumbprint' and Jackie Kay's 'Sassenachs'. The themes in these poems – of individuality, difference, identity, voice and naming – were very much those which are explored during Carnival Week. I wanted to give the children a chance to express what they felt about themselves – their backgrounds, their families, their friends, their religions, their clothes, their skin. I have listened to children discussing these topics passionately in the playground, in the dining hall, and on the way to school, but rarely in the classroom without the discussions becoming teacher-dominated. I wanted the children's writing to capture some of the passion and pride and to celebrate it explicitly.

Each session began with a quick re-cap on the readings: Were there any poems the children particularly enjoyed? What made them good? After discussing some of these elements, I re-read just one or two poems, always including one of those listed above. I asked: What did the poems make you feel? Tell me about those feelings. Spread out on the table were large pieces of paper and thick felt-tip pens. I began by listing what they felt the poems were about and then listed their responses to those issues. I have been influenced by Michael Rosen's book on writing workshops, *Did I Hear You Write?* I explained to the children that we would be writing free verse because that is the best way in poetry for getting down on paper the way we speak. I asked their permission to write down words and phrases as they talked and tried from that point onwards to restrict my contributions to asking questions rather than making statements.

In one of the first workshops, one child remarked of James Berry's poem *It's about liking who you are*. I asked *What do you like about yourselves?* The following poem more or less wrote itself with each child contributing a line of their own:

Myself

I like the way my fingers hold pencils tight.
I like how I type fast on the computer.
I like my arms saving the Year Four shots in goal.
I like the colour of my skin.
I like my behaviour because I win stars.
I like myself because I'm beautiful.
(Alan, La Tanya, Liam, Matab, Monique and Sadique)

Another morning the discussion about what children liked about themselves went much deeper into areas of social relationships, language and family:

Friendly Country

I like it when I make loads of friends
and don't get bullied.
When I read a book
and no-one disturbs me it's the best.
My country is wicked because it's Jamaican
where we can talk freely.
Talking Jamaican to my mum
is cool and nice.
If you get hurt
and you talk Jamaican to your mum
it makes you feel happy.
(Craig, Dare, Elmas, Imran and Yassen)

One of the best things about running a rolling programme of workshops was that each morning there was a fresh set of poems to read and discuss. Having used poems from the readings as initial stimulus, it was the children's own poems which evolved into starting points for discussion as the week went on. The level of maturity displayed in some of the discussions was, by the end of the week, quite startling, getting to the point where I virtually became invisible after asking my opening questions. This next poem is clearly influenced by James Berry's 'Isn't My Name Magical?' but was a huge influence on the children who read it the next day, pushing them into areas of expression they might otherwise not have thought possible.

Ourselves, How We Feel

Everyone's name is different
Your own name
Is yours
and it sticks to you only
You can keep it to yourself
You shouldn't shout it out
You mustn't let anyone
take it from you.

We like our colour
because it suits us
We love our skin
because it's on us only
Our eye colour
is special to us
our hair is beautiful
like silk.
(Anum, Amber, Bilal, Dele,
Juan and Stephen)

Our Lives Are Different From Other People

Our blood is different
and our imaginations
and our gods

You should never be ashamed
if you look different
because we all have
the same thing
inside

feelings
heart
voices
five senses

different colour eyes watering
different brains knowing
different people's names

Some people are scared
in the dark
Others help them face their fears

Some people are good tempered
They help you do what you can't do
like science and maths

Everyone has problems and secrets
We tell lies jokes and the truth
We tell lies
so we don't get into trouble
for telling the truth
(Carl, Donovan, Marcus, Messie, Nathan,
Ryan, Ryan and Sezer)

Natalie Goldberg, in her book *Wild Mind*, talks about the moment when as a young woman she knew she had been given permission to follow her dream as a writer when she met one of her literary heroes for the first time; and Ted Hughes has said that the real progress in any writer's life occurs when he manages to outwit his own inner police system. This is the kind of language I would use to describe what was going on in those writing workshops: the 'event', as Robert Lowell called it, of children being told that they could say things they didn't know were legitimate or permissible and the confident, self-aware celebration which followed it, a place where, for a moment, in all senses of the phrase, they knew they could 'talk freely':

Who I Am

My brain tells me
if I'm happy

My face tells me
to smile

My eyes pour down
raindrops
when I'm hurt

My hands show me
that I'm strong and powerful

My teeth sparkle
when the sun comes out

It melts ice on my lemonade
and you can see in your
shadow
bobbing down the street
to your mates.
(Antonia, Esther, Rodney,
Sheila, Tyrone and Whitney)

James Berry 'Isn't My Name Magical?' in John Agard and Grace Nichols eds *A Caribbean Dozen: poems from Caribbean poets*, London, Walker Books 1994; Jackie Kay 'Sassenachs' in *Two's Company*, London, Puffin 1994; Eve Merriam 'Thumbprint' in Susanna Steele and Morag Styles eds *Mother Gave a Shout: poems by women and girls*, London, A. & C. Black 1990; Michael Rosen *Did I Hear You Write?*, London, André Deutsch 1989; Natalie Goldberg *Wild Mind: living the writer's life*, Rider 1991

Drama

Watching plays – on video, in the cinema or theatre – is often seen as a way of helping children learn about texts, but it is equally important for children to read and write drama texts for themselves. Role play, simulation and group drama are acknowledged as important elements in learning, but improvised drama can become the basis for scripted work, redrafted orally and rehearsed before being written down. There is also a need to find a balance between drama as experience for children and the more performative aspects of drama. The activities suggested in Fig. 6.23 can all be used for creating drama texts with children – oral or written – and as the basis for exploring existing texts through drama.

Investigating, experimenting, presenting, responding

One of the most common drama practices involves small groups working simultaneously on a given but general storyline or event. This can lead to prepared work which is shown to other groups, but need not always end in performance. Helen Nicholson

Drama Activities

Structured drama

Role play, where individuals take on the roles of specified people, and **simulation**, where role play is extended to fulfil character outlines and scenarios prepared by the teacher for particular purposes. These can take the form of meetings to decide on actions, air opinions, discuss solutions to problems, for example, *how to get rid of the dragon without harming it*; to discuss development issues; to hold 'trials' as in *Wind in the Willows*; as guests discussing Macbeth's behaviour after the Banquo-haunted feast.

Transformations

Working with a known story can be a good scaffold for drama work. Stories need not be followed precisely; children might be asked to change parts of the story or mix up two or more stories or genres or introduce characters from one story to characters in another:

- What if Jack's Giant ate something which made him shrink?
- What if Sleeping Beauty didn't like the Prince?
- What would the story of Snow White be like as an episode of *Neighbours* or *EastEnders*?
- What might have happened if the Big Bad Wolf had met Aladdin and wanted the lamp?

Transformations might involve:

Another point of view: where an event is enacted from the point of view of different characters, for example the Ugly Sisters' version of the Cinderella story or the Minotaur's experiences in the tale of Theseus' exploits.
Hot seating: where one person in role sits in the 'hot seat' and is interviewed by the rest of the group about their character, for example, the Wolf in *Red Riding Hood* might be interrogated about what he was doing in the wood in the first place or Daedalus might be interviewed about the faults in his design system for Icarus' wings.
Teacher in role: can often model hot seating effectively as a character from a known story: Goldilocks explaining just why she broke into someone else's house, stole their food and broke up their furniture; Bottom explaining what happened while he was enchanted.
Freeze frame: the drama is either stopped at a particular moment as if it were freeze frame or a frozen picture can be set up as if in a newspaper, for example, the end of the race in the Tortoise and the Hare fable.
Thought tracking: this can be done while children are holding a freeze frame; the teacher taps a child on the shoulder who has to give voice to the thoughts of the character at the moment; what would the Hare and the Tortoise be thinking as they crossed the finishing line?

Investigative drama

This can be based on a real-life incident or one in fiction; the children have to research the background of the incident to add detail to the drama, for example extracts from Anne Frank's diary, Beverley Naidoo's novel *Journey to Jo'burg* or the events depicted in the Bayeux Tapestry.

Working with texts

This should not be seen as the traditional play-reading-round-the-class routine, but as part of learning to work with a type of text which sets out to do something different from a novel or a newspaper article. For example, group reading of plays leading to performances which concentrate on character depiction; using a short extract from *A Midsummer Night's Dream* as the basis for costume/setting design or director's instructions about how a character might be enacted; adapting part of a novel. The differences between narrative text and play text need to be discussed and made explicit; what is missed out? what is added? what happens to the narrator's voice or descriptive detail of setting when a story is adapted as a play?

P. Baldwin and L. Hendy 1994 *The Drama Box*, London, HarperCollins

Figure 6.23 Some examples of drama activities

Hiawyn Oram and Satoshi Kitamura 1993 *Angry Arthur*, London, Andersen Press

gives an example of using the picture book *Angry Arthur* by Hiawyn Oram and Satoshi Kitamura as a basis for drama work. She emphasises that this is not a matter of 'acting out the story' but a way of recreating the narrative in a different mode of expression – the artistic mode of drama. The dramatic appeal lies in the tension between the exterior world of lived experience and the inner world of the emotions:

Helen Nicholson 'Voices on stage' in Styles *et al.* *Voices off*

> The plot is simple: a boy who is not allowed to stay up late to watch a Western on television becomes increasingly angry until his mood subsides and he has forgotten the reason for his rage. But the story is a complex web of the real figures in his life – his parents and grandparents – with his imaginary and increasingly fantastic world of the emotions. As Arthur's anger grows, it is enacted, destroying his house, town, world and universe. This is, of course, an extended metaphor – the text represents abstract emotions as if they were concrete and visible. Thus the focus of the drama lies in exploring the relationship between the implied narrative of Arthur's 'real life' at home and the imaginative representation of the senses.
>
> (p. 255)

Narratives allow children to create their own visual images. Helen Nicholson explains:

> In the work on *Angry Arthur*, there are two pictorial texts available. One is Hiawyn Oram and Satoshi Kitamura's picture book, with Kitamura's wonderfully graphic interpretations of anger. The other comprises the children's own kinaesthetic dramatic images. By setting these side by side there is scope for relating one to another, of questioning how the mood has been depicted and of exploring how the formal qualities of the text make meaning. It is for this reason that I do not show the book until the words of the text have been used to create a drama.
>
> (p. 257)

This follows the work of the National Curriculum Council's Arts in Schools Project.

The process of making the drama is seen in four distinct phases: *investigating, experimenting, presenting, responding.*

Helen Nicholson's framework outlining work on *Angry Arthur* has been used successfully with pupils of all ages and illustrates the areas of learning which are associated with each stage of the artistic process of making a drama. Fig. 6.24 includes extracts from her framework. Other work might include investigating sound – both vocal and instrumental – in establishing atmosphere, experimenting with the narrative through freeze-frames of the action, drawing the mood they have created or using movement to express elements of the narrative. This process can be used to create a drama from any other text, using sound, voice, movement, language and drawing.

Non-fiction

This is often a neglected area in comparison with fiction, poetry and drama. However, just as there is a range of genres in fiction texts, there is also a wide variety of genres in non-fiction: environmental print of all kinds, including advertising and presented in a range of media; reference books and material; specialist information books, films, videos and CD-ROMs; photographs; reports in newspapers, magazines and business material; biography and autobiography; persuasive texts – often experienced as orally presented on television; instructions and explanations in leaflets, manuals, guidebooks, cookery books; maps and their keys; diagrams, tables of figures and charts; analysis, commentary and reviews. And no doubt more.

The kinds of text seen on CD-ROMs are now referred to as multimedia non-linear text.

Artistic process	Teaching strategies	Areas of learning
Investigating words	**Speaking dialogue:** in a circle, every other member of the group is given a line of dialogue from the text to memorise. They then repeat them simultaneously, in the style of: (i) a racing commentator; (ii) a weather forecaster; (iii) a slowing down tape recorder, etc.	Enhances awareness of tone in language; gives a sense of the 'tune' of the words in creating meaning
Investigating the character	**Describing feelings:** one member of the group lies on a large roll of paper and is drawn round. It is explained that this is the character who is angry. Inside the figure, words are written which express how he feels; on the paper outside the figure, the group write what he may be doing.	Seeing contrast between interior and exterior life of character. Speculation about action
Experimenting with sound, movement and poetry	**Making a dramatic sequence:** the class divides into five groups. Each group is given a different extract from the text which represents Arthur's anger: (i) 'a stormcloud exploding thunder and lightning and hailstones' (ii) 'a hurricane hurling rooftops and chimneys and church spires' etc.	Consideration of the texture and tone of poetic language Using poetry to create dramatic atmosphere in sound and movement Development of the aural and visual aspects of drama: rhythm, dynamic, pattern, pace, tone, space
Experimenting with dramatic composition	**Structuring the drama:** the groups use their work with the dialogue and the poetic language as a basis for the structure of a whole-class play. They need to decide: (i) the order of the storm (the sequence of pictures may help here) (ii) how to portray the naturalistic scenes between Arthur and others (iii) how these two interrelated elements of the drama might be woven together.	Selecting, ordering and rehearsing material Comparing the language of everyday registers with the poetic Juxtaposing two contrasting dramatic styles
Presenting to the group	**Rehearsal:** time to practise both small- and whole-group drama. Groups work in pairs, acting as directors for each other. Attention should be drawn to: (i) the way in which dramatic tension is created aurally and visually (ii) pace and delivery (iii) audience awareness.	Rehearsing and responding Consideration of theatrical and dramatic effectiveness Focus on the craft of the actor and director
Presenting to an audience	**Final performance**	Use of critical vocabulary Use of dramatic technique
Responding	**Read** *Angry Arthur.* Focus on discussion of the qualities of the pictures. Discuss the relationship between visual narrative and dramatic narrative.	Use of critical vocabulary Relationship between form, content and artistic medium

Figure 6.24 Extracts from Helen Nicholson's suggestions for making drama from *Angry Arthur*

Developing a critical eye

Whilst non-fiction materials are often used as the basis for information gathering in general learning, there is not as much emphasis put on the way they are constructed as texts. Children might be asked to write in a variety of these forms, but there may not be a great deal of explicit discussion of how an information leaflet or a guide for the local church is put together. At the same time, when children are asked to use information texts as sources for information gathering there is often a concern about them copying chunks of undigested material into their own work. This is one of the perennial concerns of teachers which can be helpfully dealt with by discussing non-fiction texts as carefully and thoroughly as teachers discuss fiction, poetry and plays.

The chart in Fig. 6.25 gives you an instant picture of the extent of your own explicit teaching of non-fiction texts. Used with colleagues, it can provide a basis for discussing continuity and progression in teaching non-fiction.

Type of text	When last read as a class	When last written by the class
Environmental print – signs, captions, advertisements, food labels	SATS week	week before half-term
Reference material: information books, films, videos, CD-ROMs	Today	continually
Reports in newspapers, magazines and business material	Term 1 (Yr 6)	
Photographs, maps, diagrams, charts, columns of figures	Maps today	Figures last week for Science
Biography and autobiography	not yet	
Persuasive texts	Before half-term →	
Instructions and explanations in leaflets, manuals, guide books, cookery books	last year →	
Analysis and commentary	continually talking about reading	continually book reviews

Figure 6.25 Types of non-fiction text taught to the whole class
(Blank provided in Appendix: A22)

In teaching about non-fiction texts, it is not only useful to consider the range of texts which might be covered, but to check out the opportunities for teaching about texts, as for fiction. p. 239

Non-fiction texts can be used as a basis for:

- studying the organisation, layout and presentation of different types of texts – including visual texts
- analysing the use of language, visual images, music, camera techniques to persuade, influence or inform
- locating, categorising and using information
- preparing questions or persuasive arguments
- offering explanations or instructions
- comparing fact and opinion or information derived from different sources
- teaching strategies for getting information from texts – skimming, scanning, indexing and fast referencing.

The charts in Figs 6.26 and 6.27 can be used to identify the ways in which you use non-fiction texts during any one term or year. Before you plan a teaching programme designed to increase the children's knowledge of the structures of non-fiction texts, it is worth finding out just how much non-fiction they read at home. The Personal Reading Profile might be a way of beginning to talk with your class about the amount pp. 260–1 of non-fiction reading they do but for more detailed information, you might ask them to complete the chart in Fig. 6.26. It would be a good idea to talk about it first, explaining that, for example, football magazines and pop magazines often have biographical articles. With younger children you might want to ask them to tell you more about environmental print and what they watch on the television (Fig. 6.27). This kind of grid on a large sheet of paper, a flipchart or a board, would be a good way to work with a whole class or group to collate information and to talk about the purposes of different kinds of non-fiction texts.

Once you have discovered what your pupils know about different kinds of non-fiction text, the next step is to plan for using that information as a strong basis for learning more about texts. Over a Key Stage or their whole primary school experience, children should be helped to analyse and understand the organisation, layout and presentation of different types of non-fiction texts – including visual texts. In a similar way to their reading of fictional material, from their earliest years children come to school with considerable knowledge drawn from the visual and print environment of the home and neighbourhood. Much of this knowledge is gained from forms of mass media.

Film, television, radio, recorded music, photographs, magazines, newspapers and advertising are essential parts of everyday life for most people. It is often through these media that information is given, persuasive arguments put forward, instructions and explanations are made. Much of our regular non-fiction reading comes from forms of mass communications media. However, just because they are so obvious and everyday they often escape the kinds of careful teaching attention which is paid to book-based literacy. The fact that they are so prominent in life means that if children are to be fully literate they need to be just as analytical and critically astute in handling these kinds of texts as the more traditional forms found in books. Added to that, new technologies associated with computers add more dimensions to the mass communications media which children need to be able to understand. They need to know how the forms of media work, how they produce meanings, how they are organised and how readers make sense of them. One significant advantage of using mass media formats to look at non-fiction texts is that they are readily available and familiar to the children.

Type of text	When did you last read it?	Give example
Signs, captions, adverts, food labels		
Information books or videos, television documentaries, CD-ROMs		
Newspaper or magazine report		
Photographs, maps, diagrams, charts, columns of figures		
Biography and autobiography – in magazines or books		
Instructions and explanations in leaflets, manuals, guide books, cookery books		

Figure 6.26 Reading non-fiction at home

Texts	Where do you see them?	What are they for?
Labels		
Signs		
Notices		
Adverts		
News		

Figure 6.27 Younger children's experience of environmental print

Persuasion and information

Many types of media seek to influence viewers or readers in some way – indeed, this is often a concern for media analysts. At the same time, however, they can be the source of information and prompt further investigation. As was clear from Helen Bromley's comments earlier in the chapter, even very young children gain a great deal of knowledge from their television watching. However, since developing discrimination is an important aspect of developing literacy, children should be encouraged to use their already critically aware senses to unpick some of the messages which are being conveyed through the mass media.

Analysing advertisements

How food is advertised: this might start with children listing the television adverts they can remember which advertise food of different kinds. The types of food can be recorded on a flipchart or board and categorised. With older children you might want to consider nutritional values and discuss proteins, carbohydrates and fats; younger children might categorise according to types of sweets, drinks, biscuits, snacks and meals. Even working from memory, children will be able to tell you something about the techniques used to persuade them and their families to buy products, but a more focused analysis will reveal even more information about techniques of persuasion. They might look at adverts which you have videoed specially or you could set homework for them to watch a certain number of adverts and note their analysis on a chart, as in Fig. 6.28. You could use a similar format (without questions on sound effects and voice-over) to analyse advertisements found in magazines and newspapers.

Children can be asked to analyse toy adverts, holidays, or just to look at all the advertisements broadcast during children's television times. Whilst doing this they are learning to identify features which are specifically aimed at persuasion and the easiest way to find out whether they have taken note of persuasive techniques is to ask them to prepare an advertisement, either for a magazine or as part of drama work, aimed to persuade a specifically chosen group of consumers to buy a particular product.

Advertising information

As an activity associated with the analysis of food advertising, children can very easily use food labelling as a resource for getting information. You might bring in some food labels and packets, or ask the children to bring some in themselves – breakfast cereal packets, for example, or tinned food labels. These can be used in a variety of ways: the lists of ingredients and tables of relative quantities of types of ingredient can be used to note the fat, carbohydrate and protein content of foods, or the minerals included in cereals, for example. This is very good practice in scanning for specific words in lists. Food labels can also be analysed according to layout – size of print, colour, etc. – to indicate what is considered the most important selling point about the food. The quantities and countries of origin are valuable information resources, too.

Post offices, doctors' and vets' waiting rooms are very good sources for information advertising. Children could be given an assignment to go and look at some of these, or you could provide some. An interesting way of using these is not just to look at the information they give, and how the sentences are written, but to compare them with, for example, the information given out by estate agents. When does information become persuasion? What kind of language is used for a notice about getting your television licence, having the cat immunised and the details of a house for sale? Is information in the form of advertisements ever 'just facts'? Informational material can be readily used as a basis for preparing questions: What would you want to ask the estate agent? What else do you need to know about immunising the cat or dog?

	Advertisement 1	Advertisement 2	Advertisement 3
What product is it advertising?			
Realistic/cartoon?			
Funny/serious?			
What kinds of characters? – adults? – children? – animals? – toys? – other?			
What words are used? – on the screen? – in the voice-over?			
What are the most obvious colours? What effect do they have?			
What kinds of music/background sounds are used?			
What did you notice about camera angles? Close-ups? Long shots?			
What are the advertisers trying to persuade you to think?			

Figure 6.28 Grid for analysing advertisements on television

Advertising is also a useful focus for looking at bias in gender or cultural stereotypes. Children might look at the number and type of adverts featuring boys and girls, men and women, or people from different ethnic backgrounds. What roles are they carrying out in the adverts? Are these realistic portrayals of life as the children experience it? However, it is important to be sensitive to home cultural arrangements when looking at these aspects. Deconstructing stereotypes can sometimes seem like criticising homes and families.

Environmental print: explanations and instructions

Scanning environmental print is a readily available way of looking at explanations or instructions. *What do the notices around the school tell you? What are the notices and labels in the classroom about? What about the instruction manual for the computer? What do you need to make instructions clear?* Children can be asked to write user-friendly instructions for the computer based on their own experience, or to make games to accompany the favourite reading books of the younger children, then to write instructions for parents. They might write explanations for the classroom about how to improve a draft copy of writing by revising, then proofreading, or how to set about writing an information book.

Comparing types of text

One of the most readily available materials for comparing fact, opinion or information derived from different sources comes in the form of newspapers – both local and national. Children can be invited to compare different versions of the same event; the language used for different kinds of article, for example sports reporting and news reporting; photographs of the same event from different papers and photographic information compared with newsprint. Magazines are equally useful and available and children can be set homework to investigate and analyse a whole range of aspects – from text organisation to use of language or informative content. Even the youngest children can talk about the magazines they like to look at – the toy pages of their parents' catalogues and magazines, perhaps.

In looking at the structures of text, a comparison between a newspaper account of an event and a story reveals the completely different ways in which information is given in each form. Where a newspaper gives the end of the story at the beginning – often in the first sentence or two – then drip-feeds details, a story book will give clues or details gradually building up to the climax or outcome of the narrative. These different structures are related to the different purposes of the texts and need to be talked about explicitly and tried out in practice. A class newspaper or magazine can do a great many jobs in helping children explore the different ways texts are put together and their own preferred newspaper and magazines act as very useful models and references.

Getting information from texts

The most common classroom experiences of non-fiction reading are getting information from books, encyclopaedias, dictionaries and thesauruses. Recently there has been a boom in non-fiction publishing of very attractive books with varied layout and detailed illustrations. However, these need to be taught about just as carefully as how to read fiction texts. There needs to be explicit discussion of how to read these texts because the way you read an information book is different from the way you read a story. The information contained in an illustrated information book is set out in a fragmented way, not arranged consistently in left to right sequence. You don't have to read the top left-hand bit of a double-page spread first as you would for printed narrative. The reading strategies are much more akin to reading a visual text like a picture book or a television screen, yet they are not very often discussed. As a result, children can often be at a loss about just how to read these texts. If you are an avid and fluent narrative reader, you may find it very confusing to have to pick up information from all over a page in a different sequence from reading from left to right and from top to bottom.

One of the benefits of the latest publishing initiatives which have introduced a wider range of Big Books is that information books are now (in small numbers) being published in this format. This means that teachers can show a whole class or a large group, of any age, just how to read a text which is displayed rather than narratively sequenced. Using a Big Book means that children can be helped to identify the kinds of information they can get from the illustrations and compare this with the information carried in the print. There are now Big Books on autobiography, development education, space exploration, science, history and geography so that it will be increasingly possible to teach children how to read these texts in exactly the same way that Big Books are used for story or poetry. After modelling how to get information from such texts and discussing the layout of pictorial text, the way it gives information, and the language used, children can be taught about contents pages, indexes, glossaries, résumés. Fig. 6.29 gives a checklist for considering the kinds of teaching which might have to accompany information gathering activities.

LEARNING TO READ INFORMATION TEXTS

Readers use a range of strategies for getting information out of different kinds of text. It is easy to assume that because children have learned to read they will be able to vary their reading for different purposes but in fact they have to be taught how to read a range of different types of text.

Before asking children to read any kind of non-fiction text independently, it is worth considering the following:

What is the purpose of the reading? What do I want them to get out of it?
– facts, opinions, instructions? concepts?

What do I want them to do when they have done the reading?
– write about it? make a diagram/flowchart? discuss issues for feedback?

What reading strategies will they need to use?
– skimming? scanning? double (fast/slow) read? picture cues?

How much time will they need?
– in the lesson? at home? over several sessions?

How will they be working?
– individually? in pairs? in groups?

How will I know what they have learned?
– by written work? oral feedback? presentations? other ways?

How will they evaluate their own learning?
– by written response? talking with others?

Figure 6.29 Checklist before using information texts in the classroom

Chapter 2 includes some suggestions for guiding children in getting information from books, but a key to their success in doing this will be the quality of the material available. Even very attractive-looking books can be almost impossible to understand or will not necessarily yield the kinds of information you want to make available to the children. It is important that you have read the books you want the children to use so that you can be sure that the texts are appropriate models. However, just getting information isn't enough; and exercises in skimming and scanning won't guarantee more informed readers. For information to become understanding or embedded knowledge, there needs to be some motivation to learn, and a chance to make something of the information gathered. p. 45

Once children have been taught strategies for getting information from texts, then they can use them in researching or making their own information texts. By making texts, children act on their knowledge and transform it into understanding. In the following case study account Ben Reave describes how some pupils in a Year 5/6 class wrote non-fiction texts. They had been given the opportunity to choose whether to write a story book or information book for a known reader.

Conveying information through texts

Case Study 10

About half the class, fifteen pupils in all, had opted to write information books. Some had chosen to write for parents or grandparents, others for younger brothers or sisters or even for friends in the same class. I wanted to see how well they could use the models of information books they had available in the classroom and the library to make texts which gave information through pictures as well as words. Before the work began I asked them to choose one book and answer questions about it (Fig. 6.30).

Working with a partner, look at the books you've chosen and decide on the answers to these questions:

Is there an index? contents page? How are the sections arranged?
Is this helpful if you want to find something?
Could it be improved?

Look at the pictures first. What information do they give you?
Are they easy to understand?
Which pictures do you think are the best at giving information?

Now look at the words used. Are they easy to understand?
What information do they give you that the pictures can't?
Are there any difficult words? Which ones?
Does the book help you to understand the words used?

How could the text be made easier to understand?
Do you need both pictures and words?

What are the ingredients of a good information book?

Figure 6.30 Survey of information books

Most of the books they were using had helpful contents pages and indexes, although these varied in the details they offered. As far as raising their awareness of pictorial text went, some felt that the pictures gave content information distinct from the verbal text; others thought that in the books they were looking at the illustrations just did the same as the verbal text:

> Just by looking at the pictures it tells me how their houses look, what clothes they wear and how they live.

Some found the pictures helpful, others didn't. They felt that *pictures with details* and *labelled pictures were the best at giving information.* When I shifted the question to *Are the pictures easy to understand?* several of them responded like this one:

> The pictures are understandable but if you want more information you have to read the writing.

In response to *What information do the words give you that the pictures can't?* most felt that in the books they were examining the words gave more information than the pictures:

> The pictures can just show you how they look like but the writing can tell you what they do and how they work.

All of them thought that a good information book needed both pictures and words as shown by their responses to the question *What are the ingredients of a good information book?*

> Pictures, contents, index and glossary
> Contents page, not too little words, lots of information about interesting things
> Lots of information but no hard words! Lots of pictures and colour. Clear words and clear pictures and clear writing
> No Latin words. Clear pictures. Clear words. Lots of pictures. Colourful pictures. Clear writing
> Good pictures and good describing words
> Mostly to be about one thing like: muscles, bones and other things

I asked these questions to raise the children's awareness of the relationship between pictorial and verbal text before they began to put their own information books together and I was interested to see how they would use the books they consulted as models for layout and presentation.

Choosing a reader and what to write about

They then had to decide on who their book was for and what it would be about. They needed to think about the audience to decide the topic. I suspect that some decided on a topic which interested them first, then chose who would be the lucky reader! It's very convenient to write for a friend in the same class if you're interested in football. One or two found it difficult to relate the idea of content to readership. One boy wanted to write about his home but was writing for his mother; when we discussed this, I suggested that she might know a lot about his home, anyway, so perhaps he might choose another topic, which he did. What became very clear, however, was that almost all of them had a particular interest which they wanted to exploit through making a book. I asked them first of all to use the *What I already know/What I need to find out* sheet (Fig. 6.31) to help them decide how they would research any extra information. Many of them seemed to have all they wanted to write about in their own heads, but I tried to encourage them to use books for research by giving them a grid (Fig. 6.32) on which they simply noted page references relating to the 'need to find out' areas. This helped them to focus their research and use indexes and contents pages to help them find things out.

Jamaica

What I already know:

I know that Jamaica is hot and lots of people go their on holiday, they have parm trees, moskito's, and quite a lot of sea-sides. They speck in a different axent. It's a small country.

What I need to find out:

If it rains a lot to. Is there flat land, not just montains, what kind of animals live there. How many people live there. What food they eat, if they eat the same things we do every day. What clothes they wear. What food they eat every day.

Figure 6.31 Using a question sheet to guide research (Year 5)

Title of book	Key word/topic	Key word/topic	Key word/topic
The World of TIGers	Habitats Tigers live in difrent parts of the world like India p.3	Camouflage Striped like shadrows in the jungles p7	Hunting they hut down there pray they hide in long grass and shadro places p.5
Lions	most lions live in open grass lands of Africa p.1	dusty color like the grass p8	Lions hont by stalking and surprising their victims. The female lions do the honting p3
The Cheetah	The cheetahs live on treesd shadro places or open plains of Africa p.2	spotted moves so fast the spots go blured p.6	when the cheetah spots it's prey it walks slowly towards it and then starts to run faster and faster p6

Figure 6.32 Grid to help research into chosen topics

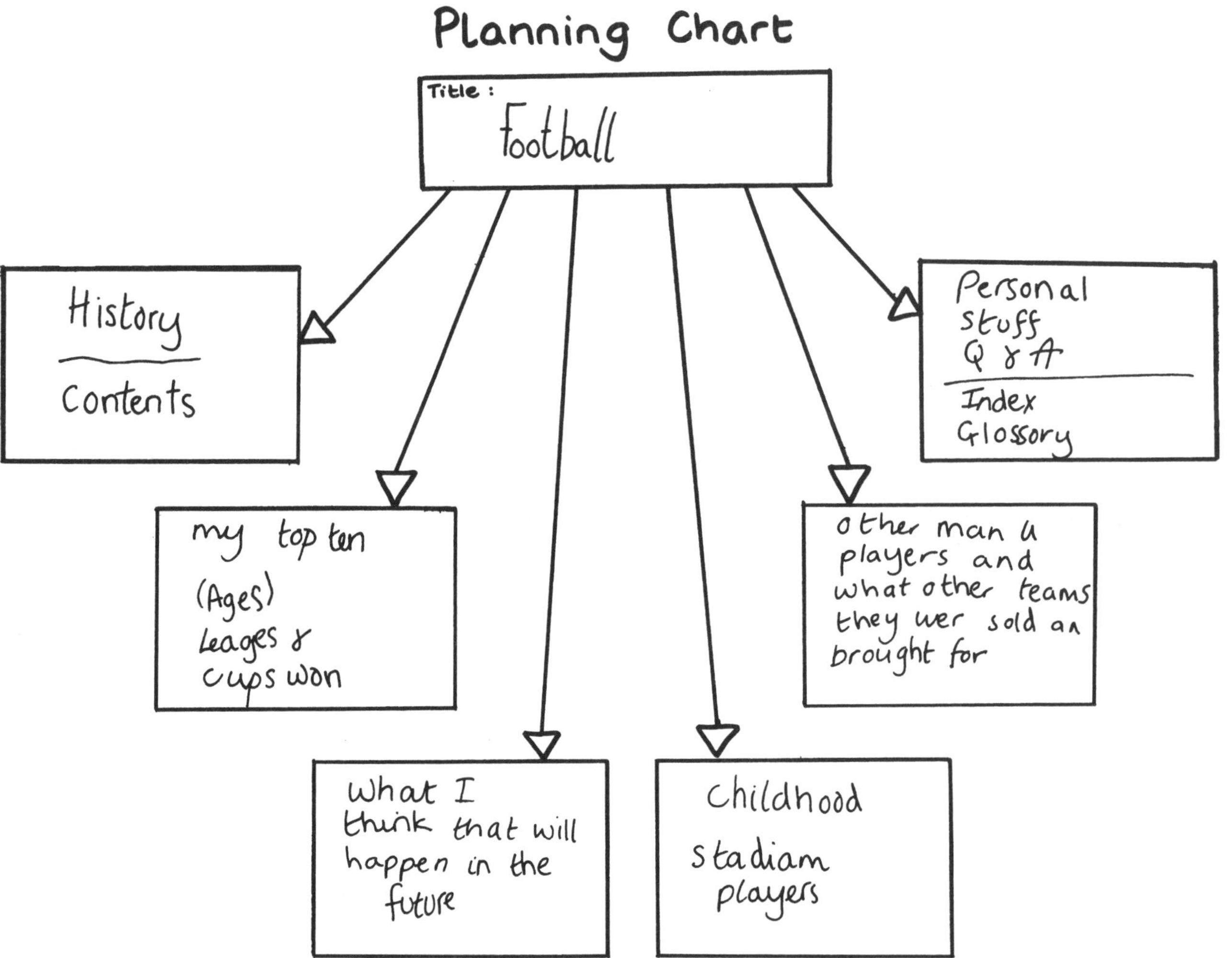

Figure 6.33 Planning chart for sections of information book (Year 5)

Once they had begun researching, I asked them to plan the sections of their books by giving them a planning diagram (Fig. 6.33). This helped them to decide how many pages they needed for the whole book and was a means of prompting them to think about categories of information. They worked individually on their books, but had partners to help them sort out ideas and, eventually, to assist in the proofreading process. After that I asked them to work out how many pages they would need and to do a layout mock-up. Annabell's (Fig. 6.34) shows just two double-page spreads for her lengthy book about football; she chose to use the whole spread for some of her illustrations. Craig (Fig. 6.35) decided to make a book about dinosaurs; his mock-up shows a very clear eye for page layout.

I was very impressed with the way the children settled to the task – quite a daunting one. We worked an hour and ten minutes every Thursday afternoon for about six weeks and they were free to continue their work at other times during the week if they had spare time. Most of them worked with unusual application. They were prepared to redraft and were ingenious about using illustration in a range of forms. They drew heavily on the models of information books they had available for illustrative detail, but very few of them showed any urge to rely on source books for the content. I think this may be related to the fact that many of them were drawing on their own knowledge as the first source of information. When the books were nearing completion the classroom assistant helped them to comb bind them. They made their own decisions about layout, but I think when I repeat the activity with the other half of the class we will all have learned a lot about actually putting the books together!

Figure 6.34 Annabell's layout mock-up for her football book (Year 5)

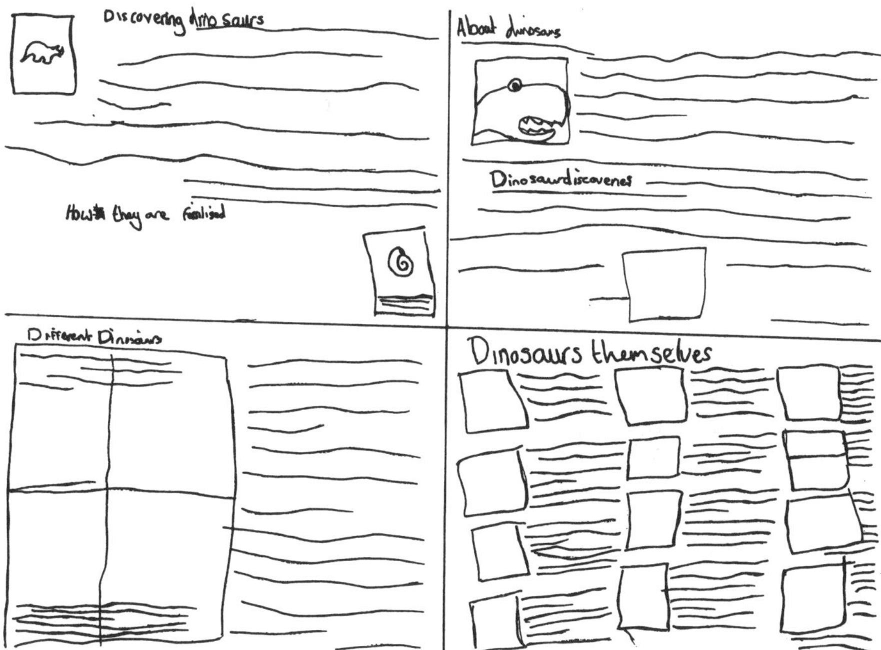

Figure 6.35 Craig's layout plans for a book about dinosaurs (Year 6)

One key area that we want to work on when we make the next set of books will be proof-reading. Interestingly, the organisation of the information was generally coherent and well thought out, so their editing and revising techniques seem fine. However, although they used their partners to help them proofread, there were still too many undetected errors of punctuation and spelling in the finished books – a useful lesson for all of us. I shall have to reinforce their own careful reading of their work and offer more focused strategies and they now realise why it is important.

Reflecting on experience

At the end of the six weeks we spent a Thursday afternoon session in groups where the fiction authors and the non-fiction authors shared their books with each other. Before they settled into their groups, I asked them to fill in Review Sheets (Figs 6.36 and 6.37) as a way of helping them to focus on evaluating the experience.

It also gave me a chance to see whether they had become more aware of using pictures to give information. All of them mentioned being pleased with their illustrations. Other features which pleased them were:

> The way I got things out of my own mind.
>
> That I did it on the deadline.
>
> The amount of work I did.
>
> I am very pleased with my final copy and the layout because I think I've got the pictures the right size.
>
> That I did it all myself.

The improvements mentioned were often technical – using different pens or colours, layout, colour of paper used – and proofreading. Several mentioned that they would like to have written more. When I ask the other half of the group to do their information books I shall put a little more emphasis on content and see if they can be more attentive to the quality of the information they have included. The advice to others was again often technical:

> Plan it well and write a bit at home.
>
> Do the most important bits first.

but there were other comments which suggested an awareness of audience:

> Use more writing but think who it is for.
>
> Don't give up and even if it's for a grown up put illustrations in it. And if it's a small child don't make the writing too complicated and don't exaggerate on the pages.
>
> Do lots of writing and pictures so that the person reading the book learns more from it.

One of the reasons for embarking on this activity was that the children should learn something about non-fiction texts by making them:

> I have learned that you don't need too many pages for a good, interesting book.
>
> How to put a book together and that I can make it funny.
>
> I have learned to proofread my work and use punctuation.

REVIEW SHEET

Title of my book:

Manchester united F.C.

What I'm most pleased with:

I am pleased with the whole book especially the illustrations and the writing.

What I'd like to do better if I did it again:

Not to get spelling mestakes in pen. and do a bit more illustrations.

Advice for people making their own book:

dont give up and even if its a grown up put illustrations in it. And if its a small child don't make the writing to complecated, and don't exagerate on the pages.

What I've learned from making my book:

allways check your spellings!

Figure 6.36 Carl reviews his experience of writing a book (Year 5)

REVIEW SHEET

Title of my book: Tropical fish.

What I'm most pleased with: I am most pleased with are the illustration because I have managed to make it look like the actual fish, which is usually quiet difficult for me. I am also really pleased with my ~~for~~ front cover, especially when I changed the writing on the cover. The other bit that I am really pleased with is the actual layout of the book, I am not usually very good a book layout.

What I'd like to do better if I did it again: I would like to put it in better order, for instance in alphabetical order.

Advice for people making their own book: The advice I would give to other people is not to make it too complicated, and don't do too many pages because it can get boring.

What I've learned from making my book:

I have learnt that you don't need too many pages for a good, interesting book.

Figure 6.37 Dijana reviews her experience of writing a book (Year 5)

I had underestimated the extent of other kinds of learning which the book-writing project promoted:

> Remember when the deadline is to finish it and not be too ambitious.
>
> I can work harder than I thought.
>
> I have learned that I can do a book and be pleased as well.
>
> That I can work independently.

Now I'm looking forward to repeating the activity with the other half of the class. The children who have already written information books are experienced authors of non-fiction texts who can advise others and who have all been able to reflect on their own authorship and the process of constructing a text, useful experience that we can build on.

Progression in teaching about texts

The way teachers talk about texts is a key to helping children get to grips with a range of genres. It is never too soon to talk with children about the ways books and other texts are constructed. When they have a vocabulary through which to explain their views, to offer opinions and to analyse aspects of a text, children are even more capable of taking their analytical understanding further. And as everyone who knows young children will be aware, they do have firmly held opinions and preferences. For these to be developed into justified analyses of texts, children will need a progressive series of experiences of responding to texts. As a starting point for thinking about progression in teaching and learning about texts, it is worth noting just when you introduce specific terminology to children. The chart in Fig. 6.38 can build to an agreed glossary of terms which will fit with schemes of work to promote understanding and knowledge of fiction and non-fiction texts. For example, when do you start talking about authors and illustrators, covers of books, the blurb on the back, the bar-code and dedication, contents pages and indexes? When do you discuss the setting, characters, plot, flashback, information structure, persuasive texts? You might want to brainstorm with a group of colleagues the kinds of terms you use which describe fiction and non-fiction texts before you try to complete the chart in Fig. 6.38.

Once you have begun to look at the terminology you use, you can then build towards a sense of progression in teaching from and about texts. The charts shown in Figs 6.39, 6.40 and 6.41 offer a framework for noting current practice in helping children respond to texts of different kinds. Using a blank chart as in Appendix p. 348 decide on a series of activities you have carried out recently with your class over a few weeks and note the ways you structured the learning.

with thanks to teachers on the Advanced Diploma in Language and Literature, Homerton College, Cambridge

The examples in Figs 6.39, 6.40 and 6.41 are drawn from work on different types of text, but show nevertheless that progression in teaching from and about texts often means a gradually closer focus on the ways in which texts are constructed and expectation that the kinds of responses to the texts will become more complex as children grow in interpretive experience.

In the early years, the emphasis is on broadening the range of experience. As children grow older, analysis becomes more important and their own writing acts as a means of analysing the structures of particular types of text. In Years 5 and 6 the texts become more demanding and the comparisons lead not only to analysis of the structure of the texts themselves, but to the ways in which different texts carry different implications and messages. Progressive outlines like these can provide a basis for looking with colleagues at the range and repertoire elements of policy and planning and feed into the development of schemes of work. Schemes can be quite

Technical terms	When introduced in discussing reading	When introduced in discussing writing
e.g. author's biography, paragraphs		
genre	Yr 5	Yr 6
narrator	Yr 3	Yr 3/4
justify opinion	Yr 4	Yr 6
flashback	Yr 5	Yr 6
glossary	Yr 3	Yr 5/6

Figure 6.38 Towards a progressive glossary of technical terms to talk about texts (Blank provided in Appendix: A23)

quickly assembled by looking at current practice in teaching from texts and teaching about texts.

The range and repertoire might include reading, writing, speaking and listening activities based on:

Fiction genres – picture books, short stories, videos and novels of:

- traditional stories from different cultures – folktales, fairy stories, fables, myths, legends
- contemporary stories from different cultures
- fantasy
- science fiction
- human interest stories
- animal stories
- adventure and mystery stories
- long-established children's fiction
- historical fiction.

Plays – traditional and modern; for radio, screen or stage
Poetry – traditional and modern, narrative and descriptive, etc., from different cultures
Non-fiction might include pictorial and print texts such as:

- biography, autobiography and reference material on the lives or backgrounds of authors
- newspapers and magazines – persuasive, argumentative, reportage, analysis
- television documentaries and video information films
- environmental print
- information books
- travel writing
- journals
- letters.

Nobody would suggest that you can only look at fairy stories in Year 2, for example, or autobiography in Year 5. There is likely to be a considerable amount of revisiting genres throughout a child's school experience. The important factor in ensuring progression is what teachers expect children to be able to do with a particular genre as they grow older. In planning for progression, a group of colleagues might decide on a genre – traditional stories, for example – and complete the planning sheet used in Figs 6.39–6.41 for each year group. This could then form the basis for discussion about just what is involved in ensuring progression in teaching from and teaching about texts. It will also provide a valuable strand for schemes and units of work.

The final chapter includes a framework for constructing policy, schemes of work and termly units.

Type of text *Poetry* | Year 1/2

Input

Which texts? How will they be introduced? What strategies can /did you use to find out what the children already knew?

A whole range of poetry books in the classroom - modern and traditional, many of them funny.
Didn't have to try too hard to find out what they knew, it came from them. In regular poetry sessions I left books lying around for their perusal.

Learning opportunities

What do I want them to learn? – about the texts themselves? through using the texts?

To enjoy the rhymes and rhythms of poems; to use rhyme as a strategy for teaching reading; to get aquainted with a range of different kinds of poems to move away from the narrow diet of Rosen and Ahlbergs.
I also wanted them to develop their oral skills by rehearsing poems in groups for 'performance' and talking about them, forming and expressing opinions etc.

Tasks

What activities? What variations in groupings?

Poem of the week – written up on the wall
Specially selected books – taken into class and left lying around.
Reading from a wider range of poets – modern, traditional, narrative, descriptive....
Video and audio tapes of performance poets
Poetry corner
Writing our own poems

Groupings: as a class, friendship, any way they choose, individual

Resources and support

People? Strategies? Technical?

Library service poetry collection
Teachers and parents as audiences prompting and encouraging, bilingual assistant to translate and talk in Punjabi, performance poet as model – and fun, audio tape, video, radio

Range of outcomes and assessments (who/what/where/when/how?)

Big book of 'Poems we like', knowledge of more and more different poems and poets, informal and formal performances of poems (in class and assembly), greater confidence, more opinions, more knowledge of names of poets, knowledge of terms like 'narrative poems', 'rhyme', rhythm, even onomatopoeia!

Assessment:

me: gave chances for Speaking and Listening assessments of group discussion and performances and for adding to reading records.

Figure 6.39 Teaching from and about texts, Year 1/2 (Blank provided in Appendix: A24)

Type of text Class Newspapers	**Year 3/4**
Input Which texts? How will they be introduced? What strategies can /did you use to find out what the children already knew? Various newspapers – children bring some in from home; teacher to supply a chosen range. Talking about newspapers and magazines read at home to find out about range.	
Learning opportunities What do I want them to learn? – about the texts themselves? through using the texts? To look at reporting in various styles – eg gardening, sport, social, sensational, adverts To practise writing in a chosen style using the text as a model To think about writing for a specific audience.	
Tasks What activities? What variations in groupings? Give examples to look at and dissect, separating into categories. Survey parents' reading tastes and preferences in newspaper articles. ~~Look at~~ headlines and talk about how they encapsulate the article. Compare gardening and sport examples and talk about the differences. Choose a kind of reporting and write an article in the style, using an example from the newspapers brought in. Invite a newspaper person in to talk about the process. Class discussion; children encouraged to share and show. Make class news wall to be added to over the next few weeks; support/encourage verbal and pictorial contributions. Groupings: mixed ability; take cognisance of ability; verbosity, leadership qualities, behaviour and gender spread.	
Support People? Strategies? Technical? Talking with parents about why they like to read particular papers. Visit from newspaper person Learning how newspaper articles are structured Access to I.T.	
Range of outcomes and assessment (who/what/where/when/how?) Articles and news wall. Knowledge of using language in different ways for different effects. Reading each others' articles; feedback from discussion with me and their friends; comparing their articles with the real thing. During the work I assessed their drafting and editing strategies. At the end I used their chosen finished articles for their portfolios. Did a lot of useful speaking and listening formative assessment, too.	

Figure 6.40 Teaching from and about texts, Year 3/4 (Blank provided in Appendix: A24)

Type of text Information: Child labour in the Fens 1830 Year 5/6
Input Which texts? How will they be introduced? What strategies can /did you use to find out what the children already knew? Diary extracts from locally written autobiography by person who had been a child labourer in the Fens. Tape by Fen character Children made notes, following teacher modelling of note-making on board. Discussed 'what else we knew.'
Learning opportunities What do I want them to learn? – about the texts themselves? through using the texts? To develop note-taking and ability to use note making in different contexts. To understand the difference between fiction & non-fiction writing. The ability to re-model information. The ability to empathise with the child Fen labourer.
Tasks What activities? What variations in groupings? Listened, read and made notes. Hot seating – each child answered two or three questions in role about child working in the Fens in 1830s. Wrote an information piece on child labour for classroom exhibition. Wrote a piece from child's point of view to accompany factual writing. The children worked in friendship pairs.
Support/resources People? Strategies? Technical? Tapes and transcripts Photos of Fen workers Diary accounts Example of how to take notes Some pairs had one as a scribe; in some pairings both wrote. Some pairs wrote their own versions then acted as response partners making helpful editorial comments.
Range of outcomes and assessments Classroom exhibition; empathy accounts. Assessment to see how successful the children were in remodelling texts and to judge whether they were more proficient either at information or story re-telling. To see what types of note-taking happened and how successfully these were transferred back to full text. Used hot-seating to assess speaking and listening for explanations and persuasive speaking; formulating and answering questions.

Figure 6.41 Teaching from and about texts, Year 5/6 (Blank provided in Appendix: A24)

Chapter Seven

The English coordinator's handbook

This chapter includes:

The role of the English coordinator:
- **Subject/teaching knowledge**
- **Developing policy and schemes of work**
- **Advice and support for colleagues**
- **Managing resources**
- **Assessing, reporting and recording**
- **Communicating with others – inside and outside school**
- **Monitoring, review and evaluation**

A framework for reviewing or developing policy:
- **Aims**
- **The environment for developing language and literacy, including equal opportunities and special educational needs**
- **The range, repertoire and resources for reading, writing, speaking and listening, including cross-curricular issues and the use of IT**
- **Assessing, reporting and recording progress**
- **Provision for under-fives**
- **Parental involvement**

Implementation, monitoring, evaluating the policy

Identifying inservice needs.

The role of the English coordinator

Ofsted 1995 *Subjects and Standards: issues for school development arising from Ofsted inspection findings 1994–95 Key Stages 1 and 2*, London, Her Majesty's Stationery Office

The influence of the subject coordinator is crucial in ensuring well-planned and coherent provision and in maintaining balanced progress.

This final chapter draws together the threads of what 'making progress in English' implies for the English coordinator. Although the job description will vary from school to school, there are general areas which are commonly understood to be part of the English coordinator's role and responsibility. While the English coordinator can be expected to be up to date in subject teaching knowledge, be responsible for collating, developing and reviewing policy and monitoring its implementation, support and inform colleagues, oversee English resources, ensure English assessments are in line with school policy and communicate effectively with parents, governors and colleagues, there are some roles which a coordinator cannot be expected to fulfil. For example, the coordinator may be able to support colleagues, but cannot be expected to enforce changes which are part of school policy; that is the role of the headteacher. The English coordinator will plan for curriculum development, but only the headteacher can arrange for time and resources to put those developments into practice.

A planned conversation with your headteacher will help to make clear just what s/he sees as your role. After such a meeting it is worth making notes from this – perhaps a list of bullet points outlining the role responsibilities of the coordinator and the headteacher – and agree these in writing before beginning on any long-term development plans. A list like this will help you to make a thoughtful audit of what you already do and what you plan to do. It is important, however, that you should plan to carry out any changes in a systematic way, remembering that if you try to do everything at once you will end up dissipating your efforts and being less effective. As a way of preparing for the meeting with your headteacher and for your own future planning, you might like to think about how much of the list on Fig. 7.1 is, or should be, part of your job. How much of it do you fulfil already? Whilst checking against current practice, it is important to remember that Rome was not built in a day!

Planning for priorities: key tasks and needs

Once you are clear about the relative responsibilities you and the headteacher carry, you will then need to identify your key tasks for the year. A three-year plan (which relates to the School Development Plan) will give you a longer-term perspective on what is realistically possible. You need to plan your priorities (see Fig. 7.2). Having established priorities, you are then in a position to look at what you need – in the way of support, management arrangements and resources – to be able to do the things you want to do. At this point you may need to return to the headteacher for further conversations about future planning. Discussion should involve looking at the School Development Plan to see where time and resources have been allocated for English inservice, bearing in mind another point made by Ofsted in the report quoted above:

'The subject coordinator must have sufficient time and opportunity, as well as adequate expertise and training, in order to be effective in promoting consistency and improving standards in all aspects of literacy.'

Ofsted *Subjects and Standards*, p. 3. Every chapter of this manual offers a range of activities and audits which can be carried out in monitoring existing practice and developing new initiatives.

At the end of the year you will need to return to your planning sheet to monitor and evaluate just how much you have achieved. From there you can begin to plan for the next year of your rolling programme.

Barriers to success

You also need to be honest (at least with yourself) about what the barriers to success are. These might be practical or to do with interpersonal relations. It is important to be realistic. You must cross off your list things which are beyond your control – be firm with yourself about this. For example, the financial constraints imposed on schools are among the greatest stress elements of the job, but you can't do anything about such funding arrangements and so you must delete this from your own list of responsibilities.

Perhaps the greatest difficulty in acknowledging barriers to success lies in the area of working with colleagues. There may be one or two who are not committed to change or whose classroom practices do not get the best out of the pupils. If they are willing to have an honest look at their own practice, all well and good. If not, you may have to decide that – for the moment at least – you cannot influence their ideas or practice. This is difficult for teachers whose main driving force is to devote time to those children who need most help to get on the road to learning; the tendency is to spend time and effort on an individual child who is proving recalcitrant. In the classroom this is absolutely right and laudable, but when working with colleagues it might be counter-effective. There are some colleagues who have perfected the art of non-development. Whilst it would be a great coup to get such a colleague to take on a new initiative aimed to raise standards, you need to be realistic about what you can do in terms of using pressure and support to create change. Start with the colleagues who are ready for a bit of uplift and effortful success; this can be the beginning of a process of gradual change where the most development-proof colleagues might also get involved and gain satisfaction from improved standards.

Working with colleagues

Teachers develop their practice as a result of any of a whole range of different prompts. Their interest may be sparked by a colleague's practice or the books written by pupils for their own/other classes. They might be moved to look carefully at their classroom work because of the needs of a particular group of children, or even an individual. Informal staffroom conversations, full staff or development/Inset meetings, interesting articles or television documentaries, out-of-school courses and conferences – and more – all play their part in the exchange of new ideas. Specially planned meetings may begin by trawling the existing good practice related to a particular area or using audit frameworks as a focus for reflection. A list of controversial statements can start up ideas or a visiting speaker can provide the impetus for considering useful change – it is sometimes difficult to be a prophet in your own land.

Many valuable exchanges come from quite hasty conversations during a school day, but it might be worth extending the value of these snatched moments by:

- actively seeking advice from colleagues about particular practices; for example, a colleague who is good at using IT may be able to offer advice about planning and drafting; or someone whose strengths lie in design technology, science or maths might be able to advise on reading and constructing concept maps or diagrams

Subject/teaching knowledge

This involves both keeping up to date with curriculum developments and developing the teaching of English within the school. This might include:

- attending courses
- attending local coordinator meetings
- leading staff meetings about English teaching
- organising, reading for and following up school-based Inset about English
- becoming involved in new initiatives offered within the local authority
- creating a supportive and effective language and literacy environment in your own classroom.

Advice and support for colleagues

You are probably carrying out these responsibilities all the time in subtle ways, but more formally, it might include:

- getting (and reading!) relevant journals
- teaching with colleagues as part of planned Inset
- leading by example – e.g. setting up your own writing area in the classroom
- keeping colleagues informed about local Inset courses or conferences.

Developing policy and schemes of work

This might include collating and being responsible for establishing policy from the outset or reviewing and monitoring existing policy documents. It will involve coordinating long-term and medium-term planning:

- producing a development plan for English
- negotiating, drafting or reviewing the school English policy document
- helping colleagues plan for English – how they teach and the quality of learning
- coordinating the writing up of Schemes of Work for English and termly Units of Work.

Resource management

You will need to be clear about the school's budgeting system and how funds are allocated to English. You may also need to find out: whether you have a role in ordering resources for needs identified in your English development plan; and whether you are responsible for monitoring the use and effectiveness of resources in raising standards of achievement or improving the quality of learning throughout the school.

You may also need to:

- audit the book stock in the school, for example, for challenging reading at KS2, useful information material and books, a wide range of texts in classroom reading areas
- be informed about the availability of audio and video tapes, CD-ROMs and other computer software

Figure 7.1 Checklist for English coordinators

- administer general stock control
- review the organisation and management of the school library.

Assessment, reporting and recording

Your role in these arrangements will vary according to your school's organisation and management, but it might include:

- meeting with the Assessment coordinator to make sure you each have a clear view of your relative roles in managing ARR
- making sure colleagues are clear about ARR arrangements in the school
- establishing, developing or monitoring the school's English ARR
- holding regular moderation meetings (as part of the English or school development plan) to help teacher assessment of work
- liaising with the SENCO over screening arrangements and referrals for children who are experiencing difficulties.

Communications and public relations

This is an essential part of the role which is perhaps the most neglected. It could mean that on your own initiative or with colleagues, you:

- develop partnerships with parents about literacy (writing as well as reading)
- keep governors and parents informed about current issues to do with English teaching
- keep an eye on, and discuss with the headteacher, the school as reflecting the value and status given to literacy and as a mirror of community languages
- make links with local industries, companies, organisations
- organise Book Weeks or invite visiting writers, storytellers, poets, etc.
- get the children involved in poetry or poster-making competitions
- help the headteacher to publish informed and useful evidence of the children's progress in English
- make links with other schools
- brief the headteacher about initiatives undertaken by colleagues in English work.

Monitoring, review and evaluation

Much of this part of the role has been mentioned in other categories, but generally, it means keeping an eye on and being aware of what is going on in English in your school. It might mean:

- holding termly planning meetings for English to avoid unhelpful repetition of experience for the pupils and to establish continuity and progression. This will relate to work in the ARR areas of the role and to the development of a negotiated and agreed policy for English
- establishing with the headteacher a means of monitoring for effective teaching in order to provide support where necessary
- developing systems for pupils to evaluate their own work.

Figure 7.1 Checklist for English coordinators (continued)

	Year One	Year Two	Year Three
Subject/teaching knowledge	Key tasks wider range of genres at KS2 Needs books - sets & enlarged texts	Key tasks information texts throughout the school KS1 & KS2 Needs INSET & books	Key tasks gender & achievement Needs analysis of SATS & INSET
Developing policy, schemes of work, etc.	Key tasks review reading ← deal with OFSTED recommendations → Needs ← staff development time →	Key tasks review writing Needs	Key tasks review speaking & listening Needs
Advice & support for colleagues	Key tasks managing group reading Needs INSET	Key tasks integrating writing with literacy hour Needs ← staff development time & INSET →	Key tasks monitoring where sp. & list. fits with literacy Needs
Resource management	Key tasks monitor classroom reading areas Needs Time	Key tasks set up classroom writing areas/ boxes Needs Money!	Key tasks Look at possibility of listening stations Needs Even more money!
Assessing, Reporting and Recording	Key tasks audit the current reading records Needs ← staff development time →	Key tasks audit writing records Needs	Key tasks audit/develop sp. & list. records Needs
Communications and public relations	Key tasks involving parents in writing the reading pamphlets partic. KS2 Needs Parent Governors support	Key tasks begin publishing literacy success information Needs Development of framework	Key tasks ← monitor & review Needs Time
Monitoring, review and evaluation	Key tasks reading (plus special needs) Needs ← specified time as part of school Development Plan →	Key tasks writing (plus special needs) Needs	Key tasks speaking & listening (plus special needs) Needs

Figure 7.2 Planning sheet: establishing priorities and planning for future development (Blank provided in Appendix: A25)

- asking to visit other teachers' classrooms to be given advice or shown pupils' work; this can also help to establish a more open view of monitoring
- inviting a colleague to team teach with you to demonstrate a particular strategy or approach
- planning visits or termly units of work together in order to discuss learning objectives.

In a similar way, opportunities for discussing shared aims can come through:

- displays/publication of pupils' work in progress as well as finished products
- joint displays in the library or other public places – in and out of school
- encouraging pupils to seek advice from other colleagues
- listening carefully in staff discussions to find common ground or to hear of colleagues' good ideas and practices.

Developing and reviewing policy

The other chapters of this manual deal with subject teaching knowledge, matters of assessment, reporting and recording and some elements of communications and public relations. The remainder of this chapter is devoted to the development and review of policy and schemes of work.

One of the most important points to bear in mind when developing or reviewing policy is just what a policy is, or represents. It is not just a set of papers in a neat folder; it is a set of live, active principles being carried out every day in the school and in each classroom. This is the strength of any thought-out, discussed, negotiated and agreed set of principles. They are still alive even when they have been captured on paper. At best, these ideas will have come from quite a lengthy process of debate – even disagreement – amongst a group of colleagues who are intent on forging a way of working with children which will challenge and support them as they make progress in English. At worst, the policy will have been hastily written down by one person who has been landed with the job to satisfy an external demand for 'something on paper'; after the individual's strenuous efforts, a document compiled like this is likely to gather dust on a shelf.

One of the clearest indicators of a school's policy about English is the extent to which texts and materials of all kinds, including children's own published work, are on public display in the school – not just in libraries and corridors, but in every classroom. Another immediate way of identifying a school's policy is to see just what happens in each classroom to help children develop their language and literacy. However, although this will show something about the value placed on reading, speaking and listening and writing, and on the readers, speakers and listeners and writers in a school, it cannot even begin to represent the complexity of what a full English curriculum should be like. Also, although there is no doubt that everyday practices about language and literacy reflect the principles which underpin them, it is important to make both the principles and the practices explicit. Any school could produce a glossy folder which draws a comprehensive picture of what 'English' ought to be, yet fails to demonstrate satisfactory standards of literacy. On the other hand, a school could have an excellent record of classroom practice and success in English, but fail to carry this through, perhaps by not making explicit to parents just what the reasons are for using the classroom methods chosen to help children make progress.

A policy document may fulfil several purposes but it should at least offer:

- a statement which explains clearly to parents, governors and others, how reading, writing, speaking and listening are valued and incorporated into the everyday work of the school (principles)
- a practical reference for staff and helpers, reflecting commonly agreed views

about the implementation of practices to ensure successful reading, writing, speaking and listening (practice).

The construction of a policy, or the review of currently existing policy, is an excellent way for colleagues to focus their ideas about how best to help children develop as successful, assured and independent language users. However, the main purpose of any policy document should be to give guidance to teachers, parents and others about how to achieve the highest standards possible. In doing this, it will reflect the important relationship between principles and practice.

Although different schools and authorities suggest different headings for sections of policy, any policy framework needs to include these major areas:

- *Aims:* an outline of the school's approach to the development of language and literacy (Section One)
- *Environment:* school and classroom management and organisation for reading, writing, speaking and listening (Section Two)
- *Range, repertoire and resources:* planning systematically for progression in using and producing a range of texts (Section Three)
- *Records of progress, assessing and reporting* achievement in language and literacy (Section Four)

An English Policy Document should also make reference to:

• equal opportunities • special needs	see Sections One and Two
• cross-curricular issues • the use of ICT	see Section Three
• provision for under-fives	Section Five
• parental involvement	Section Six

and indicate:

- the date for reviewing the policy or staged review of sections of the policy
- methods by which implementation of the policy will be monitored and evaluated
- inservice needs.

It might be worth asking the parent governors or other parents to read a draft of the document to make sure that it explains the English curriculum in a way which non-professionals will be able to understand. There might be elements of specific professional terminology which need explanation.

Carrying out a review of existing policy might reveal areas for inservice (see pp. 321–2).

Section One: Aims

Teachers sometimes feel a little ill at ease with this part of a policy document, talking about aims or principles as 'airy fairy'. Nothing could be further from the truth. The principles on which teaching is founded will determine the kinds of practices which are used. This section of the document should be a brief and precise statement of what is considered important about language and literacy in the school. It should include what the staff consider should be the child's entitlement to development in English.

When putting this section of the policy together, it is worth writing it as though explaining the school's approach to parents. The opening section of a policy document might include statements like the following extracts from a school policy:

We want the children in our school to become confident, active and committed in their language and literacy. We think our children should be entitled to experiences which enable them to:

- make choices about the sorts of texts they enjoy
- read between the lines and behind the images
- communicate clearly and with assurance . . .
- read fluently and with understanding, a range of different kinds of reading material using reading methods that are appropriate to the material and the reading purpose . . .
- be able to write for a range of purposes, organising the content and style of what is written to suit the purpose and readership. We want them to use spelling, punctuation and syntax appropriately and with confidence. We want them to develop a legible, cursive handwriting style and to be able to use word processing skills . . .
- be able to speak with confidence, clarity and fluency in appropriate forms of speech. We want them to be able to speak and listen in a variety of groupings and circumstances in both informal and formal contexts and to feel proud of their own language.

These extracts could be used as a basis for alteration, amendment and addition.

This section should also include an outline of the school's approach to provision for children who have special educational needs and issues of equal opportunities.

Section Two: The environment for language and literacy development: organising for a range of learners and issues of differentiation

The environment for learning is more than just the physical provision of books, materials and nicely mounted displays. The school and classroom environment reveal the value placed on literacy and this in turn reflects the inner environment of the teacher's mind. A rich and inventive mind will create a stimulating visual and material environment. The empty noticeboard or dog-eared display tell a visitor – and the children – a great deal about the inner environment of the teacher's mind and expectations and the opportunities which are (or are not) on offer for the children. It is worth taking another look at the environment. For example, do the notices reflect the community of the school or of the nation? Does this look like a place which values literacy? The following lists suggest areas for investigation before policy statements about the contexts and organisation of learning are written.

The school

Key questions relating to the school as a supportive environment for literacy are:

- What messages would a visitor get about the status or value given to reading, writing, speaking and listening, from first impressions of the school?
- How are resources (human and material) used in the school?

Areas to consider when auditing the literacy and language environment of the school will be:

- library provision or a school bookshop
- how much the children participate in plays, other public performances or meetings

- the way writing and reading materials are displayed
- whether reading or writing ever featured in public – e.g. assemblies, book weeks
- how ICT is used to support language and literacy
- the participation of parents or other adults in language and literacy development.

The classroom

Literacy development is to do with helping children experience greater success and satisfaction in reading and writing. Raising standards of reading and writing means setting up an environment in which learning can be most effective, rather than adhering to particular methods or materials. The context for any classroom activity will frame what it is possible for pupils to achieve.

An important first question might be:

What messages does my classroom give about the value I place on reading, writing, speaking and listening?

Think about:

- special areas for reading, writing, speaking and listening
- varied materials
- walls, displays and notices – how much do the children participate in these? are displays interactive?
- reflections of diversity – different cultures, gender images.

Then there are issues of differentiation and special educational needs – methods used for:

- managing and varying activities and groupings
- managing resources
- setting and responding to homework
- developing active and independent learners
- supporting children who have statements of special educational need.

Equal opportunities: how do you cater for diversity between:

- boys/girls
- different languages
- less/more fluent and confident learners
- physical or medical conditions?

It isn't just the physical setting of the classroom or school which contributes to an effective context; there needs also to be the *context of possibility* – that intangible area of teachers' expertise which feeds into planning for activities which will both challenge and support literacy.

cross-curricular issues
developing schemes of work
ensuring progression
the use of ICT

Teacher intervention can suggest 'interference'. This need not be the case, but in order to create a framework for colleagues to grapple with discussion about the tricky issues of literacy development, it's worth re-examining just what intervention might mean. It helps, perhaps, to shift the perspective by first making another shift in thinking: seeing teaching as *making it possible for children to learn*. This signals a broader and much more positive view of intervention – and one which starts before the teacher and pupils even reach the classroom. It makes the identification of learning objectives a priority. If you know what you want the children to learn over a Key Stage or their whole primary experience, then you will be in a better position to describe just how you will go about achieving those objectives.

When planning for children's progress in reading, writing, speaking and listening, a teacher will keep in mind both the larger-scale types or genres, forms or formats of text which s/he wants the children to experience, as well as the close focus on details of text construction or interpretation. This revisits the diagram on p. 194 of Chapter 5 which outlined the fours areas of English:

- the process of getting and conveying information
- the process of developing independence and discrimination
- the study of language at sentence and word level
- the study of texts – fiction and non-fiction.

Cross-curricular issues

The first two take place throughout the curriculum as well as during work specifically described as English. Strategies for reading texts differently for different purposes, working independently on drafting and proofreading, making choices about which resources to consult, collaborative activities and, of course, talk, are all part and parcel of the everyday uses of literacy and language. It is worth identifying just which aspects of language and literacy are taught and used throughout the curriculum so that English lessons can concentrate on the study of language and the study of texts. The chart in Fig. 7.3 will help colleagues note where processes of getting and conveying information and strategies for developing independence come into cross-curricular work.

Resources for learning

Part of the classroom context of possibility will be the teacher's consideration of what resources to use. It is easy to think that resources are those familiar ones which are regularly brought into the classroom in the physical form of books, artefacts, videos, and all the other carefully selected (and important) materials for engaging children in learning. However, one of the most fruitful resources resides in the children themselves and their existing knowledge of texts.

Awareness of pupils' competence with texts of all kinds can save much valuable time and effort which might otherwise be squandered in the assumption that the teacher has to start on a blank sheet to develop a child's literacy. Finding out what children know about reading, writing, speaking and listening not only establishes an essential knowledge base, but helps the children themselves to move their implicit

Processes: Getting and conveying information: researching, skimming, scanning, listening, note-making, informing, explaining
Developing independence and discrimination: drafting, choosing reading material, varying texts for purpose and audience

	Reading	Writing	Speaking and listening
Art	Captions in Art books. Information about artists	Comment on own & artists' work. Write about specific artists. Write imaginatively after looking at artwork	Discuss techniques, composition, content, method. Oral evaluation of own & others' work
Design Technology	Follow instructions. Use pictorial text in information books	Planning design projects. Revise and evaluate	Working out ideas in pairs & groups. Oral evaluation of own & others' work
Geography	Maps. Information seeking (incl. CD Rom)	Making maps & graphs / charts. Writing in role. Describing journeys	Story-telling involving other lands & peoples
History	Books, newspapers, photographs, cartoons, magazines, maps, information seeking. (incl. CD Rom)	Writing in role. Writing information. Note-making. Making charts e.g. family trees	Role play. Debate. Researching in groups
Maths	Reading figures. Instructions. Stories about mathematicians	Figures & graphs. Estimating	Estimating. Hypothesising. Predicting
Music	Musical notation. Words of songs. Information books about instruments and artists	Lyrics. Reflections on music. Evaluating own musical composition. Imaginative writing from music	Oral evaluation of own & others' work. Songs. Rhymes. Chants, raps
Physical Education	Instructions. Diagrams	Record & evaluate personal movement repertoire. Imaginative writing related to movement	Explanation & Evaluation. Following Instructions
Science	Instructions. Diagrams. Information books. Encyclopaedias	Predicting, Hypothesising, Evaluating } Experiments →	→

Figure 7.3 A checklist for teaching English across the curriculum (Blank provided in Appendix: A26)

knowledge into the conscious light of careful scrutiny. This means they can recognise what they already know so that they can extend this knowledge. They have a hold on those systems of thought which are so important to later learning. Talking about texts, responding carefully to those which the pupils produce, offering models and examples – not only of the range of available texts, but also, by example, of what it is like to be a developed reader, writer, speaker and listener – all contribute towards a varied context of opportunity.

However, it is not enough just to find out what children know and can do; this needs to form the basis for planned and systematic future learning. But systematic planning need not signal inflexibility. Think of the meticulous driver who insists on sitting in a traffic jam in order to stick to the planned route and so misses a lot of interesting scenery as well as losing the chance to find new ways of reaching the destination. For the children's sakes – the companions on the journey – it is just not worth missing the scenery; and sitting in a traffic jam enhances nobody's life or learning!

Using Information and Communications Technology

Whilst the children and other adults in the classroom are important resources, one of the most significant developments in classroom resourcing has come about through the greater availability of computers. ICT can contribute to English teaching and learning in a range of ways. What are the benefits of using ICT in English? Perhaps the most universally accepted form of computer application for English is word processing. From their earliest years, children can get to grips with concept keyboards, then qwerty keyboards to make their own texts. This has been particularly successful as a way of supporting children who experience difficulties with writing. Desktop publishing packages mean that books, pamphlets and newspapers can be produced to a professional standard. In terms of reading, the advent of the CD-ROM is probably the most significant shift, enabling quick referencing and, importantly, the capacity for several children to research at once. This means that the added value of discussion can enhance their learning and shift information gathering very quickly towards genuine understanding. Databases can be used to store and retrieve information about texts. In other curriculum areas, the requirement to input data in abbreviated form also means attention to language and more genuine comprehension of information texts.

concept keyboard: a means of using an overlay on a traditional (qwerty) keyboard which allows children to press a picture or a large word to call up words on the screen; **qwerty:** as on a standard typewriter keyboard (taken from the first six letters of the top row)

see Storysearch case study, Chapter 6, pp. 254–8

School-based ICT

Discussion amongst colleagues could discover the extent to which ICT is being fully exploited in English. Questions to consider would be:

How many of the following types of texts are available to the pupils in an electronic form?

Fiction	Non-fiction
Drama texts	Newspapers
Magazines	Reference books
Encyclopaedias	Dictionaries

How many of the following IT resources are available to the pupils?

Word processors	Desktop publishing
Simulations/adventures	Language development software
Talking books	Databases
CD-ROM	Internet and e-mail
Overlay (concept) keyboards	

Classroom-based ICT

- Approximately how often do your pupils have opportunities to use ICT to develop their reading, writing, speaking and listening – daily/weekly/termly/yearly?
- What do you use ICT for in developing language and literacy?
- Do all the children have equal access to using the computers?
- How do you assess the children's use of ICT in English?
- Would you like to make more use of ICT to support language and literacy?
- Are there any problems which mean that you cannot make full use of ICT to develop English? What are they?

Responses to these might feed in to an assessment of inservice needs (see final section).

Schemes of work

In order to be able to plan for flexibility and possible changes of direction, teachers need to have some idea where the learners should be at the end of a series of activities or a period of time. The range and repertoire ('key skills' in the National Curriculum) for Reading, Writing, Speaking and Listening should be clearly set out for each year group and Key Stage. These outlines will form the Schemes of Work for each year.

Reading

This should include details of learning objectives for reading:

- the range of reading – fiction and non-fiction to be covered (including media texts)
- provision for developing knowledge about language (including standard English)
- the purposes for reading
- levels of fluency/independence in becoming a reader.

All of these areas are covered in Chapters 1–6.

Writing

This should include details of learning objectives for writing:

- the range of writing – fiction and non-fiction (including media texts)
- provision for developing knowledge about the structures, forms and formats of texts (including standard English)
- the purposes and audiences for writing
- stages in the writing process towards fluency and independence.

Speaking and listening

This should include details of learning objectives for speaking and listening:

- the range of spoken texts to be covered, including drama
- levels of formality/register (including standard English)
- the purposes and audiences for speaking and listening
- levels of fluency and assurance.

Each section should also include details of:

- the use of ICT
- how English is tackled through different curriculum areas, cross-referred to other subject documentation
- provision for special needs
- issues of equal opportunities.

Ensuring progression

These Schemes of Work will be complemented by detailed Units of Work (termly or half-termly plans) and teachers' weekly (or fortnightly) and daily planning. A separate section in the policy folder should contain an overview of the agreed areas for study of texts and study of language for each class over each Key Stage (Figs. 7.4 and 7.5) and detailed Units of Work.

Each Unit of Work will need to identify:

Learning objectives: experiences, concepts/knowledge, conventions/skills, strategies and behaviours
Resources/materials: remembering that people can be resources, too
Texts
Tasks/activities
Groupings and provision for *differentiation*
Links with National Curriculum Programmes of Study
Assessment criteria: what you will use as evidence of progress.

After the unit has been covered, you should allow for *evaluation* which will inform *future learning*.

Section Four: Assessment, reporting and recording progress

Any system of record-keeping needs to be based on the collection of different kinds of evidence. It should build to a full description of a child's learning, and communicate clearly not only to teachers but also to parents and children.

Assessment of development needs to be capable of capturing:

There are sections on assessment in Reading, Writing, Speaking and Listening in Chapters 2, 3 and 4.

- detailed observations of the texts children can confidently tackle
- their knowledge reservoir of different kinds of texts
- their increasing ability to become independent in working with texts
- the gradual development of discrimination and choice.

The diversity of evidence will be made possible by the diversity of opportunity offered and in the range of texts included in the literacy curriculum. These will be matched by the variety of learning experiences and ways in to literacy. Given opportunities for

The following grid allows you to fill in the headings for each half-termly or termly Unit of Work.

	Reception		Year 1		Year 2	
Term 1	Rhymes and Patterned and predictable stories (domestic) Reading & making →	Environmental print – labels, captions, shopping. Different print. Books made from labels.	Trad. stories & tales (revisit some from R. & introduce new) storytelling Reading &	Info – books and poems about trees and forests (& role play/ drama) making	Author focus – Anthony Browne (link with work on relationships) own stories & books	Comparing books and videos written recommendations and reviews
Term 2	Traditional stories & tales with predictable patterns Reading & making →	Books about us – information; intercultural; pictorial text and alphabetical order	Jolly Postman – letters, invitations, cards, adverts (& role play/ drama) Reading &	Looking things up – directories catalogues, info. books, alphabetical order making	Information books on plants and growing things – (link with Science) Reading & making	Trad. stories – comparing versions storytelling & drama
Term 3	Poems about 'us' and homes Info texts about homes in other lands Reading & ma-	Animal stories (other than fairy tales) Story Telling -king →	Stories, poems and information about farms (& drama)	Author focus – John Burningham (link w. Science) Letters to him	Newspapers – making class newspaper – accounts – video reviews – adverts etc Reading & making	Funny stories The Class Joke Book – riddles, jokes, puzzles – Reading and making

Figure 7.4 Overview of agreed areas for study of texts and study of language – KS1 (Blank provided in Appendix: A27)

	Year 3		Year 4		Year 5		Year 6	
Term 1	Short stories about characters – (eg The Julian Stories) and homes Reading →	writing Personal experience (eg stories and poems) writing in role	Magazines – what do we read? Making group magazines according to interest	Historical stories – fiction and fact – Reading, writing & Drama	Traditional stories from other cultures – Europe (& information on Europe)	Poetry from the past – anthologies of favourites and reviews	Different games – groups reading & writing acc. to interest	The short story – examples leading to class anthology of own short stories
Term 2	Myths & legends from Asia & poetry & drama Reading	Our languages – lang. study dictionaries and phrase books writing	Narrative poetry – modern and classic Reading and writing	Other words – fantasy & Sci fi fact & fiction Reading and writing	Contemporary novels – groups reading and writing about them	Information books for younger pupils – researching and writing	Poetry of different forms – leading to class anthology	Classic stories adapted to film – reading, viewing & writing
Term 3	Author study – Dick King Smith Personal choice & class reading and writing	My Animal Adventure – writing books for the class library (Range of models)	Extracts from Shakespeare – reading, writing and performing	Author studies – group choices – reviews child recommendations	Persuasive texts – reading, writing, debating (linked to Humanities work)	Author study – Roald Dahl – reading and writing →	Short stories we like – individual choice & sharing → writing	Plays – chosen extracts performed own plays written and performed

Figure 7.5 Agreed areas for study of texts and study of language – KS2 (Blank provided in Appendix: A28)

reflection and evaluation, even very young children can be confident literary critics of their own – and other people's – texts. When this reflection and evaluation is directed towards their own reading, writing, speaking and listening, children themselves can become involved in the process of tracking their own progress, giving them not only responsibility but a framework for future development.

Three important questions to be asked when reviewing or establishing policy for assessment, reporting and recording are:

- What do we want our ideal recording and assessment system to do for us?
- How does our present system match up?
- How do we respond to and mark children's work?

The second question can be addressed through noting for each Key Stage and year:

- What records of progress are kept for:
  reading?
  writing?
  speaking and listening?
- What is the range of evidence collected?
- Are the records the same for all classes in the school?
- What records are passed on from class to class or at transition across Key Stages?
- How does the school ensure progression?
- Who else is involved in keeping records? (parents/helpers/the children themselves?)
- How do the children evaluate and comment on their own progress?
- What arrangements are there for screening for language and literacy difficulties?
- How is information given to parents?
- What formal assessments are made?
- How are the results recorded and passed on?

Section Five: Provision for under-fives

The questions to be asked about this area of school provision are similar in some ways to the areas of the whole policy document:

- How can we help children make the transition between home and school?
- How can we discover, value and build on the language and literacy experiences they bring to school?
- What language and literacy experiences should we provide for children under five?
- What kind of literacy and language learning environment will best support their introduction to full-time education?
- What resources (human and material) are necessary?

If children's progress is to be measured as they go through the school, then it makes sense to have some kind of baseline observations to use as a starting point. However, the nature of the baseline assessment is a key factor in considering the usefulness of later measures of progress. Pencil and paper tests will not necessarily reveal the reservoirs of language and literacy experience held by most children. Baseline assessment needs to be much more observationally founded if it is to yield information which will feed forward to teachers' planning. Fig. 7.6 gives a suggested outline and Fig. 7.7 offers a recording format for a Baseline Profile.

(a) Baseline: what do we need to know when children start school?

About children's **experience** of language and literacy:

- stories they have heard, seen and enjoyed
- familiarity with books and other reading materials
- experience with IT
- play involving literacy
- family relationships over language and literacy – who tells them stories, reads to them, shares books and other materials with them, watches videos with them?
- rhymes, songs, poems, jingles they enjoy
- what they know about letters and the alphabet
- whether they can recognise and read their own name.

It is also useful if parents or carers can be asked to bring in some of the children's early attempts at making marks on paper. These, combined with observations at the writing table, can help to see:

- how they use pictures, symbols and/or familiar words/letters to communicate meaning
- whether they direct their writing from left to right (in English)
- whether they use another language or script in their early writing
- whether they know about purposes for writing – cards, letters, lists
- whether they can write their names and if they use upper and lower case letters.

About children's language and literacy **behaviour**:

- the ways children handle books; assurance, directionality, orientation (independently and with the teacher)
- who they choose to read with
- how/whether they listen to and join in with stories, songs, poems
- how/when/whether they like to read to themselves
- how/whether they talk about pictures
- how/whether they read the print
- whether they understand that print carries meaning
- the vocabulary they use to talk about books, pictures, videos and television
- whether they make up their own stories
- how/whether they engage in role play, in particular if this involves literacy
- how/whether they handle writing implements
- how keen they are to use writing materials.

Figure 7.6(a) Baseline assessment checklist

(b) How do we find out about children's literacy experience and behaviours?

By creating an environment where they will feel supported
By observation:

- when reading to or with the children; when someone else is reading; when they are reading with friends or alone
- when they are playing or in the role play area
- when they are using the writing table/corner
- when they are listening to you or someone else tell a story, read poetry, sing, etc.

By listening and talking to children:

- when they are telling stories
- talking about themselves
- talking about videos or books they like
- talking about pictures
- telling you about their own drawings or writing.

When do we do make observations and assessments?

Over half a term or a reasonably lengthy period of time since genuinely informative observations cannot be done in one or two sessions. Observations need to be planned for and children need time to get used to new contexts and people.

How do we record observations?

As a progressive language and literacy profile of each child: notes, lists or narrative which include all of the features listed above can be summarised after the agreed period of observation (see Baseline Profile sheet).

Who is involved?

Parents and carers can offer a great deal of information and should be asked to contribute to the Baseline Profile. They will also be able to provide relevant medical information. They should also be informed about and perhaps involved in observing and recording. It is important to make it clear to parents and carers that what they do at home in respect of language and literacy is valuable and valued.

Figure 7.6(b) Baseline assessment checklist (continued)

Baseline Assessment Profile

Name: Marula Shah **Date:** Sept 3rd

Language and literacy experience information from parent/carer M. likes to hear and tell stories and has a range of books and videos. At the moment she watches and re-watches 101 Dalmatians. Can write her own name in English and read it. The bits of writing the family brought show experiments in both languages.

Languages spoken in the home: Gujerati and English

Languages spoken/understood by the child: Gujerati and English

Date	Observation focus	Comments	Observed by
Sept 4th	choosing books	M. very focused - took time to choose and settled on Owl Babies which she knows from Nursery.	E.B.
Oct. 7th	Role play	M. played in the Three Bears' House with N (who also speaks Gujerati) They played in both languages, doing the 'planning' in Gujerati ...	P.B.
Nov. 15th	Writing corner	M. knows upper/lower case letters, spacing, directionality and draws on phonic language a lot	E.B.

Summary:

Language and literacy experience:

In the first term, M. has shown that she has a good grasp of story texts – the shapes and language associated with them (English). She tells stories in Gujerati at home with siblings and occasionally on the tape. In her writing she draws on both phonic and graphic knowledge.

Language and literacy behaviours:

M. is a good browser. She has quite decided tastes about what she wants to read and share. In talk she is a good conversational partner. She is less ready to experiment with writing, showing signs of anxiety if she thinks it isn't right. She chooses to read rather than write.

Figure 7.7 Baseline Profile sheet (Blank provided in Appendix: A29)

Section Six: Partnerships for literacy

Since much literacy experience takes place as part of the shared culture of a community, whether it is the home, school or classroom community, then collaborations and partnerships become important ingredients of intervention for successful language and literacy development. It is important to be able to establish dialogues with parents where they can both give and receive information and ideas, but often the place of parents in the partnership is to hear about school practice in developing literacy and to do what the teachers ask them to do. Since early literacy experience is important and parents play a crucial role in supporting their children's reading and writing throughout their school lives, it is worth listening to what parents know about their children's language and literacy experience and interests.

In reviewing or beginning to establish policy for working in partnership with parents or carers, the following questions might be helpful starting points:

- What do parents think literacy is? Is it the same as teachers think? How and when do we share views on language and literacy with parents/carers and establish common ground?
- How might we include parents'/carers' views about development?
- How do we find out what children know about language and literacy when they first come to school?
- How do we gain the confidence of parents, carers and families, especially those who don't (or can't) usually get involved ? How can we show them we value their opinions and experience?
- How do we continue to involve parents with their children's education in language and literacy up to the end of Key Stage 2?
- Are parents involved in formulating policy documents, creating information booklets, choosing reading material, etc.?

Section Seven: Date for review, methods of implementation, monitoring and evaluation

Once the policy has been discussed, negotiated, agreed and drafted, it will need to be implemented for a period of time in order to see how it works. During this time, the English coordinator will arrange for monitoring and evaluation of the policy. It is often best to develop policy in stages, concentrating on a specific area first. This may have been noted as part of the process of identifying priorities and planning for future action. Policy development, implementation, review and evaluation are probably best carried out over a three- to five-year period, and this could be a rolling programme, where Reading is being implemented whilst Speaking and Listening policy is being developed (Fig. 7.8).

Year 1	Year 2	Year 3	Year 4	Year 5
Develop Reading policy including sections 5 and 6	Implement Reading policy	Monitor, evaluate and, if necessary, revise Reading policy	Use Reading policy, noting areas for future development	Use Reading policy, noting areas for future development
Use Speaking and Listening policy, noting areas for future development	Develop Speaking and Listening policy including sections 5 and 6	Implement Speaking and Listening policy	Monitor, evaluate and, if necessary, revise Speaking and Listening policy	Use Speaking and Listening policy, noting areas for future development
Use Writing policy, noting areas for future development	Use Writing policy, noting areas for future development	Develop Writing policy including sections 5 and 6	Implement Writing policy	Monitor, evaluate and, if necessary, revise Writing policy

Figure 7.8 Rolling programme of policy development, implementation, monitoring and review

	Reading	Writing	Speaking and Listening
Environment	audit all class reading areas		set up listening posts
Range and repertoire	✓	✓	plan for wider range - partic. 'redrafted' talk
Progression	staff development sessions		
Assessment, reporting and recording	✓	✓	✓
Equal opportunities	check texts in classrooms	begin looking at content.....	gender groups?
Special needs	organise bought in day's inservice for Spring Term		
Differentiation	✓	✓	✓
Cross-curricular teaching	Begin audit/review		
Using Information Technology	CD Rom info. texts for topic	✓	✓
Provision for under-fives	Review acc. to Baseline guidance		
Links with parents	KS2 priority	spelling homework	?

Figure 7.9 Identifying inservice needs of the whole staff (Blank provided in Appendix: A30)

Identifying inservice needs

The process of developing policy can often reveal areas where colleagues would like more help, but it may be worth carrying out a more systematic review in order to plan for future inservice provision. Fig. 7.9 gives a grid for noting areas which arise from policy review or discussions with the whole staff. Discussion might focus on one issue at a time, for example Equal Opportunities, noting areas of existing good practice. This then reveals gaps where further action might need to be taken which can be noted on the grid. The grid can be used over a period of time to track inservice provision in English.

Alongside the identification of inservice needs for the whole staff there will be areas you have noted where individuals need support. These often arise as a result of monitoring. This can be a tricky aspect of your role with some colleagues, since there is a long-standing fear that anyone who comes in to observe teaching is necessarily making negative judgements. One way of lessening the anguish is to ask the teacher herself or himself to identify areas of practice which are significant. This might be either because they are aspects of practice which are going well or are areas of classroom practice which the teacher would like to develop. An observant eye can offer both positive support for existing good practice and an objective eye for areas which the teacher wants to improve.

Before a programme of monitoring is decided on it is worth being explicit about what monitoring means and asking colleagues to answer a few questions (Fig. 7.10).

Subject monitoring – English

Over the next two terms I have been allocated time for monitoring English. This is to observe how the curriculum is progressing and I see it as a time when I might teach alongside you or observe you teaching. The aim is to identify good practice and to help you in the areas you want to develop. Before I work out the programme of visits, would you answer the following:

- What aspects of your classroom work are you satisfied with?
- What areas of your work are you trying to develop?
- What kinds of support would you like? (within reason!)

I can make two observation times available.

When would you like me to observe an area which you are pleased with?

When shall I come and observe an area you want to develop?

Figure 7.10 Questions to establish helpful monitoring

The material in this manual will provide some starting points. You might, for example, want to begin by asking all colleagues to complete the supportive literacy environment audit in Chapter 1 (pp. 19–20). Whatever you plan to do to support colleagues, it is worth remembering that the long-term aim is to help children make progress in English.

Appendix

The materials in this appendix may be reproduced free-of-charge for use in your school.

PERSONAL READING PROFILE

Tick in the column which represents how you feel about the different kinds of reading listed:

Type of reading	Happy	Quite comfortable	OK	Quite uncomfortable	Ugh!
Letters from home or a friend					
Diagrams					
Columns of figures					
Magazines					
Newspapers					
Handwriting					
Computer text					
Advertising hoardings					
Music					
Novels					
Maps					
Notices (e.g. in museums or staff rooms)					
Factual books					
Pictures					
Photographs					
Other					

A1 Sample proforma for profile of an experienced reader © Routledge

LANGUAGE FAMILY TREE

GRANDPARENTS' GENERATION

LANGUAGE	LITERACY

PARENTS' GENERATION

LANGUAGE	LITERACY

A2 The Language Family Tree © Routledge

INVOLVING PARENTS

Parents in my classroom

Activities	How does this support literacy?

Parents in the school

Activities	How does this support literacy?

Parents at home

Activities	How does this support literacy?

A3 Sample proforma for the different ways that parents can support literacy © Routledge

SCREENING FOR DIFFICULTIES – READING

Name: **Class:** **Year:**
Languages spoken: **Term** 1 2 3

Cause for concern:

Checks made on:	Date	Comments
hearing		
sight		
perceptual problems		
physical difficulty/impairment		
medical condition		
other		

Relevant information from home:

Most recent contact with parent/carer:

Record of evidence: focused observation period from: **to:**

Observer(s):

Existing assessments/level of progress:

Summary of observations:

Targets set:

Dates for review:

Parents' comments:

Review and suggestions for further action:

A4 Sample proforma for Screening Record for children experiencing difficulties with reading © Routledge

CLASS RECORD SHEET – READING

Teacher: **Class:**

Date (year)

Name	Age	Boy/ Girl	Languages spoken	Reading Level Term 1	Reading Level Term 2	Reading Level Term 3

A5 Grid for recording class progress in reading © Routledge

READING RECORD **Name:** **Class:** **Age:** **Languages spoken:** **DATE:**

Text chosen: (Title) by child / by teacher familiar / unfamiliar fiction / non-fiction

level of difficulty for the reader: (e.g. straightforward, a challenge . . .)

Behaviours: Talking about / approaching text:

assurance telling the story

involvement commenting on likes/dislikes

book language cross-referring

Reading aloud:

self-correcting

seeking help

reading on

reviewing

Strategies:

directionality

letter/sound matching

letter shape matching

word recognition

picture cues

meaning cues

text structure cues

Understanding of text:

predicting events

commenting on character and/or setting or plot

responding to the content

picking up details

grasping inferences

asking questions

Accuracy:

number of words read accurately:

number of self-corrections:

number of errors/miscues:

Level on Scale of Progression:

NC Level (if appropriate):

Summary and future teaching strategies:

A6 Sample proforma for termly reading record © Routledge

WRITING RECORD	**Name:**	**Class:**	**Age:**	**Languages spoken:**	**Date**

Title and type of writing:

Stage of completion: draft / notes | proofread / edited by writer | proofread by teacher | finished piece handwritten / word processed

Context: teacher directed | collaborative work | part of research | self-chosen | other (specify)

Choices made by writer about type of writing content organisation technical features	**Awareness of reader:** e.g. level of explicit detail register 'hooking' the reader in
Behaviours: assurance; self-editing; involvement; talking about writing; handwriting fluency; using appropriate language	**Text organisation** (e.g. does the structure fit the task? is it clear/logical/sequenced?) **Strategies:** directionality; attempting orthodox spelling; proofreading **Syntax:** variation in complexity: **Vocabulary:** variety and experimentation:
Accuracy in spelling number of words in piece: number spelt accurately: patterns in spelling errors: **Accuracy in punctuation** number and range of punctuation marks used: number used accurately: patterns in punctuation errors	**Summary and future teaching strategies:**
Level on Scale of Progression **NC Level** (if appropriate)	

A7 Sample proforma for termly writing record © Routledge

CLASS RECORD SHEET – WRITING

Teacher: **Class:**

Date (year):

Name	Age	Boy/ Girl	Languages spoken	Writing Level Term 1	Writing Level Term 2	Writing Level Term 3

A8 Grid for recording class progress in writing © Routledge

Name	Stage of writing confidence: guided; supported; independent	Problem – mine or the pupil's?	Possible action

A9 Problem writers © Routledge

SCREENING FOR DIFFICULTIES – WRITING

Name: **Class:** **Year:**
Languages spoken: **Term 1 2 3**

Cause for concern:

Checks made on:	Date	Comments
hearing		
sight		
perceptual problems		
physical difficulty/impairment		
medical condition		
other		

Relevant information from home:

Most recent contact with parent/carer:

Record of evidence: focused observation period from: **to:**

Observer(s):

Existing assessments/level of progress:

Summary of observations:

Targets set:

Dates for review:

Parents' comments:

Review and suggestions for further action:

A10 Sample proforma for screening record for children experiencing difficulties with writing © Routledge

WRITING MISCUE – SUMMARY OF ANALYSIS

- **Writing behaviour**

How does this child see herself/himself as a writer?

Possible future action:

- **The process of writing**

What does the writer's approach tell you about her/his fluency and independence in writing?

Possible future action:

- **Purpose/intention**

What does this piece show about the writer's success in making her/his own meaning and intentions in writing clear?

Possible future action:

- **Audience/readership**

How does this piece show the writer's understanding of the needs of a reader?

Possible future action:

A11 Sample proforma for writing miscue – summary of analysis (i) © Routledge

- **Structure/form**

What does this piece indicate about the writer's ability to present ideas clearly and coherently?

How does the form fit with the intended task?

Possible future action:

- **Technical features**

What features show the writer's competence in handling the transcription elements of syntax, punctuation, vocabulary, spelling?

How effectively has the writer varied technical features in relation to intention and readership?

Possible future action:

A11 Sample proforma for writing miscue – summary of analysis (ii) © Routledge

Activity Planning Sheet

Activity Title		Year/Group

Activity Details	Planned Learning	Organisation Resources	P of S	Assessment Opportunities

Evaluation and Extension

A12 Sample proforma for planning for assessment of speaking and listening – storymaking © Routledge

RECORD OF EVIDENCE – SPEAKING AND LISTENING

Name: **Class:** **Languages spoken:**

TEXTS AND CONTEXTS	**Term One date:** **Type of evidence:**	**Term Two date:** **Type of evidence:**	**Term Three date:** **Type of evidence:**
Learning focus:			
Groupings – indicate: • pairs/small group/large group • friendship/ability/random • child/child: child/adult: all children: children with adult • older/younger, • familiar/unfamiliar • same gender/different gender			
Range of purposes: e.g. exploring ideas; investigating; reporting; discussing; narrating; presenting			
Key skills: e.g. organising and communicating ideas; taking different views into account; listening attentively and responding accordingly; qualifying or justifying ideas			
Language awareness: e.g. reflection on own use of language; self-evaluation of key skills; use of particular register or vocabulary			
Fluency and assurance: speaking and listening behaviours according to context			
Summary			

A13 Sample proforma for a year's evidence of talk © Routledge

Speaking and Listening screening – Observation Sheet

Name: **Class:** **Year:**

Focused observation period from: **to:**

Observer:

Date:	**Talk texts:**	**Talk contexts:**	**Talk behaviours:**	**Evidence:**
	e.g. narrating, asking, explaining, clarifying, describing, reporting	e.g. collaborative learning, role play; playground grouping: pair/small group/large group friendship/ability/random familiar/unfamiliar gender	e.g. face and body language; eye movements and contact; does child initiate? are responses appropriate?	note words spoken; evidence of learning; does talk match task? other observations

A14 Sample proforma for screening for difficulties with speaking and listening Step 1: focused observation © Routledge

SCREENING FOR DIFFICULTIES – SPEAKING AND LISTENING

Name: **Class:** **Year:**
Languages spoken: **Term 1 2 3**

Cause for concern:

Checks made on:	Date	Comments
hearing		
sight		
perceptual problems		
physical difficulty/impairment		
medical condition		
other		

Relevant information from home:

Most recent contact with parent/carer:

Record of evidence: focused observation period from: **to:**

Observer(s):

Existing assessments/level of progress:

Summary of observations:

Targets set:

Dates for review:

Parents' comments:

Review and suggestions for further action:

A15 Sample proforma for screening for difficulties with speaking and listening Step 2: taking action © Routledge

Progression in Knowledge About Language 1 – Grammar				
	lexical knowledge and terminology	structuring writing	language variation	using language for effect
Nursery/Reception				
Year 1				
Year 2				
Year 3				
Year 4				
Year 5				
Year 6				

A16 Grid for compiling a progressive scheme for teaching grammar © Routledge

I Know About – Punctuation		Name:
Punctuation mark	**What it's called**	**Sentence**
		From a book: My own:
		From a book: My own:
		From a book: My own:
		From a book: My own:

A17 Sample proforma for catering for individual progress in punctuation © Routledge

Progression in Knowledge About Language 2 – Punctuation		
	Punctuation marks	**How they will be introduced**
Nursery/ Reception		
Year 1		
Year 2		
Year 3		
Year 4		
Year 5		
Year 6		

A18 Grid for compiling a progressive scheme for teaching punctuation © Routledge

Text teaching audit	
Which texts have you used over a period of time with the class?	What teaching opportunities did they offer?
1	
2	
3	
4	

A19 Sample proforma for text teaching audit – over a term © Routledge

Year	
Types of text/genre (e.g. traditional stories, narrative poems, plays, big books, classic stories, contemporary novels)	**Teaching opportunities**
Term 1	
Term 2	
Term 3	

A20 Sample proforma for the range of text experience – over a year © Routledge

Comparing versions

- Were there any differences between what happened (the plot) in the film and in the book?
- Were the characters any different? Choose one or two to compare.
- Do you think the setting shown in the film was what you had expected from the book (or the other way round, depending on which was read first)?
- How did the book and the film create atmosphere?
- What did you think about the ending (resolution) in each version?
- Which version did you prefer? Why?

Book: Film:

Different	The same
Plot	
Characters	
Atmosphere	
Resolution (ending)	

Which version do you prefer and why?

A21 Sample proforma for comparing video and book versions © Routledge

Type of text	When last read as a class	When last written by the class
Environmental print – signs, captions, advertisements, food labels		
Reference material: information books, films, videos, CD-ROMs		
Reports in newspapers, magazines and business material		
Photographs, maps, diagrams, charts, columns of figures		
Biography and autobiography		
Persuasive texts		
Instructions and explanations in leaflets, manuals, guide books, cookery books		
Analysis and commentary		

A22 Sample proforma for types of non-fiction text taught to the whole class © Routledge

Technical terms	When introduced in discussing reading	When introduced in discussing writing
e.g. author's biography, paragraphs		

A23 Towards a progressive glossary of technical terms to talk about texts © Routledge

Type of text	**Year 1/2**
Input Which texts? How will they be introduced? What strategies can /did you use to find out what the children already knew?	
Learning opportunities What do I want them to learn? – about the texts themselves? through using the texts?	
Tasks What activities? What variations in groupings?	
Resources and support **People? Strategies? Technical?**	
Range of outcomes and assessments (who/what/where/when/how?)	
Assessment:	

A24 Sample proforma for teaching from and about texts © Routledge

	Year One	Year Two	Year Three
Subject/teaching knowledge	Key tasks Needs	Key tasks Needs	Key tasks Needs
Developing policy, schemes of work, etc.	Key tasks Needs	Key tasks Needs	Key tasks Needs
Advice & support for colleagues	Key tasks Needs	Key tasks Needs	Key tasks Needs
Resource management	Key tasks Needs	Key tasks Needs	Key tasks Needs
Assessing, Reporting and Recording	Key tasks Needs	Key tasks Needs	Key tasks Needs
Communications and public relations	Key tasks Needs	Key tasks Needs	Key tasks Needs
Monitoring, review and evaluation	Key tasks Needs	Key tasks Needs	Key tasks Needs

A25 Planning sheet: establishing priorities and planning for future development © Routledge

Processes: **Getting and conveying information: researching, skimming, scanning, listening, note-making, informing, explaining**
Developing independence and discrimination: drafting, choosing reading material, varying texts for purpose and audience

	Reading	**Writing**	**Speaking and listening**
Art			
Design Technology			
Geography			
History			
Maths			
Music			
Physical Education			
Science			

A26 A checklist for teaching English across the curriculum © Routledge

The following grid allows you to fill in the headings for each half-termly or termly Unit of Work.

	Reception		**Year 1**		**Year 2**	
Term 1						
Term 2						
Term 3						

A27 Overview of agreed areas for study of texts and study of language – KS1 © Routledge

	Year 3		Year 4		Year 5		Year 6	
Term 1								
Term 2								
Term 3								

A28 Agreed areas for half-termly or termly Units of Work focussing on study of texts and study of language – KS2 © Routledge

Baseline Assessment Profile

Name: **Date:**

Language and literacy experience information from parent/carer

Languages spoken in the home: **Languages spoken/understood by the child:**

Date	Observation focus	Comments	Observed by

Summary:

Language and literacy experience:

Language and literacy behaviours:

A29 Baseline profile sheet © Routledge

	Reading	Writing	Speaking and Listening
Environment			
Range and repertoire			
Progression			
Assessment, reporting and recording			
Equal opportunities			
Special needs			
Differentiation			
Cross-curricular teaching			
Using Information Technology			
Provision for under-fives			
Links with parents			

A30 Identifying inservice needs of the whole staff © Routledge

Author Index

Children's Authors Index

Subject Index